Blockchain and IoT based Smart Healthcare Systems

Edited by

L. Ashok Kumar
Department of EEE
PSG College of Technology
Coimbatore, Tamilnadu
India

D. Karthika Renuka
Department of IT
PSG College of Technology
Coimbatore, Tamilnadu
India

Sonali Agarwal
Department of IT
Indian Institute of Information Technology
Allahabad
India

&

Sheng-Lung Peng
College of Innovative Design and Management
National Taipei University of Business
Creative Technologies and Product Design
Taiwan

Blockchain and IoT based Smart Healthcare Systems

Editors: L. Ashok Kumar, D. Karthika Renuka, Sonali Agarwal & Sheng-Lung Peng

ISBN (Online): 978-981-5196-29-0

ISBN (Print): 978-981-5196-30-6

ISBN (Paperback): 978-981-5196-31-3

need for a court order if at any point you breach any terms of this License Agreement. In no event will any delay or failure by Bentham Science Publishers in enforcing your compliance with this License Agreement constitute a waiver of any of its rights.

3. You acknowledge that you have read this License Agreement, and agree to be bound by its terms and conditions. To the extent that any other terms and conditions presented on any website of Bentham Science Publishers conflict with, or are inconsistent with, the terms and conditions set out in this License Agreement, you acknowledge that the terms and conditions set out in this License Agreement shall prevail.

Bentham Science Publishers Pte. Ltd.
80 Robinson Road #02-00
Singapore 068898
Singapore
Email: subscriptions@benthamscience.net

BENTHAM SCIENCE

CONTENTS

FOREWORD

The Electronic Health Record (EHR) of a patient is a digitized document of their health history, progression comments, symptoms, and medications. Concerns about security abound, as they do with any online digital media. In the healthcare industry, the reliance on digital devices such as IoT, generates a massive volume of patient medical data. These EHR data statistics are confidential and cannot be made public. Medical data tampering can place a person's life in danger. Because of this, EHR information is subject to severe security and privacy risks. The high prevalence of health digital platforms presents a need for a more secure EHR system enabled by blockchain. Blockchain-based technologies have been proven and approved for delivering reliable and secure decentralised solutions to address the security and privacy threats associated with EHR data. Moreover, decentralized blockchain technology is unalterable. Preserving secrecy may allow for a more effective conversation between the physician and the patient, which is crucial for providing high-quality care. It also provides doctors, patients, and insurance providers an efficient way to obtain medical information while maintaining the privacy of the patient's data. The blockchain-based architecture provides the following features: privacy, authenticity, integrity, interoperability, and accountability of electronic health records between two entities. This book covers some state-of-the-art research associated with artificial intelligence, big data, and blockchain for smart health care development. It explains the fusion between the privacy and security of a blockchain-based data analytic environment. The book provides the fundamental framework, research insights, and empirical evidence for the efficacy of these new technologies, employing practical and basic approaches to help professionals and academics reach innovative solutions and grow competitive strengths.

V. Chandrasekar
University Distinguished Professor and Associate Dean for International Programs
Fellow IEEE, AGU, AMS, URSI and US national Academy of Inventors
Colorado, State University
Colorado, United States

PREFACE

Technology is constantly changing the healthcare industry, which is a crucial aspect of daily living. The use of technologies like Internet of Things (IoT), artificial intelligence, and blockchain systems can improve the state-of-the-art in health care and general medical practise. As the Internet of Things (IoT) has grown, its applications in the field of smart health care are adapted to various real-world scenarios. An Internet of Things (IoT)-based health care is a collection of intelligent medical tools and software that communicate online with a health care information system. It has created a world of opportunities in the medical industry. Smart connected medical gadgets can gather vital health information and offer additional information about the symptoms. Smart health care IoT devices range from basic wristbands that can track blood pressure, heart rate, and sleep patterns to linked inhalers, ingestible sensors, glucose monitors, and remote patient monitoring systems. These devices must have dependable connectivity and adhere to security and privacy laws in order to meet the demands of smart health care. A patient's medical information is kept digitally in a digital health record (EHR). The electronic health record (EHR) is a piece of technology that could provide the groundwork for new patient services and functionality. They increase patient access, raise the standard of service, and cut expenses. The blockchain security architecture assures that electronic health records between two organisations are confidential, authentic, legitimate, interoperable, and accountable. A blockchain-based approach to address the issues of data management, exchange, and storage, real-time patient monitoring at remote locations, monitoring of smart IoT devices, and faster and more seamless data transfer of patient medical records are just a few benefits that will come with the adoption of blockchain-based smart healthcare. Blockchain technology is a pervasive technology utilised in many industries, including banking, finance, supply chain management, and healthcare. The IoT and blockchain appear to be the ideal combination, as there is a great demand for data security given the volume of data generated by IoT sensors. A blockchain-enabled IoT-based smart health care is also an advancement because it can lessen the burden on healthcare systems and avoidable hospital visits by connecting patients with their health care providers and enabling the safe transfer and storage of medical data through the use of the blockchain mechanism. The book employs academic and practical approaches to assist professionals and academics in coming up with novel solutions and strengthening their competitive advantages. It provides the fundamental framework, research insights, and empirical evidence regarding the efficacy of these new technologies.

L. Ashok Kumar
Department of EEE
PSG College of Technology
Coimbatore, Tamilnadu
India

D. Karthika Renuka
Department of IT
PSG College of Technology
Coimbatore, Tamilnadu
India

Sonali Agarwal
Department of IT
Indian Institute of Information Technology
Allahabad
India

&

Sheng-Lung Peng
College of Innovative Design and Management
National Taipei University of Business
Creative Technologies and Product Design
Taiwan

List of Contributors

A. Valarmathi	Department of Computer Applications Bit Campus, Anna University, Thiruchirappalli-24, India
Anand Kumar S.	Vellore Institute of Technology, Vellore, India
Akila Victor	School of Computer Science & Engineering, VIT, Vellore, India
Chaithra V.	BMS Institute of Technology and Management, Bengaluru, India
Divya Palanisamy	N.G.P. Institute of Technology (affiliated to Anna University), NGP Nagar, Kalapatti -6410648, India
D. Karthika Renuka	Department of IT, PSG College of Technology, Coimbatore, Tamilnadu, India
G. Srinivasagan	Department of Chemistry, Rajapalayam Rajus College, Rajapalayam, Tamilnadu, India
Geeta Amol Patil	BMS Institute of Technology and Management, Bengaluru, India
Geetha Narasimhan	School of Computer Science & Engineering, VIT, Vellore, India
Jaskiranjit Kaur	Panjab University, Chandigarh, India
Jayashree K.	Department of Artificial Intelligence and Data Science, Panimalar Engineering College, Chennai, India
Kumaresan Natesan	Anna University Regional Campus, Coimbatore, India
K. Karthigadevi	Department of Computer Applications, Kalasalingam Academy of Research and Education, Krishnankoil, Tamilnadu, India
L. Ashok Kumar	Department of EEE, PSG College of Technology Coimbatore, Tamilnadu, India
M. Narayana	Electronics and Communication Engineering Department, Anurag University, Hyderabad, India
M. Shanmuganantham	Tamilnadu Government Polytechnic College, Tamilnadu, India
Manoranjan Dash	Department of Artificial Intelligence, Anurag University, Hyderabad, India
Pranshu Tripathi	School of Computer Science & Engineering, VIT, Vellore, India
Parvesh Kumar	Chandigarh University, Chandigarh, Punjab, India
Pinaki Pratim Acharjya	Department of CSE, Haldia, Institute of Technology, Haldia -721607, India
Praveena Venkatesan	NGP Institute of Technology, Coimbatore, Tamil Nadu 641048, India
Partheeban Pon	Computer Science and Engineering, Stella Mary's College of Engineering, Aauthenganvilai, Kanyakumari, India
Priya Vijay	Department of Computer Science and Engineering, Rajalakshmi Engineering College, Chennai, India
R. Anusuya	Department of IT, PSG College of Technology Coimbatore, Tamilnadu, India
R. Manimegalai	Department of Computer Science and Engineering, PSG Institute of Technology and Applied Research, Neelambur, Tamil Nadu 641062, India

Ramya Easwaran	SNS College of Technology, Coimbatore, India
R. Nagarajan	Gnanamani College of Technology, Tamilnadu, India
Raghu Indrakanti	Electronics and Communication Engineering Department, Anurag University, Hyderabad, India
R. Babu	Department of Computational Intelligence, School of Computing, College of Engineering and Technology, SRMIST, Chennai, India
Surekha K.B.	BMS Institute of Technology and Management, Bengaluru, India
Saranya Rajendran	Sri Ramakrishna Engineering College, Coimbatore, Tamil Nadu 641022, India
Suresh Kumar Nagarajan	Department of Computer Applications, Kalasalingam Academy of Research and Education, Krishnankoil, Tamilnadu, India
Santanu Koley	Department of CSE, Haldia, Institute of Technology, Haldia -721607, India
S. Jayanthi	Department of Computer Science and Engineering, Bit Campus, Anna University, Thiruchirappalli-24, India
Sanjay Vasudevan	School of Computer Science and Engineering, Vellore Institute of Technology, Vellore, India
Sarvana Kumar Selvaraj	Department of Computer Science and Engineering, Jain University, Bangalore, India
S. Kannadhasan	Study World College of Engineering Coimbatore, Tamilnadu, India
V. Kavitha	Computer Science and Engineering, University College of Engineering, Kancheepuram, India
Vidhya E.	Padmavani Arts and Science College for Women, Salem, Tamil Nadu 636011, India
V. Vishu	Department of Computer Applications, Coimbatore Institute of Technology, Coimbatore, Tamil Nadu 641014, India
Vijay K.	Department of Computer Science and Engineering, Rajalakshmi Engineering College, Chennai, India
Yash Vaish	School of Computer Science & Engineering, VIT, Vellore, India

CHAPTER 1

The Role of Emerging Technologies in Smart Health Care

Jaskiranjit Kaur[1,*] and **Parvesh Kumar**[2]

[1] *Panjab University, Chandigarh, India*

[2] *Chandigarh University, Chandigarh, Punjab, India*

Abstract: Numerous technological advancements like 3-D Printing, Virtual Reality (VR), Augmented Reality (AR), Artificial Intelligence (AI), Internet of Things (IoT), Drones, Robots, and Blockchain are now being inscribed for their ability to change the health care industry and make it a more automated and effective field. Various tools related to AI, like Google, DeepMind, Atomwise, Chatbot, Enlitic, Freenome, and Buoy Health, are helpful in makingthe health industry more efficient. There is another technology which is nanomicelle that can be used for effective drug delivery to treat various cancers, including breast, colon, and lung cancer. Moreover, self-assembling peptide nanoparticles that were prepared from SARSCov-1 spike (S) protein, successfully induced neutralizing antibodies against the coronavirus, subsequently preventing infection of Vero cells. Furthermore, the application of 3D printing in medicine can provide many benefits, including the customization and personalization of medical products, drugs, and equipment; cost-effectiveness; increased productivity; democratization of design and manufacturing; and enhanced collaboration. IoT enables real-time alerting, tracking, and monitoring, which permits hands-on treatment, better accuracy, apt intervention by doctors, and improves patient care delivery results. The other most promising application isblockchain in the healthcare sector for identity management, dynamic patient consent, and management of supply chains for medical supplies and pharmaceuticals. In addition, there are several case studies that describe the benefits of emerging tools, like recently the use of Emerging Technologies for the study, diagnosis, and treatment of patients with COVID-19 by using Deep Convolutional neural networks (CNN), which is a widely used deep learning architecture, enabled distinguishing between COVID-19 and other causes of pneumonia through chest X-ray image analysis.

Keywords: AI, Blockchain, Drone, IoT, Nanotechnology, Virtual reality.

[*] **Corresponding author Jaskiranjit Kaur:** Panjab University, Chandigarh, India; E-mail: er.jaskiran@gmail.com

L. Ashok Kumar, D. Karthika Renuka, Sonali Agarwal & Sheng-Lung Peng (Eds.)
All rights reserved-© 2024 Bentham Science Publishers

INTRODUCTION

There are many technologies that are worthwhile in the healthcare sector, such as artificial intelligence (AI), bioprinting, nanotechnology, virtual reality, blockchain, and robotics. With the use of these technologies, anyone, anywhere at any time, might perform medicine in aneasy way, which makes the health industry more automated. In addition, with the use of emerging technologies, many other advantages are possible such as enabling remote monitoring of patients and their access to healthcare, health statistics collection, fast patient identification, access to medical records, and information exchange with providers and other patients.

Artificial Intelligence (AI)

Most of the AI and healthcare technologies have strong relevance to the healthcare field. Artificial intelligence in healthcare combines computer science and robust datasets to enable problem-solving related to health, such as patient care, diagnosing patients, end-to-end drug discovery and development, improving communication between physicians and patients, transcribing medical credentials, such as prescriptions, and remotely treating patients, administrative processes and helping them improve upon existing solutions and overcome challenges faster [1]. It also encompasses sub-fields of machine learning and deep learning, speech recognition, computer vision, and natural language processing which are frequently mentioned in conjunction with artificial intelligence to create expert systems that make predictions or classifications based on input data [2]. These learning algorithms evolve and become more accurate, they are likely to significantly impact healthcare services to identify diseases through diagnostic approaches, treatments, and care processes, and help develop more efficient and precise interventions. There are various tools that are based on AI to be helpful in the diagnosis of patients such as medical imaging technologies like computed tomography (CT), ultrasonography, x-rays, mammography, computed tomo-graphy (CT scans), nuclear medicine, and Magnetic resonance imaging (MRI) scan of human body parts.

INITIATIVES ON AI

A number of AI start-up companies like Google, Microsoft, and IBM have also been steadily increased investing in the development of health care with AI. There are several UK-based companies collaborating with UK universities and hospitals for better implementation of AI techniques. There are many Assisted Self-Diagnosis Apps that are based on AI methods, such as Ada, Babylon, Buoy Health, Your.MD, Mediktor, HealthTap, Apotheka Patient, Sensely, Health Buddy, *etc.*

Such paradigms are Harvard University's teaching hospitals advancing health care systems with artificial intelligence techniques to diagnose potential blood diseases at a very early stage.

Self-Diagnosis AI Apps

BioXcel Therapeutics, a biopharmaceutical company, combines proprietary machine learning algorithms, big data, and AI techniques to find and develop novel therapeutics in the areas of immuno-oncology and the brain. Moreover, BioXcel's firm works with two drug re-innovation programs which are BXCL501 and BXCL701.

Buoy Health employs AI-based system algorithms to accurately identify, treat, and analyse signs of sickness. Chabot asks a patient about their symptoms and health concerns, then, after making a diagnosis, directs the patient to the appropriate care [3].

BERG is a biotech company in the trial stages that uses artificial intelligence and its own platform, Interrogative Biology, to change treatments for oncology, neurology, and uncommon diseases and map diseases. Critical biomarkers can be found in BERG, which speeds up the identification and development of therapies directed at the most promising therapeutic targets and pathways. The elimination of hit-to-lead optimization and screening in Berg's method, which generates virtual models of healthy and diseased cells, results in clear time-saving. Berg avoids these procedures by selecting compounds that occur naturally and using them as the foundation for medication in its virtual model [4].

XtalPi's ID4 platform combines AI technology, cloud, and quantum physics that provide small molecule candidate chemicals and pharmaceutical compounds for drug design and development in days instead of weeks or months for quick prediction and development by maintaining a petabyte-scale database consisting of pharmaceutically active molecules [5].

Deep Genomics' AI platform handles the complexity of RNA biology, identifies new targets, evaluates thousands of opportunities, increases the number of successful clinical trials, and accelerates time to market. It also identifies the best treatment candidates to increase and reduce costs. Moreover, over 69 billion dissimilar cell connections were analyzed by Deep Genomics' Project Saturn. Headquartered in New York, Kaia Health offers AI-powered digital therapy via a mobile app for exercise routines related to chronic pain, soporific events, and learning assets for the treatment of chronic low back pain, chronic bronchitis, and emphysema (COPD). We operate a digital treatment platform that we provide [6].

Analysis of Medical Imaging: The instrument of AI is utilized for case triage. It helps a doctor review scans and photos. In order to prioritize crucial cases, avoid errors while analyzing EHRs (electronic health records), and create more accurate diagnoses, radiologists or cardiologists might use this information.

Large amounts of data and photos from a clinical trial may need to be analyzed, so AI systems can quickly examine these datasets and relate data from other studies in order to find undetectable relationships and patterns. Medical imaging specialists can immediately track critical information. Patient Synopsis provides radiologists and cardiologists with a summary that focuses on the context of these images by delving into previous diagnostics and medical procedures, lab results, medical history, and known allergies [7].

Decrease the Cost to Develop Medicines: The effectiveness of possible medications for a variety of ailments has been predicted by supercomputers using databases of molecular structures. AtomNet's technology, convolutional neural networks, could predict the binding of tiny chemicals to proteins by examining cues from millions of experimental measurements and thousands of protein shapes. Convolutional neural networks were able to find a potential drug candidate that was both safe and effective using this technique, which decreased the cost of creating new medications.

In 2015, when the Ebola virus was outbreak in the West Africa, Atomwise with IBM and the University of Toronto worked together to find the best vaccine to stop the Ebola virus entry into body cells. The cure for the Ebola virus was made possible by this AI analysis, which was completed in less than a day instead of the typical month or year.

Analyzes Unstructured Data: Due to the vast volume of health data and medical records, clinicians frequently struggle to keep up with the most recent medical advancements while still providing high-quality patient-centered treatment. ML systems can swiftly scan EHRs and biomedical data organised by healthcare organizations and medical specialists to give clinicians timely, accurate answers. Health information and patient medical records are frequently kept as complex unstructured information, which makes them challenging to access and comprehend [8].

AI can find, gather, store, and standardize medical data, assisting with repetitive tasks and assisting clinicians with quick, precise, and customized treatment plans and medications for their patients instead of being overburdened with the burden of searching, identifying, gathering, and transcribing the solutions they need.

AI is a Useful Tool for Emergency Medical Personnel

The period between dialing 911 and the ambulance's arrival is crucial for recovery from a sudden heart attack. Emergency dispatchers must be able to recognise the symptoms of cardiac arrest in order to take the necessary action and increase the patient's chance of life. AI is capable of analyzing both verbal and nonverbal cues to establish a diagnosis remotely. An artificial intelligence tool called Corti helps emergency medical professionals. In order to determine whether a heart attack is occurring, Corti analyses the caller's speech, background noise, and pertinent data from the patient's medical records. In a heart attack, Corti alerts the appropriate authorities. Same as different ML tools, Corti no longer looks for specific signals; however, it trains itself by being attentive to many calls with a view to stumble on essential points. Corti continuously develops its version based on what it has learned. Approximately 73% of the time in Copenhagen, emergency dispatchers can identify a cardiac arrest based solely on the caller's description. However, AI can do higher. A small-scale look carried out in 2019 discovered that ML fashion had been capable of diagnosing cardiac arrest calls higher than human dispatchers through the usage of the speech reputation software app, ML, and different history clues. ML has a significant role to play in aiding emergency medical professionals. Future medical devices could leverage technology to send drones equipped with automatic defibrillators or trained volunteers to respond to emergency calls, increasing the chances of survival in cardiac arrests that happen in the community.

Speeds Up the Invention and Improvement Of Genetic Remedy

With the help of altered molecular phenotypes, such as protein binding, genetic disorders are preferred. Predicting those changes involves estimating the likelihood that hereditary diseases may develop. This is feasible with the aid of gathering information on all recognized compounds and biomarkers applicable to apply on scientific trials. This information is processed, for example, with the aid of using the AI gadget of Deep Genomics. The company develops its own proprietary AI and uses it to learn new ways to fix the effects of genetic mutations while developing specially crafted treatments for people suffering from rare Mendelian and complex diseases. The organisation exams recognized compounds to broaden a quicker genetic remedy for situations with excessive unmet needs. The organisation's professionals are running on "Project Saturn," a drug gadget primarily based totally on AI molecular biology that assesses extra than sixty-nine billion oligonucleotide molecules *in silico* (carried out or produced through pc modeling or pc simulation) towards 1 million goal web sites for you to screen mobileular biology to free up extra ability remedies and cures. By lowering the costs associated with treating rare illnesses, the development of genetic medicine benefits both patients and medical professionals.

AI in Pandemic

It checks the improvement of COVID-19 patients and shares patient information to make the surgeon's job easy. This helps to manage the emergency condition of the patient by demonstrating several intelligent approaches. It alerts the patient to take proper medication through the utilization of the app. This technology performs the required medical tasks with less involvement of humans. It allows us to follow more critical aspects of patient care. AI-enabled robots are used for the communication of COVID-19 patients without the physical presence of doctors. The major roles of AI during the COVID-19 pandemic are contact tracing, preventing the spread of the COVID-19 virus, better understanding the nature of this virus, fever detection, predicting future outcomes, proper management of COVID-19 cases, controlling misinformation, vaccine development, detecting the probability of symptoms and proper surveillance systems [7]. It is used for the assessment of patient images and helps to predict the results. In the upcoming days, AI will provide an excellent source to identify problems and reduce the shortage of doctors. Some AI-related tools are summarized in Table 1.

Table 1. AI tools and description.

Tools	Description
Google DeepMind	Process CT and MRI scans, detect malignant cells, and other medical data to find novel, simple ways to diagnose and treat disease.
Atomwise	Used to develop effective medicines by analysing billions of chemicals and conducting preclinical drug trials.
Chatbot	Listens to a patient's symptoms and health concerns, diagnosis and then guidelines [50].
Enlitic	Tools to streamline radiology diagnosis, and it works to analyzing unstructured medical data.
Freenome	Blood tests, diagnostic procedures, and screenings are used to detect cancer at an early stage and provide more effective therapy.
Buoy Health	AI-based symptom and cure checker that uses algorithms to diagnose and treat illness

NANOTECHNOLOGY

Nanotechnology is a branch of technology that studies materials of extremely small structures, having a size of 0.1 to 100 nm. The use of nanotechnology widely ranges from industrial and medicinal to energy use due to its unique properties such as high photostability, high level of brightness, and absorption coefficients [9]. Moreover, these materials include more durable construction materials, effective bioavailability, minimal side effects, therapeutic drug delivery, and higher-density hydrogen fuel cells that are environmentally friendly and less costly. Nanotherapeutics and nanomedicines are available for clinical use, including treatments for cancer, high cholesterol, autoimmune diseases, fungal infections, macular degeneration, hepatitis, and many other conditions. Doxorubicin HCl liposome injection (Doxil, Ortho Biotech) for ovarian cancer, daunorubicin citrate liposome injection (DaunoXome, Diatos) for advanced AIDS-related Kaposi's sarcoma, and amphotericin B liposome injection (AmBisome, Gilead) for fungus infections are among the nanomedicines currently available on the market. The following Table **2** describes the Approved Cancer Drug Therapies Based on Nanotechnology [10].

Table 2. Drug name and its description.

Drug name	Where it is used
Irinotecan	To treat colon or rectal cancer (cancer that begins in the large intestine)
Paclitaxel	To treat breast cancer, ovarian cancer
Doxorubicin	To treat cancer of the blood, lymph system, bladder, breast, stomach, lungs
Cimzia	To reduce pain and swelling due to certain inflammatory conditions [2]
Rapamune	To prevent organ rejection after transplantation [2]
Emend	To prevent nausea and vomiting that may be caused by chemotherapy [2]
Cabenuva	To help control HIV infection

How Nano-medicines or Smart Pills Work?

Nano-medicines use smart nanoparticles for better drug delivery. Such systems are embedded with technological components such as microchips, cameras, or sensors that wirelessly communicate with wearable software or mobile apps and send information to computers at pharmacies or doctor's offices. This technology diagnoses similar data as conventional diagnostic techniques such as endoscopy.

A brief explanation of the pharmaceutical nanosystem is as follows which is mentioned in Fig. (**1**):

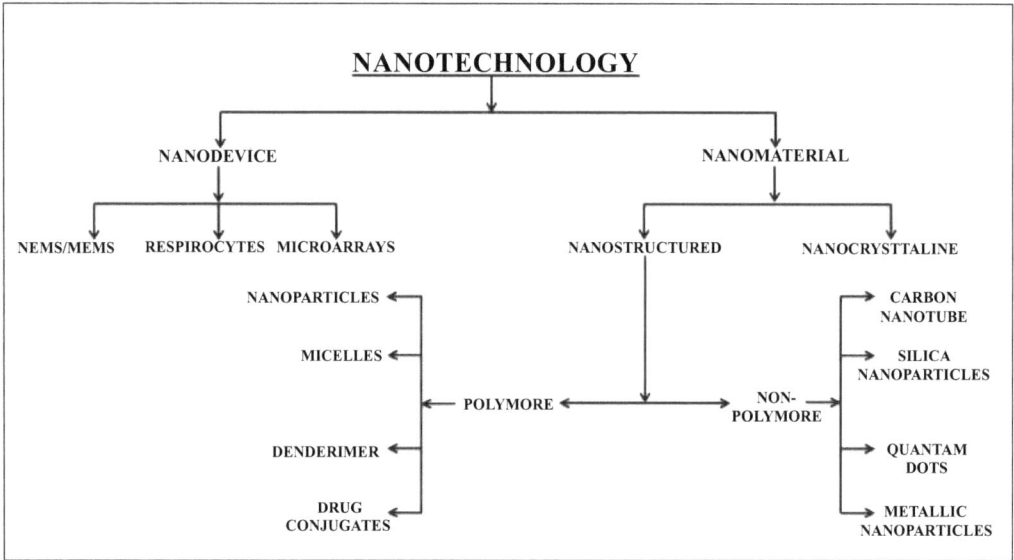

Fig. (1). Pharmaceutical Nano System.

As shown in the schematic diagram, pharmaceutical nanotechnology is divided into two basic types, which are nanomaterials and nanodevices.

Nanomaterials are materials of which a single unit is sized (in at least one dimension) between 1 and 100 nm and its some chemical properties include composition, structure, molecular weight, boiling and melting points, vapor pressure, octanol-water partition coefficient, water solubility, reactivity, and stability that are important in characterizing materials. These materials may be in the form of particles, tubes, rods, or fibres. Further, nanomaterails are categories of nanocrystalline and nanostructures. These nanostructures may be in the form of polymers or nonpolymers according to their properties. Nanostructured polymers may be nanoparticles, micelles, and drug conjugates, and nonpolymers are carbon nanotubes, silica nanoparticles, quantum dots, *etc* [12].

A nanocrystalline (NC) material is a polycrystalline material with a crystallite size of only a few nanometers and mostly used for treating wounds, especially burns and chronic wounds due to its effective antimicrobial properties. Other properties of nanocrystalline materials like increased strength/hardness, enhanced diffusivity, improved ductility/toughness, reduced density, reduced elastic modulus, higher electrical resistivity, increased specific heat, higher thermal expansion coefficient, and lower thermal conductivity make them more effective than conventional polycrystalline coarse-grained materials.

Nanodevices, including high electron mobility transistors, heterojunction bipolar transistors, resonant tunnelling diodes, and quantum optoelectronic devices like lasers and detectors, are also part of nanotechnology. Some nanodevices with their uses are described briefly in Tables **3** & **4**.

Table 3. Uses of Nanodevices.

PillCam	**The most recent PillCam model can take over 50,000 photos in a 12-hour period by shooting two to six frames per second. UT Southwestern began using PillCam technology in 2005 for diagnosing inflammation and pre-cancerous or dilated veins in the esophagus [3].**
Atmo Gas Capsule	Atmo Gas Capsule sensors can help detect the levels of oxygen and carbon dioxide in the body and any harmful substances. Additionally, it is utilised to track food sensitivity, find cancerous digestive organs, and diagnose gastrointestinal illnesses. The improved signal-to-noise ratio of the capsule as compared to breath testing is caused by the fact that gas concentrations in the gut are 5,000–10,000 times higher than those in the breath [4].
Intelligent Sensor Capsules	Eliminates the necessity for stomach injection of medications. When administered orally, it unfolds before settling on the organ, tracking vital signs for diagnostic and therapeutic vigilance.
NanoFlares	NanoFlares are small, light-emitting particles that are made to bind to specific genetic targets in cancer cells, aiding in the detection of these cells. Exospores of the nanoscale are being collected and analysed by UC San Diego researchers in order to look for biomarkers for pancreatic cancer [5].
Nanobots	The magnitude of a nanobot is smaller than a human cell in the field of medicine to deliver drugs, operate on internal injuries, and even combat cancer. These tiny bots are controlled by precise magnetic fields generated by an array of electromagnets and used to collect tissue biopsies or carry drug capsules inside the body [5].
NanoSENSE	Nanowear, the leading nanotechnology-based connected-care, and remote monitoring platform, today announced the clinical launch of NanoSENSE, a Heart Failure Management and Alert Diagnostic Validation Study. The unique and exceptional properties of nanomaterials (large surface area to volume ratio, composition, charge, reactive sites, physical structure, and potential) are exploited for sensing purposes.

Table 4. List of nano mission sanctioned new projects for fy 2018-2019.

S no.	Project name	Date of Sanction
1.	Development of Nanoconjugates for site-specific delivery of Curcumin and siRNA to lung Cancer cells [6].	21.02.2019
2.	Development of a vesicular stomatitis virus glycoprotein based virus-like nanoparticles platform for targeted drug deliver [6].	11.02.2019
3.	Nanoscale interfacial magnetic skyrmion and its applications in memory devices [7].	04.02.2019
4.	Electric field-controlled spin dynamics in nanomagnets [6].	14.01.2019

(Table 4) cont.....

S no.	Project name	Date of Sanction
5.	Nanostructured cathodes and Interlayers for Na-S and Mg-S batteries [6, 7].	11.01.2019
6.	Emergent electronic phases by interface and lattice engineering of complex oxides [6].	11.01.2019
7.	Investigations of organic nano- materials memory applicatons [6]	28.02.2019

IoT

The Internet of Things (IoT) is a network of wireless systems that are connected to one another and networked digital devices like sensors and internet devices that can collect, send, and store data without the assistance of a human or computer [18], as shown in Table **5**.

The Internet of Things (IoT) promises a number of benefits for streamlining and enhancing the delivery of healthcare, including the capacity to diagnose, treat, and monitor patients both within and outside of hospitals. There are more such advantages of using IoT like remote monitoring, medical data accessibility, improved treatment management, and instant and reliable treatment [19]. In 2022, during the pandemic period, IoT's sensor-based technology has the potential to lower the danger of surgery in difficult instances, which could be useful in COVID-19 [20 - 22]. In the medical field, IoT's focus is to help perform the treatment of different COVID-19 cases precisely. By 2025, 75 billion IoT devices are anticipated to exist [22 - 24].

Table 5. IoT integrated with other techniques.

IoT integrated with other techniques	Benefits
5G-IoT communication	The upcoming 5G network is anticipated to serve smart healthcare applications that can generally meet the requirements, such as ultra-low latency, high bandwidth, ultra-high reliability, high density, and high energy efficiency. In order to enhance network performance, increase cellular coverage, and address security-related challenges, future smart healthcare networks are projected to integrate 5G and IoT devices. Speed up the system which is 100 times faster than the 4G network and it improves communication in the system [8].
AI- IoT	Manage, analyze, and obtain meaningful insights from data with fast and accurate analysis. It tends to improve the quality and effectiveness of the specific service offered by integrating AI-driven IoT and tools with data mining features into individual medical devices [9].
IoT with blockchain	prevent unscrupulous attackers from accessing the network and make it more secure to ensure data integrity and availability. It is a threat breaker for computerized medical records [10].

(Table 5) cont.....

IoT integrated with other techniques	Benefits
IoNT(nanotechnology)	By integrating nano-communication capabilities with nano devices and enabling them to smoothly communicate with current micro- and macro devices, as well as by overcoming a number of other technological challenges, the IoNT vision may be fulfilled. Healthcare has resulted in more personalized, timely, and convenient health monitoring and treatment [11].
cloud-based IoT	The main benefits are device connection management, secure device connection, data transfer and access control, real-time data management, and rich analytics and insights are easier than ever [12].

Five-Layer Architecture of IoT

All IoT-related services inevitably follow five basic steps called create, communicate, aggregate, analyze, and act. All these are done by some specific layer and each layer transfers data to the next layer in a meaningful way [25]. These 5 layers are as followed:-

The perception layer is the lowest layer of the conventional architecture of IoT and is called the recognition layer, which includes sensors (Humidity Sensors, Pressure Sensors, Proximity Sensors, and Level Sensors) for perceiving and acquiring environmental data and transform them in a digital setup [25, 26].

The transport layer is the next layer of IoT architecture which mainly focuses on transferring end-to-end sensor data from the perception layer to the processing layer and vice versa through networks such as wireless 3G, LAN(Local Area Network), Bluetooth, RFID (Radio-frequency identification), and NFC (Radio-frequency identification) with reliability, congestion avoidance. Ordering of packets, error detection, and correction in the delivery of data packets are the other main functions which this layer performs [26].

The Processing Layer is referred to as the IOT system's middleware layer. It stores, analyzes, and processes large amounts of data that come from the upper layer, that is, the transport layer. It is capable of managing and giving the lower layers a wide range of services [26, 27]. It makes use of a variety of technologies, including big data processing modules, cloud computing, and databases.

The Application Layer is responsible for delivering application-specific services to the clients with their prior requests. It describes several applications for the Internet of Things, such as smart homes, smart cities, and smart health.

The Business Layer oversees the entire Internet of Things (IoT) system, including all apps, business and revenue models, and user privacy, and it produces data-driven decision-making analysis. It is the most upper layer of IOT which interacts with the user [25]. All layers are shown in stack form in Fig. (**2**).

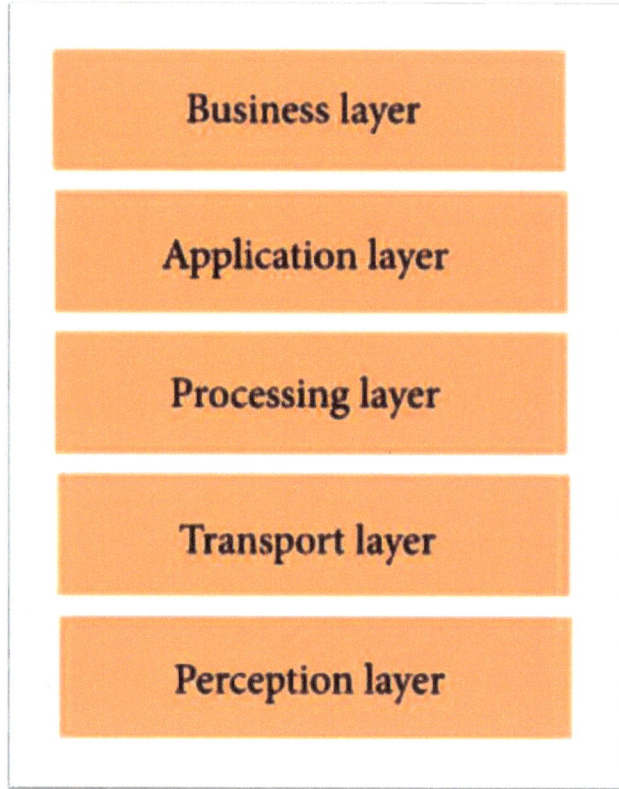

Fig. (2). Architecture of IoT.

Sensors and Actuators: Context awareness is one of the key components of the Internet of Things and is impossible without sensor technology, and these IoT sensors are mostly capable of wired and wireless transmission, providing real-time, continuous data feed from assets and processes [28-30]. They increase accuracy while also ensuring faster **transmission** of measurement data, which enhances process control and asset health [31, 32].

Healthcare Monitoring Devices, Embedded Sensors

Table 6. Embedded Sensors in Health Devices.

Sensors	Working of sensors
Glucose monitoring	Glucose monitoring is wearable technology that makes it easier to track your blood sugar levels over time by inserting the sensor properly under your skin, usually on your belly or arm [13].
Heart-rate monitoring	Sensors integrated into a smartwatch or wearable like a ring, necklace, earbud, shoe, or item of clothing, many modern heart rate monitors are quite accurate [14].
Hand hygiene monitoring	Sensors embedded help in hand hygiene is one of the most effective ways of reducing the transmission of pathogens that cause healthcare–associated infections [15].
Depression and mood monitoring	The wristband that monitors for symptoms of a panic attack. When an imminent attack is detected, the 'Breathe Watch' alerts the wearer and/or their carers, and provides calming techniques [16].
Connected inhalers	Digital inhalers or smart inhalers embedded with sensors are used to collect, rescue, and control data virtually and in real-time, track adherence, and often include clinical platforms that aid patient self-management [16].
Ingestible sensors	The pill broadcasts a real-time video stream as it goes down your oesophagus and into your stomach [17].
Gyroscope sensors	They are also used in medical devices used to assist with the diagnosis, prevention, monitoring, and treatment of a disease or injury.

IoT Device Trends and Anticipated Growth

The estimations for the future growth of IoT devices have been fast and furious. One of the fastest-growing segments of the IoT market is healthcare devices, as shown in Table **6**. In fact, it is anticipated that the market for this industry, commonly referred to as the Internet of Medical Things (IoMT), will reach $176 billion by 2026 [33].

According to Intel's predictions, the number of internet-enabled gadgets would increase from 2 billion in 2006 to 200 billion by 2020, or approximately 26 smart devices for every person on Earth.IHS Mark predicted that there will be 75.4 billion connected devices in 2025 and 125 billion by 2030, which is a little more conservative.

Other businesses have adjusted their statistics by excluding PCs, tablets, and smartphones from the calculation. By 2020, 20.8 billion connected things are predicted to be in use by Gartner, IDC, and BI Intelligence, respectively [33].

IDC forecasts that spending on IoT devices and services will total $772.5 billion in 2018, up 14.6 percent from the $674 billion it predicted would be spent in

2017, and then $1 trillion and $1.1 trillion in 2020 and 2021, respectively. Total spending on IoT devices and services was estimated by Gartner to be close to $2 trillion in 2017.

The Global IoT estimation was USD 72.91 billion in 2020 and is expected to reach USD 89.40 billion in 2021, projected to grow at a CAGR of 22.95% reaching USD 251.90 billion by 2026 in Healthcare Market size.

In 2020, COVID-19 is anticipated to be the third most common cause of mortality in the country, and the pandemic is anticipated to result in a deficit of 3.3 trillion dollars, or around 15% of GDP [33].

Virtual Reality (VR): Virtual reality (VR) is a simulated reality created by computer techniques to make a user completely immersed in a digital environment, and this environment is perceived through a device known as a Virtual Reality headset or helmet [34]. Virtual technologies can replicate various sensations, including vision, hearing, smelling, and even touching and other behaviours. Additionally, research from Statista indicates that the AR/VR market share would be approximately 193 billion dollars, or nearly 16 times what it was in 2018, As shown in Fig. (**3**).

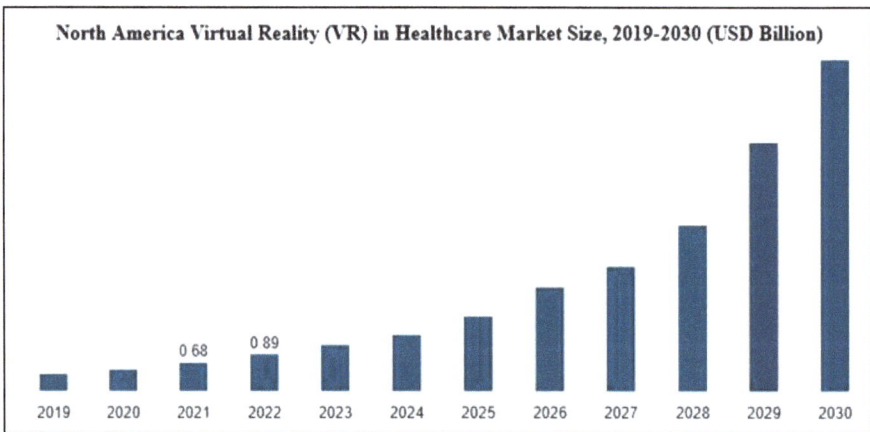

Fig. (3). VR healthcare market size.

Key Market Insights

According to our analysis, the global market for virtual reality in healthcare grew by an average of 36.0 percent in 2020 compared to 2019. In 2021, the market for virtual reality (VR) in healthcare was estimated to be worth USD 459.0 million. The market is anticipated to increase by USD 6.20 by 2029, representing a CAGR of 38.7% over the forecast period, from USD 628.0 million in 2022. By 2025,

NewGenApps, a provider of AI, machine learning, big data analytics, and AR/VR solutions, predicts that 216 million people will be playing AR and VR games worldwide [35, 36].

Some of the most practical and pioneered ways virtual reality tools are helpful in the healthcare field are the following:-

1. **Treatment in a VR Clinic**:- Treatment for specific illnesses like phobias (flying, driving, public speaking, *etc.*), PTSD from car accidents, panic disorder, and agoraphobia is made simple or even possible due to VR Clinics. The skill to conduct the exposure session in a virtual environment, allowing for the stimulation of multiple senses (visual, auditory, and tactile), while still enabling the monitoring of the patient's physiology, allowed therapy to advance more quickly and, in the majority of cases, more successfully [37].

For instance, Cambridge University researchers developed and used a navigation test that employs virtual reality to identify individuals with early Alzheimer's disease and is more accurate than a traditional cognitive evaluation.

Phobia patients are treated by cognitive behavioral therapy in VR Clinic to recognize the thoughts causing negative feelings surrounding their fears and through thoughts, the patient learns how to replace those undesirable beliefs with more positive ones with fear in a controlled way and in small doses. By taking small steps, they can confront and gradually conquer their phobia.

2. **Surgical Training**:- Virtual reality enables cost-effective practice of practical skills without having to deal with consequences in real life. Due to the realistic graphics and feedback, it has used simulation as well as other technologies and procedures to attain an incredibly high bar for safety and give students a beneficial learning experience. After passing the VR training, healthcare professionals report improved accuracy and confidence when dealing with high-risk conditions for patients. As a result, specialised VR training platforms, such as OssoVR, Google VR, SteamVR, and Cluster, are enabled for more frequent and routine practise of various surgical operations with changeable settings and pre-set scenarios to develop skills and learn from mistakes [38, 39].

3. **Dentistry treatment**:- Virtual reality (VR) and augmented reality (AR) have many uses in the field of dentistry such as relaxation and pain management, preparing for a dental procedure in advance, and the best way to give training.VR tools enable dentists to practice their skills on virtual patients or even 3D models of teeth through special drills configured to imitate real-life tactile feedback. In place of the traditional teaching method using mannequins with plastic teeth, hapTEL, an example of such a virtual dental training system, was introduced in

2010. Modern dental training devices using haptic technology from the company MOOG provide an extraordinarily accurate virtual reality simulation of dental treatments [40].

In 2014, the University of Pennsylvania School of Dental Medicine became the first dental school in North America to incorporate this technology into its curriculum. These units are already in use at dental schools around Europe and Asia.

4. **Healthy lifestyle promotion with 3D models**:- The tremendous visual impact of virtual reality can be used to educate and aware people, especially youth regarding the harmful effects of such bad habits as smoking, alcohol and drug abuse, an unwholesome diet, sedentary lifestyle, and others and the right path of life. Illustrative 3D models can show how the human body gradually changes under the effect of such habits and how long it takes to recover, fully or partially, from the damage. Such visualization presents an intelligible and relatable method of promoting a healthy life and urging people to change their lives before it's too late [39].

5. **Helping patients with Alzheimer's**:- VR tools help manage psychological and behavioural symptoms of the disease such as Alzheimer's, agitation, aberrant motor behavior, anxiety, and elation. Around the globe today, 50 million individuals are affected with dementia. By the year 2050, this number is projected to be more than triple from its current level andis expected to reach $2 trillion by 2030. Virtual and augmented reality (VR and AR) uses computer-generated environments for diagnosing and treatment of Alzheimer's disease for relieving its symptoms. VR stimulation provided by the virtual reality tours helped dementia patients tap into old memories and help in faster recovery of lost memory and improve communication between patients and their families or carers. The researchers suggest this may show a correlation between VR and positive mood and motivation to engage in the art class.

6. **Feel stay-at-home via VR during long in-hospital treatment**:- Virtual reality goggles can assist in relieving any stress brought on by long-term hospitalisation, which is difficult and unpleasant for all patients, especially youngsters who miss their parents and friends. Recently, we can see in the COVID-19 pandemic VR tools such as psychological intervention techniques for good mental health without physical contact. In these situations, medical virtual reality makes it simpler for friends and family to be in constant contact with their hospitalised friends and family members [41].

Drone

A drone is an unmanned aircraft known as unmanned aerial vehicles (UAVs) or an unmanned aircraft system that can be remotely controlled or fly autonomously using software-controlled flight plans in its embedded system integrated with onboard sensors and a global positioning system (GPS) [42]. Navigational systems, such as GPS drones use autopilot functions to travel along a path that is predetermined and sensors for the purpose to detecting obstacles and avoiding collisions, which makes it a more effective system. Drones have proven to be beneficial to various fields such as the agriculture industry, military, public safety, commercial shipping, law enforcement and traffic surveillance, and education. Drones in medicine and healthcare are often used in public health and disaster relief, telemedicine, and medical transport.

They include (1) Prehospital Emergency Care, (2) Expediting Laboratory Diagnostic Testing, and (3) Surveillance.

Prehospital Emergency Care:- Prehospital care is provided by emergency medical services (EMS) responders, who are the initial healthcare providers at the scene of the disaster. Medical drones can be flown to deliver medical supplies such as automated external defibrillators (AED), red blood cells, medicine, or vaccines, to save emergency patients in remote areas.

Transporting Devices and Materials

In the past, it took a lot of time and money to carry medical items to and from patients. Now drones are widely used by providers to send products like hazardous materials and small medical gadgets to the required places in short time span. In addition, touchless communication is made possible by drones, which slows the spread of contagious diseases such as pandemic cases [43]. For this purpose fixed-wing drones are used due to their superior engine efficiency and their ability to cover great distances covering around 400 hectares. Fixed-wing drones resemble airplanes, and fixed-wing hybrids, which incorporate wings and rotors on a single battery. These types of drones are better suited for flying long distances. A proof-of-concept unmanned system was put to test in 2007 by researchers from the National Health Laboratory Service (NHLS) and Denel Dynamics (UAV division) to transport microbiological samples from remote clinics to NHLS centres more effectively for quick Human Immunodeficiency Virus (HIV) testing.

Enable Backup Transport System in the Pandemic

Global health providers are now looking for different ways of transmitting vaccines to rural and remote areas—and drones are helping the cause. Drones allow safe, easy, and efficient access to places that are difficult or dangerous to reach through traditional delivery means. By using drones, providers can ensure that people who need vaccines can obtain them in a timely manner.

With the clear need to avoid all unnecessary direct human contact, an increased interest in contactless transportation and delivery modes emerged. Drones are a promising alternative in this regard, especially for the delivery of essential goods, such as COVID-19 viral tests [44].

Delivering Organ Transfers

Transportation often depends on the distance involved and can include ambulances, helicopters, and airplanes. Organs must frequently be transported quickly by medical professionals, making conventional methods like flight and cars unworkable. Instead, medical professionals are increasingly adopting drones to transport organs quickly between institutions. Drones increase the likelihood that valuable items will reach their destinations on schedule while enabling faster and safer deliveries. Once organs are recovered from donors, they will only remain healthy for a short period of time, so every minute counts.

Blockchain

A blockchain in health care is a distributed database or ledger that is shared among the nodes of a computer network to preserve and exchange patient medical records through hospitals, which manage the medicine supply chain, diagnostic laboratories, pharmacy firms,and physicians [45]. It also helps to pick up the performance, security of data, accountability, and transparency of sharing medical information in the health care system.

Current blockchain systems are categorized into four types: public, private, consortium, and hybrid blockchains.

Public Blockchain: Public blockchains provide a fully decentralized open network, where every member can access the blockchain content, *i.e.*, the public blockchain is permissionless and anyone can join the network to read, write, or participate within the blockchain. For validating transactions this network tends to use proof-of-Work or proof-of-Stake consensus algorithms. There are some of the key advantages of the public blockchain, such as Greater Transparency, User Empowerment, and immutability [46].

Private Blockchain: Private blockchains are centralized dedicated networks for single enterprise solutions and are utilized to keep track of data exchanges occurring between different departments or individuals, which quickens the transaction process. If one needs to join a private blockchain that allows only the selected entries of verified participants, like that for a private business. A participant can join such a private network with only an authentic and verified invitation. A validation is also necessary either by the network operator(s) or by a clearly defined set protocol implemented by the network [46].

Consortium Blockchain: A consortium blockchain (also called federated blockchain) is a permissioned network and public only to a privileged group. It serves as a distributed database that can be consistently synchronised and audited, keeping track of participant data transfers under one central authority or we can say more than one organization involved that provides access to preselected nodes for reading, writing, and auditing the blockchain. It provides a significant degree of control, offers scalability, control over resources, and faster processing which makes it more efficient and secure in many ways.

Hybrid Blockchain: Blockchains that are hybrids combine the advantages of private and public blockchains. As a result, a private blockchain is used in the background to regulate access to the ledger's alterations, while a public blockchain is used to make the ledger completely accessible. Table **7** describes the comparison of different blockchains.

Table 7. Comparison table of different types of blockchain.

Characteristics	Public blockchain	Private blockchain	Consortium blockchain	Hybrid Blockchain
Accessibility	Public Class	Public or restricted	May be public or restricted	combination of the public and private blockchain
Determination of consensus	All miners	Only one organization	A designated set of nodes	PoW miners
Efficiency	Low	High	High	vary depending on the design choices and implementation details
Immutability	Impossible to tamper	Could be tamped	Could be tampered	Impossible to tamper
Decentralized	Yes	No	Partial	Depends on the implementation details and the trade-offs made to address the specific requirements of the blockchain solution.

(Table 7) cont.....

Characteristics	Public blockchain	Private blockchain	Consortium blockchain	Hybrid Blockchain
Transaction speed	Slow	Lighter and Faster	Lighter and Faster	Improved than private and public chain
Scalability	Scalability issues	Highly scalable	Offers scalability and much secured	Highly scalable
Transaction throughput	Low	Very high	High	higher transaction speeds and throughput compared to public Blockchain.
Example	Bitcoin and Ethereum	Ripple (XRP) and Hyperledger	Hyperledger, Corda, Ripple	Hyperledger Fabric framework

Centralized Electronic Health Records:- Blockchain technology is used to securely store digital health records of patients due to this feature year Between 2009 and 2017, more than 176 million patient records were exposed to data breaches. It also makes patient information more secure, incorruptible, and transparent. In addition, the decentralized nature of the technology also allows patients, doctors, and healthcare providers to share the same information quickly and safely. There are many companies such as Akiri, BurstIQ Factom, and Medical Chain, which adopt blockchain technology to prevent cyber attacks on healthcare data. Guardtime is one of these companies which is located in California and recently signed a deal with a private healthcare provider in the United Arab Emirates to bring blockchain to its data privacy systems [47].

Medical Supply Chain Management and End-to-end secure traceability of drug products:- Blockchain is a virtual regulatory analytics platform that provides fast-track drug development to help in monitoring labor costs and waste emissions. This approach leverages smart contracts and decentralized off-chain storage for efficient product traceability in the healthcare supply chain which provides a secure, immutable history of transactions to all stakeholders [48]. This all is possible to leverage the cryptographic properties of blockchain to achieve a decentralized, verifiable track and trace system for pharmaceutical drugs. Encrypt messages in a P2P (Point-to-Point) network is the main part of cryptography, which prevent the system from a third party from accessing and gaining knowledge of the data.

Empowering Genomics data:- Genomic drugs open the world of genetic data for providing an accurate diagnosis, prognosis, and appropriate treatment of several genetic diseases to determine their susceptibility to the disease and appropriate treatment options for their personalized medicine. Some companies are using blockchain by using digital currency Bitcoin to help create a fair marketplace for genetic information. An ideal implementation of personal genomic data storage would (1) protect from loss and manipulation, (2) provide appropriate access to clinicians and biomedical researchers, and (3) allow individuals control over their own genomic data [49]. Some companies like Nebula Genomics are helping to build a giant genetic database by eliminating expensive middlemen and incentivizing users to safely sell their encrypted genetic data. EncrypGen makes next-generation software to aid in safely storing and sharing, buying, and selling of genomic data for research and science, and to allow users to manage their own data and sell it to researchers. EncrypGen plans to expand its user profile to include self-reported medical and behavioral data [47].

Machine Learning

It is increasingly being used in more recent healthcare systems to enhance various facets of patient care, diagnosis, treatment, and healthcare administration [50]. Here are some notable applications of machine learning in the field of medicine:

Medical Image Analysis: Medical image analysis: Machine learning algorithms have been applied to image data from X-rays, CT scans, MRIs, and other types of medical imaging to help with the early detection and diagnosis of diseases [51].

In medical image classification, deep learning algorithms, such as convolutional neural networks (CNNs), have shown promise in accurately identifying and classifying abnormalities, such as tumors or fractures [52].

Early disease detection using predictive analytics and analytics: Machine learning models can be trained on patient data to make predictions about the likelihood of developing specific diseases or conditions. there are some frameworks that are used to predict COVID diseases. COVIDX-Net will let radiologists identify COVID-19 in X-ray pictures automatically [53]. Machine learning algorithms can identify people who may be at higher risk for conditions like diabetes, cardiovascular diseases, or certain types of cancer by analyzing a combination of patient demographics, data, medical history, genetic information, information, and lifestyle factors. Timely intervention and preventive measures are made possible by early detection.

Treatment optimization and personalized medicine: Machine learning methods can help in the customization of treatment regimens for specific patients [54]. Machine learning algorithms can find patterns and forecast the best course of treatment based on variables like genetic profiles, treatment response patterns, and co-existing conditions by analyzing large datasets and patient characteristics. This may result in more focused treatments, fewer negative effects, and better patient outcomes.

The analysis of continuous streams of patient data gathered from wearables, IoT devices, or electronic health records (EHRs) using machine learning algorithms is possible in the context of health monitoring and remote patient care. Machine learning models can recognize anomalies, forecast health deterioration, and enable early intervention by tracking vital signs, activity levels, sleep patterns, and other physiological data. This aids in the management of chronic diseases, remote patient monitoring, and the provision of individualized care.

Drug Discovery and Development: The use of machine learning algorithms in pharmaceutical research and development processes is growing. Machine learning can help with drug discovery, target identification, drug repurposing, and clinical trial design optimization by examining large volumes of biomedical data, including genomics, proteomics, and chemical structures. New medications and treatments may develop faster as a result.

Resource Allocation and Healthcare Operations Optimization: Machine learning techniques can help with resource allocation and healthcare operations optimization. Forecasting patient admissions, length of stays, and demand for healthcare services allows hospitals to allocate resources more effectively [55]. Additionally, administrative tasks can be automated, medical coding can be simplified, and billing errors can be decreased with the help of machine learning algorithms.

These are merely a few instances of how machine learning is currently being applied in modern healthcare systems. Machine learning is anticipated to have a bigger impact on patient care, clinical judgment, and the delivery of healthcare as technology develops.

CONCLUSION

Emerging technologies have transformed the way of our living by changing almost every sector of life. The adoption and deployment of these technologies in the healthcare industry benefit all related fields involved in providing healthcare, including those who need access to cost-effective healthcare, and other services. The main technologies such as 3-D Printing, Virtual Reality (VR), Augmented Reality (AR), Artificial Intelligence (AI), Internet of Things (IoT), Drones, Robots, and Blockchain make it an automatedand effective field. There are several projects initiated by governments of different countries to improve the delivery of healthcare services and management of the public health system. In Addition, Deep Genomics' XtalPi's ID4 Buoy Health BioXcel biotech companies in the clinical stage are using their exclusive platform, Interrogative Biology, driven by artificial intelligence to map diseases and change treatments for oncology, neurology, and uncommon disorders.

REFERENCES

[1]   T. Davenport, and R. Kalakota, "The potential for artificial intelligence in healthcare", *Future Healthc. J.,* vol. 6, no. 2, pp. 94-98, 2019.
[http://dx.doi.org/10.7861/futurehosp.6-2-94] [PMID: 31363513]

[2]   "Future of artificial intelligence in health care | deloitte ", Available from: https://www2. deloitte.com/us/en/pages/life-sciences-and-health-care/articles/future-of-artificial-intelligence-in-health-care.html (Accessed Jul. 12, 2022).

[3]   A. Ćirković, "Evaluation of four artificial intelligence-assisted self-diagnosis apps on three diagnoses: Two-year follow-up study", *J. Med. Internet Res.,* vol. 22, no. 12, p. e18097, 2020.
[http://dx.doi.org/10.2196/18097] [PMID: 33275113]

[4]   "Berg backs AI-driven discovery platform to save time, money in R&D | Fierce Biotech", Available from: https://www.fiercebiotech.com/r-d/berg-backs-ai-driven-discovery-platform-to-save-time-money-r-d (Accessed Jul. 13, 2022).

[5]   "ID4 platform (Intelligent Digital Drug Discovery and Development platform XtalPi Inc. - [LSUS] Life-Sciences-USA.com - The Transatlantic Life Sciences Web Portal", Available from: https:// www.life-sciences-usa.com/product/id4-platform-intelligent-digital-xtalpi-inc-mit-massachusetts-2001-32571.html (Accessed Jul. 13, 2022).

[6]   "Mila announces collaboration with leading ai therapeutics company deep genomics | deep genomics", Available   from: https://www.deepgenomics.com/news/mila-announces-collaboration-leadin--ai-therapeutics-company-deep-genomics/ (Accessed Jul. 13, 2022).

[7]   Karthikeyan B. Advantages of AI in medical field. Bodhi.:43, 2021.

[8]   D. Technology, *Artificial intelligence in healthcare : Transforming the practice of medicine digital technology* vol. 8. , 2021, no. 2, pp. 188-194.
[http://dx.doi.org/10.7861/fhj.2021-0095]

[9]   "Nanotechnologies: 1. What is nanotechnology", Available from: https://ec.europa.eu/health/ scientific_committees/opinions_layman/en/nanotechnologies/l-2/1-introduction.htm (Accessed Jul. 07, 2022).

[10]   "Current Nanotechnology Treatments - NCI", Available from: https://www.cancer.gov/nano/cancer-nanotechnology/current-treatments (Accessed Jul. 07, 2022).

[11]   V. Weissig, T. Pettinger, and N. Murdock, "Nanopharmaceuticals (part 1): Products on the market", *Int. J. Nanomedicine,* vol. 9, pp. 4357-4373, 2014.
[http://dx.doi.org/10.2147/IJN.S46900] [PMID: 25258527]

[12]   A.M. Khidir, M. Alsayid, and A.A. Saeed, "Pharmaceutical nanotechnology and application", *World J. Pharm. Pharm. Sci.,* vol. 9, no. 2, pp. 202-211, 2020.
[http://dx.doi.org/10.20959/wjpps20202-15466]

[13]   Available   from: https://utswmed.org/medblog/pillcam-gets-close-and-intestinal-spot-gi-bleeding/ (Accessed Jul. 11, 2022).

[14]   K.J. Berean, N. Ha, J.Z. Ou, A.F. Chrimes, D. Grando, C.K. Yao, J.G. Muir, S.A. Ward, R.E. Burgell, P.R. Gibson, and K. Kalantar-Zadeh, "The safety and sensitivity of a telemetric capsule to monitor gastrointestinal hydrogen production in vivo in healthy subjects: a pilot trial comparison to concurrent breath analysis", *Aliment. Pharmacol. Ther.,* vol. 48, no. 6, pp. 646-654, 2018.
[http://dx.doi.org/10.1111/apt.14923] [PMID: 30067289]

[15]   Available from: https://www.netscribes.com/nanotechnology-in-healthcare/ (Accessed Jul. 11, 2022).

[16]   Available   from: https://dst.gov.in/news/new-projects-sanctioned-during-fy-2018-2019-nano-mission (Accessed Jul. 7, 2022).

[17]   Available from: https://ece.iisc.ac.in/list-of-ongoing-projects/ (Accessed Jul. 7, 2022).

[18]   Available from: https://www.researchgate.net/publication/297141894_Towards_Internet_of_Things_Survey_and_Future_Vision (Accessed Jul. 10, 2022).

[19]   B. Al-Shargabi, and S. Abuarqoub, "IoT-enabled healthcare: Benefits, issues and challenges", *ACM Int. Conf. Proceeding Ser,* 2020.
[http://dx.doi.org/10.1145/3440749.3442596]

[20]   A. Ahad, M. Tahir, and K.L.A. Yau, "5G-based smart healthcare network: Architecture, taxonomy, challenges and future research directions", *IEEE Access,* vol. 7, no. July, pp. 100747-100762, 2019.
[http://dx.doi.org/10.1109/ACCESS.2019.2930628]

[21]   I. Keshta, "AI-driven IoT for smart health care: Security and privacy issues", *Informatics in Medicine Unlocked,* vol. 30, p. 100903, 2022.
[http://dx.doi.org/10.1016/j.imu.2022.100903]

[22]   "Monitoring and Securing the Healthcare Data Harnessing IOT and Blockchain Technology", *Turkish J. Comput. Math. Educ.,* vol. 12, no. 2, pp. 2554-2561, 2021.
[http://dx.doi.org/10.17762/turcomat.v12i2.2213]

[23]   P.K.D. Pramanik, A. Solanki, A. Debnath, A. Nayyar, S. El-Sappagh, and K.S. Kwak, "Advancing modern healthcare with nanotechnology, nanobiosensors, and internet of nano things: Taxonomies, applications, architecture, and challenges", *IEEE Access,* vol. 8, no. April, pp. 65230-65266, 2020.
[http://dx.doi.org/10.1109/ACCESS.2020.2984269]

[24]   J.L. Shah, H.F. Bhat, and A.I. Khan, *"Integration of Cloud and IoT for smart e-healthcare," in Healthcare Paradigms in the Internet of Things Ecosystem.* Elsevier, 2020, pp. 101-136.
[http://dx.doi.org/10.1016/B978-0-12-819664-9.00006-5]

[25]   N. Verma, S. Singh, and D. Prasad, "A review on existing iot architecture and communication protocols used in healthcare monitoring system", *Journal of The Institution of Engineers (India): Series B,* vol. 103, no. 1, pp. 245-257, 2022.
[http://dx.doi.org/10.1007/s40031-021-00632-3]

[26]   H.F. Atlam, R.J. Walters, and G.B. Wills, "Internet of Things: State-of-the-art, Challenges, Applications, and Open Issues", *International Journal of Intelligent Computing Research,* vol. 9, no. 3, pp. 928-938, 2018.
[http://dx.doi.org/10.20533/ijicr.2042.4655.2018.0112]

[27]   "5 Layer Architecture of Internet of Things - GeeksforGeeks", Available from: https://www.geeksforgeeks.org/5-layer-architecture-of-internet-of-things/ (Accessed Jul. 10, 2022).

[28]   T.N. Gia, M. Ali, I.B. Dhaou, A.M. Rahmani, T. Westerlund, P. Liljeberg, and H. Tenhunen, "IoT-based continuous glucose monitoring system: A feasibility study", *Procedia Comput. Sci.,* vol. 109, pp. 327-334, 2017.
[http://dx.doi.org/10.1016/j.procs.2017.05.359]

[29]   S.S. Khamitkar, and P.M. Rafi, *IoT based System for Heart Rate Monitoring* vol. 9. , 2020, no. 7, pp. 1563-1571.
[http://dx.doi.org/10.17577/IJERTV9IS070673]

[30]   Challenge FG. WHO Guidelines on Hand Hygiene in Health Care. Retrieved from: whqlibdoc who int/publications/009 pdf. 2009.

[31]   Available from: https://ordr.net/article/iot-healthcare-examples/ (Accessed Jul. 10, 2022).

[32]   "Health IoT: Ingestible sensor can help diagnose disease | internet of business", Available from: https://internetofbusiness.com/health-iot-ingestible-sensor-can-help-diagnose-disease/ (Accessed Jul. 10, 2022).

[33]   "IoT in Healthcare Market Size, Industry Share & Trends – 2032", Available from: https://www.futuremarketinsights.com/reports/iot-in-healthcare-market (Accessed Jul. 10, 2022).

[34]   "What Is Virtual Reality And How Does It Work", Available from: https://www.softwaretest

inghelp.com/what-is-virtual-reality/ (Accessed Jul. 11, 2022).

[35]   "Virtual Reality in Healthcare Market Size, Share | Growth", Available from: https://www.fortunebusinessinsights.com/industry-reports/virtual-reality-vr-in-healthcare-market-101679 (Accessed Jul. 11, 2022).

[36]   "Virtual Reality Applications in Healthcare - Flatworld Solutions", Available from: https://www.flatworldsolutions.com/healthcare/articles/virtual-reality-applications-in-healthcare.php (Accessed Jul. 11, 2022).

[37]   L. Li, "Application of virtual reality technology in clinical medicine", *American Journal of Translational Research,* vol. 9, pp. 3867-3880, 2017.

[38]   T.S. Puntambekar, "Awareness of Virtual reality in Surgical Training in India", *Indian J. Public Health Res. Dev.,* vol. 10, no. 5, p. 702, 2019.
[http://dx.doi.org/10.5958/0976-5506.2019.01093.3]

[39]   "Virtual Reality (VR) in Medicine: Top 10 Use Cases | LIGHT-IT", Available from: https://light-it.net/blog/virtual-reality-in-medicine/ (Accessed Jul. 11, 2022).

[40]   B. Tse, W. Harwin, A. Barrow, B. Quinn, J. San Diego, and M. Cox, "Design and development of a haptic dental training system - HapTEL", In: *in Lecture Notes in Computer Science (including subseries Lecture Notes in Artificial Intelligence and Lecture Notes in Bioinformatics*, 2010, pp. 101-108.
[http://dx.doi.org/10.1007/978-3-642-14075-4_15]

[41]   M.H. Hatta, H. Sidi, C. Siew Koon, N.A. Che Roos, S. Sharip, F.D. Abdul Samad, O. Wan Xi, S. Das, and S. Mohamed Saini, "Virtual Reality (VR) technology for treatment of mental health problems during covid-19: A systematic review", *Int. J. Environ. Res. Public Health,* vol. 19, no. 9, p. 5389, 2022.
[http://dx.doi.org/10.3390/ijerph19095389] [PMID: 35564784]

[42]   "What is a Drone? - Definition from WhatIs.com", Available from: https://www.techtarget.com/iotagenda/definition/drone (Accessed Jul. 11, 2022).

[43]   T. Mesar, A. Lessig, and D.R. King, "Use of drone technology for delivery of medical supplies during prolonged field care", *J. Spec. Oper. Med.,* vol. 18, no. 4, pp. 34-35, 2018.
[http://dx.doi.org/10.55460/M63P-H7DM] [PMID: 30566722]

[44]   M. Kunovjanek, and C. Wankmüller, "Containing the COVID-19 pandemic with drones - Feasibility of a drone enabled back-up transport system", *Transp. Policy,* vol. 106, pp. 141-152, 2021.
[http://dx.doi.org/10.1016/j.tranpol.2021.03.015] [PMID: 33846672]

[45]   "What Is a Blockchain? How does it work", Available from: https://www.investopedia.com/terms/b/blockchain.asp (Accessed Jul. 11, 2022).

[46]   R.M. Stulz, "Public versus private equity", *Oxf. Rev. Econ. Policy,* vol. 36, no. 2, pp. 275-290, 2020.
[http://dx.doi.org/10.1093/oxrep/graa003]

[47]   "18 Top blockchain in healthcare examples helping revive the industry", Available from: https://builtin.com/blockchain/blockchain-healthcare-applications-companies (Accessed Jul. 12, 2022).

[48]   A. Musamih, K. Salah, R. Jayaraman, and J. Arshad, *A Blockchain-based Approach for Drug Traceability in Healthcare Supply Chain* in IEEE Access, vol. 9, pp. 9728-9743, 2021.
[http://dx.doi.org/10.1109/ACCESS.2021.3049920]

[49]   B. A. Dedeturk, A. Soran, and B. Bakir-gungor, "Blockchain for genomics and healthcare : A literature review, current status, classification and open issues", *PeerJ,* vol. 9, p. 12130, 2021.
[http://dx.doi.org/10.7717/peerj.12130]

[50]   E. H. Weissler, "The role of machine learning in clinical research: transforming the future of evidence generation", *Commentary*. vol. 22, no. 1, pp. 1–15, 2021.
[http://dx.doi.org/10.1186/s13063-021-05489-x]

[51]   O. Access, *Research_in_Medical_Imaging_Using_Image_Processing 2019.pdf.*

[52]   M. Badawy, *Healthcare Predictive Analytics Using Machine Learning and Deep Learning Techniques: A Survey,* 2022.

[53]   E.E-D. Hemdan, M.A. Shouman, and M.E. Karar, "COVIDX-Net: A Framework of Deep Learning Classifiers to Diagnose COVID-19 in X-Ray Images", http://arxiv.org/abs/2003.11055 Online

[54]   R.F. Mansour, A.E. Amraoui, I. Nouaouri, V.G. Diaz, D. Gupta, and S. Kumar, "Artificial intelligence and internet of things enabled disease diagnosis model for smart healthcare systems", *IEEE Access,* vol. 9, pp. 45137-45146, 2021.
[http://dx.doi.org/10.1109/ACCESS.2021.3066365]

[55]   R. Leon Sanz, and P. Leon-Sanz, "Modeling health data using machine learning techniques applied to financial management predictions", *Appl. Sci.,* vol. 12, no. 23, p. 12148, 2022.
[http://dx.doi.org/10.3390/app122312148]

CHAPTER 2

An Overview of Blockchain in the Field of Smart Healthcare System

Ramya Easwaran[1,*] and **Kumaresan Natesan**[2]

[1] *SNS College of Technology, Coimbatore, India*

[2] *Anna University Regional Campus, Coimbatore, India*

Abstract: Rapid Blockchain is one of the most talked about technologies in the world at the moment. The origin of blockchain is a cryptocurrency called "bitcoin". It is a secure currency that can be used as a medium of exchange worldwide. Blockchain itself is a decentralised, peer-to-peer distributed ledger capable of storing all transactions that take place on the network. This property makes blockchain useful for any type of exchange, such as data, currency and information. Blockchain protects against potential data theft or corruption in the healthcare network. It is important to maintain the integrity and validity of patient records to ensure wellness. Artificial intelligence and blockchain will provide a smart healthcare system for people around the world by extracting useful information, protecting medical data, simplifying claims processing, using patient self-generated data and systematising procedures.

Keywords: Bitcoin, Distributed Ledger, Peer to peer, Smart Healthcare, Systematized procedures.

INTRODUCTION

The foundation of blockchain technology is bitcoin. It was first introduced by Satoshi Nakamoto in January 2009. Blockchain uses an innovation that is a mix of mathematics and software engineering called cryptography. Blockchain is a distributed database used to store an infinite number of records, called chunks. Blockchain is a distributed record. It is an open currency that anyone can buy; however, once the information is created, it cannot be corrected and does not allow for correction in the form of computerised trust [1]. Hashes or cryptographic signatures play an important role; they are used to record transactions. There are four types of blockchains. The first type is an open blockchain where anyone can participate. The second type is a reserved blockchain, where anyone can join after applying for membership. The third is a

---

* **Corresponding author Ramya Easwaran:** SNS College of Technology, Coimbatore, India E-mail: ramya.e.ece@snsct.org

semi-private blockchain, which combines public and private blockchains, and the fourth is a side chain, which manages the idea of running a different conveyed record off the primary chain. However, exchanges are ready to take place in a similar currency [2].

Blockchain is the use of cryptography to create an immutable, decentralised, dynamic or evolving record of bits of records, called blocks, that are linked and bound together in a sequential request. Fig. (**1**) shows the hash functions in blockchain.

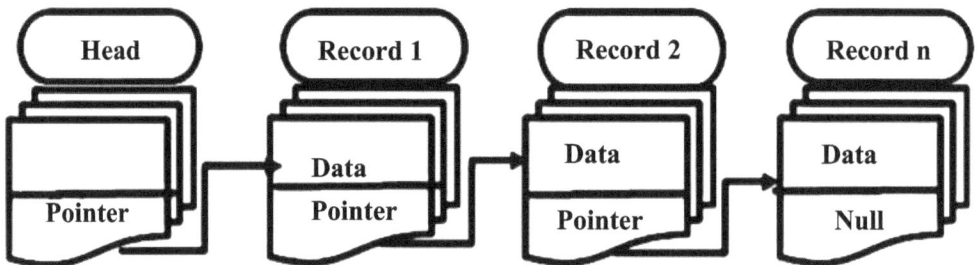

Fig. (1). Structure of records associated together, each record has the hash of an earlier record.

There are numerous blockchain platforms, such as IBM Blockchain, IOTA, Multichain, Open Chain, Quorum, R3 Corda, Ripple, Steller and Symbiont Assembly. The Ripple and Corda protocols are primarily used in the financial industry. Blockchain has many features, such as immutability of stored information, scalability, unanimity and high security. There are many efficient algorithms, such as proof of work (Pow), proof of stake (PoS), and proof of activity (PoA), which are used in blockchain [2]. In Fig. (**2**), the typical structure of a blockchain has the following elements in each block: current hash, nonce, timestamp, transaction details, and previous hash.

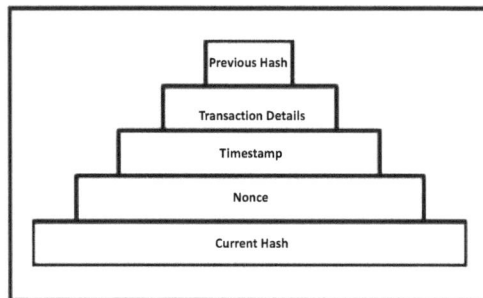

Fig. (2). Typical Structure of the block in Blockchain.

The block is a basic unit of the blockchain created by miners. The typical structure of a block is very simple, as shown in Fig. (**2**), and includes a chunk form that forms a chunk header [1].

MAJOR ISSUES AND CHALLENGES OF HEALTHCARE SYSTEMS

The healthcare system is made up of five stakeholders. For example, it shapes the framework for medical care between providers, patients, payers, the supply chain (manufacturers, distributors and pharmacies) and research organisations [3]. The issues and challenges in the healthcare system are illustrated in Fig. (**3**).

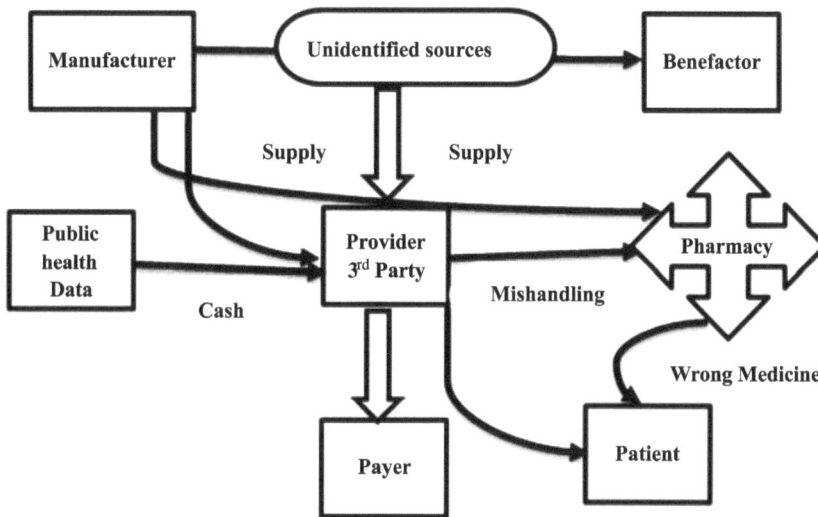

Fig. (3). Outline the links between the top five healthcare investors (providers and manufacturers and dispensers from a single unit of the pharmaceutical supply chain).

Benefactor: The provider is a key competitor in the healthcare sector. The provider is the main intermediary between patients, customers and pharmacies (Fig. **3**). The implementation of automated medication registers and health records is one of the biggest challenges for healthcare providers [4]. It is also expensive, both in terms of time and money. The lack of interoperability guidelines for the exchange of health information between research and clinical settings risks increasing the cost of time [5].

Patients: Patients are an important parameter in healthcare systems. Providers hold patients' health information. Patients are generally concerned about the security of their health information, but their privacy is exploited in many ways. Information can be used for drug promotion, research, general medical care and other purposes [6]. HIPAA (Health Insurance Portability and Accountability Act) security regulations restrict the use of patient health information. In addition, the confidential moderator receives financial benefits by selling patients to outsiders [6], as shown in Fig. (**3**). Similarly, separate repositories of patient wellbeing data or non-interoperability affect the lack of correspondence between medical service groups, resulting in poor quality of care, extra time and increased costs of re-testing [7].

Payers: Insurance claims on behalf of patients by the payer (insurer or employer) must also be audited by central organisations, which are extremely vulnerable to doubts and planned untrue changes [8]. Records (invoices, prescriptions, *etc.*) can be falsified by forged medical cards, false invoices, falsified tests, *etc.* Verification and determination of the origin of data is crucial when following Honest Assurance Privilege procedures [9].

Research Organizations: General wellbeing information is expected by research associations and drug organisations to track new infections, create drugs and make drug disclosures. Sharing medical information is essential for public information assortment, clinical review and exploration [10]. Patient information documented by a supplier is shared with these associations without the patient's consent, which is a violation of the patient's rights [11]. Patient assent, executive information on the board, information respectability and straightforward outcomes are the main pressing issues of a trustworthy and useful framework.

Pharmaceutical Supply Chain Management: The key players in the drug production network are suppliers, dealers, manufacturers and drug shops. It is a complex process involving a variety of activities, such as purchasing of materials, manufacturing, packaging, distribution, *etc.* Proper management and monitoring are required to ensure reliability. Drug seizures can be concluded on several bases. The onset and nature of the seizure are not assured. Unacceptable ingredients and poorly designed bases can play a significant role in the development of new drugs [12]. It is, therefore, necessary to trace the origin of information through verifiable registers, confirmed article data and ownership in the drug supply chain. In any case, current frameworks need to keep pace with authentic data to address the problem of counterfeit medicines [13].

The problems faced by health systems around the world are listed in Table **1**. Tick-boxes are a major problem for health workers. Healthcare systems have several disadvantages in the areas of confidentiality and monetisation.

Table 1. Major issues in healthcare systems.

Issues faced by healthcare systems	Healthcare Patrons				
	Benefactor	Patient	Investor	Research Groups	Resource chain
Record Management	✓	✓	✓	✓	✓
Information Exchange	✓	✓	✓	✓	✓
Safety	✓	✓	✓	✗	✓
Absence of information provenance	✗	✓	✓	✓	✓
Secrecy	✓	✓	✓	✗	✗
Monetization	✓	✓	✗	✗	✗

ROLE OF BLOCKCHAIN IN THE HEALTHCARE SYSTEM

In healthcare services, blockchain networks can be useful for storing and trading patient information. Blockchain applications can accurately distinguish between serious and dangerous errors in clinical settings. Blockchain has a crucial impact on managing trickery in clinical preliminaries for better medical service outcomes [14]. The conveyed blockchain stage offers the wellbeing area chances to follow extortion, reduces above-average costs, reliably produces occupations, dispenses with duplication of work, and authorises transparency in the wellbeing climate. It is also used to hold resources, such as the immutability and security of decentralisation.

Distributed communication between all medical staff can be efficient, as the relevant records are replicated by authorisation centres with virtually no representative. Controlled access and persistent information in records can increase the detection of misrepresentation, combat counterfeit drugs, guarantee billing, and promote reproducibility in research [15].

Blockchain innovation is a problematic development that cuts across sectors without uncertainty. Fig. (4) explains the problems and solutions to partners in medical services, who are similarly excited about the valuable open doors managed by blockchain in medical services, and are vigorously putting into circulated record advancements to advance more proficient medical service frameworks [16]. The intelligent work process stream began with the distributed organisation stream, digitised exchanges, and circulated information and records, empowering blockchain drivers to work more stressed to make medical care administration better and more imaginative than before [17].

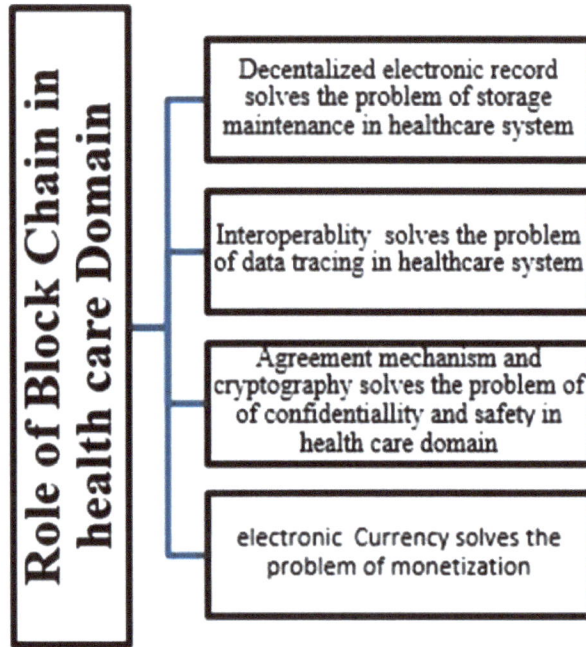

Fig. (4). Major challenges faced by the healthcare industry resolved using blockchain technology.

BLOCKCHAIN APPLICATIONS IN HEALTHCARE

Blockchain technology is playing an important role in healthcare systems around the world. Blockchain integrates the healthcare system into various work processes. The integration phase of the blockchain architecture is shown in Fig. (**5**). Blockchain innovation provides a decentralised arrangement for trading well-being information, which secures and validates well-being data. In addition, blockchain removes the weight and cost associated with compromising information by enabling easy access to constant well-being data. Blockchain technology has captured the attention of healthcare advocates and biomedical experts in numerous healthcare areas, such as longitudinal health records, electronic claims, prescription development and interoperability in population health, customer health, patient gateways, medical investigations and data security.

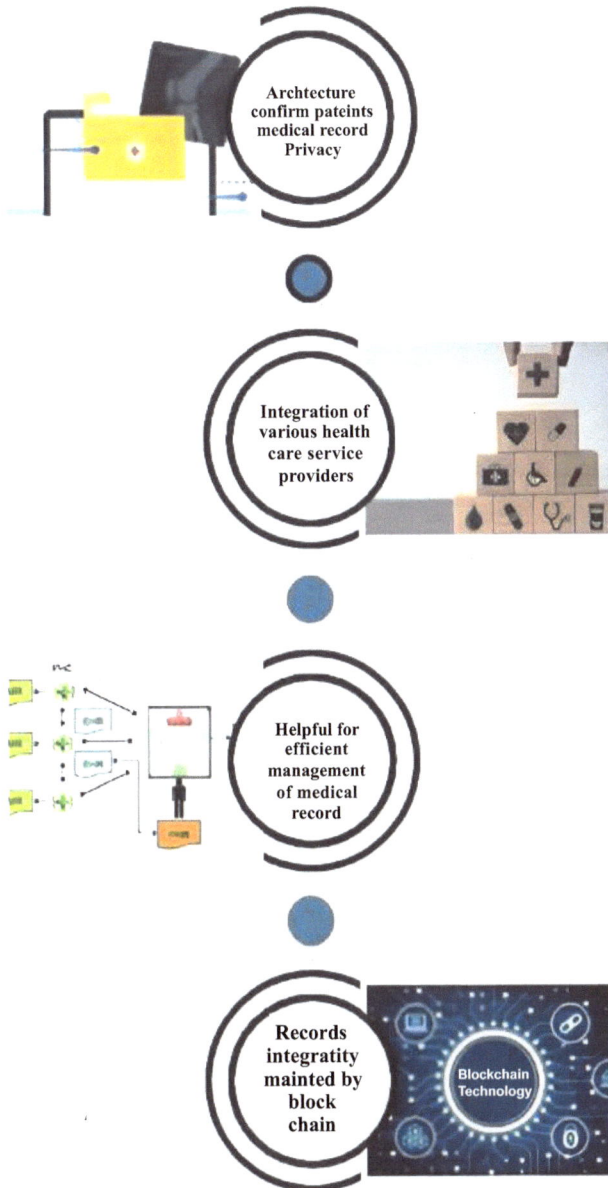

Fig. (5). Blockchain integration phases in different phases of the healthcare system.

Table **2** summarises the real applications of blockchain in the healthcare industry. The extent of Blockchain in medical care is rising, coming and energising as it enhances the resolution of some major commercial difficulties.

Table 2. Real-life applications of Blockchain in healthcare.

S.No	Uses	Descriptions	References
1.	Data collection of a Distinct patient	Blockchain is based on current cryptographic methods that integrate the appropriate system for cryptography for data distribution. The patient's identity, birthday, analysis, tablets and mobile antiquity are reserved in the EHR design by the patient's intricacies by the health care provider. These statistics are stored in dispersed, calculated or constant records.	[18, 19]
2	Analyze the special effects of a specific method	Blockchain makes the life of the drug supply less complex, because it has every bit of data on it. Patients will be expertly educated on the best way to take care of these consequences.	[20, 21]
3	Validation	Exchanges are accepted on a blockchain until they are related to the sequence and completed by calculations. The legitimacy is fixed until the substance is twisted, carefully marked and protected.	[22, 23]
4.	Identification of false content	The innovation has initially accepted the entire population to intensively screen what happens in a medical preliminary. The rationale behind this innovation is that it is consumer-facing and offers patients secure access to wellbeing and safety registers as they progress.	[24, 25]
5.	Keep up with fiscal summaries in emergency clinics	Blockchain companies have developed methods to restructure the secretarial and recording processes. With this request, anyone can formulate a plan to go to a healthcare benefactor and go through the administration in advance.	[26, 27]

ROLE OF ARTIFICIAL INTELLIGENCE AND BLOCKCHAIN IN SMART HEALTHCARE SYSTEMS

By consolidating the two technical networks, computer-based intelligence and blockchain imperfections can be skilfully taken care of [28]. AI procedures rely on documents or information to absorb, construct and sort the decisions. When information is obtained from an information repository or a reliable, protected, confidential, and credible source, AI computations are superior. A blockchain is a distributed record where information can be stored and traded in a cryptographically secure, approved, and settled way through all the extraction hubs.

The combination of AI and blockchain can lead to a harmless, incontrovertible, and dispersed method for penetrating records that AI-driven methods are essential to collect, and consume [29]. This method leads to principal data and data safekeeping improvements in various diligences, including therapeutic, delicate, lending and monetary transactions, and permitted data [30]. Such incorporation entails intellectually dispersed independent agents to authenticate facts, values, and ability transfers among abundant powers that are routine and fast [31]. For example, Google, Microsoft, Apple, and Amazon, as well as a large number of new companies, are effectively investigating artificial intelligence for clinical applications to work on, among other things, more persuasive use of patient information, determination accuracy, and better suggestions given evidence-based research discoveries. Clinical records and other data can be transferred to the blockchain using the EHR framework [32].

Fig. (6) explains the combination of the two technologies: while blockchain can guarantee safety and uprightness, the addition of simulated intelligence capacity to the area of well-being can be beneficial. Currently, artificial intelligence is essentially used to detect anomalies in X-rays and CT scans, a task that artificial intelligence can perform in addition to humans, guaranteeing a higher level of personalised treatment.

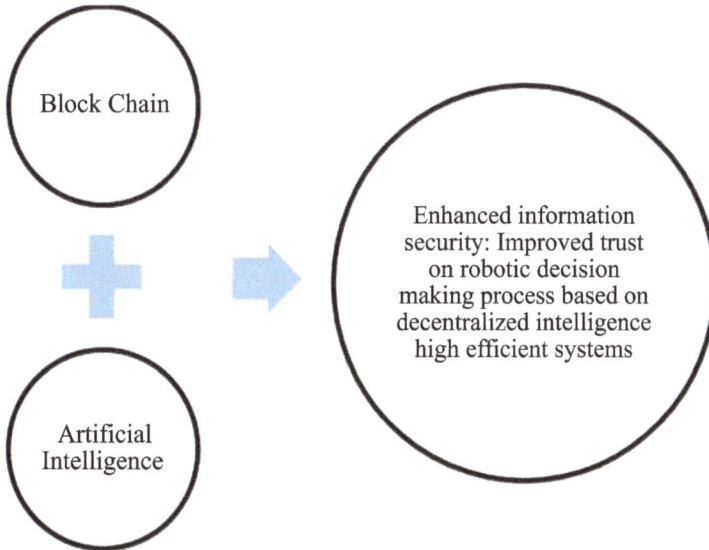

Fig. (6). Combining AI and blockchain for highly efficient systems.

RECENT CHALLENGES TO BLOCKCHAIN IMPLEMENTATION IN IN THE HEALTHCARE SYSTEMS

Blockchain is an innovation that has not yet been fully successful. As blockchain is another innovation, there are many difficulties of blockchain in the medical field [33]:

i. **Privation of Practical Awareness**: It's not normal for all customers to have expensive equipment and programming resources. Many clients are not familiar with the latest innovations. For example, many older people don't use workstations or PCs. GPUs are expected for digital money mining, which are not available on all PCs. This is an important test for blockchain.

ii. **Absence of Paperless Method Implementation**: Many clients and professionals prefer paper records. They like to keep clinical records in a document framework. Some pharmacies are not 100% paperless. Most pharmacies use remedies to track their medicines.

iii. Patients also keep the paperwork for their own convenience. Therefore, adapting to a completely paperless blockchain network is a difficult undertaking.

iv. **Lack of Government Participation**: Most hospitals are government-owned. So there is government involvement in the implementation of guidelines. Some governments are too inflexible to accept the latest technologies. Therefore, blockchain cannot be applied in government-owned hospitals because it is an extremely localised, distributed ledger. There is no central authority or third party to make the decisions. The decisions are typically made by blockchains.

v. **Lack of Crypt currency Acceptance**: Most specialists don't recognise digital currency as a means of payment. So far, with the reception of blockchain innovation, virtual instalments have not been fully settled. The income occurs. In this way, a legitimate execution of the online instalments should be taken over. Then, at that point, the blockchain innovation should be adopted.

vi. **Lack of Privacy**: The data is stored in the blockchain's record, and each client has a duplicate of the record, so if one part of the organisation goes bust, the information remains secure and can very well be updated later. Many clients like to keep their clinical issues hidden. Therefore, it complicates an individual's security.

CONCLUSION AND FUTURE WORK OF BLOCKCHAIN IN THE FIELD OF SMART HEALTHCARE SYSTEMS

Blockchain innovation is constantly changing, rather than being complete. If the biomedical and healthcare frameworks want to embrace this innovation, there are some potential issues that need to be addressed. One of the most interesting aspects of blockchain innovation is the underpinning of its development and specificity. However, its underlying execution will face similar limitations to current innovation, and the open nature of blockchain will stimulate and sustain expansive development in the future. BIS Exploration has uncovered assessed reports that the quick application and joining of blockchain in medical services could save more than $100 billion every year in costs related to IT, tasks, support capabilities, staff and well-being information by 2025 [34].

REFERENCES

[1]　M. Faisal, and S. Naz, "Amjad A li and Zahida Parveen, "Bloch chain in the healthcare system" Sci. Int. (Lahore) 32(1), ISSN1013-5316", *CoDEN,* vol. SINTE8, pp. 181-186, 2020.

[2]　J Indhumathi, Shankar Achyut, Rukunuddin Ghalib Mohamed, J Gitanjali, Hua Qiaozhai, Wen Zheng, and Qi XIn, "Blockchain-based internet of things for uninterrupted, Ubiquitous, User-friendly, unflappable, unblemished, unlimited healthcare services (BC IoMT U6 HCS)", *IEEE Access,* vol. 8, 2020.

[3]　M. Arumugam, G. Deepa.S Sreekanth, and S Nailesh. Arun, ""Counterfeit drugs prevention using Blockchain techniques", IOP Conf. series", *Mater. Sci. Eng.,* vol. 1055, p. 012109, 2021.

[4]　https://www.healthcareitnews.com/news/here-are-major-issues-facing-healthcare-2021-according-pwc

[5]　S. Yaqoob, M. Murad, R. Talib, A. Dawood, S. Saleem, F. Arif, and A. Nadeem, "Use of Blockchain in Healthcare: A Systematic Literature Review", *Int. J. Adv. Comput. Sci. Appl.,* vol. 10, no. 5, pp. 644-653, 2019.
[http://dx.doi.org/10.14569/IJACSA.2019.0100581]

[6]　E. Karafiloski, and A. Mishev, "Blockchain solutions for big data challenges: A literature review", In: *IEEE EUROCON 2017-17th International Conference on Smart Technologies,* 2017, pp. 763-768.
[http://dx.doi.org/10.1109/EUROCON.2017.8011213]

[7]　D.J. Skiba, "The potential of Blockchain in education and healthcare", *Nurs. Educ. Perspect.,* vol. 38, no. 4, pp. 220-221, 2017.
[http://dx.doi.org/10.1097/01.NEP.0000000000000190] [PMID: 28622267]

[8]　C. Brodersen, B. Kalis, C. Leong, E. Mitchell, E. Pupo, A. Truscott, and L. Accenture, *Blockchain: Securing a New Health Interoperability Experience.* Accenture LLP, 2016.

[9]　M.A. Engelhardt, "Hitching healthcare to the chain: An introduction to Blockchain technology in the healthcare sector", *Technol. Innov. Manag. Rev.,* vol. 7, no. 10, pp. 22-34, 2017.
[http://dx.doi.org/10.22215/timreview/1111]

[10]　Jin Park, and Jong Park, "Blockchain security in cloud computing: Use cases, challenges, and solutions", *Symmetry,* vol. 8, 2017.
[http://dx.doi.org/10.3390/sym9080164]

[11]　A. Dubovitskaya, Z. Xu, S. Ryu, M. Schumacher, and F. Wang, "Secure and trustable electronic medical records sharing using Blockchain", *AMIA Annu. Symp. Proc.,* vol. 2017, American Medical Informatics Association, p. 650, 2017.

[12]　T.K. Mackey, and G. Nayyar, "A review of existing and emerging digital technologies to combat the global trade in fake medicines", *Expert Opin. Drug Saf.,* vol. 16, no. 5, pp. 587-602, 2017.
[http://dx.doi.org/10.1080/14740338.2017.1313227] [PMID: 28349715]

[13]　Kevin A. Clauson, Elizabeth A. Breeden, Cameron Davidson, and Timothy K. Mackey, "Leveraging Blockchain technology to enhance supply chain management in healthcare", *Blockchain in Healthcare Today,* 2018.
[http://dx.doi.org/10.30953/bhty.v1.20]

[14]　A. Haleem, M. Javaid, R.P. Singh, R. Suman, and S. Rab, "Blockchain technology applications in healthcare: An overview", *International Journal of Intelligent Networks,* vol. 2, pp. 130-139, 2021.
[http://dx.doi.org/10.1016/j.ijin.2021.09.005]

[15]　K. Rabah, "Challenges & opportunities for Blockchain-powered healthcare systems: A review", *Mara Research Journal of Medicine & Health Sciences,* pp. 45-52, 2017.

[16]　https://www.magazine.medicaltourism.com/article/Blockchain-technology-can-transform-healthcare

[17]　A. Sharma, S. Bahl, A.K. Bagha, M. Javaid, and D.K. Shukla, A, "Haleem Blockchain technology and its applications to combat COVID-19 pandemic", *Res. Biomed. Eng.,* pp. 1-8, 2020.

[18]   M. Ejaz, T. Kumar, I. Kovacevic, M. Ylianttila, and E. Harjula, "Health-BlockEdge: Blockchain-edge framework for reliable low-latency digital healthcare applications Sensors", 21 (7) 2021, p. 2502.

[19]   T.K. Mackey, T.T. Kuo, B. Gummadi, K.A. Clauson, G. Church, D. Grishin, K. Obbad, R. Barkovich, and M. Palombini, "'Fit-for-purpose?' – challenges and opportunities for applications of blockchain technology in the future of healthcare", *BMC Med.,* vol. 17, no. 1, p. 68, 2019.
[http://dx.doi.org/10.1186/s12916-019-1296-7] [PMID: 30914045]

[20]   R. Vaishya, M. Javaid, I.H. Khan, A. Vaish, and K.P. Iyengar, "Significant role of modern technologies for COVID-19 pandemic Journal of Industrial Integration and Management", 2021, pp. 1-3.

[21]   H.M. Hussien, S.M. Yasin, N.I. Udzir, M.I.H. Ninggal, and S. Salman, "Blockchain technology in the healthcare industry: Trends and opportunities", *J. Ind. Inf. Integr.,* vol. 22, p. 100217, 2021.
[http://dx.doi.org/10.1016/j.jii.2021.100217]

[22]   "M.A. Engelhardt Hitching Healthcare to the Chain: an introduction to Blockchain technology in the healthcare sector", *Technol. Innov. Manag. Rev.,* vol. 7, no. 10, 2017.

[23]   H.L. Pham, and T.H. Tran, "Y. Nakashima A secure remote healthcare system for hospital using Blockchain smart contract In2018 IEEE Globecom Workshops (GC Wkshps)", *IEEE,* pp. 1-6, 2018.

[24]   L. Ismail, H. Materwala, and S. Zeadally, "Lightweight Blockchain for Healthcare", *IEEE Access,* vol. 7, pp. 149935-149951, 2019.
[http://dx.doi.org/10.1109/ACCESS.2019.2947613]

[25]   C.C. Agbo, Q.H. Mahmoud, and J.M. Eklund, "Blockchain technology in healthcare: a systematic review Healthcare", *7,* Multidisciplinary Digital Publishing Institute , p. 56, 2019.

[26]   R.W. Ahmad, K. Salah, R. Jayaraman, I. Yaqoob, and S. Ellahham, "M. Omar the role of Blockchain technology in Telehealth and Telemedicine", *Int. J. Med. Inf.,* p. 104399, 2021.

[27]   V. Ramani, T. Kumar, A. Bracken, M. Liyanage, M. Ylianttila, and M. Ylianttila, "Secure and efficient data accessibility in Blockchain-based healthcare systems", In: *IEEE* Global Communications Conference (GLOBECOM), 2018, pp. 206-212.
[http://dx.doi.org/10.1109/GLOCOM.2018.8647221]

[28]   D. Campbell, "Combining ai and Blockchain to push frontiers in healthcare", http://www. macadamia. com/2018/03/16/combining-ai-andBlockchain-in-healthcare/

[29]   T. Marwala, and B. Xing, "Blockchain and artificial intelligence", arXiv preprint arXiv:1802.04451.

[30]   P. Mamoshina, L. Ojomoko, Y. Yanovich, A. Ostrovski, A. Botezatu, P. Prikhodko, E. Izumchenko, A. Aliper, K. Romantsov, A. Zhebrak, I.O. Ogu, and A. Zhavoronkov, "Converging blockchain and next-generation artificial intelligence technologies to decentralize and accelerate biomedical research and healthcare", *Oncotarget,* vol. 9, no. 5, pp. 5665-5690, 2018.
[http://dx.doi.org/10.18632/oncotarget.22345] [PMID: 29464026]

[31]   D. Magazzeni, P. McBurney, and W. Nash, "Validation and verification of smart contracts: a research agenda", *Computer,* vol. 50, no. 9, pp. 50-57, 2017.
[http://dx.doi.org/10.1109/MC.2017.3571045]

[32]   A.S. Ahuja, "The impact of artificial intelligence in medicine on the future role of the physician", *PeerJ,* vol. 7, p. e7702, 2019.
[http://dx.doi.org/10.7717/peerj.7702] [PMID: 31592346]

[33]   https://www.geeksforgeeks.org/challenges-of-Blockchain-in-healthcare/

[34]   https://www.forbes.com/sites/forbestechcouncil/2021/10/25/the-future-of-Blockchain-in-healthcare/ ?sh=7841133a541f

CHAPTER 3

Integration of Blockchain and Internet of Things

R. Babu[1,*], Jayashree K.[2], Priya Vijay[3] and Vijay K.[3]

[1] *Department of Computational Intelligence, School of Computing, College of Engineering and Technology, SRMIST, Chennai, India*

[2] *Department of Artificial Intelligence and Data Science, Panimalar Engineering College, Chennai, India*

[3] *Department of Computer Science and Engineering, Rajalakshmi Engineering College, Chennai, India*

Abstract: Customers can benefit from the Internet of Things in a number of ways, and it has the potential to transform the fundamental ways that consumers interact with technology. The pervasiveness and correspondences maintained for IoT might provide various conveniences and aids for people, but also open up many security loopholes. Blockchain, a distributed digital ledger, is finding uses in industries as diverse as finance, healthcare, utilities, agriculture, real estate, and Supplier Management. The middleman acting as guardians for specific applications in these enterprises can be removed in order to provide security and those equivalent applications can be run in a distributed way with practically no centralized power. Blockchain technology makes this feasible without sacrificing efficiency or safety, which was previously impossible. Blockchain and IoT seem to be best on their own in the respective sector in which it is applied, so businesses can try and exploit this powerful combination known as Blockchain Internet of Things (BIoT) to bring immense advancements, progressions and cutting edge innovations in the area of their interest. The term "BIoT" was created by fusing blockchain with IoT applications.

Keywords: Blockchain IoT, Covid-19, Digital Ledger, Machine Learning, Quarantine Tracking.

INTRODUCTION

Many current devices can be connected to the internet using a potential new technology known as the Internet of Things (IoT). The development of IoT devices is facilitated by the seamless integration of RFID, remote connectivity, and sensors [1]. Using clever features in conjunction with IoT services gets incor-

* **Corresponding author R. Babu:** Department of Computational Intelligence, School of Computing, College of Engineering and Technology, SRMIST, Chennai, India; Tel: +91 9403615809 E-mail: babu.rajen17@gmail.com

L. Ashok Kumar, D. Karthika Renuka, Sonali Agarwal & Sheng-Lung Peng (Eds.)

porated for providing excellent types of aid, using regulators and electromechanical frameworks to lay out harmony between the internet and the real world. Clinical medical care frameworks are the newest invention that is redefining the way people live today. Blockchain technology uses an online electronic personal records system to take quality information [2]. Blockchain technology is frequently described as a sort of design that stores trade records. The public information base's "blocks" are another name for the records. An organization's chain is connected *via* distributed hubs. In order to do blockchain jobs, a variety of regulations and work methods are used. Prior to adding the entire block to the communication organisation, it is important to regularly examine the organisation framework's hubs.

With its distributed ledger, public-key authentication, and consensus procedures, blockchain technology is a perfect fit for protecting IoT networks. Due to the distributed structure of the Blockchain, the data can be shown in a straightforward and unambiguous manner. Cryptocurrency and the IoT together have become cutting-edge instruments for decentralised healthcare data sharing, patient monitoring, record integrity assurance, protection level forecasting, and supply chain management [3].

Therefore, this section analyses the fundamentals of blockchain and IoT, as well as their various applications, components, and highlights. The advantages and drawbacks of coordinating blockchain with IoT, as well as how the two ideas might be joined, will be discussed. In the next parts, you can expect to read about the various connected works and planned research courses for Integrating IoT with Blockchain.

BLOCKCHAIN

A distributed ledger known as blockchain is comparable to an electronic book that stores the past. Due to encryption, data on this system is stored decentralized across all network users and is very challenging to delete or manage [4]. The advancement of blockchain technology has a lot of advantages, including dependability, security, quickness, robustness, correctness, and usefulness [5, 6].

Components of Blockchain

A number of potential advantages of blockchain technology over existing methods have been proposed. The blockchain is made up of several simple aspects, including the records, blocks, hashes, transactions, minors, and agreements and this has been represented in the diagrammatic form in Fig. (**1**).

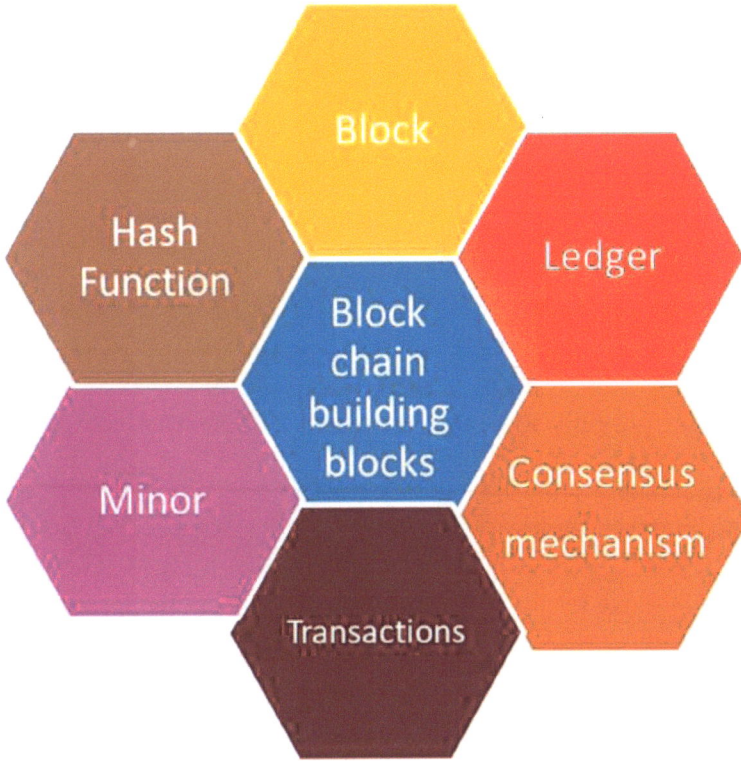

Fig. (1). Components of Blockchain.

The record is an information structure that is used to store different sorts of data. There are massive contrasts between the old-style data set and the record. A data set framework stores information as tables with segments and columns. Besides, it involves a social model for questioning and assembling information by interfacing data from a few sources [7]. Then again, the record is used to store every one of the exchanges produced using all taking part clients in the organization.

The block serves as the fundamental building block of the blockchain. Within each block, numerous exchanges take place. They were combined by including a one-of-a-kind hash of the information from the previous block in the one being processed now. Just like that chain, this union is a roadblock to development. This feature is attractive since it has no obvious effect and can be utilised without anxiety, given that it is exceedingly impossible to construct two different hashes for two separate bits of advanced data. Providing a hash reward for the block is one way to verify its identity and contents [8].

An exchange is a collection of related financial dealings that have been treated as a single entity for the purposes of record-keeping. Adding a new exchange to the block is only possible if the majority of nodes in the blockchain accepts it. Particularly relevant for minors is the fact that the difficulty with which an exchange can be permitted increases in direct proportion to its size [9].

Blockchain's Features

The primary features [10] that make blockchain technology something that can radically reshape a few businesses are:

Non-segmentation techniques [43] and abstraction layers are typical DL classifier methodologies for skin identification. Menegola *et al.* [44] classified lesion pictures using six publicly available datasets. To detect bulbous hydroxyl, basal cell carcinoma, and nevus, both original conception and Good predictive topologies were used. They also confirmed that integrating datasets enhances classification accuracy by increasing training data. Resnet-152 was proposed by Han *et al.* [45] for the identification of pathologies images. The lesions include basal cell carcinoma, colon cancers, metal halides keratosis, fibrotic sarcomas, and myeloid. Two factors influence the reliability of skin lesion detection: visual contrast and ancestry.

Using the Inception v3 architecture, Esteva *et al.* [46] divided the lesion into three types. Before differentiating benign and malignant seborrheic keratoses and keratinocyte carcinoma types, the method distinguishes between them. It can aid in the differentiation of nevi from malignant melanomas.

1) **Decentralization**: Knowledge transfers in centralised network designs are reviewed and approved by central, external authorities. Consequently, this results in overhead for in-built server compatibility and delays in execution. No centralised authority (such as a database) is relied upon for either record-keeping or approval purposes in blockchain-based systems, allowing for decentralised and thrustless interactions between nodes.

2) **Immutability:** The blockchain is impossible to alter because all new blocks must be agreed upon by the network's peers, making it safe from censorship and tampering. In essence, all recently housed information in the blockchain is also immutable, and an attacker would have to reevaluate the involvement of the great majority of nodes in the blockchain system to change any historical records. Any changes to the data in a blockchain are instantly apparent.

3) **Auditability:** Another perk is that everyone in a group can access the blockchain and see every transaction made, complete with a timestamp. This

means that each transaction involving a given blockchain address can be quickly verified by a trusted buddy. Since blockchain addresses aren't tied to actual people, it's possible to maintain anonymity when transacting using this system. There is no way to trace the owner of a blockchain domain back to their transactions, but specific addresses can be assumed to be at fault, and assumptions can be made about the types of transactions in which that address engages.

4) Fault resilience: A blockchain is highly resilient since all nodes have a copy of all records from all previous blocks. The replicas kept in the blockchain's peers can be used to prevent leaks of sensitive information, and consensus can be used to identify problems with the blockchain's architecture.

Types of Blockchain

Standardization and consensus mechanisms in a blockchain can take several forms. It's important to note that private blockchains aren't the only option; public blockchains are also a thing. The extent to which a blockchain is kept secret and how it is communicated is the primary difference between private and public blockchains [11]. It's also possible for blockchains to be partially decentralised, creating a situation known as a "continuum," in which a given framework is neither fully unified nor fully transmitted [12].

The public blockchains have an open public ledger that is freely accessible for reading and writing and is transparent. An example of a public ledger where any organisation member can submit information and ensure that it is consistent with earlier blocks on the chain is Bitcoin. If multiple operational hubs have access to the organization's check exchanges and data trading, there is no requirement for trust between them. A blockchain of this type is regarded as completely disseminated [13].

In contrast, private blockchains/secure databases occupy the opposite end of the system. Because they reinstate intermediaries, private blockchains work against the blockchain's original intent. However, private blockchains benefit from increased productivity, faster transactions, and lower costs than traditional systems because the governing organisation composes and verifies each transaction. They use secret paperwork to keep tabs on members and make it difficult for newcomers to join. The organisation has restrictions on things like the ability to change, read, and create data. Due to the concentration of power, there is often no need for an agreement convention when these liberties are maintained contained to a single party such as an rganisation. Less is known about private blockchains than public ones.

Consortium records exist at the intersection of the public and private spheres, and these records may be overseen by a number of different unified groups rather than either no focal association or a single focal association. It's a cross between low trust (public) and great confidence in a particular association (private) [14], and the reading and writing permissions may be clearly established for certain hubs.

INTERNET OF THINGS

The Internet of Things framework is a cutting-edge technology that has the ability to improve our daily lives, our businesses, and the economy as a whole. Numerous new options for digital service providers and app developers to give users benefits over the status quo are created by the proliferation of connected devices.

Features of IoT System

Applications and administrations share a few normal highlights, which incorporate [15 - 17], Fig. (**2**).

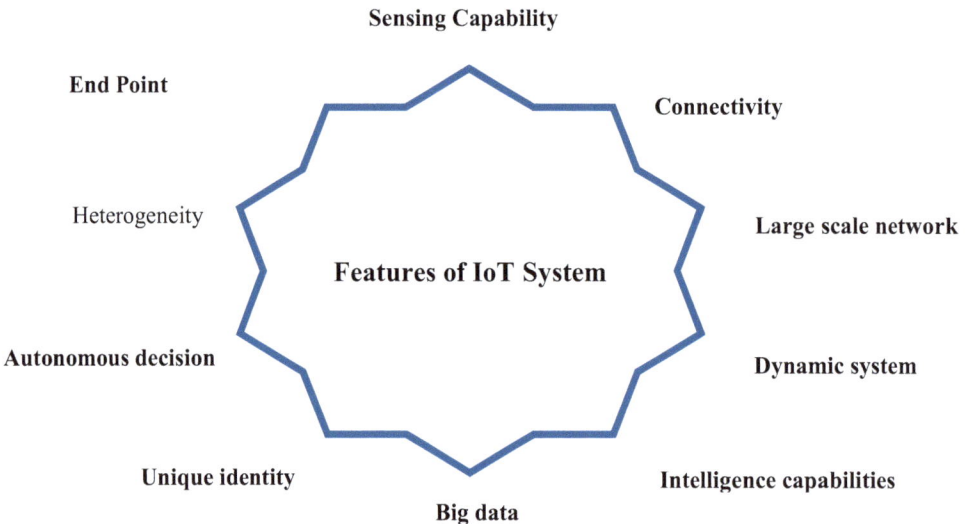

Fig. (2). Features of IoT System.

Detection Abilities: In many applications of the Internet of Things (IoT), the Remote Sensor Organization is the foundational invention that propels development (RSO). Commonly, an RSO takes the shape of a network of sensors that monitors its immediate surroundings and relays that data to a central location. The collecting of all continuous and crucial data about the elements of the environment is made possible by sensors, making them the backbone of the IoT and empowering heads to make quick, accurate decisions based on that data.

Availability: The IoT architecture depends on several critical features, one of the most significant being availability, to make billions of devices and products available from a distance. Furthermore, it permits the interconnection and exchange of a wide range of climate-related goods through the Internet, opening the door to the creation of new applications and services.

Massive Scale Administration: 75 billion gadgets are expected to be in operation by the end of 2025, proving that the IoT framework comprises a staggering number of interconnected pieces of technology. Conventional techniques of management are insufficient for this complex network, which is comprised of a vast number of devices and goods.

Dynamic Framework: The IoT is a resilient and ever-changing structure in the wild. Connecting publications from different fields is within its capabilities. In addition, sensors that capture numerous consistent and relevant data about environmental variables allow IoT devices to be powerfully adjusted to changing scenarios and settings.

Knowledge Capacities: The sophisticated hardware, software, and sensing capacity of IoT devices enable them to collect a vast quantity of logical data, from which they may draw inferences and optimise their performance in specific scenarios and in concert with other collaborating items.

Large Information: Conventional data mining techniques cannot be used to analyse the vast amounts of data produced by IoT devices. There are enormous amounts of information suggested. The Internet of Things (IoT) generates large amounts of data, making it one of the most abundant sources of big information, but in order to fully benefit from it, you'll need to come up with creative research plans.

Unique Characteristics: All sorts of gadgets can now talk to one another over the internet thanks to the IoT architecture. All devices can connect to the internet if they have a unique identifier (such as an IP address) that allows them to do so. To facilitate updating devices following a security breach, manufacturers in the IoT infrastructure provide each one a unique identifier. Thus, while the total number of IoT devices may number in the billions, each one is distinct in its own way.

Independent Choice: Countless sensors built into the Internet of Things backbone allow for the collection of massive volumes of accurate, timely weather information. With this one-of-a-kind information, IoT gadgets may make autonomous, well-considered choices.

Heterogeneity: A large number of gadgets and items can be connected and made to communicate with one another thanks to the Internet of Things framework. Each device has a distinct operating system, platform, and software and hardware component mix. The Internet of Things infrastructure enables a wide range of devices to converse usefully despite their peculiarities.

Significant Utilization of IoT during the Covid-19 Pandemic

Recognizing and preventing the transmission of Corona Virus, as well as assisting clinical specialists [18], staff medical technicians, healthcare labourers, *etc.*, in providing their therapies in a captivating and beneficial manner, is a challenging endeavour at present. In this article, a look at the current state of this epidemic and the results of some recent exploration projects that have used the Internet of Things to address it is considered. People are willing to put up with a lot during this epidemic, including maintaining social distance, benefiting from clinical offices, monitoring and monitoring the isolated, and so on. Fig. (**3**) depicts the various roles played by the Internet of Things throughout this pandemic. These roles include Exemplary disease identification and equivalence.

• Objectives Reducing the number of new cases and deaths caused by disease.

• Monitoring the ICU's solitary patients.

• Contact tracing among infected individuals.

• Assisting Workers in the Healthcare Industry.

• Prescriptions, medical supplies, and hospital cuisine are all readily available.

• Patient monitoring from afar.

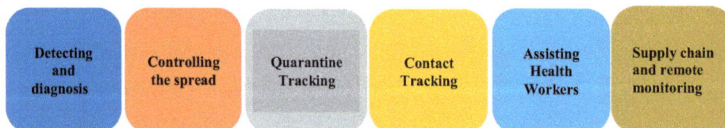

Fig. (3). Application of IoT during Covid 19 Pandemic.

INTEGRATION OF BLOCKCHAIN AND INTERNET OF THINGS

The Internet of Things (IoT) is making waves in today's globe due to its substantial commitment to several industries like commerce, healthcare, resource monitoring, agriculture, telemetry, and more. The information is shared across devices using IoT gadgets. Over 20 billion IoT devices and portable digital assistants are in use now, according to a recent study [19]. As a result of many devices being linked together and sharing vital data, it helps maintain availability and heterogeneity [20]. Due to its properties, the Internet of Things creates particular difficulties in the areas of trust, security, validity, and protection, to name just a few. Only a few examples of how these issues affect sensitive data are financial transactions, military correspondence, and medical services [21]. By enabling the safe and open flow of personal data amongst its users, blockchain, a recently developed technical development, has the ability to overcome these issues [22]. It has various inherent qualities, such as uprightness, validation, protection, and extortion assurance [23] that can help in defining the requirements for trust, security and safety in the Internet of Things (IoT). Reliability and security problems hamper the Internet of Things, but blockchain technology could help by monitoring billions of devices simultaneously and facilitating communication and transactions between numerous parties [24].

The blockchain represents a potential innovation in terms of the problems (trust, enemy attack, *etc*.) that plague IoT and IIoT-based frameworks [25]. As the number of patients in the nation keeps expanding, it is getting harder to provide individualised care. The recent improvement in wearable technology's quality has benefitted healthcare [26]. Long-distance observational understanding is the essential approach for resolving healthcare difficulties. Remote patient monitoring relies heavily on IoT devices and wearable technology [27]. Data transmission of vital signs to healthcare professionals is the main purpose of these devices [28]. This information may include the patient's heart rate, blood sugar levels, and breathing patterns. One use of the Internet of Things in medicine is remote patient monitoring. Specialists can remotely monitor patients who need routine treatment but can't always be present for it by implanting Internet of Things sensors in a patient's body and in their environment. In the healthcare sector, blockchain technology has the potential to address concerns with drug readability, clinical record sharing, *etc*. The numerous security threats that can be launched against the IoT put users' confidence, safety, privacy, and/or access at risk. Therefore, using IoT exclusively in the healthcare industry for applications like remote patient checks could, in the worst scenario, result in patient information loss, information management during its transfer, and other problems. Through the use of the Internet of Things, blockchain technology can be applied to the healthcare industry to enhance its capabilities and secure patient data (IoT).

There are three techniques for coordinating blockchain with IoT. The techniques utilized are affected by the awareness of the information, the lawful prerequisites, how much the information is, and the framework's dormancy and throughput necessities. The level of connection between IoT gadgets and how much blockchain is coordinated into frameworks, as well as the degree of accentuation put on the blockchain, act as the reason for ordering combination instruments. By these measures, blockchain's effect on the primary strategy—call it the Internet of Things or the Convergence of Blockchains—is negligible at best. IoT-blockchain, also known as BoC, is the next step, and it makes extensive use of blockchain for data storage; the hybrid model, on the other hand, incorporates an edge, hazy, or conformance into the incredible structure. It's important to note that these approaches don't work for every conceivable scenario; subsequently, a few conditions require a mix of them. Regardless, a few commonplace works are displayed in an even design above, considering the essential characterization measures. As opposed to different spaces, the show exhibits that the ruling engineering in HIoT is the main kind wherein blockchain is used as a store for the metadata related to genuine records. As was recently observed, this is usually because of radiology-related data being present. This combination solves the data transmission capacity problem associated with storing a document on the blockchain, which is an advantage when applied to the healthcare industry [29]. The difficulties of applying a single rule to a blockchain system are explored. A high degree of inertness is required in certain cases, but hybrid integration, which makes use of blockchain and IoT, is ideally suited to such circumstances. It also makes sense in situations where a lot of sensors are involved.

RELATED WORK

Because of the ceaselessly expanding total populace, the well-being area becomes quite possibly of the main social-monetary issue [30]. The quantities of clinics and assets in the medical clinics are extremely restricted and, in certain areas, there are no medical clinics. At present, wearable wellbeing gadgets assume a significant part in far-off persistent's treatment. These devices monitor the patient continuously, collecting data on their health that will be used to inform the planned treatment. The medical services team and the specialists can benefit from this approach because they can get access to the data at any time, regardless of their location. However, keeping these wearable devices safe and secure is no easy task. Although the healthcare industry has several challenges, they may all be surmounted by integrating blockchain technology. The authors have given a broad study in regard to security challenges and their arrangement in the IoT [31].

Better patient care and a slower shift from centralised to decentralised health systems [32 - 34] are possible outcomes of eHealth's acceptance of the Blockchain perspective. Analysts in this sector focus on planning eHealth engineering with IoT/Fog/Cloud/Blockchain to provide secure data sharing and monitoring of data storage and organisation. Utilizing medical services that leverage blockchain technology can improve a variety of areas, including interoperability, authorised access to patient healthcare data, secure tracking of solutions, emergency clinic resources, wearable sensors over the course of their entire life cycle, and more. The clinician usually assumes they will have access to the patient's medical history, including any descriptions of symptoms recorded during earlier doctor visits. In today's eHealth environments, patients no longer have access to doctors' electronic medical records. However, a patient who reviews his medical history can reduce the likelihood of duplicate clinical records and unneeded clinical trials. The Blockchain has the ability to drastically alter the efficiency with which medical services are given and paid for by placing the patient in command of their own medical history. Patients can now contribute to the validation and reliability of their own health records thanks to the blockchain.

In [35], Jamil *et al.* created a Blockchain-based infrastructure for monitoring vital signs in emergency clinic waiting rooms. Patients in the medical centre are equipped with wearable sensors that transmit data on their vital signs to validated hubs affiliated with the BLOCKCHAIN networks. To improve resource management in the proposed system, further development was done based on a Cloud-driven paradigm, and Cloud front-end advancements were created using HTML5 and JavaScript. The BLOCKCHAIN uses the Representational State Transfer Application Programming Interfaces (REST API) to offer item-centric administrations, which can be triggered by either IoT gadgets or a web client. To ensure the privacy and integrity of patients' vital sign data, a savvy agreement backed regulated admission to the BLOCKCHAIN record. This deal also made it possible for BLOCKCHAIN records to be kept anywhere in the future network. In addition, the entry control method was put in place so that system participants and customers could have access to the restricted data and interactions necessary to run the IoT gadget's essential authorised specialists. The primary sign exchanges were stored in a couch information database created by the BLOCKCHAIN P2P network nodes. To add to this, Celesti *et al.* [36] presented an eHealth architecture that would build a telemedical research centre by utilising an Ethereum Blockchain to connect the Clouds of a unified emergency clinic. While the authors did a good job of illustrating the healthcare work technique as part of the conceptual methodology, a thorough implementation evaluation has not been done to prove that the framework is feasible.

The Internet of Things and the multiple security challenges relating to IoT-layered systems are summarised by Khan and Salah [37]. As a result, the writers were able to fully appreciate the significance of the security requirements of the IoT framework and adopt the finest solutions. In the study, blockchain technology was also proposed as a potential remedy for a number of concerns about the security of the IoT infrastructure. For instance, Sengupta *et al.* [38] reviewed security breaches and problems in the modern Internet of Things (IoT). Additionally, the planning took into account the possible risks. The authors then went on to describe how blockchain innovation can help with some of the security issues that they had previously raised. They also demonstrated some of the challenges associated with applying blockchain technology to the Industrial Internet of Things. By utilising the advancements made possible by blockchain technology, Dorri *et al.* [39] developed a lightweight architecture for the Internet of Things. The goal of the design was to save IoT devices from the onerous processing requirements and data storage requirements of blockchain. In his high-level overview of blockchain technology, Tandon [40] discussed how it provides a complete solution to the security and safety problems posed by the IoT framework. The report also discussed the advantages and disadvantages of using blockchain technology in the IoT. To prevent drug extortion, researchers in [41] describe a system that monitors all the medications in a distribution network. We intend to lessen the accessibility of phoney pharmaceuticals by using blockchain. Currently, the two most popular technologies used to improve the traceability and identification of medications are blockchain and radio frequency identification (RFID).

RESEARCH CHALLENGES OF IOT DATA ON BLOCKCHAIN

However, Blockchain's complexity presents a challenge when combined with IoTs due to the latter's restricted power and capacity capacities [42]. Fig. (**4**) depicts the problems in handling IoT data on the Blockchain, and the summary of these difficulties is provided below.

• **The compromise between power utilization, execution, and security:**

The massive amount of computing power needed to execute Blockchain computations has hindered the growth of these innovation solutions for asset-driven devices. Bitcoin's energy needs are the same as the annual energy usage of Ireland [43, 44]. Some have suggested that doing away with the Proof of Work (PoW) contract in blockchains is a viable option for reducing energy usage and increasing throughput [45, 46]. As opposed to the norm, PoW protects the Blocks from malicious Sybil attacks and ensures they are built properly. Because of this, we seek to optimise the parameters of blockchain cycles in terms of both security and efficiency [47].

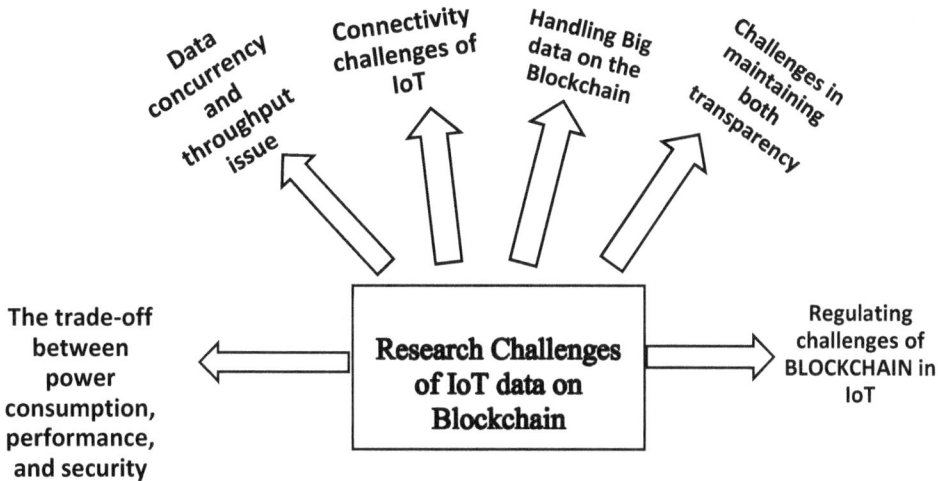

Fig. (4). Research Challenges of IoT data on Blockchain.

• Information simultaneousness and throughput issue:

Since IoT frameworks rely on data continuously pouring from IoT devices, they are inherently highly concurrent [48]. Complex cryptographic security standards and agreement procedures restrict the Blockchain's scalability. Because of this, blockchain throughput may be increased even more [49]. The purpose of this evaluation is to ascertain how well Blockchain's capacity can deal with the problem of routine exchanges in IoT devices.

• Availability difficulties of IoT:

Connecting IoT devices [50] to high-density storage arrays and system management tasks enables the dissemination of information about the IoT to potential business partners. Despite the fact that there is only preliminary backing for combining blockchain technology with the Internet of Things, this may present exciting new potential for enterprises in a wide variety of sectors.

• Taking care of big information on the Blockchain:

Each member of the Blockchain network keeps a local copy of the entire record that is being transferred. Every node in the network updates its local neighbourhood record to reflect the inclusion of the new Block when a new Block is validated by sending out a broadcast to the entire network. Although this decentralised inventory structure boosts efficiency, solves the bottleneck issue, and removes the need to rely on a third party [51], members may find it time-consuming and difficult to manage IoT data on the Blockchain. According to researchers, a Blockchain node needs about 730 GB of storage every year (see their paper at [52] for more details). This was calculated by assuming that 1,000 individuals would use the same 2 MB image in a Blockchain app each day. As a result, difficulty arises from meeting the Internet of Things' (IoT) constantly expanding data storage needs while Blockchain is in charge of the data.

Difficulties in maintaining both Transparency and Safety:

Utilizing blockchain technology is a great way to guarantee transactional transparency, which is particularly important in monetary applications. Storing IoT information on the blockchain and obtaining it through specific IoT modules such as eHealth [53] may violate the client's privacy. If you want to keep things somewhat open and secure while simultaneously enhancing practical access control for IoT, you need to employ Blockchain technology.

• Managing difficulties of Blockchain in IoT:

Blockchains' decentralisation, immutability, opacity, and computerization offer promising security solutions for several Internet of Things applications; nonetheless, their combination presents a number of additional managerial problems [54]. Immutability is highlighted to emphasise that information about the linked organisation has been sent permanently in Datagram Transport Layer (DTL) and can never be changed. Furthermore, records cannot be partitioned for the goal of retaining sufficient security before being disseminated on the blockchain due to a lack of organisational resources. Since the DTL operates in secret, pinpointing those responsible for illegal service trades could be challenging. Because of this, tracing down the culprits will be more difficult. Blockchain's capacity to automate activities has many practical implications; nevertheless, comedians who utilise several acting and memory skills may not be familiar with how to jumble their code and may make mistakes when programming. Since the introduction of new disruptive technologies like Blockchain necessitates a reevaluation of the existing norms and principles for the Internet of Things, it is imperative that this be done before attempting the DTL [55].

FUTURE RESEARCH DIRECTIONS

Although BIoT deployment and setup have advanced significantly over the past several years, there are still some areas that require further consideration. To further improve BIoT applications and arrangements, additional studies and analyzes should be conducted in specific areas. As a result, businesses will be able to increase their stability, adaptability, and safety [56]. These are the following:

i. Machine Machine Learning-Based Solutions for BIoT Applications' Security and Privacy

Better disruption identification and security protection require proactively analysing AI deployments for BIoT privacy and enforcement, as well as evaluating other AI calculations like K-NN and other profound training and clumping approaches.

ii. Problems Arising from Decentralization's Technical Implementation

The majority of proposed Implementations have entailed centralising the blockchain in order to address difficulties with flexibility, security, and privacy. To lessen the propensity for centralization and speed the transition to truly decentralised, nimble organisations suitable for BIoT rollouts, more research and study are required.

iii. Blockchain Infrastructure

Due to the sensitive nature of the data generated by IoT devices, a blockchain network that effectively addresses the lack of trust in IoT installations is crucial. This is because the successful implementation of IoTs on blockchains depends on trust. A number of solutions have been proposed to deal with this issue, however, they primarily rely on control systems and cross-domain techniques.

iv. Governance, Regulations, and Legal Aspects

They don't know what to do or where to start in the blockchain's decentralised ecosystem. The fact that blockchains can be implemented and used at this point without significant obstacles or reasonable objections is cause for optimism. Without proper oversight, the introduction of IoT devices can significantly increase the vulnerability of a system. Blockchains demand standardised specialists, but there should also be baseline standards for integrating IoT-based contracts and apps.

v. Adaptability

One of the most contentious aspects of merging the two is the blockchain's scalability and ability to operate effectively within a network of enormous scale, like the Internet of Things (IoT). By examining the throughput of times per second, the scalability of blockchain may be compared to that of the quantity of IoT devices. Being intermediate steps in the blockchain network, they are by nature slow. Consider the fact that Bitcoin can execute seven transactions per second. Additionally, Ethereum can manage 20 transactions at once. While VISA can process approximately 2000 transactions per second, PayPal can only process 170 transactions per second [57]. The Internet of Things' expectations, which encompass billions of transactions, cannot be met by this form of data processing. Since Bitcoin has a low throughput and some Internet of Things (IoT) applications, in particular, rely heavily on accurate data, this makes it challenging to design such apps. Despite the fact that a number of solutions have been put forth, including more flexible agreement computations and private blockchains prepared for the Internet of Things (IoT) [58], further study is required to adequately address the elasticity issue in blockchain technology. We just cannot afford to wait any longer for a solution to this urgent problem.

CONCLUSION AND FUTURE WORK

A network in which everyday things are integrated with wireless identification chips and other technologies that enable people to connect and interact with one another is referred to as the "Internet of Things" (IoT). Applications for the Internet of Things (IoT) are being utilised in the healthcare sector [59] for a variety of activities, such as real-time monitoring of a patient's vital signs and ensuring that their prescription is simple to interpret. Despite this, there are a number of security issues with the IoT that can be resolved by using blockchain technology. The Blockchain, a distributed ledger, might be used to enhance security. Patients can feel secure knowing that their medical records are safe by integrating blockchain technology with conventional medical procedures.

REFERENCES

[1]   V.K. Aggarwal, N. Sharma, I. Kaushik, B. Bhushan, and Himanshu, "Integration of Blockchain and IoT (B-IoT): Architecture, Solutions, & Future Research Direction", *IOP Conf. Series Mater. Sci. Eng.,* vol. 1022, no. 1, p. 012103, 2021.
       [http://dx.doi.org/10.1088/1757-899X/1022/1/012103]

[2]   J.E. BEULAH, Tokenizing Patient medical records on the blockchain.

[3]   B. Sivasankari, and P. Varalakshmi, "Blockchain and IoT Technology in Healthcare: A Review", *Stud. Health Technol. Inform.,* vol. 294, pp. 277-278, 2022.
       [http://dx.doi.org/10.3233/SHTI220455] [PMID: 35612074]

[4]   D. Drescher, *Blockchain Basics, A Non-Technical Introduction in 25 Steps.* Apress: Frankfurt am Main, Germany, 2017.
[http://dx.doi.org/10.1007/978-1-4842-2604-9]

[5]   P. Akhavan, M. Philsoophian, L. Rajabion, and M. Namvar, "Developing a Block-chained knowledge management model (BLOCKCHAINKMM): Beyond traditional knowledge management", *Proceedings of the 19th European Conference on Knowledge Management (ECKM 2018)* Padua, Italy, 6–7 2018.

[6]   V. Morabito, *Business Innovation through Blockchain.* Springer: Cham, Switzerland, 2017.

[7]   J.J. Sikorski, J. Haughton, and M. Kraft, "Blockchain technology in the chemical industry: Machine-to-machine electricity market", *Appl. Energy,* vol. 195, pp. 234-246, 2017.
[http://dx.doi.org/10.1016/j.apenergy.2017.03.039]

[8]   H.F. Atlam, and G.B. Wills, "An e_cient security risk estimation technique for Risk-based access control model for IoT. Internet Things 2019, 6, 1–20. 18. Atlam, H.F.;Wills, G.B. An efficient security risk estimation technique for Risk-based access control model for IoT", *Internet Things,* vol. 6, pp. 1-20, 2019.

[9]   K. Biswas, and V. Muthukkumarasamy, "Securing Smart Cities Using Blockchain Technology", *Proceedings of the 2016 IEEE 18th International Conference on High Performance Computing and Communications and IEEE 14th International Conference on Smart City and IEEE 2nd International Conference on Data Science and Systems (HPCC/SmartCity/DSS) Sydney, Australia,* pp. 5-6, 2016.

[10]   M.S. Ali, M. Vecchio, M. Pincheira, K. Dolui, F. Antonelli, and M.H. Rehmani, "Applications of Blockchains in the Internet of Things: A Comprehensive Survey", *IEEE Commun. Surv. Tutor.,* vol. 21, no. 2, pp. 1676-1717, 2019.
[http://dx.doi.org/10.1109/COMST.2018.2886932]

[11]   M. Pilkington, "Blockchain Technology: Principles and Applications", In: *Research Handbook on Digital Transformations* Edward Elgar Publishing, 2016.

[12]   R. Brown, "Unbundling of trust": How to identify good cryptocurrency opportunities?: Bitcoin-a--envisaged isn't what we have", Available From: https://gendal.me/2014/11/14/the-unbundling--f-trust-how-to-identify-good-cryptocurrencyopportunities/

[13]   V. Buterin, "Slasher: A punitive proof-of-stake algorithm", Available From: https://blog. ethereum. org/2014/01/15/ slasher-a-punitive-proof-of-stake -algorithm/

[14]   V. Buterin, "On public and private blockchains", Available From: https://blog. ethereum.org / 2015/08/07/on-public-and- private- blockchains/

[15]   H.F. Atlam, R.J. Walters, and G.B. Wills, "Internet of Things: State-of-the-art, Challenges, Applications, and Open Issues", *International Journal of Intelligent Computing Research,* vol. 9, no. 3, pp. 928-938, 2018.
[http://dx.doi.org/10.20533/ijicr.2042.4655.2018.0112]

[16]   H.F. Atlam, and G.B. Wills, Intersections between IoT and distributed ledger.*Advances in Organometallic Chemistry.* vol. Vol. 60. Elsevier BV: Amsterdam, The Netherlands, 2019, pp. 73-113.

[17]   H.F. Atlam, and G.B. Wills, "Technical aspects of blockchain and iot", In: *Advances in Computers.* vol. Vol. 115. Elsevier, 2019, pp. 1-39.

[18]   S. Malliga, S.V. Kogilavani, and P.S. Nandhini, "A comprehensive review of applications of internet of things for COVID-19 pandemic", *IOP Conf. Ser.: Mater,* vol. 1055, no. 1, p. 012083, 2021.
[http://dx.doi.org/10.1088/1757-899X/1055/1/012083]

[19]   "Internet of things (IoT) connected devices installed base worldwide from 2015 to 2025 (in billions)", Available From: https ://www. statista. com/statistics/471264/ iotnumber-of-connected-devi-es-worldwide/

[20] T.T. Kuo, H.E. Kim, and L. Ohno-Machado, "Blockchain distributed ledger technologies for biomedical and health care applications", *J. Am. Med. Inform. Assoc.,* vol. 24, no. 6, pp. 1211-1220, 2017.
[http://dx.doi.org/10.1093/jamia/ocx068] [PMID: 29016974]

[21] M. Chakarverti, N. Sharma, and R.R. Divivedi, "Prediction analysis techniques of data mining: A review", *Proceedings of 2nd International Conference on Advanced Computing and Software Engineering (ICACSE),* 2019.
[http://dx.doi.org/10.2139/ssrn.3350303]

[22] D.C. Nguyen, P.N. Pathirana, M. Ding, and A. Seneviratne, "Blockchain for Secure EHRs Sharing of Mobile Cloud Based E-Health Systems", *IEEE Access,* vol. 7, pp. 66792-66806, 2019.
[http://dx.doi.org/10.1109/ACCESS.2019.2917555]

[23] A. Reyna, C. Martín, J. Chen, E. Soler, and M. Díaz, "On blockchain and its integration with IoT. Challenges and opportunities", *Future Gener. Comput. Syst.,* vol. 88, pp. 173-190, 2018.
[http://dx.doi.org/10.1016/j.future.2018.05.046]

[24] I. Eyal, "Blockchain technology: Transforming libertarian cryptocurrency dreams to finance and banking realities", *Computer,* vol. 50, no. 9, pp. 38-49, 2017.
[http://dx.doi.org/10.1109/MC.2017.3571042]

[25] P.P. Ray, D. Dash, K. Salah, and N. Kumar, "Blockchain for IoT-based healthcare: background, consensus, platforms, and use cases", *IEEE Systems Journal,* vol. 15, 2020.

[26] S. Parvathavarthini, "An improved crow search based intuitionistic fuzzy clustering algorithm for healthcare applications", *Intelligent Automation and Soft Computing,* vol. 26, no. 2, pp. 253-260, 2020.

[27] V-S. Naresh, "Internet of things in healthcare: architecture, applications, challenges, and solutions", *Comput. Syst. Sci. Eng.,* vol. 35, no. 6, pp. 411-421, 2020.
[http://dx.doi.org/10.32604/csse.2020.35.411]

[28] P. Yu, Z. Xia, J. Fei, and S. Kumar Jha, "An application review of artificial intelligence in prevention and cure of COVID-19 pandemic", *Comput. Mater. Continua,* vol. 65, no. 1, pp. 743-760, 2020.
[http://dx.doi.org/10.32604/cmc.2020.011391]

[29] P. Zhang, J. White, D.C. Schmidt, G. Lenz, and S.T. Rosenbloom, "FHIRChain: applying blockchain to securely and scalably share clinical data", *Comput. Struct. Biotechnol. J.,* vol. 16, pp. 267-278, 2018.
[http://dx.doi.org/10.1016/j.csbj.2018.07.004] [PMID: 30108685]

[30] Sanjeev Kumar Dwivedi, Priyadarshini Roy, Chinky Karda, and Shalini Agrawal, "Blockchain-Based Internet of Things and Industrial IoT: A Comprehensive Survey", *Security and Communication Networks,* vol. 2021, 2021.
[http://dx.doi.org/10.1155/2021/7142048]

[31] K. Jayashree, "An Extensive Survey of Privacy in the Internet of Things", In: *IoT Protocols and Applications for Improving Industry, Environment, and Society,* 2021, pp. 78-100.
[http://dx.doi.org/10.4018/978-1-7998-6463-9.ch004]

[32] S. Khezr, M. Moniruzzaman, A. Yassine, and R. Benlamri, "Blockchain technology in healthcare: A comprehensive review and directions for future research", *Appl. Sci. (Basel),* vol. 9, no. 9, p. 1736, 2019.
[http://dx.doi.org/10.3390/app9091736]

[33] M. Hölbl, M. Kompara, A. Kamišalić, and L. Nemec Zlatolas, "Aida Kamišalić, and Lili Nemec Zlatolas. A systematic review of the use of blockchain in healthcare", *Symmetry (Basel),* vol. 10, no. 10, p. 470, 2018.
[http://dx.doi.org/10.3390/sym10100470]

[34] H-T. Pham, and P.N. Pathirana, "Measurement and assessment of hand functionality via a cloud-based implementation", *International Conference on Smart Homes and Health Telematics Springer,* pp. 289-

294, 2015.

[35]   F. Jamil, S. Ahmad, N. Iqbal, and D.H. Kim, "Towards a remote monitoring of patient vital signs based on iot-based blockchain integrity management platforms in smart hospitals", *Sensors (Basel),* vol. 20, no. 8, p. 2195, 2020.
[http://dx.doi.org/10.3390/s20082195] [PMID: 32294989]

[36]   A. Celesti, A. Ruggeri, M. Fazio, A. Galletta, M. Villari, and A. Romano, "Blockchain-based healthcare workflow for tele-medical laboratory in federated hospital iot clouds", *Sensors (Basel),* vol. 20, no. 9, p. 2590, 2020.
[http://dx.doi.org/10.3390/s20092590] [PMID: 32370129]

[37]   M.A. Khan, and K. Salah, "IoT security: Review, blockchain solutions, and open challenges", *Future Gener. Comput. Syst.,* vol. 82, pp. 395-411, 2018.
[http://dx.doi.org/10.1016/j.future.2017.11.022]

[38]   J. Sengupta, S. Ruj, and S. Das Bit, "A Comprehensive Survey on Attacks, Security Issues and Blockchain Solutions for IoT and IIoT", *J. Netw. Comput. Appl.,* vol. 149, p. 102481, 2020.
[http://dx.doi.org/10.1016/j.jnca.2019.102481]

[39]   A. Dorri, S.S. Kanhere, and R. Jurdak, "Blockchain in internet of things: Challenges and Solutions", *arXiv:1608.05187,* 2016.

[40]   A. Tandon, "An empirical analysis of using blockchain technology with internet of things and its application", *Int. J. Innov. Technol. Explor. Eng.,* vol. 8, pp. 1470-1475, 2019.

[41]   V. Ahmadi, "Drug governance: IoT-based blockchain implementation in the pharmaceutical supply chain", *Proceedings of the 2020 Sixth International Conference on Mobile and Secure Services (MobiSecServ),* 2020.
[http://dx.doi.org/10.1109/MobiSecServ48690.2020.9042950]

[42]   K.R. Özyılmaz, and A. Yurdakul, "Work-in-progress: integrating low-power iot devices to a blockchain-based infrastructure", *2017 International Conference on Embedded Software (EMSOFT) IEEE,* pp. 1-2, 2017.

[43]   K.J. O'Dwyer, and D. Malone, "Bitcoin mining and its energy footprint", *25th IET Irish Signals & Systems Conference 2014 and 2014 China-Ireland International Conference on Information and Communications Technologies (ISSC 2014/CIICT 2014)* Limerick, 2014, pp. 280-285.

[44]   Q. Zhou, H. Huang, Z. Zheng, and J. Bian, "Solutions to scalability of blockchain: A survey", *IEEE Access,* vol. 8, pp. 16440-16455, 2020.
[http://dx.doi.org/10.1109/ACCESS.2020.2967218]

[45]   A. Panarello, N. Tapas, G. Merlino, F. Longo, and A. Puliafito, "Blockchain and iot integration: A systematic survey", *Sensors,* vol. 18, no. 8, p. 2575, 2018.
[http://dx.doi.org/10.3390/s18082575] [PMID: 30082633]

[46]   A. Uddin, A. Stranieri, I. Gondal, and V. Balasubramanian, "An efficient selective miner consensus protocol in blockchain oriented iot smart monitoring", *ICIT,* pp. 1135-1142, 2019.

[47]   J. Huang, L. Kong, G. Chen, M.Y. Wu, X. Liu, and P. Zeng, "Towards secure industrial iot: Blockchain system with credit-based consensus mechanism", *IEEE Trans. Industr. Inform.,* vol. 15, no. 6, pp. 3680-3689, 2019.
[http://dx.doi.org/10.1109/TII.2019.2903342]

[48]   P.K. Sharma, N. Kumar, and J.H. Park, "Blockchain technology toward green iot: Opportunities and challenges", *IEEE Netw.,* vol. 34, no. 4, pp. 263-269, 2020.
[http://dx.doi.org/10.1109/MNET.001.1900526]

[49]   A.D. Dwivedi, L. Malina, P. Dzurenda, and G. Srivastava, "Optimized blockchain model for internet of things based healthcare applications", *2019 42nd International Conference on Telecommunications and Signal Processing (TSP),* pp. 135-139, 2019.
[http://dx.doi.org/10.1109/TSP.2019.8769060]

[50] A. Stanciu, "Technical aspects of blockchain and iot", In: *In Advances in Computers* vol. 115. Elsevier, 2019, pp. 1-39.

[51] E. Karafiloski, and A. Mishev, "Blockchain solutions for big data challenges: A literature review", *IEEE EUROCON 2017-17th International Conference on Smart Technologies,* pp. 763-768, 2017.

[52] Kyle, "Blockchain issues | #1: Data storage", Available From: https://medium.com/@Kyle.May/blockchain-issues-1-data-storage-40fb9812c9a2

[53] Tianqi Yu, Xianbin Wang, and Yongxu Zhu, "Blockchain technology for the 5G-enabled internet of things systems: Principle, applications and challenges", In: *5G-Enabled Internet of Things*, 2019, pp. 301-321.

[54] E.R.A. Forum, Ed., *Joshua Ellul, Jonathan Galea, Max Ganado, Stephen Mccarthy, and Gordon J Pace. Regulating blockchain, dlt and smart contracts: a technology regulator's perspective.* vol. Vol. 21. Springer, 2020, pp. 209-220.

[55] M. Díaz, C. Martín, and B. Rubio, "State-of-the-art, challenges, and open issues in the integration of internet of things and cloud computing", *J. Netw. Comput. Appl.,* vol. 67, pp. 99-117, 2016. [http://dx.doi.org/10.1016/j.future.2018.05.046]

[56] C. Nartey, E.T. Tchao, J.D. Gadze, E. Keelson, and G.S. Klogo, "On blockchain and IoT integration platforms: Current implementation challenges and future perspectives", *Wirel Commun Mob Comput,* 2021. [http://dx.doi.org/10.1155/2021/6672482]

[57] M. Samaniego, U. Jamsrandorj, and R. Deters, "Blockchain as a Service for IoT", *Proceedings of the 2016 IEEE International Conference on Internet of Things (iThings) and IEEE Green Computing and Communications (GreenCom) and IEEE Cyber, Physical and Social Computing (CPSCom) and IEEE Smart Data (SmartData)* Chengdu, China, 15–18 December 2016; pp. 433–436. [http://dx.doi.org/10.1109/iThings-GreenCom-CPSCom-SmartData.2016.102]

[58] H.F. Atlam, R.J. Walters, G.B. Wills, and J. Daniel, "Fuzzy Logic with Expert Judgment to Implement an Adaptive Risk-Based Access Control Model for IoT", *Mobile Net. Appl,* pp. 1-13, 2019.

[59] P. Ratta, A. Kaur, S. Sharma, M. Shabaz, G. Dhiman, and S. Sharma, "Application of blockchain and internet of things in healthcare and medical sector: Applications, challenges, and future perspectives", *J. Food Qual,* vol. 2021, pp. 1-20, 2021. [http://dx.doi.org/10.1155/2021/7608296]

CHAPTER 4

Consequences and Deliberations in Implementation of Blockchain and Internet of Things Integration

K. Karthigadevi[1,*] and **G. Srinivasagan**[2]

[1] *Department of Computer Applications, Kalasalingam Academy of Research and Education, Krishnankoil, Tamilnadu, India*

[2] *Department of Chemistry, Rajapalayam Rajus College, Rajapalayam, Tamilnadu, India*

Abstract: Blockchain technology proposes security facilities to the Internet of Things (IoT). The things or objects used in daily life are connected to the internet to form IoT. The blockchain integral safety mechanism can deliver amenities, such as authentication, accessibility, integrity, secrecy, and authorization to the IoT applications. The uses of IoT applications are the dream turning into reality. But using this IoT still faces some challenges, mainly in the areas of security such as data consistency and reliability. The objects have interacted over the internet; they can also be supervised and controlled remotely. The use of IoT reduces time, manual work, tracking and money. With the evolution of IoT, it is essential to deliver more security for enormous amounts of data. Blockchain is a circulated network with the properties of integrity and secrecy. The blockchain maintains data security in the network of IoT. Here to discover the challenges associated with the combination of IoT and blockchain, a study is taken first, then a blockchain introduction is offered, followed by the Blockchain-based IoT requirements, demand and Quality of Service (QoS) discussed. Then, tasks faced while applying this blockchain-based IoT, such as plan, progress and deployment, are discussed. Then applications of blockchain-based IoT such as throughput, efficiency, latency, privacy, fork problem, smart contracts, legal issues, security, storage and proposed solutions are deliberated. Finally, upcoming research guidelines for the combination of IoT and blockchain are designated.

Keywords: Blockchain Technology, Challenges in Blockchain IoT Applications, Internet of Things, Quality of Service, Smart Contracts.

INTRODUCTION

These days, IoT and blockchain technologies are crucial to technology. The combination of blockchain and IoT may open up new avenues as well as allow for

* **Corresponding author K. Karthigadevi:** Department of Computer Applications, Kalasalingam Academy of Research and Education, Krishnankoil, Tamilnadu, India; E-mail: k.karthikrish@gmail.com

L. Ashok Kumar, D. Karthika Renuka, Sonali Agarwal & Sheng-Lung Peng (Eds.)

the development of apps that can benefit from the blockchain's distributed work. Connecting physical objects to communication networks like the internet is referred to as the Internet of Things (IoT). Currently, communication networks like the internet have connected not just computers but also devices like refrigerators, TVs, laptops, stoves, washing machines, automated doors, air conditioners, electrical appliances, vehicles, bikes, motorbikes, and cellphones, among others. According to the IoT utilization projection, the communication network may connect 50 to 60 billion devices [1]. There are many different claims made in the IoT space.

The implementation of privacy and security solutions would be done in accordance with IoT device characteristics. Equivalent degrees of security must be provided for different types of devices, and systems that can audit and regulate access are required in these environments. Data created by devices can be authorized, audited, and authenticated using blockchain technology. The trust protocol is another name for blockchain technology. It tries to reorganize security measures in order to produce a global index for every transaction that takes place in a particular network. Applications of blockchain technology include smart contracts, digital management and supply chain management [2].

Blockchain is a protocol that can be trusted, and it is called "the protocol of trust". The fundamental idea of blockchain is to delegate the safety mechanism, and a new role has to provide an unambiguous file for all the deals or dealings and take the place of a certain link. It functions as a shared, open, and global ledger. Without the involvement of a third party, it generates agreement and assurance *via* direct communication between two diverse parties. In certain other applications, blockchain can be utilized for contracts, supply chain management and identity administration [3].

This article contains the most current requests in safety and secrecy and discusses what can impact the Internet of Things. It also intends to update some understanding of blockchain technology. The technique will be a review of cutting-edge publications that leverage the blockchain to deliver some amount of security and confidentiality and will propose a different type of egotistic mining attack [4], which we refer to as a follower. A hostile technique known as "stalker" seeks to prevent a particular miner from publishing their blocks.

We planned this article into five different sections. Section 1 is an introduction to blockchain. Section 2 represents the fundamentals of the proposed solutions that is a literature survey for understanding purposes. Section 3 represents the working mechanisms and implementation and design of the technology of blockchain. Delegates use cases, results and discussion of blockchain technology to deliver safety cum security and confidentiality at IoT. It describes the conclusion of deliberations and open queries.

The step-by-step operation of blockchain and provides the following explanation:

(1) A block is used to indicate transactions that a node wants to execute.

(2) The P2P network is informed of the deal.

(3) The network nodes verify the transaction (PoS).

(4) The block is further to the blockchain after validation.

(5) The deal is finished.

Despite being introduced in 2008, blockchain technology wasn't actually put into use until 2009 [14]. It has the capacity to monitor and archive data from several nodes. Blockchain's decentralized architecture can handle trillions of transactions between IoT devices. It can avoid constructing and operating pricey centralized servers in this way. In contrast to the centralized Internet of Things design, it manages with all complexity in the network, providing an inducement to effective colliers (devices or nodes). IoT designs of the current nodes are taking the risk of failure that would be eliminated by the BIoT [5, 6]. Since the values are validated and confirmed by entire devices in the network and using a method before a deal is carried out, the blockchain is particularly reliable for IoT devices (users). How agreement is reached among entire devices in the verifying net to attach a new block is determined by the consensus algorithm. With the help of blockchain capabilities like secrecy and anonymity, IoT devices may help hide sensitive data [7, 8]. To enable the IoT with blockchain combination, the blockchain advocates employing smart contracts to increase the functionality and intelligence of devices [9]. The use of IoT and blockchain technology will enable bulges to buy and sell power routinely [10].

LITERATURE REVIEW

The future is defined by the IoT. The physical elements will be connected to the internet and be capable of identifying other gadgets as their own. IoT is a brand-new Internet revolution. Numerous applications, such as smart manufacturing, logistics, home appliances, lifestyles, and healthcare systems, will be impacted. The author reviews, incorporates, and summarizes hybrid approaches that can be applied to healthcare applications in an IoT setting [11, 12].

The cybersecurity of IoT has already drawn more examine of cyber security because of the Internet of Things' (IoT) steadily growing relationship. It is believed [8] that identity management is the foundation upon which safety systems must be built. Identification forgery and failure are problems with the predictable and centralized identity management system. Using blockchain technology as the main infrastructure to uniquely identify the devices in sensors, a safe IoT system framework has been suggested. They developed a plan to enhance the system for identity authentication. Experiments showed that our defense has grown stronger and more comfortable with assaults [13, 14].

Due to the unreliable internet connection, cloud packages are at an unclear stage and are vulnerable to cybercrime events including node failure [15], injection, data tampering and structured query language (SQL). The IoT claims of reliable data availability and integrity [16, 17] cannot be supported by cloud packages. Because blockchain is a distributed ledger that cannot be exploited and is impervious to tampering, it can be employed. Blockchain is also largely utilized to uncover the severe safety issues with IoT, particularly with regard to data consistency and integrity [18, 19].

Blockchain gives users access to software that enables distributed, dependable data communications and actions. Due to the use of distributed storage [20], smart contracts [21], and digital assertions, the blockchain is currently gaining more respect. The primary purpose of using IoT in blockchain technology is for the recording of actions, like changes in weight, moisture, location, or temperature. It also has ledgers that are impenetrably secure and that can only be viewed by authorized individuals. Blockchain technology is used to satisfy the IoT's safety feature needs [18]. IoT apps and blockchain characteristics work together to increase IoT security and safety.

Ledger-based blockchain technology is also called shared ledger technology. The underlying concept behind distributed ledger technology (DLT) is the replication and distribution of an agreement across several network nodes [22]. In the network, each node functions as a peer. When the database ledger is sent to this peer-to-peer network, each node copies it and stores an undistinguishable copy, allowing the node to update itself independently. Since there is no centralized power in this system, it is totally decentralized. The blockchain is unique from other distributed ledgers in that it has ordered blocks of grouped data within its special structure. Cryptographic primitives are used to encrypt the connections between these blocks [23].

When neither confirmation nor audit tools are offered, the problem of hope in data systems is further exacerbated, especially when they have to deal with sensitive data, such as financial transactions involving fictitious currencies. In this case, Satoshi Nakamoto provided two essential ideas in 2008 [24] that had a significant impact. The first of these is Bitcoin, a virtual money that maintains its value devoid of assistance from any governmental body or financial institution. Instead, a decentralized P2P network of actors that makes up an auditable and verifiable network holds bitcoin collectively and safely. The second idea is blockchain, whose acceptance has grown even more than that of cryptocurrencies.

TYPES OF BLOCKCHAIN AND DIFFICULTIES FACED WHILE IMPLEMENTING BLOCKCHAIN TECHNOLOGY IN IOT

Recently, researchers have had more ideas and released a lot of studies in the area of e-Health systems in IoT fully automation homes/cities, agriculture, supply chain management and applied blockchain technology in various industries. We analyzed the most current publications on blockchain technology in the situation of the IoT and the Internet of Energy in order to give readers a thorough grasp of the potential future applications and uses of blockchain technology.

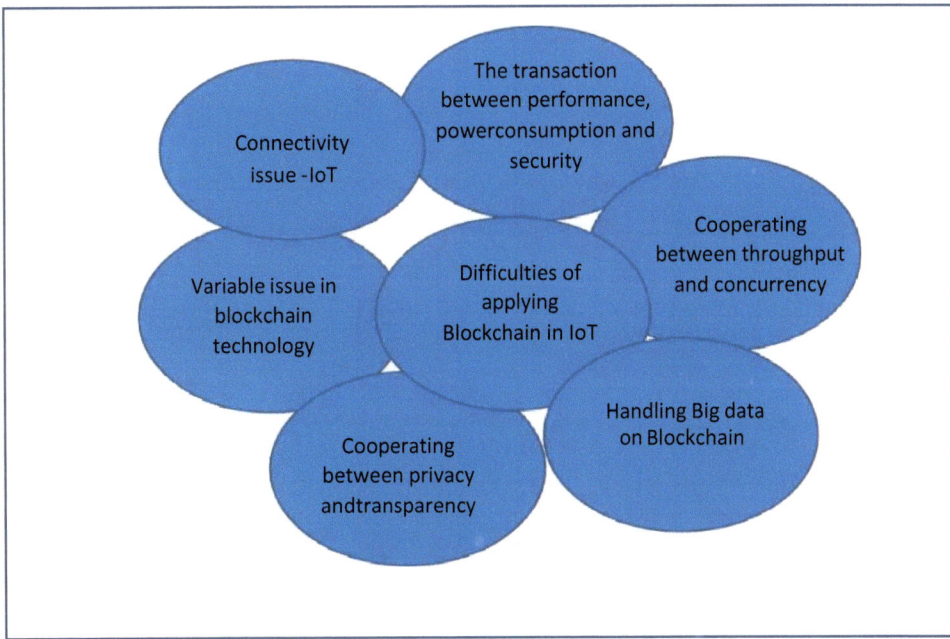

Fig. (1). Difficulties faced while implementing blockchain technology in IoT.

Fig. **(1)** represents the various difficulties faced while implementing blockchain technology in IoT.

Blockchain Types

Three categories can be used to categorise blockchain technology.

a. Public Blockchain

Everyone can access the public blockchain without any limitations. As soon as a user (node) joins the blockchain, it can reach a consensus without the contribution of another party. In public blockchains, users (miners/nodes) receive incentives. Ethereum, Litecoin and bitcoin are a few community blockchains.

b. Blockchain Consortium

Blockchain for consortiums might be private or public. A node is predetermined to act as the central authority in this blockchain. This blockchain may occasionally also be partially decentralized. A few instances of a consortium blockchain are R3CEV and Hyperledger.

c. Personalized Blockchain

A private blockchain is not accessible to all users. In this instance, the owner has restricted access to the network (node). A private blockchain is considered to be permission if it permits just a small group of chosen nodes to execute transactions or engage in other activities.

i. The Transaction Between Performance, Power Consumption and Security

Blockchain algorithms require a lot of computing power to run, which has slowed down the development of technology-based services that largely use physical resources. The energy use of Bitcoin is related to internal electricity, here the IoT sensor devices cannot handle [25]. According to Zhou *et al.* [26], the complete network of Bitcoin can consume more power energy than many countries, like Europe, South America and Europe. Additionally, experts have enquired about how well the blockchain processes data from the IoT and recommended improving its algorithms to upgrade the rate at which established blocks are created [27]. As an illustration, removing blockchain technology POW agreement will decrease energy usage and enhance the concert [28]. The POW shields of the blocks against intruder sybil attacks make them impenetrable. Therefore, the objective is to increase blockchain actions such that effectiveness and security are appropriately aligned [29].

ii. Cooperating Between Throughput and Concurrency:

IoT nodes have high concurrency because IoT nodes continuously communicate information [30]. The blockchain's sophisticated science security protocol and agreement procedures limit its throughput. The next amount of information measure is required for quick synchronization of the most recent blockchain devices in a chain link structured ledger, which could increase blockchain output [31]. The issue is to increase blockchain throughput in order to encounter the demand for recurrent communications in IoT devices.

iii. Property Tests of IoT:

In order to communicate IoT knowledge with imaginable investors, the IoT nodes are expected to be associated with high computational, networking and storage capabilities. IoT devices have limited capabilities when it comes to connecting with blockchain technology to create fresh corporate openings for the adoption of the newest claims and facilities across many industries. Managing massive amounts of facts on blockchain technology: All the handlers of the network retain a resident duplicate copy of the whole circulated ledger. A new block is a transmission over the whole P2P network upon confirmation, and each device adds the confirmed block to its local ledger. A new block is broadcast over the whole P2P network upon confirmation, and each node adds the established block to its resident ledger. The administration of IoT facts on blockchain technology places a cost on contributors' storage space, even the localized storage construction increases proficiency, resolves the block issue and does away with the necessity for third-party faith. The research is legitimate. Blockchain technology device wants 730 Giga Byte of the memory storage area each year; 1,000 users exchange 1-2 MB images every day in a high-performance blockchain technology application. So, once blockchain deals with IoT knowledge, the problem is to deal with the growing knowledge storage requirements.

iv. Difficulties for Preserving Transparency and Confidentiality in IoT

Transparency and confidentiality of communications are critical in some of the applications of blockchain technology, like finance, will be ensured by blockchain. However, individuals' privacy is also compromised once IoT facts from specific IoT devices, like IoT in eHealth, is stored and accessed on the blockchain [32]. The creation of a blockchain-based access control system that is both affordable and effective is required to maintain a balance between transparency and privacy in IoT applications.

v. Regulation and Difficulties of Blockchain Technology in IoT

A number of blockchain technology alternatives, such as immutability, decentralization, automation and anonymity, are capable of security resolutions for different IoT claims. These options collectively introduce a number of new onerous restrictions [33]. According to the unchangingness feature, information disclosed in the distributed deals ledger on the Peer-to-peer network cannot be altered or removed. Additionally, there are no records examined for secrecy before being commercially used on the blockchain.

Laws will be broken by actions resulting from the rules against corporal punishment, such as rational contracts on a DTL. It is, therefore difficult to differentiate the parties' closing dealings for illicit services due to the DTL's obscurity. While the blockchain's automation function has several advantages, it is unclear who is responsible for certain actions like obfuscating code and coding errors. Current IoT laws and regulations need to be updated in order to implement the DTL, especially in light of the introduction of the most disruptive technology to date, blockchain [34].

The core of blockchain technology is the virtual currency known as Bitcoin, developed by Satoshi Nakamoto in 2008. It is frequently referred to as "blockchain" and is naturally described as a clear, transparent, reliable, and distributed ledger on a Peer-to-Peer network [35]. The fundamental building blocks of the blockchain are transactions, which are grouped together to form blocks. A distributed ledger of blockchain is formed using entire validated blocks. The disseminated ledger block is connected to the block that was formerly accepted by utilizing the cryptologic hash code. Numerous uses outside of virtual currencies have already been developed using this new technology, which has previously been thoroughly studied. Every user in a P2P network can create, verify, and confirm statements made about the behavior of other users.

Fig. (**2**) represents blockchain technology. Here, a transaction is requested first, and then it is transmitted to a point-to-point network of mainframes, or devices, that consist of the requested transactions. The number of nodes in a network uses famous techniques to authenticate the deal and the user's status. A confirmed deal may involve digital currency, agreements, documents, or other data. Once the transaction has been validated, it is joined with other transactions to provide a fresh set of data for the ledger. The novel block is then enduringly integrated into the current blockchain. The deal has finally finished.

A look at

blockchain technology

What is it?

The blockchain is a decentralized ledger of all transactions across a peer-to-peer network. Using this technology, participants can confirm transactions without the need for a central certifying authority. Potential applications include fund transfers, settling trades, voting, and many other uses.

How it works:

Someone requests a transaction.

The requested transaction is broadcast to a P2P network consisting of computers, known as nodes.

Validation

The network of nodes validates the transaction and the user's status using known algorithms.

A verified transaction can involve **cryptocurrency** contracts, records, or other information.

The transaction is complete

The new block is then added to the existing blockchain, in a way that is permanent and unalterable.

Once verified, the transaction is combined with other transactions to create a new block of data for the ledger.

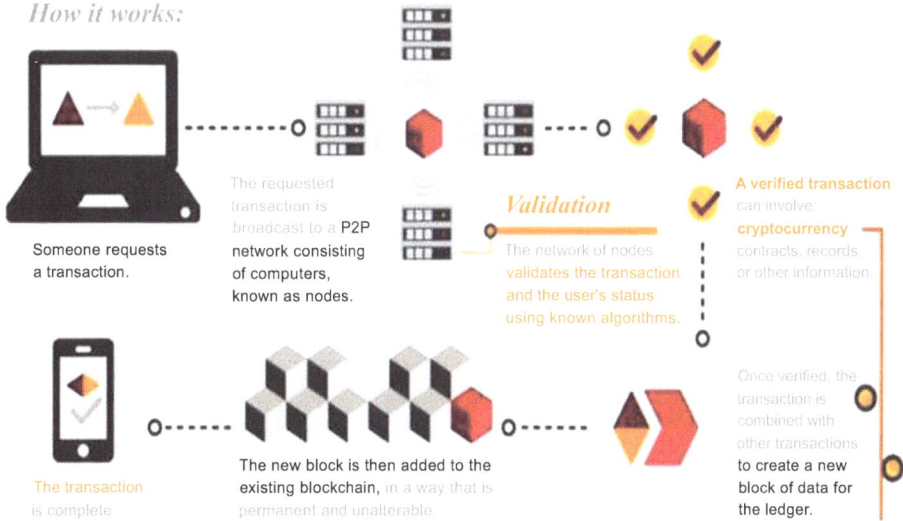

Fig. (2). Blockchain Technology.

LIMITATIONS AND IOT APPLICATION ATTACKS

The IoT has the capacity to inhibit entire features and plays a major role in the monotonous life of a human. The various areas of the IoT have differed as transportation, smart environment and healthcare, such as logistics, IoT house, and personal or social applications. To encounter the difficulties and goals of exact applications in IoT, actuators and various sensors are used to collect the data and transfer with other nodes in a network with the help of an interacting network. The key features of modifications made are as follows:

i. High volume and low-cost presentation

ii. Mobility and stable topology

iii. Decentralization

iv. Unpredictable and unstable connections

v. More number of nodes and enormous IoT data

Limitations in IoT of Wireless Sensor

Fig. (**3**) represents the concept of blockchain with IoT technology. The power of IoT communication is the capability to interconnect with a great number of nodes in various sensing and calculating capabilities which work with fewer human dealing. Several requirements are established in the IoT to get intelligence and activate the systems in an assorted manner. Such kinds of requests are smart transport, home, grid and eHealth. The IoT planning contains of these layers, service, interface, perception and network layer.

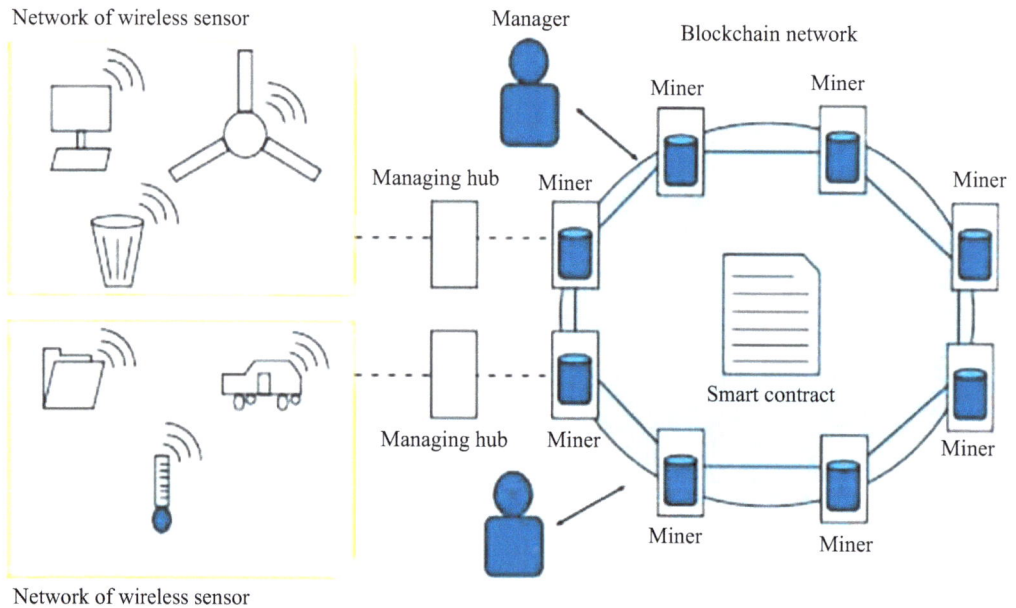

Fig. (3). Blockchain with IoT technology.

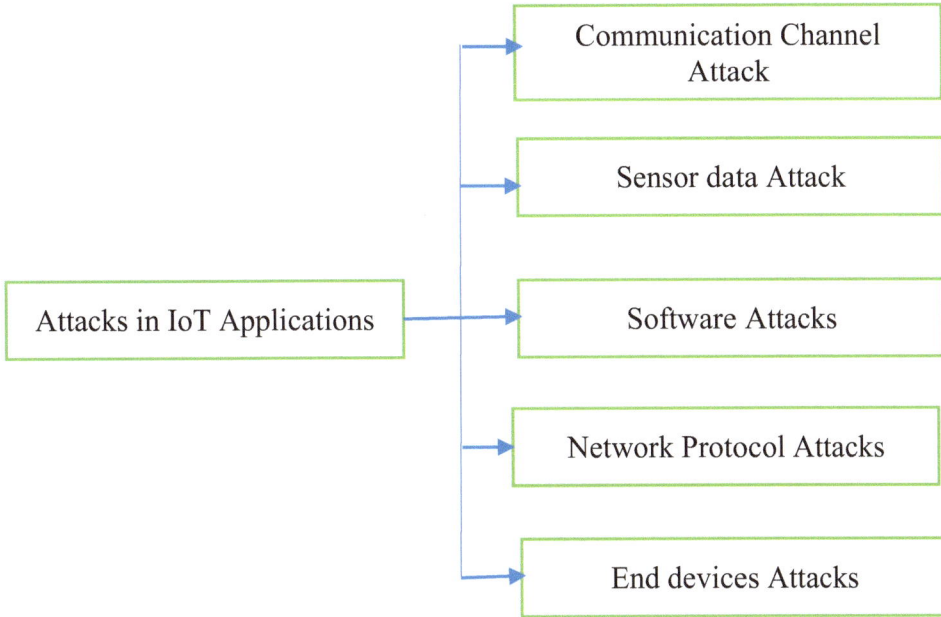

Fig. (4). IoT application attacks.

Fig. (**4**) represents the IoT attacks applications. Some of the IoT application assaults produced in IoT communication networks are communication channel attacks, sensor data attacks, software attacks, network protocol attacks and end devices attacks.

Fig. (**5**) represents the usage of IoT with blockchain technology. There is a need for a distributed ledger technology, trustworthy, private and secure IoT network. Blockchain has become a potent technology in recent years, both for business and the scientific community. Community validation is used by blockchain technology to synchronize replicated ledger content among various users.

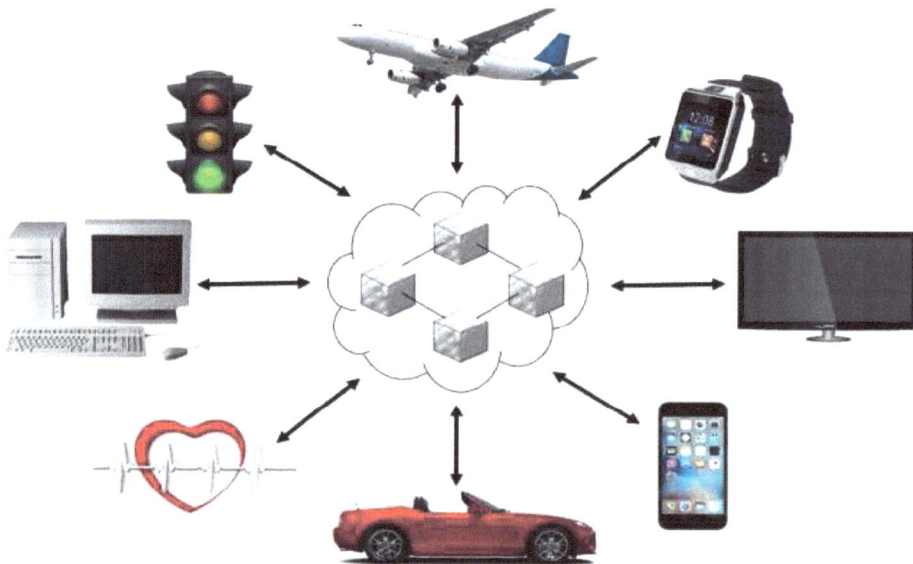

Fig. (5). IoT with Blockchain technology.

BLOCKCHAIN SECURITY ANALYSIS

The involvement of numerous peers is essential for a blockchain to be secure. For instance, the security of the Bitcoin blockchain is dependent on the massive hash power generated by many nodes participating in the proof of work, which prevents an attacker from providing a higher quantity of computation.

Improved Blockchain Security

Compared to traditional record-keeping systems, new IoT and blockchain technology is more dependable and safer [8]. An agreement between the network participants is required before a transaction can be logged. A transaction is converted and related to the earlier transaction once it has been approved. Additionally, rather than being held on a single server, data is distributed throughout a network of processers, preventing hackers from fast access to transaction data. The main security measure in blockchains is PKI (private/public key infrastructure). Blockchain systems use asymmetric cryptography to secure participant-to-participant transactions. Since these keys are produced using characters which are choosing a random manner and integers such as numerals, it is impossible to determine the isolated key from the public key. By doing this, data leakage is reduced and blockchain documents are protected from potential dangers.

Additionally, blockchain has the potential to alter how private information is shared in sectors like finance, government, and healthcare, where protecting private information from several applications is essential to preventing fraud and criminal activity. Additionally, BCTIoT is able to provide customers with reliable access control, which routinely authorizes all the IoT device functions [14]. Users of smart contract services can also get data provenance. Blockchain enables data owners to control the exchange of their data as a result. On the blockchain, self-executing smart contracts are ensured to be private and to belong to their respective owners. The confirmation and denial of malicious access are made possible *via* smart contract-based permission.

Decentralization

Blockchain's decentralized nature offers a workable solution to the block and failure challenges in the IoT network by removing the need for a trustworthy third party [8, 15]. Even if one of the blockchain nodes is offline, the BCIoT network still runs well. Blockchain data is often dispersed among a large number of P2P nodes, and the device is particularly resilient to malicious attempts and technical blunders. The security or availability of the network cannot, under any circumstances, be compromised. An offline node occurs. Contrarily, many conventional records trust more than one server. More susceptible to malfunctions and online occurrences. Additionally, the peer to peer (P2P) nature of blockchain technology grants all system users reasonable authentication rights to ensure and verify the accuracy of IoT data.

Higher Traceability

Unlike Blockchain, previous systems do not allow for the rapid tracing of properties imported in a convoluted supply chain to their point of origin. Blockchain transactions, including historical data can help in confirming the legitimacy of assets and preventing fraud. Similar to this, the Blockchain can stock and trail a patient's past records, which are crucial for their maintenance.

Reduced Cost

One of many businesses' main goals is to minimize costs. Due to the lack of middlemen and mediators' expenses for communal BC, blockchain technology can decrease the charge of running a corporate. Blockchain technology users do not want to read a lot of literature. A transaction may be completed because the separate party has contact to a single, immutable ledger. Blockchain requires significant investment in specialized infrastructure for private and for the processing of transactions, the association of blockchain technology and public blockchain still controls a fee compared to the charge of third-party amenities.

Data Privacy

Due to their immutable and dependable characteristics, storage solutions on the blockchain are highly successful in preventing the alteration of IoT data [19]. Blockchain uses digital signatures and immutable hash chains to protect the authenticity and integrity of data exchanges. In essence, the blockchain gives users the ability to monitor network activity in order to safeguard computer and data rights.

Immutability

Data about transactions is never changed on a blockchain. Technically, utilizing the blockchain network, transactions are hashed, timestamped, and then joined into a block. By using block hashing techniques to connect blocks together, a consecutive blockchain is also produced. The chain is virtually unalterable since the block hash value of the information from the preceding block is always saved in one field of the header of a new Block. Data cannot be edited, modified, or removed once it has been confirmed and put into the blockchain. Any attempts to alter or amend a transaction can be resisted by the cryptographic connections of the subsequent Blocks. Even if a transaction is changed, the change will be clear.

Greater Transparency

Since all network users have access to the transaction histories in the blockchain, they are more visible. In contrast to individual copies in a traditional network, participants in a distributed network known as a blockchain share the same documents. Only a consensus, which requires unanimous agreement, may change this shared text. In other words, a solo copy of the information in blockchain technology is distributed throughout a large network for public verification. As a result, everyone using the blockchain has equal access to the network to link, confirm, and trace transaction activities. The entire network would need to collaborate in order to change a single transaction record, which requires changing all future records as well. As a final result, the information on blockchain technology is more secure.

CONCLUSION

Here they examined research from a variety of areas, including IoT eHealth, smart homes and vehicles, in order to report security and secrecy challenges. Blockchain, Edge, Fog, Cloud, and other technologies were utilized in these applications. But there are still a lot of technical and security issues in IoT. Several challenges to deploying blockchain technology in the IoT space are listed in this paper, along with information on how these challenges are being resolved.

In order to identify their advantages and disadvantages, numerous characteristics of recent blockchain and IoT publications are taken into consideration. The study also includes a detailed analysis of blockchain components and a number of widely used consensus mechanisms.

REFERENCES

[1]   D. Evans, "The Internet of Things: How the next evolution of the internet is changing everything", *CISCO IBSG,* 2011.

[2]   Ali Dorri; Salil S. Kanhere; Raja Jurdak; and Praveen Gauravaram, *"Blockchain for IoT security and privacy: The case study of a smart home"*, 2017 IEEE International Conference on Pervasive Computing and Communications, 2017.
       [http://dx.doi.org/10.1109/PERCOMW.2017.7917634]

[3]   Alfonso Panarello, Nachiket Tapas, Giovanni Merlino, Francesco Longo and Antonio Puliafito I, *Blockchain and IoT Integration: A Systematic Survey*, Sensors 18, 2575; pp. 1-37, 2018.
       [http://dx.doi.org/10.3390/s18082575]

[4]   I. Eyal, and E.G. Sirer, "Majority is not enough: Bitcoin mining is vulnerable", In: *Financial Cryptography and Data Security* Springer: Berlin, Heidelberg, 2014.

[5]   K. Ashton, "That 'internet of things' thing", *RFID Journal,* vol. 22, no. 7, pp. 97-114, 2009.

[6]   Zhixiang Li, "Physical unclonable function based identity management for IoT with blockchain", *Procedia Computer Science,* vol. 198, no. 2022, pp. 454-459, 2022.

[7]   K. Karthigadevi, S. Balamurali, and M. Venkatesulu, "Wormhole attack detection and prevention using EIGRP protocol based on roundtriptime", *J. Cyber Secur,* vol. 7, no. 1 & 2, pp. 215-218, 2018.

[8]   K. Karthigadevi, S. Balamurali, and M. Venkatesulu, "Improving quality of service in wireless sensor networks using neighbor constraint transmission centric distributed sink hole detection and network simulator 2", *J. Eng. Appl. Sci. (Asian Res. Publ. Netw.),* vol. 12, no. 4, pp. 1197-1201, 2017.

[9]   K. Karthigadevi, S. Balamurali, and M. Venkatesulu, "Watchdog- Round trip time method to detect and prevent the wormhole attack using AODV routing protocol", *J. Web Eng.,* vol. 17, no. 6, pp. 3619-3628, 2018.

[10]   K. Karthigadevi, S. Balamurali, and M. Venkatesulu, "Based on neighbor density estimation technique to improve the quality of serviceand to detect and prevent the sinkhole attack in wireless sensor network", *2019 IEEE International Conference on Intelligent Techniquesin Control, Optimization and Signal Processing (INCOS) IEEE,* pp. 1-4, 2020.

[11]   N. Chidambaram, P. Raj, K. Thenmozhi, and R. Amirtharajan, "Enhancing the security of customer data in cloud environments using a novel digital fingerprinting technique", *Int. J. Digit. Multimed. Broadcast.,* vol. 2016, pp. 1-6, 2016.
       [http://dx.doi.org/10.1155/2016/8789397]

[12]   G. Booth, A. Soknacki, and A. Somayaji, "Cloud security: attacks and current defenses, in: Proceedings 8th Annual Symposium Information Assurance (ASIA13), 2013, pp. 45; N. Kshetri, Can blockchain strengthen the internet of things?", *IT Prof.,* vol. 19, no. 4, pp. 68-72, 2017.

[13]   N. Kshetri, "Can blockchain strengthen the internet of things?", *IT Prof.,* vol. 19, no. 4, pp. 68-72, 2017.
       [http://dx.doi.org/10.1109/MITP.2017.3051335]

[14]   E. Rani, "An automated cost prediction in uber/call taxi using machine learning algorithm", *2022 2nd International Conference on Advance Computing and Innovative Technologies in Engineering,* 2022.
       [http://dx.doi.org/10.1109/ICACITE53722.2022.9823852]

[15]   M. Sakthimohan, "An automated cost prediction in uber/call taxi using machine learning algorithm",

2022 2nd International Conference on Advance Computing and Innovative Technologies in Engineering (ICACITE) Greater Noida, India, 2022, pp. 764-767.
[http://dx.doi.org/10.1109/ICACITE53722.2022.9823777]

[16]   Z. Zheng, S. Xie, H.N. Dai, X. Chen, and H. Wang, "Blockchain challenges and opportunities: A survey", *Int. J. Web Grid Serv.,* vol. 14, no. 4, pp. 352-375, 2018.
[http://dx.doi.org/10.1504/IJWGS.2018.095647]

[17]   B. Betts, "Blockchain and the promise of cooperative cloud storage", Available From: ComputerWeekly.com.

[18]   Available From: https://www.computerweekly.com/feature/Blockchain-and-the-promise-of-

[19]   A. Dorri, S.S. Kanhere, and R. Jurdak, "Towards an optimized blockchain for iot", *Proc. 2rd Int. Conf. Internet-of-Things Design Implementation ACM,* pp. 173-178, 2017.
[http://dx.doi.org/10.1145/3054977.3055003]

[20]   K. Christidis, and M. Devetsikiotis, "Blockchains and smart contracts for the internet of things", *IEEE Access,* vol. 4, pp. 2292-2303, 2016.
[http://dx.doi.org/10.1109/ACCESS.2016.2566339]

[21]   X. Zha, X. Wang, W. Ni, R.P. Liu, Y.J. Guo, and X. Niu, "Blockchain for IoT: the tradeoff between consistency and capacity", *Chin. J. Internet Things,* vol. 1, no. 1, 2017.

[22]   M. Isaja, and J. Soldatos, "Distributed ledger technology for decentralization of manufacturing processes", *Proceedings of the 1st IEEE industrial cyber-physical systems (ICPS) Saint Petersburg,* pp. 696-701, 2018.
[http://dx.doi.org/10.1109/ICPHYS.2018.8390792]

[23]   "Litecoins", Available From: https://litecoin.com

[24]   S. Nakamoto, "Bitcoin: A peer-to-peer electronic cash system", Available From: https://bitcoin.org/ 1240 bitcoin.pdf

[25]   A. Panarello, N. Tapas, G. Merlino, F. Longo, and A. Puliafito, "Blockchain and IoT integration: A systematic survey", *Sensors,* vol. 18, no. 8, p. 2575, 2018.
[http://dx.doi.org/10.3390/s18082575] [PMID: 30082633]

[26]   J. Huang, L. Kong, G. Chen, M-Y. Wu, X. Liu, and P. Zeng, "Towards secure industrial IoT: blockchain system with credit-based consensus mechanism", *IEEE Trans. Industr. Inform.,* vol. 15, no. 6, pp. 3680-3689, 2019.
[http://dx.doi.org/10.1109/TII.2019.2903342]

[27]   Q. Zhou, H. Huang, Z. Zheng, and J. Bian, "Solutions to scalability of blockchain: a survey", *IEEE Access,* vol. 8, pp. 16440-16455, 2020.
[http://dx.doi.org/10.1109/ACCESS.2020.2967218]

[28]   K.J. O'Dwyer, and D. Malone, "Bitcoin mining and its energy footprint", *25th IET Irish Signals & Systems Conference 2014 and 2014 China–Ireland International Conference on Information and Communications Technologies* 26–27 Jun 2014; Limerick, Ireland, IET, London, 2014, pp. 280–285.
[http://dx.doi.org/10.1049/cp.2014.0699]

[29]   M.A. Uddin, A. Stranieri, and I. Gondal, "An efficient selective miner consensus protocol in blockchain oriented IoT smart monitoring", *2019 IEEE International Conference on Industrial Technology Melbourne, Australia,* pp. 1135-1142, 2019.
[http://dx.doi.org/10.1109/ICIT.2019.8754936]

[30]   P.K. Sharma, N. Kumar, and J.H. Park, "Blockchain technology toward green IoT: opportunities and challenges", *IEEE Netw.,* vol. 34, no. 4, pp. 263-269, 2020.
[http://dx.doi.org/10.1109/MNET.001.1900526]

[31]   K. Karthigadevi, and G. Srinivasagan, "Study of agricultural analysis of soil using random forest classification in tirunelveli district", *Indian J. Environ,* vol. 42, no. 1, pp. 52-58, 2022.

[32]   A.D. Dwivedi, L. Malina, and P. Dzurenda, "Optimized blockchain model for Internet of Things based healthcare applications", *2019 42nd International Conference on Telecommunications and Signal Processing* 1–3 Jul 2019; Budapest, Hungary, IEEE, Piscataway, NJ, USA, 2019, pp. 135–139. [http://dx.doi.org/10.1109/TSP.2019.8769060]

[33]   K. Karthigadevi, and G. Srinivasagan, "Random Forest Classification Algorithm for Agricultural Data Analysis in Tirunelveli District", *J. Xian Univ. Archit. Technol,* vol. 12, no. 8, pp. 418-432, 2020.

[34]   K. Karthigadevi, "S BalaMurali, M Venkatesulu, "Neighbor Constraint Transmission Centric Distributed Sink Hole Detection and Mitigation Approach for Quality of Service Improvement in Wireless Sensor Networks"", *International Journal of Wireless Networks and Communications,* vol. 9, no. 1, pp. 1-11, 2017. [IJWNC].

[35]   S. Porkodi, and D. Kesavaraja, Integration of Blockchain and Internet of Things.*Handbook of Research on Blockchain Technology.* Academic Press, 2020, pp. 61-94. [http://dx.doi.org/10.1016/B978-0-12-819816-2.00003-4]

CHAPTER 5

Blockchain Integrated with Internet of Things-benefits, Challenges

Geeta Amol Patil[1,*], **Surekha K.B.**[1], **Chaithra V.**[1] and **Anand Kumar S.**[2]

[1] *BMS Institute of Technology and Management, Bengaluru, India*

[2] *Vellore Institute of Technology, Vellore, India*

Abstract: All sectors are now using digital ways to facilitate humans. Be it health, finance, supply chain, communication, transport, IT, or education, all the sectors are now relying on technologies and the internet for providing facilities and also using them as sources of information. These sectors, when using traditional ways, faced a lot of challenges. For example, people earlier going to railway stations to book train tickets had to wait for long durations in queues, and if all the seats are filled by the time they reach or their turn comes to reserve seats, it goes all in vain to spend time traveling to the station and time in queues. Coming to the finance sector, people had to go to banks to create a bank account and for all the formalities. They had to spend time going to banks and then wait in queues to get their work done. Also, it took around 1-2 weeks for every task to complete in banks. So, the process was quite time-consuming, monotonous and unreliable in practice. Thus many sectors started looking for alternative methods to perform their daily tasks. Slowly, the sectors started digitizing, and started using computers to perform tasks, to store and update their data. They also started using the internet in their daily applications. Each organization of industry is now available on the internet. All of their information is present and one can apply for their services using their websites. Thus, IoT comes into the picture here. All the sectors using the internet to access and provide information, using the cloud to store their data are using IoT services. Internet of Things (IoT) technology will soon become an integral part of our daily lives to facilitate the control and monitoring of processes and objects and to change the way man interacts with the physical world. For all aspects of IoT to be fully functional, there are a few obstacles to overcome and important challenges to overcome. These include, but are not limited to, cyber security, data privacy, power consumption, and metrics. The dedicated Blockchain environment and its various processes provide a useful way to address these few IoT challenges.

Keywords: Cyber Security, Computer Vision, IoT Challenges.

* **Corresponding author Geeta Amol Patil:** BMS Institute of Technology and Management, Bengaluru, India; E-mail: geetapatil@bmsit.in

L. Ashok Kumar, D. Karthika Renuka, Sonali Agarwal & Sheng-Lung Peng (Eds.)

INTRODUCTION

Today, around 5 billion devices are connected to Internet of Things (IoT) systems, and this number is increasing day by day [1]. Every device on the Internet generates and exchanges data. In light of this enormous number of gadgets, significant and continuous data is created. Addressing the basic security concerns of such a large-scale information structure is challenging. The distributed architecture of the IoT presents a significant difficulty. In an IoT network, each node can be a potential failure point. A node can be a source to launch cyber-attacks such as Distributed Denial-of-Service (DDoS) [2]. A network with increasing infected nodes acting simultaneously may swiftly come to an end. Another concern is regarding its centralized configuration [3]. Nodes in the network which are vulnerable to threats have to be addressed. Maintaining confidentiality and authentication of the sensed data becomes important in the entire IoT system [4].

IoT data can be misused and exploited without data security. Data security also becomes crucial with the introduction of systems where IoT devices can exchange data resources, computational power resources and electricity resources on their own. The IoT has several important uses, including decision support systems. Timely judgments can be made using the data compiled from the fleet of sensors. Hence, it becomes important to defend the system against attacks and include safety measures to protect the nodes and the data.

Automated systems that handle real-time information, such as smart grids, manufacturing industry unit, and transportation networks, availability is essential. Losses from sensor outages can range from financial to potentially fatal. Trust building among participating organizations is a critical difficulty in the emerging economy of machines. Data-generating sensors can sell their data in data marketplaces and through end-to-end autonomous systems [5]. Instead of having a third party, a publicly verifiable audit mechanism can handle the issue of non-repudiation.

Thus integrating IoT with blockchain provides a solution to these challenges. Since blockchain uses a decentralized way of storing data in nodes and linking those nodes with hashing algorithms, thus it makes it secure to store data in IoT devices. These are also other motivations for integrating IoT with blockchain:

– Security and safety in accessing data and devices.

– Reliability of connecting devices.

– Data storage's long-term viability.

The inherent security of the blockchain technology is typically acceptable for various IoT applications when the primary goal is to keep the user's identity confidential.

Objectives of IoT integration with Blockchain are as follows:

– The objective of integrating IoT with Blockchain is to provide a reliable way to connect devices over a network that is secure, safe and reliable with storing data.

– To provide proper power resources so that devices do not have to face the consequences of power outrage or current unavailability is one of the objectives of integrating IoT with blockchain.

– To store data in a secure way so that it is accessible within an organization but cannot be tampered with.

AN OVERVIEW OF THE INTERNET OF THINGS

The current craze of internet-connected devices is the Internet of Things with built-in computing capabilities. The term refers to a wide range of devices, including internet-connected surveillance devices, security cameras, sensors, networked industrial equipment, and consumer electronics, like refrigerators and autos [6]. Pervasive computing has increased the appeal of the IoT in the technological age of today. The usage of IoT devices has benefitted smart-cities, smart-homes and smart-transportation. In 2008, the number of IoT devices outnumbered the world's population. The IoT system's multiple features allow for the creation of new apps and services on a daily basis. According to Statista [1], by the end of 2025, the number of things connected will be crossed over 19 billion. Statista estimates that by the end of 2028, the total number of IoT objects will have surpassed 25 billion. As can be seen in Fig. (**1**), by 2030, this number will have risen to almost 29 billion devices. In addition, the Internet of Things industry is expanding at a fast pace [7].

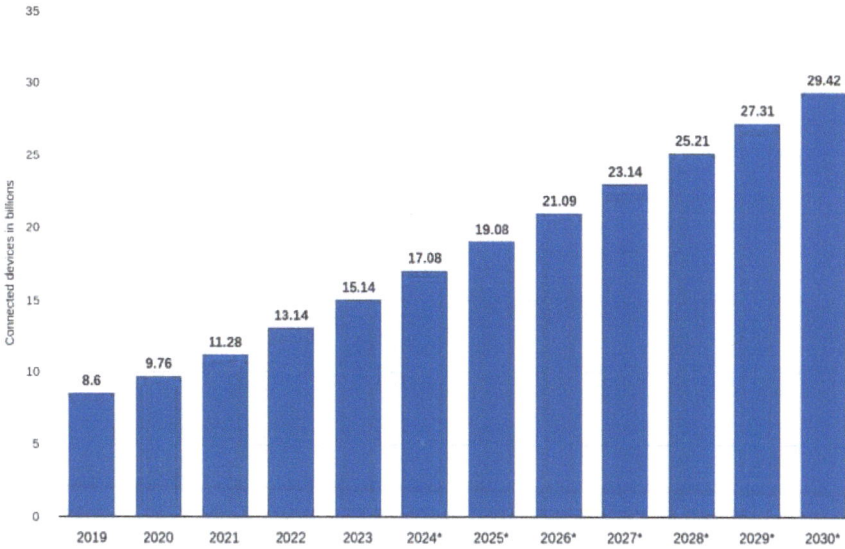

Fig. (1). Estimation of connected devices in the Internet of Things (IoT) System [1].

IoT Features

The Internet of things is indeed a cutting-edge innovation with the potential to drastically alter our lives, companies, and economies. IoT provides a slew of digital services and apps that outperform traditional alternatives in a variety of ways. These programmes and services have some characteristics:

– Sensing Capabilities: The wireless sensor network (WSN) is the fundamental technology for IoT domains. WSNs typically consist of a network of sensors which gather data on their environment and send it *via* a communication link to be processed. The IoT's building blocks are sensors, which enable the collection of all real-time and contextual data.

– Connectivity: Controlling the devices remotely, which are thousands in numbers, depends on the connectivity. It is the key element which allows thousands of remotely operated gadgets and products. It also allows a variety of items to communicate and converse over the Internet, enabling the creation of services and applications.

– Large-scale network: A massive network is made up of a huge number of devices and things which cannot be controlled using traditional methods.

– Dynamic systems: In the day to day life, IoT can be viewed as a system with dynamic in nature. It is a known fact that IoT has the capacity to connect a large number of things in various locations. These devices adapt flexibly to changing settings and circumstances. Sensors collect a range of real time and context information about their surroundings and communicate it to higher layers.

– Intelligence capabilities: IoT devices which can make smart judgments in a variety of situations and collaborate intelligently with other cooperating items to enhance hardware, software, and sensor capabilities.

– Big data: IoT devices generate large amounts of data which cannot be stored in traditional databases. A massive amount of data has to be processed by the applications. Hence there is a need for a Big Data Analysis approach.

– Autonomous Decision: Due to the acquisition of massive volumes of contextual and real time data generated by IoT devices, the devices may take autonomous and context-aware decisions.

– Heterogeneity: IoT technology enables many sorts of devices and things to be addressed and connected to one another over the Internet. Protocols, software platforms, and other hardware/software components are among these devices. Despite these differences, the IoT system enables all devices to connect with one another in a timely and efficient manner.

Centralized Architecture of IoT

A specific architecture design is required when managing a group of nodes to build a system. The centralized architecture, which uses a centralized server which controls and administers a collection of nodes, is one of the most prevalent systems. These nodes include powerful computer systems, laptops, mobile phones, and other devices capable of performing a variety of tasks. The manager of the entire system is a central server that handles all requests from various nodes and plans and distributes jobs around the network. The perception, network, and application layers make up the centralized IoT architecture [8].

The perception layer is the top layer of the IoT architecture (also called the sensing layer). This layer includes actuators, wireless sensor networks, radio frequency identification (RFID), and sensors.

IoT architecture is shown in Fig. (**2**). The fundamental role of this layer is to sense and perceive the surrounding world, as well as to gather important data that can be analyzed and extracted to help us comprehend and govern our physical surroundings. Actuators may be used by IoT devices to make context-aware and independent decisions based on data collected.

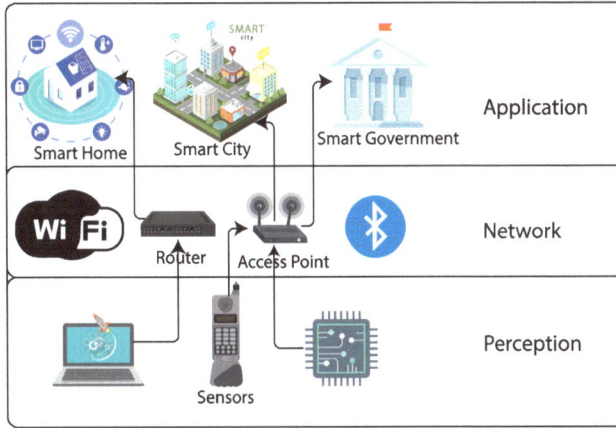

Fig. (2). The Three-layer architecture of IoT system [10].

The network layer connects PCs and other IoT products and devices to the centralized server through the Internet. The layer contains gateways, which are communication points between the perceptions and the network layer. To communicate data between the application and perception levels, 3G/4G, Bluetooth, Wi-Fi, and broadband were all used.

The application layer is made up of a variety of Internet of Things (IoT) applications that use enormous amounts of data gathered and analyzed at the perception and network layers to create digitized services in a variety of domains, including smart parking, healthcare, home automation, sustainable city, wearable, agriculture, smart grid, and many others.

The existing centralized IoT system provides a considerable amount of benefits by connecting and interacting with a large variety of heterogeneous devices. As a consequence, a single server handles the whole charge of the IoT network, making it easier to administer and maintain. It also saves money because the majority of processing processes are done by the centralized server, obviating the need for many complete workstations on the network.

As a result, the majority of network nodes can establish a terminal connection to the main server. The centralized IoT design also offers superior physical security because the majority of IoT data is kept in a single location, making it easier to defend against physical attacks.

The centralized IoT architecture, on the other hand, poses several issues. It, for example, has scalability concerns since it can't keep up with the increasing influx of IoT devices. Furthermore, it poses various security and privacy concerns.

AN OVERVIEW OF BLOCKCHAIN

The advantage of Blockchain Technology in handling security issues compared to previous solutions has drawn the attention of multiple researchers and other application developers. The entire history of transactions between two communicating peers is kept on a Blockchain, where a ledger is maintained, which is distributed, decentralized and immutable. Most nodes should register their agreement in order to store all transactions in a distributed ledger.

When a new transaction happens in the application, the initiator of the transaction will broadcast it to all the stakeholders, saying that the transaction is new and yet to be verified. When the other nodes in the Blockchain receive this, they validate and maintain it in the ledger. A set of transactions is gathered and assigned to a ledger block [9]. Each block has a timestamp and a hash function that are used to connect it to the block before it. As a result, many blocks are joined together and dubbed blockchain. Contents of a block are often verified using the hash function. Information exchange in a secure manner will be promoted by Blockchain technology by ensuring each node in the Blockchain network has a copy of the original ledger and allowing every node to maintain the updated transaction details.

Components of Blockchain

The basic components of the blockchain are shown in Fig. (**3**). Blockchain comprises the block, ledger, hashing, transaction, minor, and consensus procedures.

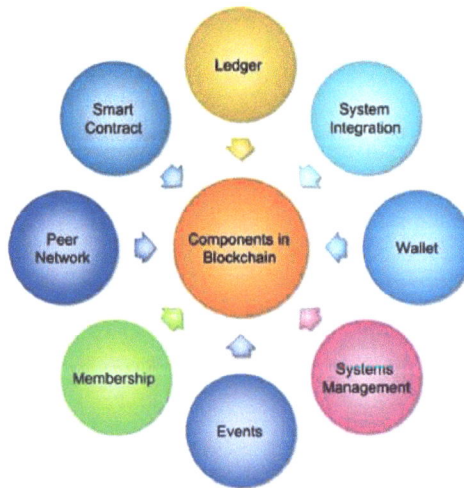

Fig. (3). Main components of Blockchain.

– The ledger, which is a data structure that may be used to hold a variety of data. The ledger and the traditional database have substantial distinctions. Tables containing columns and rows are used to store data in a database system. Furthermore, it employs a relational paradigm for accessing and aggregating data by linking data from many sources. The ledger, on the other hand, is used to keep track of all transactions that have ever been made by all members of the network.

– The block is one of the most important elements of the blockchain. Each block is made up of transactions. By placing the prior block's unique hash value in the current block, the blocks were connected. This connection forms a chain of blocks. The hash function is employed to ensure that each block's content is data-integrity-checked. Minors must solve a mathematical challenge called the hash function in order to locate a block. The hash function is utilized because it is collision-free, which means that producing two identical hashes for two different digital data sets is extremely difficult. Each block's contents may be identified and validated by assigning a hash value to it.

– The smallest element of a process or activity that is aggregated and stored in a block is called a transaction. A transaction may only be included in a block if a majority of the participating nodes in the blockchain network agree. Smaller transactions cost less power and are easier to authenticate, which is vital for minors [11].

– Minors are computers or agents that attempt to solve a tough mathematical problem in order to move on to the next block. The process of discovering a new block begins with all nodes broadcasting new transactions, following which each node combines a series of transactions into a block and executes operations to determine the proof-of-work for the block. When a node discovers a block, it joins the network.

Features of Blockchain

– Decentralization: Without having a centralized system, a single point of failure of the system can be avoided. With decentralization, robustness and scalability can be achieved by utilizing the resources of all participating nodes, which will eliminate the many to one traffic flow. This, in turn, reduces the latency between the communicating entities.

– Transparency: Blockchain enables a high level of transparency, which will allow all the nodes in the network to access the data in a transparent manner, which was lacking in the central server where the server has total control and access to all data. Each node maintains a copy of the distributed ledger in order to keep up with changes. The absence of a third party promotes the friendliness and trustworthiness of the commercial relationship.

– Better security: One of the benefits of blockchain technology is that it is more secure than previous systems. Blockchain provides a safe environment against numerous forms of assaults by utilizing public key infrastructure. The consensus mechanism provides a reliable approach for enhancing blockchain security. Since it lacks a single point of failure that may disrupt whole networks, blockchain technology is more secure than a centralized system.

– Anonymity: Despite the fact that blockchain uses a distributed ledger that is shared by all users, the nodes' security is protected by an invisible identity. Anonymity may be used to make voting more secure and private.

Design, Architecture and Methodology

To get around the drawbacks of centralized IoT design and make use of all that blockchain technology has to offer, blockchain and IoT integration is now required. Fig. (4) shows IoT architecture with blockchain. There are numerous approaches to integrating blockchain technology with IoT. This section explores one of the layered architectural strategies for integrating blockchain into IoT. Four layers make up the basic layered blockchain with IoT design.

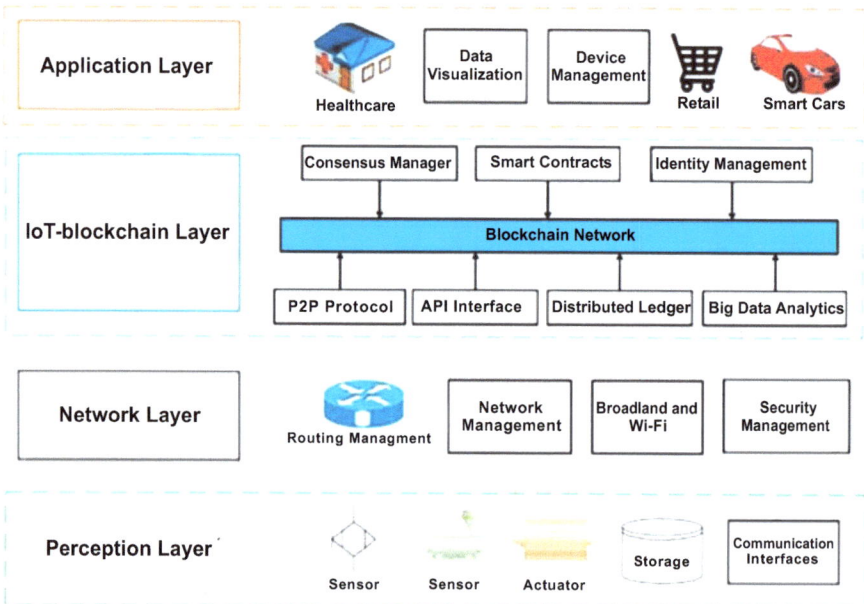

Fig. (4). Integrated IoT - blockchain architecture.

The perception layer, which can be considered the basic layer of IoT architecture, includes the components like sensors and actuators. These components are required to sense the surrounding environment's physical aspects and perceive it. The perception layer will also be used to gather the relevant data. The network layer links and communicates all IoT gadgets through the Internet, handling network and routing management. This layer is made up of networking and security components that facilitate communication and security administration.

To integrate Blockchain with IoT, an IoT Blockchain layer is added, which includes all the various features of Blockchain technology required, so that the technology can be used in the Internet of Things system. The layer includes components like distributed ledger, smart contracts, an API, big data analytics, consensus management, and identity management, among others. To make it possible for decentralized communication between IoT devices, P2P protocols are required. Whenever changes happen in the IoT network, the devices need to have a replica of the data in the distributed ledger. The ledger can be built either with or without authority. The IoT context and quantity of IoT network nodes will have a significant impact.

IoT devices generate enormous amounts of data that standard database techniques are unable to handle. Hence, a big data analytics module is introduced here, which will effectively handle on-line data storage and processing.

Furthermore, because many transactions are kept in structured ledgers, further data analysis is required. Another important aspect of blockchain technology is smart contracts, which allow for autonomous decisions based on specified criteria. When specific requirements are met or approved, a smart contract is a piece of software that leverages blockchain to carry out a set of actions. Consensus management is one of the most crucial elements for combining IoT and blockchain. It serves as the network's central server, ensuring that all connected nodes are trustworthy.

BENEFITS AND APPLICATIONS

Benefits of Integrating IoT and Blockchain

– Elimination of central authority- Blockchain eliminates the concept of central authority as it is a decentralized network. It improves scalability and fault tolerance as the updated copies of data are stored in the nodes. Also, blockchain provides authentication of IoT devices so that participants can identify each device properly.

– Direct peer to peer messaging- The distributed peer-to-peer architecture of blockchain provides and fastens the peer-to-peer messaging which is beneficial in decoupled applications. Data, storage flow and interaction become easier and there is easier integration between the devices.

– Resource usage and Automation- Blockchain concepts enable direct and automated interaction between IoT devices. It also facilitates resource usage by running an on-demand code and the payment is automated when the transaction is completed. The smart contract also enables IoT device authentication in the distributed network.

– Deployment of secure code- IoT device status can be checked periodically and updates are performed securely. Codes are also pushed in a secure manner because blockchain provides a distributed ledger and secure transaction storage.

– Built-in trust- Blockchain builds trust in IoT data since all the participants have tamper-proof copy of the data. Since all the nodes have the data and means to verify the data, trustworthiness increases.

– Security- Since blockchain stores IoT and otherwise any data in nodes which are all connected through hashes. That is, each node has its own hash value and also contains hash values of its previous and next node, so it is impossible to tamper with the data of any one node. Also, integrating IoT and blockchain automatically updates the firmware of devices which ensures security.

– Data Privacy- In blockchain, only the person having the private to access the node and its data can access it. Therefore, data privacy is also ensured and enabled by smart contracts in blockchain.

– Improve IoT system interoperability- interoperability refers to the ability of IoT devices to communicate with one another and with the physical environment. Blockchain compresses and transforms data into uniform blocks, allowing all blocks linked as peers to have the same level of access.

– Access and identity governance- Blockchain facilitates IoT governance and monitoring throughout the system's lifespan since it registers, assigns IDs to IoT devices in a complicated connection, and securely stores all data.

– Stability and robustness- IoT devices and their deployment make digitization easier, while the blockchain eliminates the need for central servers, increasing the system's reliability. The process is also more resilient as a result of trustworthy integration.

– Historical transaction records- All transaction data records are recorded in the blockchain and may be tracked back to the initial transaction by any node. By allowing customers and IoT service providers to track resources and confirm service level agreements, Blockchain's traceability feature increases the quality of service for IoT devices.

– Infrastructure development costs are reduced since the decentralized blockchain structure does not rely on any underlying network infrastructure to deliver networking features.

– Transparency- With blockchain, participants know exactly where their data is going and how it will be utilized.

Applications of Integration of IoT a Blockchain

Supply Chain Management and Logistics- Delay in the delivery of the products to the intended place is the biggest challenge in the Supply Chain Management domain. A supply chain network involves numerous stakeholders, and this is primarily the reason why delivery delay becomes one of the biggest challenges in the supply chain and logistics industry. Thus there is a need for blockchain and IoT in this sector to speed up the process of product delivery. Blockchain will provide transparency in the entire process to track the order placement, the vendors accepting the orders and putting all the products in the correct quantity for delivery and will track the delivery of the products. IoT- enabled devices will allow the companies to track the shipment of products at every stage. Motion sensors, temperature sensors and GPS are a few of the IoT devices that will help in the process to check the products and location of the shipment. For transparency, the collected data is then saved in the blockchain and can be seen by management, stakeholders, vendors, and consumers. They can also change the information if they have permission to do so. As a result, the combination of blockchain with IoT will give supply chain traceability, dependability, and integrity.

– Automotive Supply Chain- When blockchain and IoT are combined in the automotive supply chain, a new type of incoming logistic service emerges, in which smart IoT sensors and other devices track useful information in real time, resulting in a planned production schedule, improved material and information flow, and improved goods tracking. Improvements in the system result in several benefits in outgoing deliveries, such as improved just-in-time logistics, fewer damaged trucks, and so on.

– Pharmaceutical Supply Chain- Blockchain Technology helps in identifying each medical product by assigning a unique Global Trade Item (GTIN, which can be accessed by any stakeholder in the supply chain market. The integration of Blockchain and IoT technologies helps trace the medical product from the time it is made until it expires.

– Food Supply Chain- Food safety and food-borne illness are among the biggest issues faced these days which not only affect the food supply chain but also the country or the world as a whole. This is because of not having a proper transparent, traceable and supply chain management for food supply. Blockchain integrated IoT systems will enable a transparent system and also remove the dependency of third parties in the network. Most of the work will be carried out on the basis of the set of rules and consensus protocol in the food supply system. Food manufacturers can confirm that the quality of supplies has not been tampered with in the supply chain. The system is transparent, so fraud detection is immediately reported to the retailer. On the retailer side, it's easier to track down tampered food without checking the entire inventory. The advantage for consumers is that the final will give you an idea of the quality of the food one consumes.

– Retail Supply Chain- the customers are usually worried about the source and the quality of the product they are getting. A transparent system enables the trust of the customer, which is not available now. With the blockchain enabled IoT system, each product will be having a digital identification with it which will give all the information of the product along with its manufacture and expiry date.

– Automotive Industry: Different sectors like financial, health, agriculture, communication, transport have started digitizing now and are now using digital ways to enable communication with customers and with the industries among themselves. The automotive industry is also not an exception to digitization. This industry is now leveraging IoT-enabled sensors in vehicles to develop fully enabled automatic vehicles. It is also now integrating blockchain with IoT to fasten up the process and exchange information quickly. Also, they are looking for integration with blockchain to transform autonomous cars, smart vehicle parking and automated traffic control. A few companies are using this technology to detect vehicle information using the sensors in the license plate of vehicles and then they find an apt place to park the vehicle in the parking lot. The integration also enables payments using crypto-wallets in the parking system.

– Smart Homes: IoT-enabled devices integrated with blockchain enhance the security and privacy concerns of people. It is also looked upon as an option because it provides authentication/authorization, confidentiality, integrity, and availability for users. All the IoT-enabled smart devices record the information of the device and this information is recorded in their respective nodes of the blockchain. Thus any new device can be added at any time for a particular application easily and it just needs the addition of nodes in the blockchain. One device in a node can act as a supervisor to look at all the devices and their performance. Thus it will also enable automatic switching off and on of the electric appliances in the system and it will also verify the billing information or the device repairing information through blockchain.

– Construction sector: It is the least digitized sector today with most of the work still being carried out on paper. Thus all the information of the construction site, whether onsite or offsite is needed to be verified by the project manager by physically coming to the site and also after every particular duration. Thus using IoT enabled sensors in the materials or construction panels which will record the information of that object along with the environment, such as temperature, humidity and other environment variables will automate the process. Also, this information will be recorded in the blockchain and it can be checked by project managers. Also, the workers can also update the information in the blockchain given the privileges. Thus it will help in automating some parts of the onsite work of the customer, enhance security and traceability and fasten up the entire process.

CONCLUSION & FUTURE WORK

Using IoT devices in various sectors poses a lot of challenges in security, data privacy and reliability and scalability. However, most of the issues may be handled by combining IoT with blockchain. Integrating with blockchain provides a lot of benefits such as elimination of central authority, data security, privacy, authentication and authorization, transparency, automation and resource utilization, direct peer to peer messaging (one IoT device to another), cost reduction in the development of infrastructure, reliability and robustness. Thus today, many of the sectors are now inclined not only to digitize with IoT devices but also integrate with blockchain in it to provide security and transparency and to fasten up their process. A few of the sectors using it are supply chain, health sector, cryptocurrency and others, such as the financial sector, smart homes, smart agriculture, and automotive industry. However, there are a few obstacles to overcome in the integration of blockchain and IoT. When using distributed blockchain technology to store data, the data is safe and private. However, while utilizing blockchain to preserve data, data processing and saving become sluggish. Any data query in the system is sent through the network layer, which contains the blockchain nodes. The data is then accessed based on the rights granted to the user re- questing the data. Furthermore, although combining blockchain with IoT saves computing costs, adding blockchain into the system alone is costly. Thus the future scopes of integrating blockchain into IoT-enabled systems are:

– Reducing the cost of integrating blockchain with IoT devices in the system.

– Speeding the data processing and querying.

REFERENCES

[1] S. Kumar, P. Tiwari, and M. Zymbler, "Internet of Things is a revolutionary approach for future technology enhancement: a review", *J. Big Data,* vol. 6, no. 1, p. 111, 2019.
[http://dx.doi.org/10.1186/s40537-019-0268-2]

[2] R. Singh, and T.P. Sharma, "Present status of distributed denial of service (DDoS) attacks in internet world", *Int. J. Math. Eng. Manag,* vol. 4, no. 4, pp. 1008-1017, 2019.
[http://dx.doi.org/10.33889/IJMEMS.2019.4.4-080]

[3] Yaroslav Krainyk, Andrii Razzhyvin, Olena Bondarenko, and Irina Simakova, "Internet-of-things device set configuration for connection to wireless local area network", *Second International Workshop on Computer Modeling and Intelligent Systems (CMIS-2019)* Zaporizhzhia, Ukraine, April 15-19, 2019
[http://dx.doi.org/10.32782/cmis/2353-70]

[4] W. Alnahari, "Authentication of IoT Device and IoT Server Using Security Key", *2021 International Congress of Advanced Technology and Engineering (ICOTEN)* Taiz, Yemen, 2021, pp. 1-9.
[http://dx.doi.org/10.1109/ICOTEN52080.2021.9493492]

[5] D Nabil, D Tandjaoui, F. Medjek, and I Romdhani, "Trust management in internet of things", In: *Security and Privacy in Smart Sensor Networks* IGI Global, 2018.
[http://dx.doi.org/10.4018/978-1-5225-5736-4.ch007]

[6] S. Maitra, V.P. Yanambaka, A. Abdelgawad, D. Puthal, and K. Yelamarthi, "Proof- of-authentication consensus algorithm: Blockchain-based IoT implementation", *2020 IEEE 6th World Forum on Internet of Things (WF-IoT)* New Orleans, LA, USA, 2020, pp. 1-2.
[http://dx.doi.org/10.1109/WF-IoT48130.2020.9221187]

[7] P. Gupta, V. Dedeoglu, S.S. Kanhere, and R. Jurdak, "Towards a blockchain powered IoT data marketplace", *2021 International Conference on COMmunication Systems & NETworkS (COMSNETS),* pp. 366-368, 2021.
[http://dx.doi.org/10.1109/COMSNETS51098.2021.9352865]

[8] R. Premkumar, and P.S. Sathya, "A blockchain based framework for IoT security", *2021 5th International Conference on Computing Methodologies and Communication (ICCMC)* Erode, India, 2021, pp. 409-413.
[http://dx.doi.org/10.1109/ICCMC51019.2021.9418485]

[9] K. Ata¸sen, "Designing a Secure IoT Network by Using Blockchain", *2019 3rd International Symposium on Multidisciplinary Studies and Innovative Technologies (ISMSIT)* 2019, pp. 1-4.
[http://dx.doi.org/10.1109/ISMSIT.2019.8932728]

[10] R. Mahmoud, T. Yousuf, F. Aloul, and I. Zualkernan, "Internet of things (IoT) security: Current status, challenges and prospective measures", *2015 10th International Conference for Internet Technology and Secured Transactions (ICITST)* London, UK, 2015, pp. 336-341.
[http://dx.doi.org/10.1109/ICITST.2015.7412116]

[11] P.K. Sadhu, V.P. Yanambaka, and A. Abdelgawad, "Internet of Things: Security and solutions survey", *Sensors,* vol. 22, no. 19, p. 7433, 2022.
[http://dx.doi.org/10.3390/s22197433] [PMID: 36236531]

CHAPTER 6

Blockchain Powered Medical Sector – Application, Challenges and Future Research Scope

Divya Palanisamy [1,*], **Saranya Rajendran** [2] and **Praveena Venkatesan** [3]

[1] *N.G.P. Institute of Technology (affiliated to Anna University), NGP Nagar, Kalapatti -6410648, India*

[2] *Sri Ramakrishna Engineering College, Coimbatore, Tamil Nadu 641022, India*

[3] *NGP Institute of Technology, Coimbatore, Tamil Nadu 641048, India*

Abstract: The recent research in the healthcare sector using computer technologies in the fourth industrial revolution helps to improve the quality of life by accessing the medical data to monitor, diagnose and treat the patient at the right time from anywhere in the world. Blockchain is one of the major recent innovations and trending research topics that plays a vital role in diverse applications like Smart cities, Healthcare industry, Smart grid, *etc*. Blockchain, which is fascinated with its features like secure data sharing, immutability, decentralization, and reliability in data management, has made it a prominent technology in the healthcare industry. This chapter discusses 1) The working principle of blockchain technology with its different prospectus in healthcare. 2) Advantages of blockchain technology over the Internet of Things in secured patient data management, efficient data sharing with decentralized data management accessible for authorized users using cryptography techniques. 3) Various applications of blockchain technology in healthcare, like remote patient monitoring using Internet of Things (IoT) devices for cardiac and electroencephalogram (EEG) signal monitoring to diagnose life-threatening diseases. 4) Drug traceability in the pharmaceutical drug supply chain to ensure product safety with an end-to-end tracking system and immutable transaction record. Finally, this chapter also presents the blockchain based challenges and solutions that advocate the future research scope in healthcare systems.

Keywords: Blockchain, Challenges, Drug Traceability, Healthcare, Smart Cities.

INTRODUCTION

Blockchain is the next horizontal breakthrough in healthcare, following horizontal advancements such as the Internet, Cloud computing, and image processing. Simply explained, a blockchain is a network of computers that are not owned by

* **Corresponding author Divya Palanisamy:** N.G.P. Institute of Technology (affiliated to Anna University), NGP Nagar, Kalapatti -6410648, India; E-mail: divya@drngpit.ac.in

L. Ashok Kumar, D. Karthika Renuka, Sonali Agarwal & Sheng-Lung Peng (Eds.)

one single entity that is in charge of a time-stamped repository of permanent data records. Each block of this data *(e.g.*, block) is encrypted and linked together using cryptographic principles *(e.g.*, chain). The Blockchain is greatly regarded because of the following reasons such as it is not owned by a single entity, making it distributed, the data is secured cryptographically, irreversible, and the transparency can be supervised at any time and from anywhere in the world [1].

Traditional paper-based medical records have a number of flaws, prompting medical institutions to switch to electronic health records (EHR). From transferring medical records to real-time data from multiple patient body sensors, e-Health technology has come a long way. This technology creates a new paradigm for transferring medical data, resulting in EHRs that are more efficient, accurate, and secure. As the healthcare industry grows, the quantity of electronic health records (EHRs) generated increased. Immutability, cryptography, distribution, transparency, non-repudiation, audibility, and decentralisation are all blockchain principles, as shown in Fig. (**1**), which made this technology more suitable for healthcare industry [2].

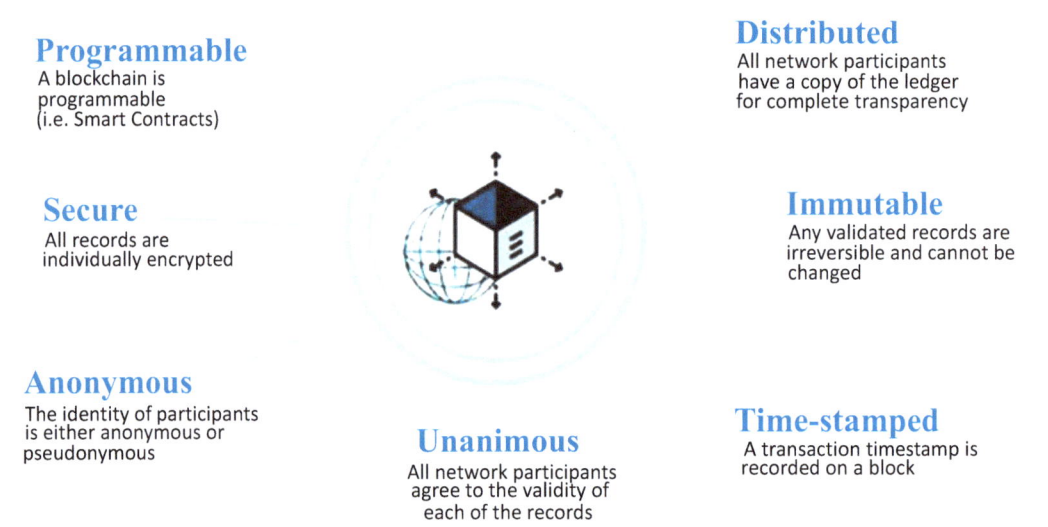

Programmable
A blockchain is programmable (i.e. Smart Contracts)

Secure
All records are individually encrypted

Anonymous
The identity of participants is either anonymous or pseudonymous

Unanimous
All network participants agree to the validity of each of the records

Distributed
All network participants have a copy of the ledger for complete transparency

Immutable
Any validated records are irreversible and cannot be changed

Time-stamped
A transaction timestamp is recorded on a block

Fig. (1). Property of Blockchain Networks.

Healthcare is an important element for both developing and wealthy countries since it is closely related to people's social welfare and daily life. In the healthcare sector, research and development should be a continuous process because it will help to improve the quality of life by combating numerous health conditions and diseases. It has been simple to observe the improvement in the healthcare sector owing to recent technological advancements. The most advanced and cutting-edge computer technology can be used to significantly improve the capabilities now available to the healthcare and medical sectors. These cutting-edge computer technologies can aid doctors and medical professionals in the early detection of a variety of ailments [3]. Nowadays, the word "Blockchain" has become one of the unavoidable terms in e-health records in the field of medical technology. As abundant data are available in the healthcare sector, the blockchain networks help to preserve, secure, exchange and provide transparency in sharing medical data [4].

The contribution of this chapter includes a discussion of the components of blockchain, application of blockchain in healthcare and challenges faced by blockchain in the healthcare industry and finally, the conclusion and future scope.

COMPONENTS OF BLOCKCHAIN

A blockchain requires four components in order to take on a life of its own. A peer-to-peer network is the primary requirement for a blockchain to function. Equally privileged nodes are a type of computer network. Anyone and everyone can attend. This network allows nodes to connect and share information from a distance. Cryptography is the second component. The technique of secure communication in a hostile environment is known as cryptography. It enables a node to communicate with other nodes. Fig. (**2**) clearly explains the design flow of the blockchain, which includes the step flow starting from the data transmission to key verification, including the transaction fee, transfer and distribution of the block [5].

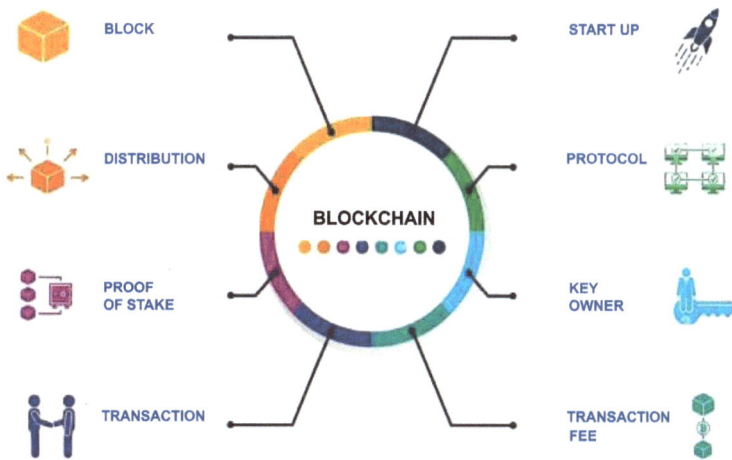

Fig. (2). Blockchain Vector Design.

A consensus algorithm is the third component. It means that the participating nodes must come to an agreement on how to add a block to the existing Blockchain. Proof of Work (PoW), Proof of Stake (PoS), Proof of Authority (PoA), Proof of Elapsed Time (PoET), and more consensus rules exist. For someone to be permitted to add a block to the current Blockchain, according to these approaches, all participating nodes must verify something [6].

Last and fourth are punishment and reward. This aspect is drawn from game theory, and it ensures that following the rules is always in the best interests of all nodes [7].

LITERATURE REVIEW

Blockchain is used in a single application sector, such as healthcare, as well as in other fields, where blockchain and IoT are used at the same time. This is done with a focus on smart cities and medication supply chains as a major part, which is the two most well-known blockchain applications in IoT and healthcare, respectively.

The tracking of medicinal products is made easier by marketers thanks to blockchain technology. The health and pharmaceutical sectors will be able to eradicate counterfeit drugs using Blockchain technology, which will also enable full product tracing. It assists in identifying the origin of the fabrication. When a medical history is generated, it can also be saved by Blockchain and is permanently preserved, protecting the confidentiality of patient records. This decentralised network connects all of the hospital's common hardware. The time and money saved by these tools can be used by researchers to measure the effectiveness of various treatments, medications, and cures. (17,18).

Several large corporations and agencies, such as American Express and Microsoft, are experimenting with blockchain technology. There are most significant events that have resulted in advancements in either blockchain architecture or industrial applications. The first Bitcoin block was created in 2009. Satoshi vanished in December of 2010 – Last public post. Estonian Blockchain Technology - e-Estonia Ethereum and Hyperledger both go operational in 2015. 2018 — the need for blockchain technology is growing, with 14 open positions for every blockchain developer. 2019 - Walmart mandates that produce suppliers use blockchain technology.

BLOCKCHAIN TECHNOLOGY IN MEDICAL SECTOR

Blockchain has an extended application and function in the healthcare sector. This technology helps healthcare researchers to transfer the patient medical record safely and securely, managing the drug supply chain, various electronic data in healthcare, digital tracking, exchange of information, *etc.* These are some of the remarkable features that make blockchain technology to adopt, practice and progress in the healthcare sector. Fig. (**3**) [66] details the involvement of blockchain in the smart healthcare system.

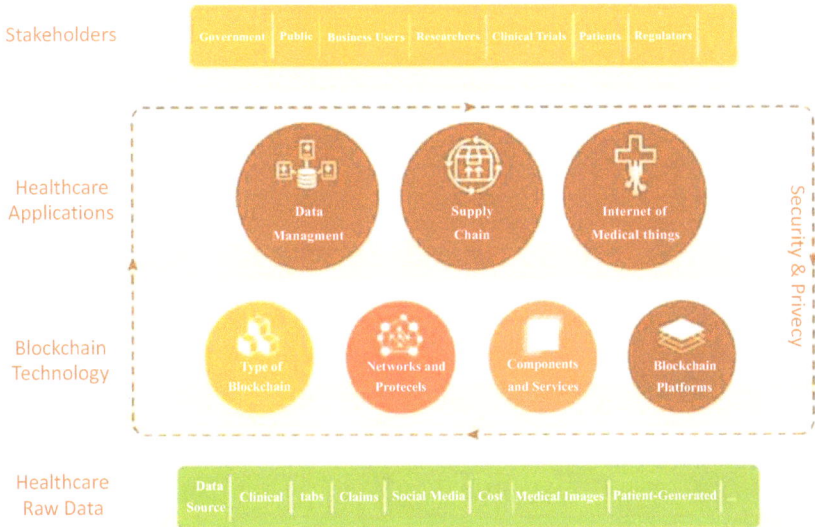

Fig. (3). Workflow of Blockchain in Smart Healthcare Sector.

Significant Applications Blockchain for Healthcare

Integration of IoT and Blockchain has taken healthcare to another level. The prevalence of chronic diseases among the ageing population is on the rise, and this is causing deep concern due to a lack of suitable facilities and sky-high expenditures. People who live in isolated places far from medical facilities face an even direr situation, as delays in diagnosis and treatment can lead to death. These problems can be solved to a large extent if they are diagnosed and treated in a timely manner. As wireless communications and wearable sensor technology advance, real-time healthcare monitoring systems are increasingly feasible. For cardiac patients at far-off locations, a real-time heart monitoring device has been proposed. In the event of an emergency, the devised system would alert the physician, albeit inadequate 3G network signals in some remote locations could cause alarm delays, as shown in Fig. (**4**). Future research should consider it, even if the delayed alarming time is still within the golden period. As wireless technology develops, it may be possible to use the newest wireless technology to get beyond these restrictions, which would increase the usefulness and usability of the suggested remote monitoring system. Furthermore, false alerts may be triggered as a result of sensor and smartphone battery difficulties. Further work can be expanded to address the battery and false alarm issues.

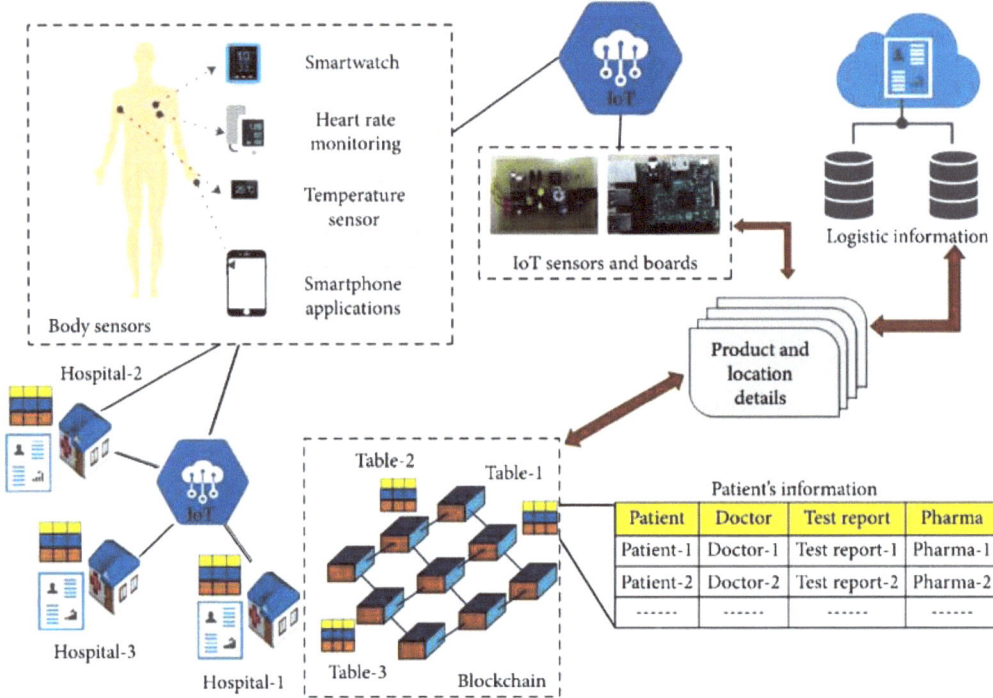

Fig. (4). Smart Contracts of Blockchain in Healthcare.

Information Storage of a Patient

Both before and during the various clinical trial phases, a considerable amount of patient information and health data is obtained. Numerous people's blood tests, quality assessments, projections, and health surveys are accessible. It might produce outcomes that demonstrate the existence of a document or record. The accuracy of the recorded data will be examined and questioned by healthcare specialists. By comparing it to the actual data stored on the Blockchain system, they will afterwards verify this. An appropriate basis for data sharing cryptography is one of the cryptographic methods on which blockchain is built. The healthcare professional also records the basic patient information like patient's name, date of birth and other necessary data like diagnosis, therapies, and ambulatory history under patient details in the EHR format. This data is stored in databases that are currently in use or on the cloud [8 - 11]. Fig. (**5**) shows the individual patient monitoring using blockchain.

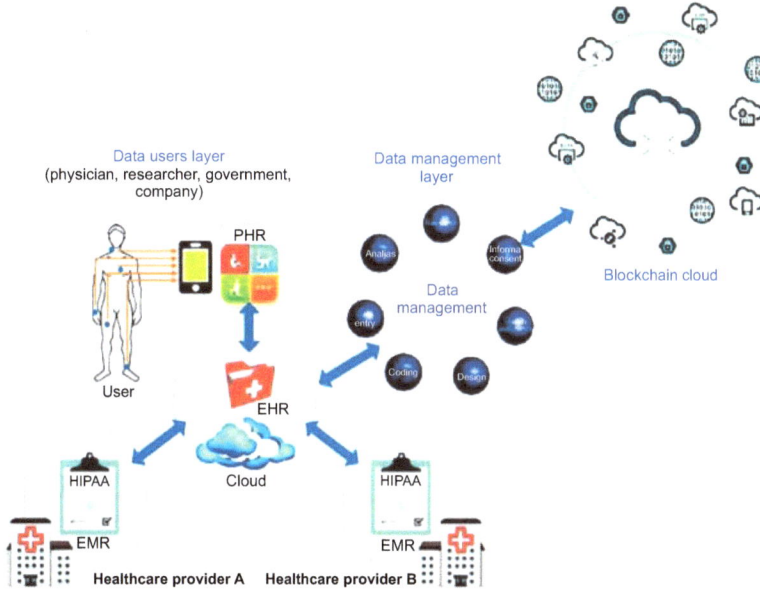

Fig. (5). Individual Patient Monitoring using Blockchain.

Analyse the Effects of a Particular Procedure

With verified access to patient data, researchers can efficiently evaluate any operation on a substantial segment of the patient population. This capitulates important outcomes that improve the management of these patients. Pharmaceutical companies will use the Blockchain architecture (as shown in Fig. (**6**)) to collect data in real-time and supply a wide range of precisely tailored prescription drugs or services to patients. Because it has all of the data on top of it, blockchain makes the job of pharmacists easier. From these results, they will effectively guide patients on how to take the prescription. It will provide professionals with real-time updates on the patient's condition and notify them of any emergencies *via* wearable data [12 - 15].

Validation

In a Blockchain, transactions are vetted by algorithms until they are linked to the chain. The authenticity is sealed as long as the data is encrypted, signed digitally and saved. Fig. (**7**) [19] explains the workflow of the blockchain from transaction request to completion of transaction which includes validation. Healthcare firms, technical innovators, and the healthcare sector are all looking for ways to learn more about what they can do now and, in the future, to make healthcare safer and more affordable. Blockchain technology has the potential to transform the health ecosystem when healthcare management is able to successfully validate the results [16 - 20].

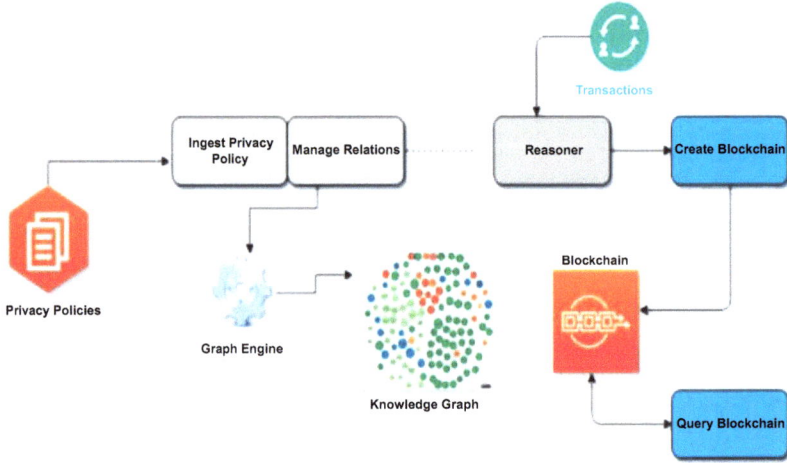

Fig. (6). Architecture of Blockchain in Pharmaceutical.

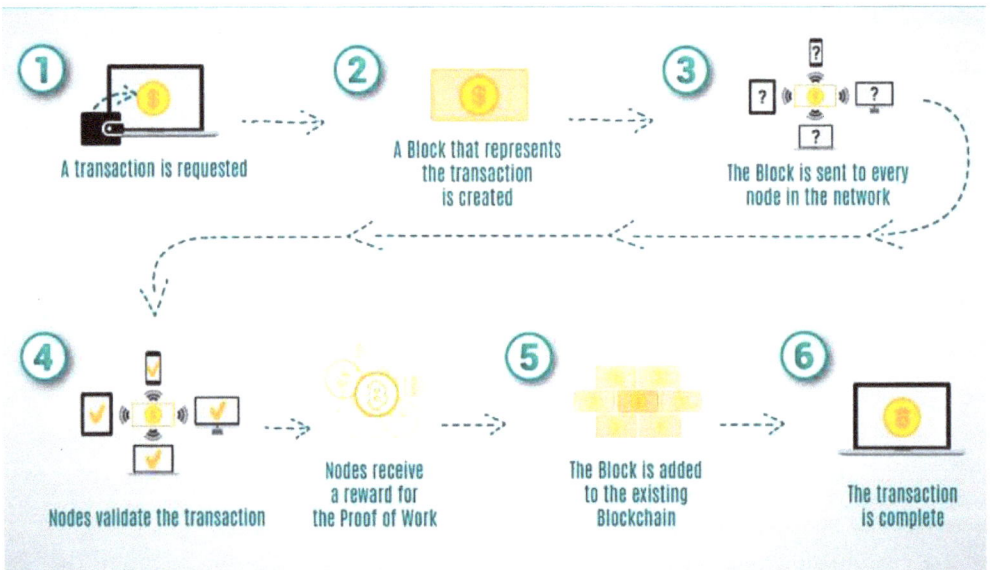

Fig. (7). Working of Blockchain.

Safety and Transparency

This permits clinicians to spend more time on patient care while maintaining high standards of security and openness. Additionally, it would make it possible to finance clinical research and therapy for any rare condition. Smooth data exchange across medical solution providers in a healthcare system can aid in accurate diagnosis, effective treatments, and cost-effective ecosystems. Blockchain enables communication and information exchange amongst many health ecosystem organisations on a single distributed leader for increased safety and transparency (as in Fig. (**8**)). Users don't need to hunt for extra solutions to guarantee integrity and confidentiality because they may interchange and monitor their data as well as other system functions [21 - 24].

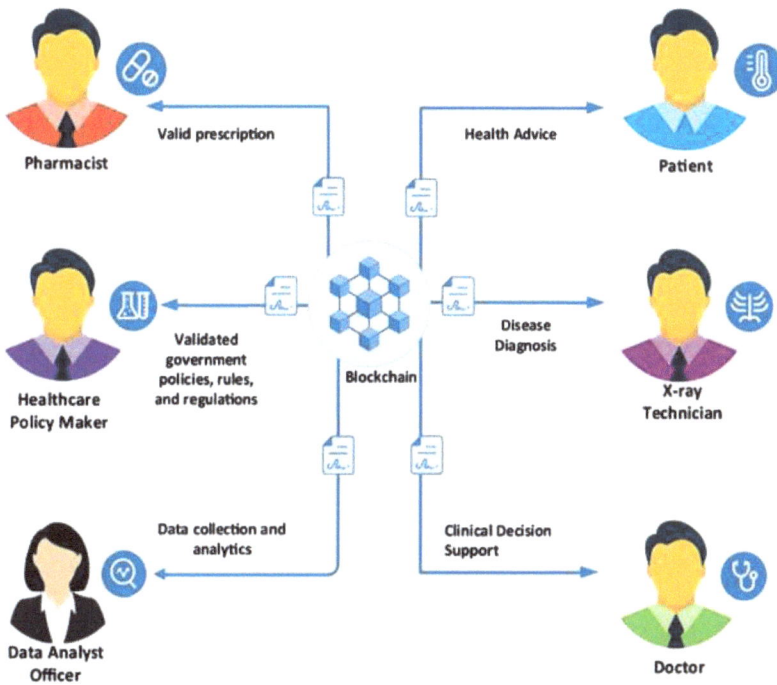

Fig. (8). Transparency of Blockchain in Healthcare System.

Health Record Keeping

Blockchain has the ability to revolutionise the process of healthcare record-keeping. Its features comprise the ability to share healthcare data, maintain electronic health records, manage insurance, and complete administrative chores. Patients can use an app to send their health data to a Blockchain network. Sensor and intelligent device collaboration is facilitated by digital Blockchain contracts. In the majority of cases, electronic health records are disseminated among numerous health-care organisations. All information will be centralised on the blockchain, and patients will have historical access, as shown in Fig. (**9**). The ability to connect all information in one place will allow us to gain a clear perception of a patient's status. Consequently, the Blockchain idea is to ensure that the data is real and legitimate, along with safeguarding the privacy of consumers [25 - 29].

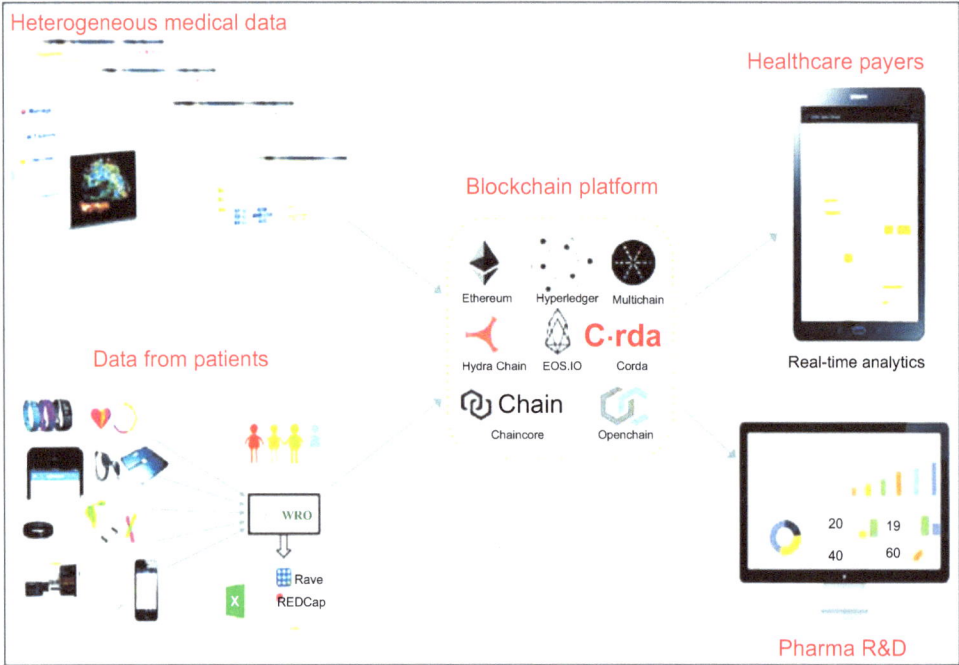

Fig. (9). Health Record Monitoring in Healthcare.

Clinical Trial

Clinical trials use blockchain technology to solve problems like data disintegration and misleading results that don't achieve the intended aims and objectives. Clinical trials will be more trustworthy thanks to blockchain. The business analysis tool looks into changing market dynamics so that the healthcare industry can see what's out there. Fig. (**10**) shows that the management of medications on the Blockchain is merely another way to use Blockchain credibility to establish and monitor the chain from the maker to the customer [30 - 33].

Display Information

To guarantee high quality and that the drug is given by the company that created the licensed medicine, the Blockchain system will reveal information about the medication's origins. Blockchain offers more robust protection for sensitive data than ever before, if handled properly. In order to display information, many industries, like banking, retail, and immobilisation, have started to use the Blockchain app trend. These businesses have reaped various advantages. Similarly, it is believed that healthcare is intricate and sophisticated. This proclamation will result in significant arguments. Due to its complexity and sophistication, the market has undergone significant changes in a number of industries, including cloud computing and the use of pharmaceutical items, medications, vaccines, and clinical trials [34 - 37].

Clinical Trials and Blockchain

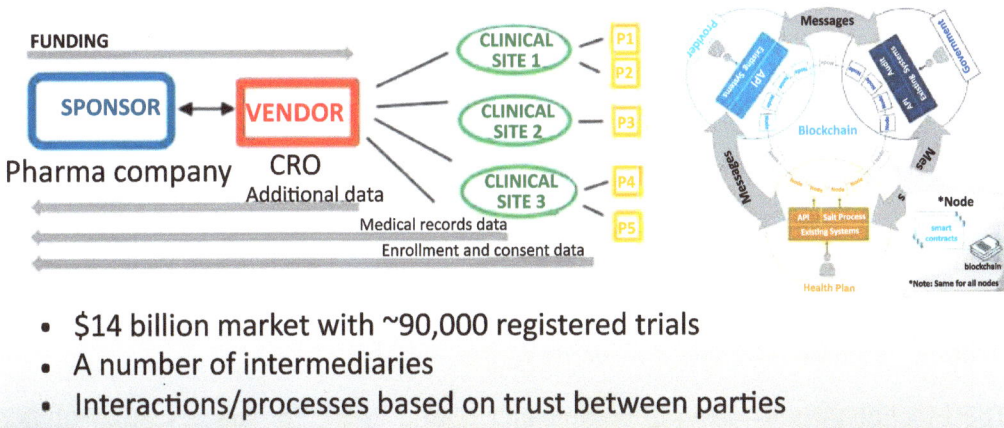

- $14 billion market with ~90,000 registered trials
- A number of intermediaries
- Interactions/processes based on trust between parties

Fig. (10). Clinical Trial and Blockchain.

Identification of False Content

Fig. (**11**) [42] shows the flow of false control identification. The blockchain will increase transparency and make it possible to spot misleading content. Clinical research should continue to be straightforward to validate for participants and consumers. An intelligent agreement is the best way to get approval and guarantee that protocol paperwork and findings are made public. Technology now makes it possible for the general public to monitor a clinical investigation carefully for the first time. This system was developed because it is user-friendly and gives patients secure, real-time access to their medical and insurance information [38 - 42].

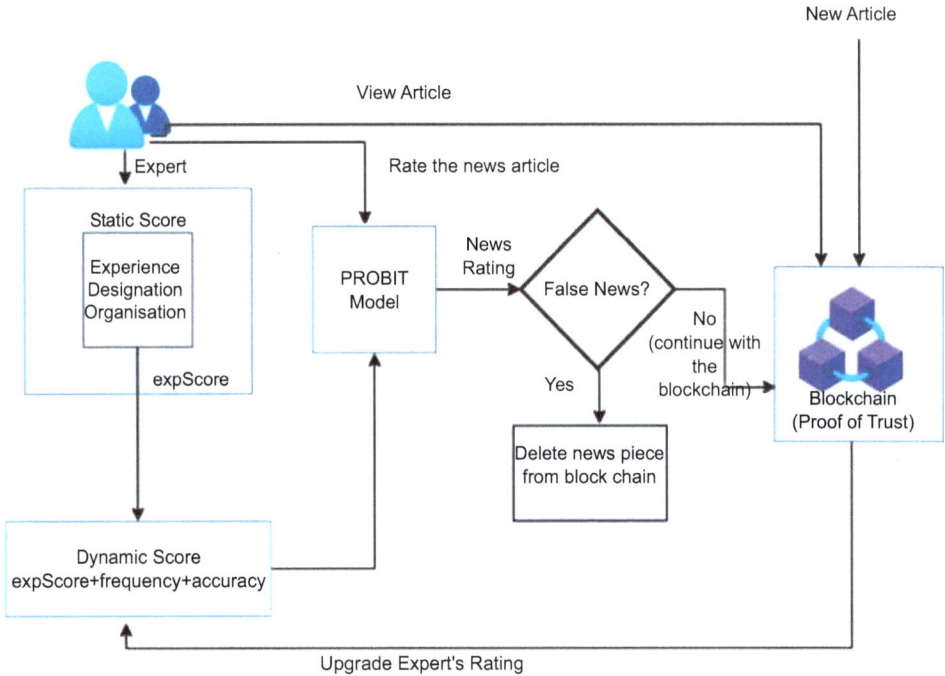

Fig. (11). Frameworks for Identification of False Control.

Reduces Needless Overhead Expenses

The blockchain will provide greater clarity and allow for the detection of fake material. Validation of clinical research for participants and consumers should remain simple. An intelligent agreement is ideal for securing approval and ensuring that protocol documentation and conclusions are exposed to public scrutiny. For the first time, technology has allowed the general public to closely follow what happens in a clinical experiment. This system was developed as it is user-friendly and gives patients secure, real-time access to their medical and insurance information [39 - 42].

Patient Monitoring

Medical professionals can rely on a Blockchain's trust to ensure they have access to medical equipment when they need it. It may also take more time for doctors to keep an eye on patients and respond to health-related occurrences from afar.

Improvements can be made to patient room temperatures, bed usage, and supply availability using blockchain technology in healthcare. A blockchain-based healthcare network assists hospitals and other healthcare organisations in creating a reliable digital identity, and improves supply chain responsiveness and traceability by combining blockchain and internet of things technology, increasing the transparency of healthcare logistics for efficient patient monitoring, which is detailly shown in Fig. (**12**) [43 - 47].

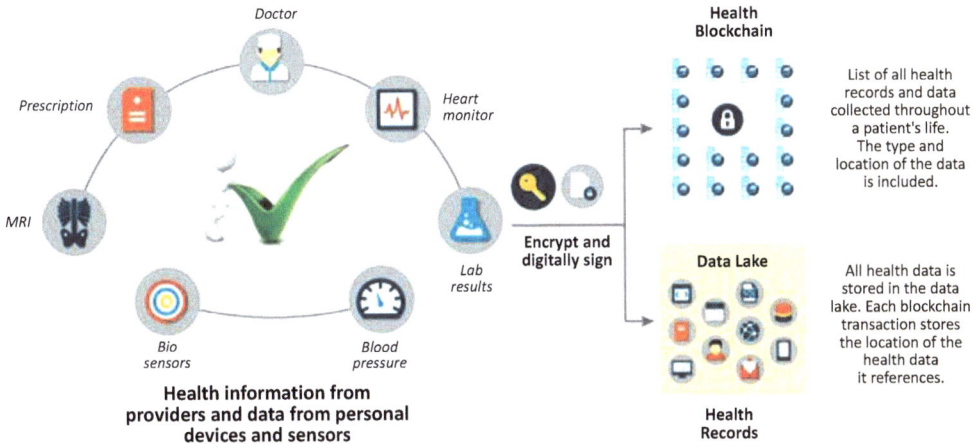

Fig. (12). Smart Healthcare system using Blockchain and IoT Technology.

Create Research Initiatives

Blockchains may offer a trustworthy data source. Blockchain has the power to alter how membership claims and disputes are now handled manually. Blockchains have the capacity to launch new and innovative research initiatives by exchanging patient data generally. A more in-depth exchange of patient data will also generate new and innovative research. As a result, participants and academics have worked together in a spectacular way. This technology could also help with patient referral management. Once a patient interacts with a doctor and establishes a therapy routine, the therapy package will be added to the Blockchain as part of the patient's medical record [48 - 51].

Maintain Financial Statements

The maintenance of correct records of financial statements during the bookkeeping procedure is important. Clinical trials are well-suited to running and evaluating efficiently. In this sector, blockchain businesses have found methods to expedite the accounting and reporting process. This app can be used by anyone to prepare for a doctor's appointment and fill out papers ahead of time. They will save time because they will not have to stand in line. However, the risks and benefits of Blockchain may be learned from its actual implementations and the types of problems it solves in the healthcare sector [52 - 55].

Improves Safety

By addressing concerns with medication validity and drug traceability and enabling secure interoperability, blockchain enhances patient safety overall. It is the only way to upgrade the existing supply chain management system and stop manufacturers of fake medications from more securely distributing their goods to consumers. Regardless of the medical institutions and organisations involved, all data would be stored in a central location using blockchains. Doctors will be able to see extensive medical records more easily thanks to Blockchain technology's interoperability, which will aid in diagnosis and the development of a better and more precise operation [56 - 59].

Reduce Data Transformation Time and Cost

Blockchain networks speed up and lower the cost of changing data. Blockchain networks have the ability to quickly and effectively address the issue of medical credential verification. The security and anonymity of patients are guaranteed by blockchain networks. This will lead to significant new insights and discoveries that could completely alter how healthcare is provided globally. Networks of monetized data sharing that are both useful and private will be created as a result of using blockchain. A distributed network computer system called blockchain makes it possible to store transaction history and supporting documentation with time stamps. In this network, each node verifies and records the information it gets [60 - 63].

Drug Traceability

The pharmaceutical cold chain and the healthcare supply chainare both part of the medical supply chain, and are linked to pharmaceutical companies, hospitals, health centres, and pharmacies. A temperature-controlled supply chain is known as a cold chain. Pharmaceuticals are typically transported in chilled containers onboard planes, which are stacked in pallets. Onboard aircraft, flowers and other agricultural items in cardboard boxes are stacked in layers in well-ventilated pallets.

One major application of blockchain is drug supply and management. The EthereumBlockchain is being used in the drug supply chain to store data and make it publicly accessible while maintaining immutability. They proposed using thermal sensitive devices to communicate temperature data during the transport of therapeutic ingredients in their solution. A smart contract including particular temperature requirements is configured for each new shipment in order to assure temperature data compliance during the shipping. Blockchain-based system for drug traceability and regulation was conducted in another study. The technology is known as Drug ledger, and it is a permissioned Blockchain that is based on an enhanced unspent transaction outputs process for the package, repackage, and unpackage adapted to the pharmaceutical supply chain. Using a permissioned Blockchain, a framework for tracking counterfeit pharmaceuticals was designed. The goal of this framework is to secure medications and verify manufacturers. They recommended creating an encrypted QR (Quick Response) for manufacturers to store details and add transactions to the Blockchain; only authorised entities will be able to access this QR (14).

Prevention of fraudulent: Blockchain can be used to keep track of how far fraud prevention has progressed. It can also handle and improve the following aspects of the pharmaceutical. Fig. (**13**) explains the drug supply chain.

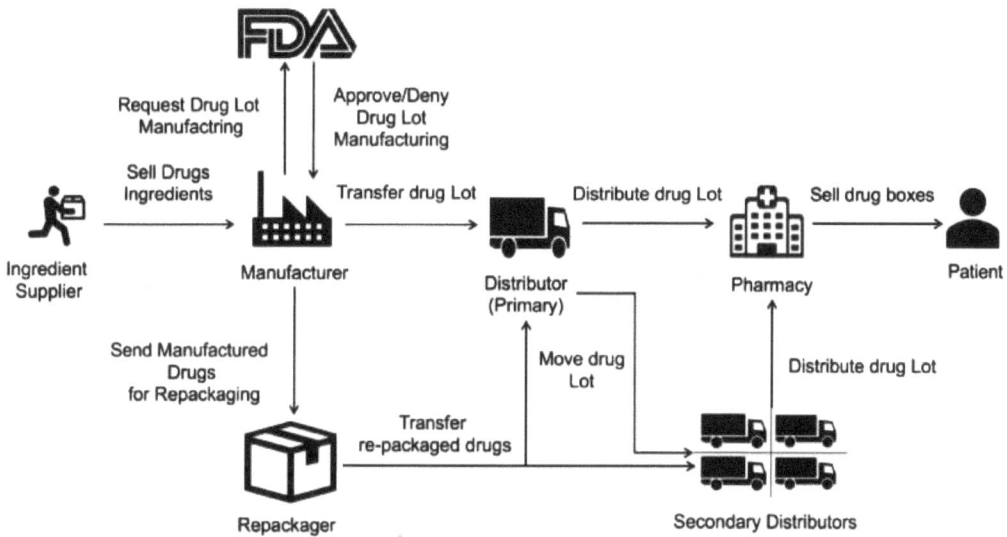

Fig. (13). Drug Supply Chain.

• First is Possession: Once a product is received, each distribution participant is liable for it.

• Second is Unification: A unique serial number must be assigned to each package of pharmaceuticals that can be sold independently.

• Third is Information coordination: Where each component is in charge of coordinating its data with a central regulating body.

CHALLENGES IN HEALTHCARE BLOCKCHAIN ADAPTATION

It is difficult to comprehend why the industry hasn't already figured out how to share patient data in a secure, distributed manner, provided the many benefits it offers. But, like with many other things in the business world, there are some specific reasons why it is difficult to share healthcare data. Before blockchain is adopted by the industry, it is believed the following challenges must be resolved: As shown in Table **1** [64-69].

Data Collection and Storage

Wearables and other healthcare monitoring technology produce a huge amount of information about a person's health. For our healthcare system to make data-driven decisions, proper data management and secure data retrieval are essential. Data is also produced by our current healthcare system's routine business operations and service delivery. Throughout their lives, patients engage with a variety of healthcare professionals, leaving a trail of data in each one's system. Providers frequently maintain primary data stewardship, which results in a fragmented data trail and declining patient access. A huge volume, variability, and speed define healthcare data. They demand real-time data analysis since they are non-uniform, include several variables, and are complex. The majority of this data is unavailable, not system-standard, and challenging to understand, use, and distribute.

Data Sharing and Interoperability

Two sorts of issues arise from ineffective interoperability: information blocking, where healthcare providers place an excessive restriction on the interchange of patient data or electronic health information, and the difficulty of accurately identifying patients. A major hindrance to effective healthcare is the absence of globally accepted patient identities and information blocking policies. Interoperability is important as well, especially during an epidemic like the corona pandemic. The timing of the epidemic highlights the critical need for a more comprehensive data-sharing infrastructure that might aid in streamlining patient-provider interactions and facilitating information flow to manage public health hazards. If patients visit a doctor who is not their primary care physician, they should have simple access to their medical records. Additionally, bettering the flow of health data would make it possible for doctors to conduct telemedicine consultations and remote monitoring. This gives patients the ability to inform their doctors of their medical background. Fast and clear information, particularly information on how patients may estimate their risk, present symptoms, and respond to therapy, is essential as the number of cases of the coronavirus rises.

The absence of interoperability in the current system is further highlighted by public health emergencies.

The Need for a Socioeconomic Database

The significance of the link between socioeconomic circumstances and individual health has been acknowledged by researchers and clinicians alike. They contend that solely individual traits might not adequately account for all factors affecting health status. The focus of socioeconomic statistics is on community, social, and environmental elements. It is crucial to the creation of health management plans that cater to the various demands of a particular population. Socioeconomic data, a rich source of information, can be used by public health professionals to evaluate the kind and regularity of illegal drug use, acts of interpersonal violence, and economic imbalances at all levels of administration [36]. Furthermore, it will be crucial to have thorough and accurate socioeconomic data to help close gaps across various socioeconomic and racial groups. If providers are to have a chance to implement successful population health management strategies, they must have access to this data [37]. Claims data, which include dates of specific service, diagnosis codes, and cost, is another important socially anchored data set for health informatics specialists. These statistics give medical personnel a clearer idea of the people they are treating and the main health problems they are dealing with. The ability to analyse how patients are managing chronic health conditions and diseases is based on the information on prescription drugs to medical professionals and decision-makers. The healthcare sector needs a strong public health system that can gather, store, score, and protect population health data.

Table 1. Various aspects and challenges in implementing Blockchain.

Aspects	Challenges
Technical	• Lack of storage capacity for significant amounts of data. • A network of linked computers (called nodes) exists to provide computational power for building blocks. • The development of blockchain software is still in its early stages. • Lack of uniformity and scalability. • Risk of information deterioration. • Throughput capacity problems and storage limitations. • Compatibility issues with existing business systems and systems of record. • Choosing a blockchain protocol, the framework that governs the design of the blockchain and the creation of applications, is necessary.

(Table 1) cont.....

Aspects	Challenges
Organizational	• Concerns over the adoption of blockchain owing to cultural and trust difficulties. • Companies are urged to use technology and connect to a common network. • Issues with interoperability. • It is unknown how much it will cost to operate a blockchain. • It can be challenging to calculate the Return on Investment (ROI).
Drivers for Adoption	• Technology adoption in society is hesitant. • There aren't enough blockchain-based projects that are profitable to go around. • Uncertainty around using the technology and connecting to a network that is shared. • Information Gap.
Government Regulations/Privacy	• The distributed storage feature of the blockchain has implications. • There is a lack of legislation that considers the special features of data exchange using blockchain. • Who owns the records? • How is consent given?

CONCLUSION AND FUTURE WORK

According to the literature analysis, the investigation into the potential applications of blockchain technology in healthcare is still in its early phases, but the number of solutions that have been suggested is rapidly increasing. With its unique approach to decentralised administration, increased security, and immutable audit trail, blockchain technology was described in this article as a paradigm shift. In addition, the report looked into the many case studies and applications of blockchain in healthcare. The findings suggest that blockchain can help healthcare organisations to advance in their healthcare quality through improved access control, interoperability, provenance, and data integrity. According to the report, the overall cost of these tasks can be decreased thanks to the distributed nature of blockchain, its clear information structure, and the immutable records preserved and retained by all participating users. In addition to improving patient participation, ensuring patient information is accessible, enabling direct and secure contact between patients and clinicians, and enhancing patient safety, the technology may be used to securely coordinate and combine information from various providers. Before using blockchain to restructure the healthcare system, legal and regulatory challenges as well as blockchain technical issues must be solved. Although blockchain in healthcare is still in its infancy, it has a lot of promise for the industry. While the technology has not yet been widely accepted in the healthcare industry, its scope of use will only expand in the future. There is a scarcity of studies on the subject in terms of future study; further research in real-world applications is needed.

REFERENCES

[1]   T. Ahram, A. Sargolzaei, S. Sargolzaei, J. Daniels, and B. Amaba, "Blockchain technology innovations. 2017 IEEE Technol", *Eng. Manag. Soc. Conf. TEMSCON,* vol. 2017, pp. 137-141, 2017.

[2]   A. Sharma, S. Kaur, and M. Singh, "A comprehensive review on blockchain and Internet of Things in healthcare", *Trans. Emerg. Telecommun. Technol.,* vol. 32, no. 10, pp. 1-53, 2021.
[http://dx.doi.org/10.1002/ett.4333]

[3]   P. Ratta, A. Kaur, S. Sharma, M. Shabaz, and G. Dhiman, "Application of blockchain and internet of things in healthcare and medical sector: Applications, challenges, and future perspectives", *J. Food Qual.,* vol. 2021, pp. 1-20, 2021.
[http://dx.doi.org/10.1155/2021/7608296]

[4]   S. Jeong, J.H. Shen, and B. Ahn, "A study on smart healthcare monitoring using IoT based on blockchain", *Wirel. Commun. Mob. Comput.,* vol. 2021, pp. 1-9, 2021.
[http://dx.doi.org/10.1155/2021/9932091]

[5]   A. Banotra, J. S. Sharma, S. Gupta, S. K. Gupta, and M. Rashid, "Use of blockchain and internet of things for securing data in healthcare systems", In: *Multimedia Security: Algorithm Development, Analysis and Applications* Springer, 2021.
[http://dx.doi.org/10.1007/978-981-15-8711-5_13]

[6]   I. Lee, "Big data: Dimensions, evolution, impacts, and challenges", *Bus. Horiz.,* vol. 60, no. 3, pp. 293-303, 2017.
[http://dx.doi.org/10.1016/j.bushor.2017.01.004]

[7]   Y. Ma, "An efficient index for massive IoT data in cloud environment", *ACM Int. Conf. Proceeding Ser,* pp. 2129-2133, 2012.
[http://dx.doi.org/10.1145/2396761.2398587]

[8]   M. Ejaz, T. Kumar, I. Kovacevic, M. Ylianttila, and E. Harjula, "Health-BlockEdge: blockchain-edge framework for reliable low-latency digital healthcare applications", *Sensors,* vol. 21, no. 7, p. 2502, 2021.
[http://dx.doi.org/10.3390/s21072502] [PMID: 33916700]

[9]   E.J. De Aguiar, B.S. Faiçal, B. Krishnamachari, and J. Ueyama, "A survey of blockchain- based strategies for healthcare", *ACM Comput. Surv.,* vol. 53, no. 2, pp. 1-27, 2021.
[http://dx.doi.org/10.1145/3376915]

[10]   S. Aggarwal, N. Kumar, M. Alhussein, and G. Muhammad, "Blockchain-based UAV path planning for healthcare 4.0: current challenges and the way ahead", *IEEE Netw.,* vol. 35, no. 1, pp. 20-29, 2021.
[http://dx.doi.org/10.1109/MNET.011.2000069]

[11]   T.K. Mackey, T.T. Kuo, B. Gummadi, K.A. Clauson, G. Church, D. Grishin, K. Obbad, R. Barkovich, and M. Palombini, "'Fit-for-purpose?' – challenges and opportunities for applications of blockchain technology in the future of healthcare", *BMC Med.,* vol. 17, no. 1, p. 68, 2019.
[http://dx.doi.org/10.1186/s12916-019-1296-7] [PMID: 30914045]

[12]   A. Khatoon, "A blockchain-based innovative contract system for healthcare management", *Electronics,* vol. 9, no. 1, p. 94, 2020.
[http://dx.doi.org/10.3390/electronics9010094]

[13]   I. Abu-Elezz, A. Hassan, A. Nazeemudeen, M. Household, and A. Abd-Alrazaq, "The benefits and threats of blockchain technology in healthcare: A scoping review", *Int. J. Med. Inf.,* vol. 142, p. 104246, 2020.

[14]   R. Vaishya, M. Javaid, I.H. Khan, A. Vaish, and K.P. Iyengar, "Significant role of modern technologies for COVID-19 pandemic", *J. Ind. Integr. Management.,* pp. 1-3, 2021.

[15]   H.M. Hussien, S.M. Yasin, N.I. Udzir, M.I. Ninggal, and S. Salman, "Blockchaintechnology in the healthcare industry: trends and opportunities", *J. Ind. Inf. Integr.,* vol. 22, p. 100217, 2021.

[16]   R. Bhuvana, L.M. Madhushree, and P.S. Aithal, "Blockchain as a disruptive technology in healthcare and financial services-A review-based analysis on current implementations", *Int. J. Appl. Eng. Manag. Lett.,* vol. 4, no. 1, pp. 142-155, 2020.

[17]   M.M. Onik, S. Aich, J. Yang, C.S. Kim, and H.C. Kim, Blockchain in healthcare: challenges and solutions.*Big Data Analytics for Intelligent Healthcare Management.* Academic Press, 2019, pp. 197-226.

[18]   C.C. Agbo, Q.H. Mahmoud, and J.M. Eklund, "Blockchain technology in healthcare: Asystematic review", In: *Healthcare* Multidisciplinary Digital Publishing Institute, 2019, p. 56.
[http://dx.doi.org/10.3390/healthcare7020056]

[19]   S. Ferdous, F. Chowdhury, and O. Madini, "In search of self-sovereign identity leveraging blockchain technology", *IEEE Access,* vol. 7, pp. 103059-103079, 2019.

[20]   S. Tanwar, K. Parekh, and R. Evans, "Blockchain-based electronic healthcare record system for healthcare 4.0 applications", *Journal of Information Security and Applications,* vol. 50, p. 102407, 2020.
[http://dx.doi.org/10.1016/j.jisa.2019.102407]

[21]   S. Wang, J. Wang, X. Wang, T. Qiu, Y. Yuan, L. Ouyang, Y. Guo, and F.Y. Wang, "Blockchain-powered parallel healthcare systems based on the ACP approach", *IEEE Trans. Comput. Soc. Syst.,* vol. 5, no. 4, pp. 942-950, 2018.
[http://dx.doi.org/10.1109/TCSS.2018.2865526]

[22]   S. Jiang, J. Cao, H. Wu, Y. Yang, M. Ma, and J. He, "Blochie: A blockchain-basedplatform for healthcare information exchange", *2018 IEEE International Conference on Smart Computing (SMARTCOMP)* Taormina, Italy, 2018, pp. 49-56.

[23]   P. Zhang, M.A. Walker, J. White, D.C. Schmidt, and G. Lenz, "Metrics for assessing blockchain-based healthcare decentralized apps", *2017 IEEE 19th International Conference on e-Health Networking, Applications and Services (Healthcom)* Dalian, China, 2017, pp. 1-4.
[http://dx.doi.org/10.1109/HealthCom.2017.8210842]

[24]   J. Hathaliya, P. Sharma, S. Tanwar, and R. Gupta, "Blockchain-Based Remote Patient Monitoring in Healthcare 4.0", *2019 IEEE 9th International Conference on Advanced Computing (IACC)* Tiruchirappalli, India, 2019, pp. 87-91.

[25]   D. Berdik, S. Otoum, N. Schmidt, D. Porter, and Y. Jararweh, "A survey on Blockchainfor information systems management and security", *Inf. Process. Manage.,* vol. 58, no. 1, p. 102397, 2021.
[http://dx.doi.org/10.1016/j.ipm.2020.102397]

[26]   X. Du, B. Chen, M. Ma, and Y. Zhang, "Research on the application of blockchain in smart healthcare: constructing a hierarchical framework", *J. Healthc. Eng.,* vol. 2021, pp. 1-13, 2021.
[http://dx.doi.org/10.1155/2021/6698122] [PMID: 33505644]

[27]   K. Peterson, R. Deeduvanu, P. Kanjamala, and K. Boles, "A blockchain-based approach to health information exchange networks", *Proc. NIST Workshop Blockchain Healthcare,* vol. 1, no. 1, pp. 1-10, 2016.

[28]   A. Celesti, A. Ruggeri, M. Fazio, A. Galletta, M. Villari, and A. Romano, "Blockchain-based healthcare workflow for telemedical laboratory in federated hospital IoT clouds", *Sensors,* vol. 20, no. 9, p. 2590, 2020.
[http://dx.doi.org/10.3390/s20092590] [PMID: 32370129]

[29]   P. Zhang, and M.N. Boulos, Blockchain solutions for healthcare.*Precision Medicine for Investigators, Practitioners and Providers.* Academic Press, 2020, pp. 519-524.
[http://dx.doi.org/10.1016/B978-0-12-819178-1.00050-2]

[30]   E. Go€kalp, M.O. Go€kalp, S. Coban, P.E. Eren, Analysing opportunities and challenges of integrated blockchain technologies in healthcare.*InEurosymposium on Systems Analysis and Design.* Springer: Cham, 2018, pp. 174-183.

[31]   G. Leeming, J. Cunningham, and J. Ainsworth, "A ledger of me: Personalizing healthcare using blockchain technology", *Front. Med.,* vol. 6, p. 171, 2019.
[http://dx.doi.org/10.3389/fmed.2019.00171] [PMID: 31396516]

[32]   M. Javaid, and A. Haleem, "Industry 4.0 applications in medical field: A brief review", *Current Medicine Research and Practice,* vol. 9, no. 3, pp. 102-109, 2019.
[http://dx.doi.org/10.1016/j.cmrp.2019.04.001]

[33]   P. Bhattacharya, S. Tanwar, U. Bodkhe, S. Tyagi, and N. Kumar, "Bindaas: blockchain- based deep-learning as-a-service in healthcare 4.0 applications", *IEEE Trans. Netw. Sci. Eng.,* vol. 8, no. 2, pp. 1242-1255, 2021.
[http://dx.doi.org/10.1109/TNSE.2019.2961932]

[34]   A.A. Omar, M.Z.A. Bhuiyan, A. Basu, S. Kiyomoto, and M.S. Rahman, "Privacy-friendly platform for healthcare data in cloud based on blockchain environment", *Future Gener. Comput. Syst.,* vol. 95, pp. 511-521, 2019.
[http://dx.doi.org/10.1016/j.future.2018.12.044]

[35]   M. Zarour, M.T.J. Ansari, M. Alenezi, A.K. Sarkar, M. Faizan, A. Agrawal, R. Kumar, and R.A. Khan, "Evaluating the impact of blockchain models for secure and trustworthy electronic healthcare records", *IEEE Access,* vol. 8, pp. 157959-157973, 2020.
[http://dx.doi.org/10.1109/ACCESS.2020.3019829]

[36]   R. Ribitzky, J.S. Clair, D.I. Houlding, C.T. McFarlane, B. Ahier, M. Gould, H.L. Flannery, E. Pupo, and K.A. Clauson, "Pragmatic, interdisciplinary perspectives on Blockchain and distributed ledger technology: paving the future for healthcare", *Blockchain Healthc Today,* vol. 1, p. 24, 2018.
[http://dx.doi.org/10.30953/bhty.v1.24]

[37]   K. Khujamatov, E. Reypnazarov, N. Akhmedov, and D. Khasanov, "Blockchain for 5G healthcare architecture", *2020 International Conference on Information Science and Communications Technologies (ICISCT) IEEE,* pp. 1-5, 2020.

[38]   C.C. Agbo, and Q.H. Mahmoud, "Comparison of blockchain frameworks for healthcare applications", *Internet Technol. Lett.,* vol. 2, no. 5, p. e122, 2019.
[http://dx.doi.org/10.1002/itl2.122]

[39]   Y. Sun, R. Zhang, X. Wang, K. Gao, and L. Liu, "A decentralising attribute-based signature for healthcare blockchain", *2018 27th International Conference on Computer Communication and Networks (ICCCN),* pp. 1-9, 2018.

[40]   K. Zheng, Y. Liu, C. Dai, Y. Duan, and X. Huang, "Model checking PBFT consensusmechanism in healthcare blockchain network", *2018 9th International Conference on Information Technology in Medicine and Education (ITME)* Hangzhou, China, 2018, pp. 877-881.

[41]   H.L. Pham, T.H. Tran, and Y. Nakashima, A secure remote healthcare system forhospital using blockchain smart contract.*In2018 IEEE Globecom Workshops (GC Wkshps).* IEEE, 2018, pp. 1-6.
[http://dx.doi.org/10.1109/GLOCOMW.2018.8644164]

[42]   E. Sengupta, R. Nagpal, and D. Mehrotra, "ProBlock: A novel approach for fake news detection", *Cluster Comput.,* vol. 24, 2021.

[43]   L. Ismail, H. Materwala, and S. Zeadally, "Lightweight blockchain for healthcare", *IEEE Access,* vol. 7, pp. 149935-149951, 2019.
[http://dx.doi.org/10.1109/ACCESS.2019.2947613]

[44]   C.C. Agbo, and Q.H. Mahmoud, "Blockchain in Healthcare", *Int. J. Healthc. Inf. Syst. Inform.,* vol. 15, no. 3, pp. 82-97, 2020.
[http://dx.doi.org/10.4018/IJHISI.2020070105]

[45] F. Curbera, D.M. Dias, V. Simonyan, W.A. Yoon, and A. Casella, "Blockchain: An enabler for healthcare and life sciences transformation", *IBM J. Res. Develop.,* vol. 63, no. 2/3, pp. 8:1-8:9, 2019. [http://dx.doi.org/10.1147/JRD.2019.2913622]

[46] G. Srivastava, J. Crichigno, and S. Dhar, "A light and secure healthcare blockchain for IoT medical devices", *2019 IEEE Canadian Conference of Electrical and Computer Engineering (CCECE) IEEE,* pp. 1-5, 2019. [http://dx.doi.org/10.1109/CCECE.2019.8861593]

[47] P.P. Ray, D. Dash, K. Salah, and N. Kumar, "Blockchain for IoT-based healthcare: background, consensus, platforms, and use cases", *IEEE Syst. J.,* vol. 15, no. 1, pp. 85-94, 2021. [http://dx.doi.org/10.1109/JSYST.2020.2963840]

[48] P. Mamoshina, L. Ojomoko, Y. Yanovich, A. Ostrovski, A. Botezatu, P. Prikhodko, E. Izumchenko, A. Aliper, K. Romantsov, A. Zhebrak, I.O. Ogu, and A. Zhavoronkov, "Converging blockchain and next-generation artificial intelligence technologies to decentralize and accelerate biomedical research and healthcare", *Oncotarget,* vol. 9, no. 5, pp. 5665-5690, 2018. [http://dx.doi.org/10.18632/oncotarget.22345] [PMID: 29464026]

[49] D.J. Munoz, D.A. Constantinescu, R. Asenjo, and L. Fuentes, "Clinicappchain: A low-cost blockchain hyperledger solution for healthcare", *International Congress on Blockchain and Applications Springer Cham,* pp. 36-44, 2019.

[50] L. Soltanisehat, R. Alizadeh, H. Hao, and K.K. Choo, "Technical, temporal, and spatialresearch challenges and opportunities in blockchain-based healthcare: a systematic literature review", *IEEE Trans. Eng. Manage.,* vol. 70, pp. 1-16, 2020.

[51] M.A. Cyran, "Blockchain as a foundation for sharing healthcare data", *Blockchain in Healthcare Today,* vol. 1, pp. 1-6, 2018. [http://dx.doi.org/10.30953/bhty.v1.13]

[52] H.S. Chen, J.T. Jarrell, K.A. Carpenter, D.S. Cohen, and X. Huang, "Blockchain inhealthcare: a patient-centred model", *Biomed. J. Sci. Tech. Res.,* vol. 20, no. 3, pp. 15017-15022, 2019. [PMID: 31565696]

[53] A.A. Mazlan, S. Mohd Daud, S. Mohd Sam, H. Abas, S.Z. Abdul Rasid, and M.F. Yusof, "Scalability challenges in healthcare blockchain system—a systematic review", *IEEE Access,* vol. 8, pp. 23663-23673, 2020. [http://dx.doi.org/10.1109/ACCESS.2020.2969230]

[54] R. Vaishya, A. Haleem, A. Vaish, and M. Javaid, "Emerging technologies to combat the COVID-19 pandemic", *J. Clin. Exp. Hepatol.,* vol. 10, no. 4, pp. 409-411, 2020. [http://dx.doi.org/10.1016/j.jceh.2020.04.019] [PMID: 32377057]

[55] T. Ali Syed, A. Alzahrani, S. Jan, M.S. Siddiqui, A. Nadeem, and T. Alghamdi, "A comparative analysis of blockchain architecture and its applications: problems and recommendations", *IEEE Access,* vol. 7, pp. 176838-176869, 2019. [http://dx.doi.org/10.1109/ACCESS.2019.2957660]

[56] A. Al Omar, M.S. Rahman, A. Basu, and S. Kiyomoto, "Medibchain: a Blockchain-based privacy-preserving platform for healthcare data", *International Conference on Security, Privacy and Anonymity in Computation, Communication and Storage Springer Cham,* pp. 534-543, 2017. [http://dx.doi.org/10.1007/978-3-319-72395-2_49]

[57] R.W. Ahmad, K. Salah, R. Jayaraman, I. Yaqoob, S. Ellahham, and M. Omar, "The role of blockchain technology in telehealth and telemedicine", *Int. J. Med. Inf.,* vol. 148, p. 104399, 2021.

[58] V. Ramani, T. Kumar, A. Bracken, M. Liyanage, and M. Ylianttila, "Secure and efficient data accessibility in Blockchain-based healthcare systems", *2018 IEEE Global Communications Conference (GLOBECOM) IEEE,* pp. 206-212, 2018. [http://dx.doi.org/10.1109/GLOCOM.2018.8647221]

[59]   D.C. Nguyen, P.N. Pathirana, M. Ding, and A. Seneviratne, "BEdgeHealth: adecentralized architecture for edge-based IoMT networks using blockchain", *IEEE Internet Things J.,* vol. 8, no. 14, pp. 11743-11757, 2021.
[http://dx.doi.org/10.1109/JIOT.2021.3058953]

[60]   M.J. Gul, B. Subramanian, A. Paul, and J. Kim, "Blockchain for public health care in smart society", *Microprocess. Microsyst.,* vol. 80, p. 103524, 2021.
[http://dx.doi.org/10.1016/j.micpro.2020.103524]

[61]   A. Islam, and S. Young Shin, "A blockchain-based secure healthcare scheme with the assistance of unmanned aerial vehicle in Internet of Things", *Comput. Electr. Eng.,* vol. 84, p. 106627, 2020.
[http://dx.doi.org/10.1016/j.compeleceng.2020.106627]

[62]   D. Dhagarra, M. Goswami, P.R. Sarma, and A. Choudhury, "Big Data and blockchain supported conceptual model for enhanced healthcare coverage", *Bus. Process. Manag. J.,* 2019.

[63]   N. Islam, Y. Faheem, I.U. Din, M. Talha, M. Guizani, and M. Khalil, "A blockchain-based fog computing framework for activity recognition as an application to e-Healthcare services", *Future Gener. Comput. Syst.,* vol. 100, pp. 569-578, 2019.
[http://dx.doi.org/10.1016/j.future.2019.05.059]

[64]   M. Attaran, and A. Gunasekaran, *Applications of blockchain technology in business: challenges and opportunities.* Springer Briefs in Operations Management: Cham, Switzerland, 2019.
[http://dx.doi.org/10.1007/978-3-030-27798-7]

[65]   "Sayadnimakhezr, MdMoniruzzaman, AbdulsalamYassine, Blockchain technology in healthcare: A comprehensive review and directions for future research", *Appl. Sci. (Basel),* vol. 9, no. 9, 2019.

[66]   K. Yaeger, M. Martini, J. Rasouli, and A. Costa, "Emerging blockchain technology solutions for modern healthcare infrastructure", *Journal of Scientific Innovation in Medicine,* vol. 2, no. 1, p. 1, 2019.
[http://dx.doi.org/10.29024/jsim.7]

[67]   A. Roehrs, C.A. da Costa, and R. da Rosa Righi, "OmniPHR: A distributed architecture model to integrate personal health records", *J. Biomed. Inform.,* vol. 71, pp. 70-81, 2017.
[http://dx.doi.org/10.1016/j.jbi.2017.05.012] [PMID: 28545835]

[68]   D. Ichikawa, M. Kashiyama, and T. Ueno, "Tamper-resistant mobile health using blockchain technology", *JMIR Mhealth Uhealth,* vol. 5, no. 7, p. e111, 2017.
[http://dx.doi.org/10.2196/mhealth.7938] [PMID: 28747296]

[69]   T. Kumari, R. Kumar, and R.K. Dwivedi, "Designing Blockchain Based Consensus Mechanism for Smart Healthcare IoT", *2023 International Conference on Intelligent and Innovative Technologies in Computing, Electrical and Electronics (IITCEE) Bengaluru, India,* pp. 878-884, 2023.
[http://dx.doi.org/10.1109/IITCEE57236.2023.10090882]

CHAPTER 7

Blockchain in the Healthcare Domain and Performing Various Security Analysis

Suresh Kumar Nagarajan[1,*], **Geetha Narasimhan**[2], **Akila Victor**[2], **Yash Vaish**[2] and **Pranshu Tripathi**[2]

[1] *Department of Computer Applications, Kalasalingam Academy of Research and Education, Krishnankoil, Tamilnadu, India*

[2] *School of Computer Science & Engineering, VIT, Vellore, India*

Abstract: Blockchain is a promising technology that can be used to improve the healthcare system. It can be used to store patient data securely and prevent tampering. It can also be used to improve supply chain management by increasing transparency and interoperability. This work proposes a web-based application that uses blockchain to store patient's data and retailer's information. The application will also be able to send encrypted messages securely and anonymously. The application will be deployed on the Ethereum platform. The benefits of using blockchain in healthcare are Security: Blockchain is a secure way to store data because it is decentralized and encrypted. This makes it difficult for unauthorized users to access or tamper with data. Transparency: Blockchain is transparent, which means that all transactions are recorded on the blockchain and can be viewed by anyone. This can help to increase trust and accountability in the healthcare system. Interoperability: Blockchain can be used to connect different healthcare systems together, which can improve the flow of information. This can help to improve patient care. Immutability: Blockchain is immutable, which means that data cannot be changed once it is added to the blockchain. This can help to ensure the accuracy of data. The challenges of using blockchain in healthcare are Complexity, Cost, and Regulation. Despite these challenges, blockchain is a promising technology that has the potential to improve the healthcare system. This work is a step towards realizing the potential of blockchain in healthcare.

Keywords: Blockchain, Bitcoin, Decentralization, Ethereum, HealthCare System, Security.

INTRODUCTION

Blockchain is a technology that makes data records secure and tamper- proof. It is a distributed ledger that is shared among a network of computers. This makes it

---

* **Corresponding author Suresh Kumar Nagarajan:** Department of Computer Applications, Kalasalingam Academy of Research and Education, Krishnankoil, Tamilnadu, India; E-mail: sureshkumar@klu.ac.in

L. Ashok Kumar, D. Karthika Renuka, Sonali Agarwal & Sheng-Lung Peng (Eds.)

difficult for unauthorized users to access or modify the data. The healthcare industry is increasingly adopting blockchain technology. This is because blockchain can be used to address a number of challenges in the healthcare industry, such as:

Data security: Blockchain can be used to secure patient's data from unauthorized access or modification.

Identity management: Blockchain can be used to create a secure and reliable way to identify patients.

Supply chain management: Blockchain can be used to track the movement of drugs and other medical products through the supply chain.

Clinical trials: Blockchain can be used to record and track data from clinical trials.

Payments: Blockchain can be used to make secure and efficient payments for healthcare services [1 - 9].

The healthcare industry is still in the early stages of adopting blockchain technology. However, the potential benefits of blockchain are significant, and it is likely to play an increasingly important role in the future of healthcare. Here are some specific examples of how blockchain is being used in the healthcare industry today:

MediLedger: MediLedger is a blockchain-based platform that is used to track the movement of prescription drugs through the supply chain. This helps to ensure that patients receive genuine and safe medications.

Chronically: Chronically is a blockchain-based platform that is used to manage patient health records. This allows patients to share their health records with their healthcare providers securely and easily.

Doc.ai: Doc.ai is a blockchain-based platform that is used to make secure and efficient payments for healthcare services. This can help to reduce the administrative costs of healthcare.

These are just a few examples of how blockchain is being used in the healthcare industry. As the technology continues to develop, we can expect to see even more innovative applications of blockchain in healthcare in the future [11].

Preventing Fraud: Blockchain technology can be used to address the problem of fraud in the healthcare industry. Fraud can occur in the form of false medical records, claims, and proof of work. Blockchain is a tamper-proof ledger of hashes that can be used to track and verify all healthcare data.

The healthcare industry is rapidly adopting digital technologies, such as electronic health records (EHRs). EHRs store a wide variety of patient data, including clinical records, statistical data, prescriptions, vaccination status, lab test reports, and other sensitive data. Blockchain can be used to secure and protect EHR data from unauthorized access and tampering [18].

In addition to securing EHR data, blockchain can also be used to improve the efficiency and transparency of the healthcare industry. For example, blockchain can be used to create a decentralized network for sharing healthcare data between different stakeholders, such as doctors, hospitals, and insurance companies. This would make it easier to access and share patient data, which could improve the quality of care.

Blockchain is a promising new technology that has the potential to revolutionize the healthcare industry. By addressing the challenges of fraud, security, and efficiency, blockchain can help to improve the quality of care and make healthcare more affordable.

Here are some specific examples of how blockchain can be used in the healthcare industry:

Secure electronic health records: Blockchain can be used to create a tamper-proof ledger of all healthcare data, making it more difficult for fraudsters to alter or steal patient records.

Manage the supply chain of drugs: Blockchain can be used to track the movement of drugs from the manufacturer to the patient, ensuring that patients receive genuine and safe medications.

Pay for healthcare services: Blockchain can be used to create a decentralized payment system for healthcare services, making it easier for patients to pay for care and for providers to get paid.

Research and development: Blockchain can be used to store and share data for medical research, making it easier to conduct clinical trials and develop new treatments.

Blockchain is still a new technology, and there are some challenges that need to be addressed before it can be widely adopted in the healthcare industry. However, the potential benefits of blockchain are significant, and it is likely to play an increasingly important role in the future of healthcare.

LITERATURE SURVEY

The authors discuss the use of blockchain technology in two different applications: decentralized chat apps and electronic health records (EHRs). In the case of decentralized chat apps, the authors argue that blockchain can be used to create a more secure and private communication platform. This is because blockchain is a decentralized ledger that is not controlled by any single entity [1]. This makes it difficult for unauthorized users to access or tamper with data. The authors propose a decentralized chat app called DCS that uses blockchain to secure messages. In DCS, messages are encrypted and distributed to all nodes on the network. This makes it impossible for anyone to read the messages without the correct key [2].

The authors also discuss the use of blockchain in EHRs. They argue that blockchain can be used to create a more secure and efficient way to store and share patient data. This is because blockchain is immutable, which means that data cannot be changed once it is added to the blockchain. This can help to ensure the accuracy and integrity of patient data. The authors propose a blockchain-based EHR system that would allow patients to control their own data. In this system, patients would have the ability to share their data with doctors and other healthcare providers, but only with their consent. The authors conclude by discussing the potential benefits of using blockchain technology in both decentralized chat apps and EHRs. They argue that blockchain can help to create more secure, private, and efficient communication and data sharing platforms [3 - 9].

The author discusses the use of blockchain technology in healthcare. They argue that blockchain can be used to improve the security and efficiency of healthcare data sharing. The author discusses the following potential benefits of using blockchain in healthcare:

Improved security: Blockchain is a secure way to store data because it is decentralized and encrypted. This makes it difficult for unauthorized users to access or tamper with data.

Increased efficiency: Blockchain can be used to automate the exchange of data between healthcare providers. This can help to improve the efficiency of healthcare delivery.

Improved transparency: Blockchain can be used to make data more transparent. This can help to improve trust between patients and healthcare providers.

The author also discusses some of the challenges of using blockchain in healthcare:

Lack of interoperability: Blockchain is still a new technology, and there is not yet a standard way to implement it. This can make it difficult for different healthcare providers to share data.

Cost: Blockchain can be expensive to implement and maintain.

Security risks: Blockchain is a complex technology and there are still some security risks associated with it.

The author concludes by arguing that the potential benefits of using blockchain in healthcare outweigh the challenges. They call for further research and development in this area.

Blockchain is a distributed ledger technology that can be used to record transactions in a secure and transparent way. This makes it a promising solution for a variety of applications, including healthcare and supply chain management.

In healthcare, blockchain can be used to store patient records in a secure and immutable way. This would prevent unauthorized access to patient data and make it easier to share data between healthcare providers. Blockchain could also be used to track the provenance of medical products, ensuring that they are safe and reliable. In supply chain management, blockchain can be used to track the movement of goods from the point of origin to the point of sale. This would improve visibility and transparency in the supply chain, which could help to reduce fraud and improve efficiency. Of course, blockchain is still a new technology and there are some challenges that need to be addressed before it can be widely adopted. These challenges include scalability, security, and privacy. However, the potential benefits of blockchain are significant, and it is likely to play an increasingly important role in a variety of industries in the future [10 - 18].

PROBLEM STATEMENT

The author found that the existing research on blockchain-based healthcare systems has some flaws, such as a lack of monitoring of transactions, a lack of decentralized peer-to-peer chat services, and vulnerability to DOS-DDoS attacks. To address these flaws, the author proposes a new blockchain-based healthcare system that would have the following features:

Web-based application: The web-based application would store patient and user data in a blockchain. This would make the data more secure and tamper-proof.

Decentralized peer-to-peer chat service: The decentralized peer-to-peer chat service would allow users to communicate securely and anonymously. This would protect users' privacy and prevent unauthorized access to their communications.

Reward system: The reward system would reward patients with cryptocurrency for participating in the system. This would encourage patients to use the system and provide them with an incentive to share their data.

Smart contract: The smart contract would allow retailers to register their medications and sell them directly to end users. This would improve the efficiency of the pharmaceutical supply chain and make it easier for patients to get the medications they need. The author plans to implement the system using the Ethereum platform, JavaScript for the web application and Python for the chat service. The author also plans to test the system for security vulnerabilities and attack vectors. The proposed system would address the flaws of existing blockchain-based healthcare systems and provide a more secure and efficient way to manage healthcare data, as shown in Fig. (**1**).

RESEARCH FRAMEWORK

This project will use JavaScript to store all patient data in a blockchain. Blockchain is a secure and tamper-proof way to store data, making it ideal for sensitive information like patient records. The project will use cryptography algorithms to secure the blockchain and prevent unauthorized access. Each block in the chain will be assigned a new hash, which makes it difficult to tamper with the data. The project will use MongoDB to store the blockchain after each block is verified as legitimate. This will be documented in the project's work documentation. The project will also create a digital currency or virtual currency. This currency will be used to reward miners for verifying transactions on the blockchain. The project will create a transaction class that will store the address, forwarders, and amount of each transaction. This class will also store a pending transaction array, which will store all transactions that are made between blocks. Each client will be assigned a public key and a private key. The public key will be used to receive funds, and the private key will be used to spend funds. The project will import the elliptic library to create keys. Before a transaction is signed, the public key must be equal to the address. Each class will require various proofs of work to ensure that the client always has valid transactions.

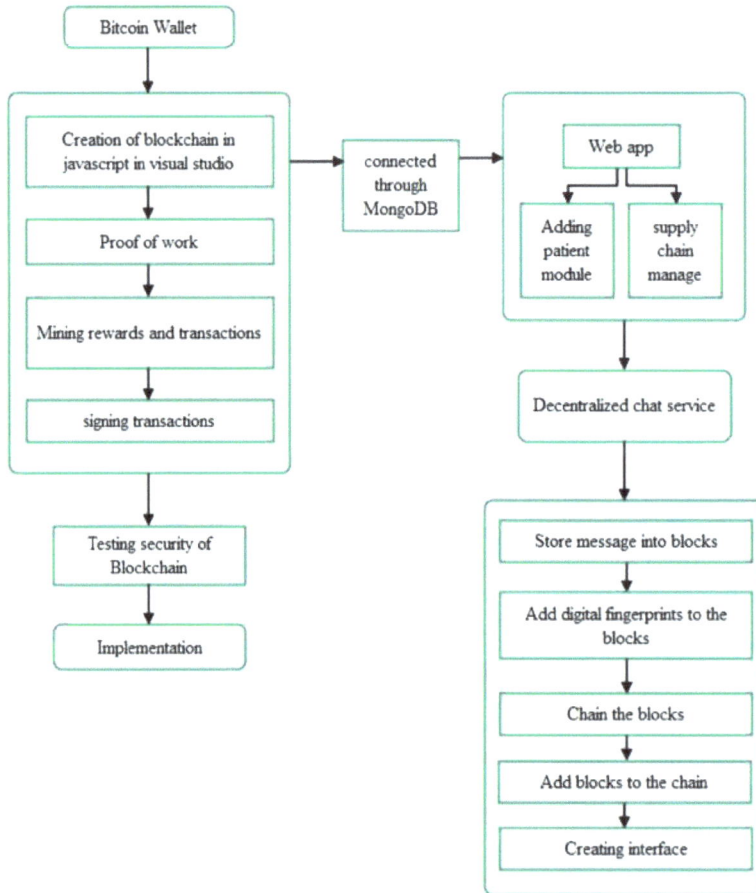

Fig. (1). Architecture Diagram.

This project will build a simple peer-to-peer chat application using Python programming and blockchain implementation. The chat application will be decentralized, meaning that it will not be controlled by a central authority. The chat application will use blockchain technology to secure the messages that are sent between users. This means that the messages cannot be tampered with or read by unauthorized users. The client's identity will be used as the public key instead of using multiple client IDs. This will prevent users from creating fake identities to do illegal activities. To overcome the lack of identity, the project will use a lottery or raffle system. Instead of requiring users to provide their identity and verifying it, the project will simply ask which user has which public key and port being used. This will allow the project to randomly select a user to communicate with and perform other tasks shown in Fig. (**2**).

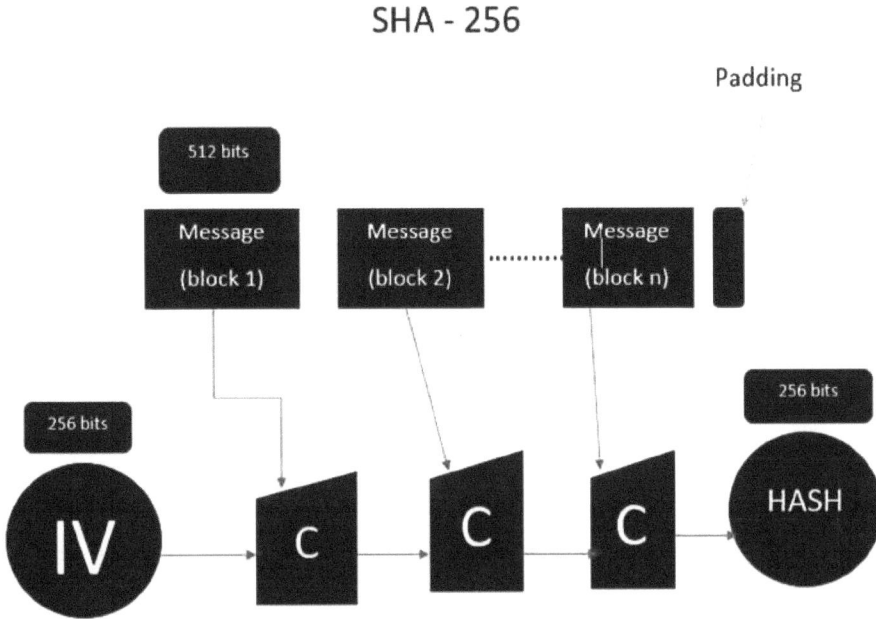

Fig. (2). SHA256 Work Flow.

This system is designed to be resistant to cyber attacks. A cyber attack is an attack where an attacker creates multiple fake identities to gain control of a network. In this project, if an attacker tries to create multiple cyber identities, they will all be assigned the same identity key. This will prevent the attacker from multiplying their power by creating new nodes. The project will also test the security of the blockchain. The project will use encryption, signatures, and other security measures to protect the blockchain. The project will also test the security of the chat application by launching various attacks, such as malware attacks. The goal of this project is to create a secure and decentralized chat application that can be used by users around the world. The project will also contribute to the development of blockchain technology by testing the security of blockchain-based applications.

- Acting similarly to spyware; some types of adware track your movement and activities online to fit precise adverts to you.
- Operating as a middleman; redirect your activities through them to share adverts with you.
- Uses up your data with every pop-up; downloads consuming your allowance.
- Slowing down your computer; running DOS uses power and network channels, affecting your device's performance. Attacks like double spending cost the user an extra amount, aka the double-spending attack, denial of service attack

stealing, restricting the user from using blockchain and making any request, and if possible, stealing the cryptocurrency.

This project will create a blockchain-based healthcare system that will be used to track the movement of medications. The system will be secure and reliable, and it will allow patients to buy prescriptions with the assurance that the supply chain information is stored. The system will use a variety of security measures to protect the data, including cryptography, anonymization, and consensus algorithms. The system will also be resistant to attacks like double spending and denial of service attacks. The system will have three main components: a login/signup page, a profile module, and a medicine supply chain management module. The login/signup page will collect data from users, such as their name, age, email address, date of birth, address, marital status, and contact number. Doctors and retailers will also need to provide proof of their credentials.

The profile module will store all of the information that was collected during the signup process, as well as additional information that is needed to access the coin. The page will also display a label that indicates whether the user is a doctor, retailer, or patient. The medicine supply chain management module will allow retailers to register their medications and track their movement. The system will also display a path of intermediaries so that patients can easily divert to buy the medications. This system will help to create a secure and reliable environment for the purchase of medications. It will also help to improve the traceability of medications and prevent counterfeit drugs from entering the supply chain.

The medications can be straightforwardly seen by the patients, and they can get the data of the medication straightforwardly or the patient can choose to create a QR code for purchasing the medication. The QR code will divert the patient to the retailer. This will help in trusted drug supply according to patients' necessities and will guarantee that the generic medication is given, as shown in Fig. (**3**).

IMPLEMENTATION

BitCoin Wallet

The author will create a simple blockchain in JavaScript. The blockchain will have three main components: blocks, transactions, and miners.

Blocks: Blocks are units of data that contain information about transactions. Each block contains a timestamp, a data field, and a hash of the previous block. The hash of the previous block ensures that the blocks are linked together in a chain, making it difficult to change or tamper with the data.

Transactions: Transactions are records of transfers of value between users. Each transaction includes the sender's address, the recipient's address, and the amount of value being transferred.

Miners: Miners are computers that verify transactions and add new blocks to the blockchain. Miners are rewarded with cryptocurrency for their work.

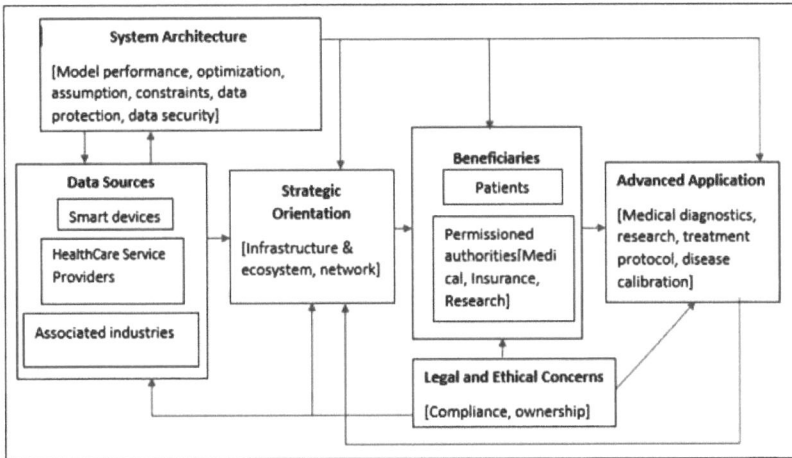

Fig. (3). Blockchain-based Healthcare ecosystem.

The author will use a proof-of-work mechanism to secure the blockchain. Proof-of-work is a system that requires miners to solve a mathematical puzzle in order to add a new block to the blockchain. The puzzle is designed to be difficult to solve but easy to verify. This ensures that only legitimate transactions are added to the blockchain. The author will also implement a mining reward system. The mining reward is a payment that is given to miners for adding new blocks to the blockchain. The mining reward is used to incentivize miners to participate in the network and secure the blockchain. The author will also create a key-generator system. The key-generator system will allow users to generate public and private keys. Public keys are used to receive cryptocurrency, and private keys are used to spend cryptocurrency.

The author's Bitcoin wallet will have the following features:

Proof of work: The blockchain is secured by a proof-of-work mechanism.

Mining reward: Users are rewarded with cryptocurrency for mining new blocks.

Difficulty: The difficulty of mining new blocks is adjusted to ensure that blocks are mined at regular intervals.

Key-generator: Users can generate public and private keys using the key-generator system.

The author's Bitcoin wallet is a simple but secure way to store and manage cryptocurrency. It is a valuable tool for users who want to participate in the blockchain economy.

TESTING

This project aims to use blockchain technology to create a user-centric electronic health record (EHR) that maintains a true version of the user's data. The project will address the following flaws in the existing EHR systems:

Lack of monitoring of the transactions: The project will use blockchain technology to create a secure and transparent ledger of all transactions. This will allow for better monitoring and auditing of the system.

Lack of decentralized peer-to-peer chat service: The project will use the Ethereum library Web3 to create a decentralized chat service that does not require a third party. This will allow for more secure and private communication between users.

Vulnerability to DOS-DDoS attacks or a RUDY attack: The project will use blockchain technology to make the system more secure against these attacks.

The project will also implement the following features:

Medical supply chain management: The project will track the movement of medicines and medical equipment through the supply chain. This will help to ensure the validity of the products and facilitate needed safety recalls.

Rewarding patients: The project will reward patients for using the system. This will encourage patients to participate and help to improve the quality of the data.

Encryption of medical health records: The project will use strong encryption to protect the privacy of medical health records.

Decentralized peer-to-peer chat service: The project will create a decentralized chat service that does not require a third party. This will allow for more secure and private communication between users.

The project is still in the early stages of development, but it has the potential to revolutionize the way EHRs are used. The project will address the major flaws in the existing systems and provide a more secure, transparent, and user-centric EHR solution.

RESULTS AND DISCUSSION

Summary of the Website

This is a test version of a website that can be used to connect patients and doctors from all over the world. The website can allocate a doctor to a patient based on the patient's needs. The doctor can then be added to the patient's private chat group for consultation.

In addition, the patient's award (score) and the medications they use are recorded and sent to the blockchain supply chain. The length of time patients wait is analyzed, and the severity of the patient's illness is determined by the number of medications they have previously taken. This information can be used to dynamically match patients and doctors to ensure that patients who are more valuable in terms of their medical scores are prioritized. These are explained in Figs. (**5-18**).

Website Screenshot

The sign-in portal that verifies the username/email and password of the user trying to access the site is shown in Fig. (**4**).

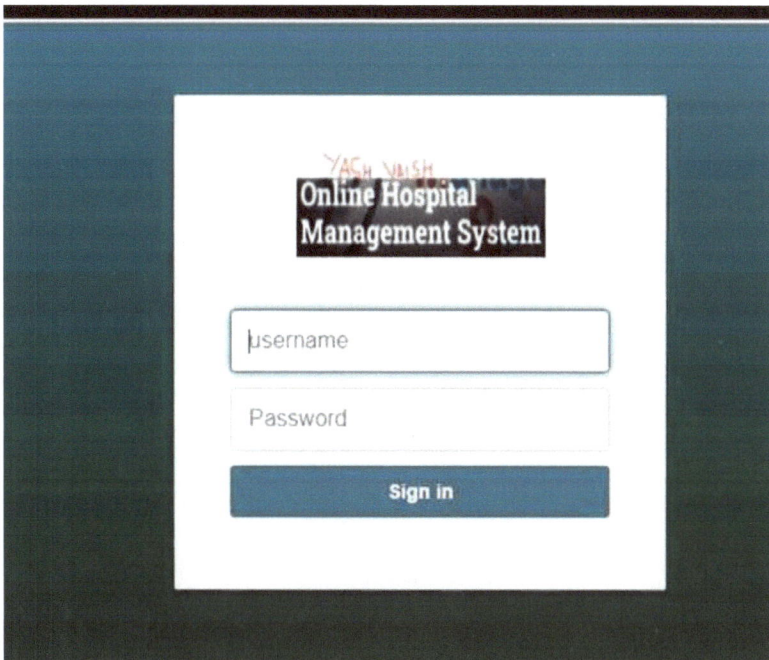

Fig. (4). Signup Page.

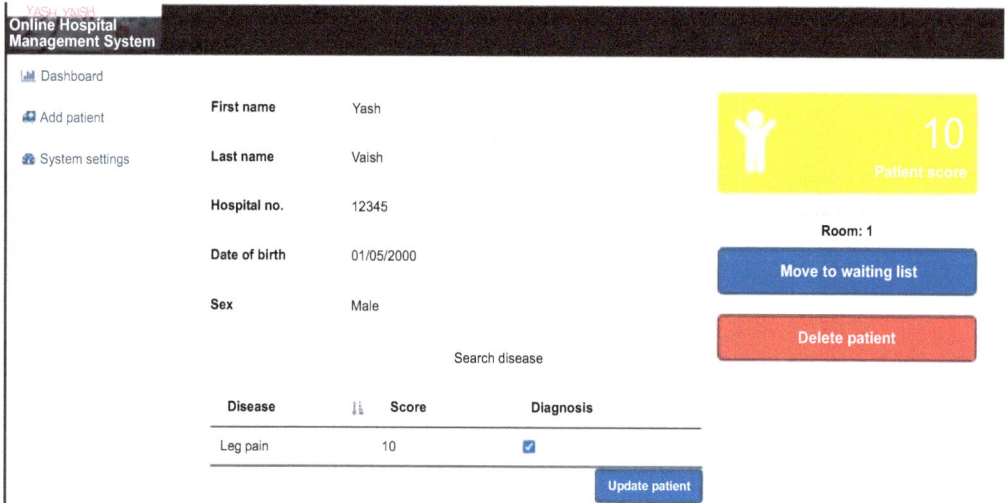

Fig. (5). Patient Dashboard.

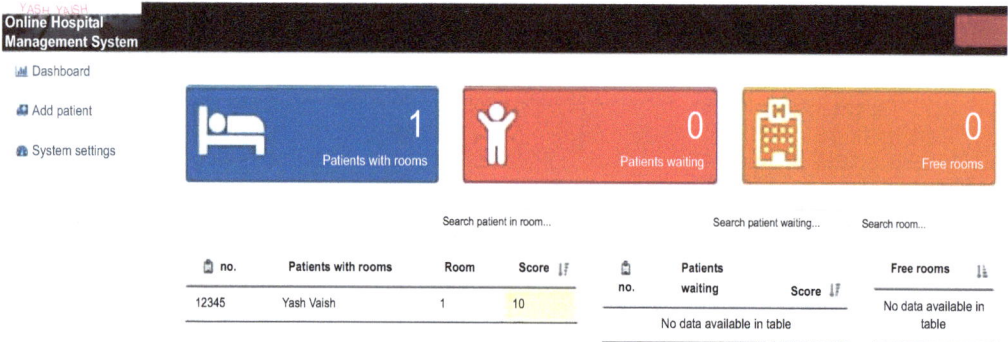

Fig. (6). Main Page.

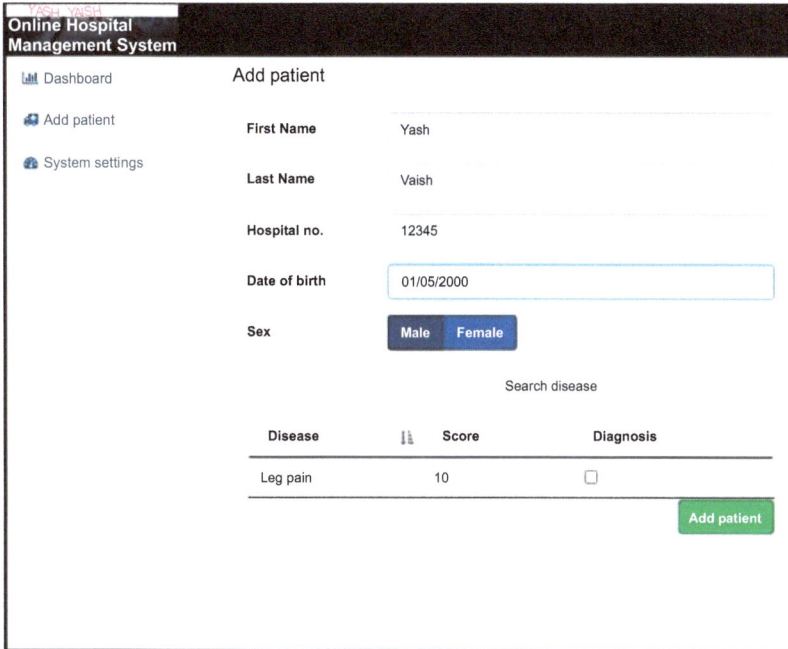

Fig. (7). Adding Patient Module.

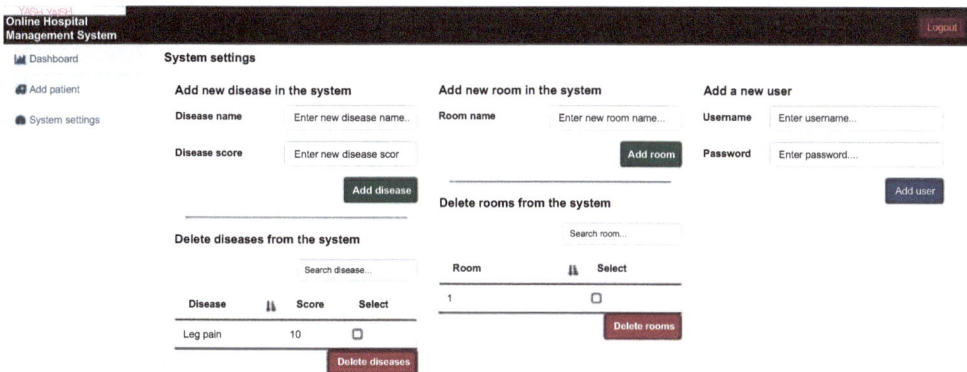

Fig. (8). Review Page.

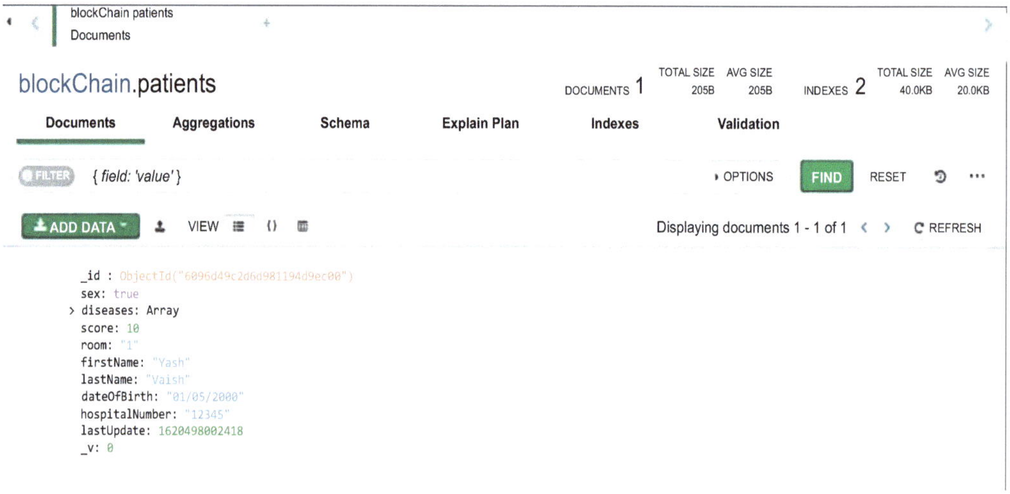

Fig. (9). Patient Database.

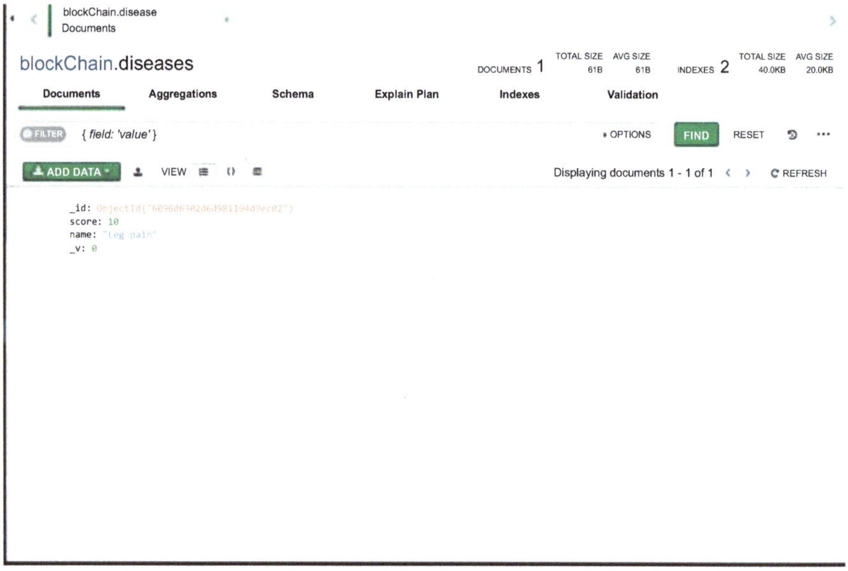

Fig. (10). Disease Database.

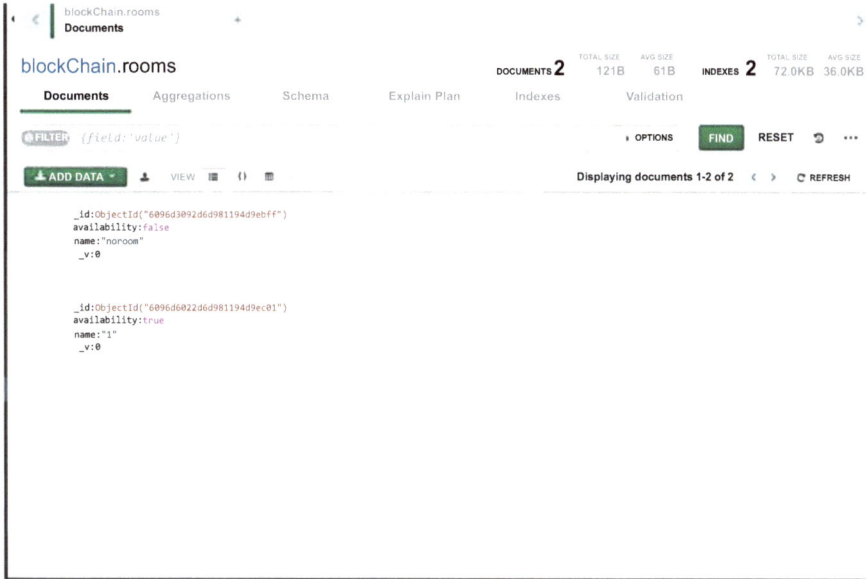

Fig. (11). Room Database.

Fig. (12). Genesis Block.

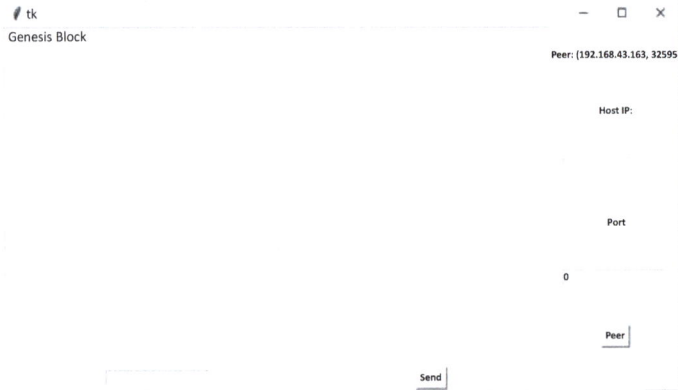

Fig. (13). User Chat Application on one terminal.

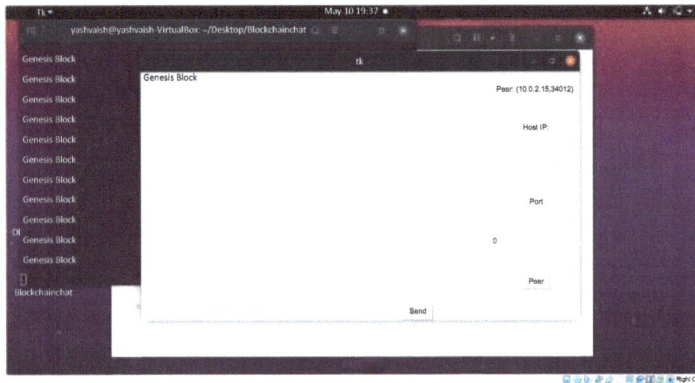

Fig. (14). User Chat Application on another terminal.

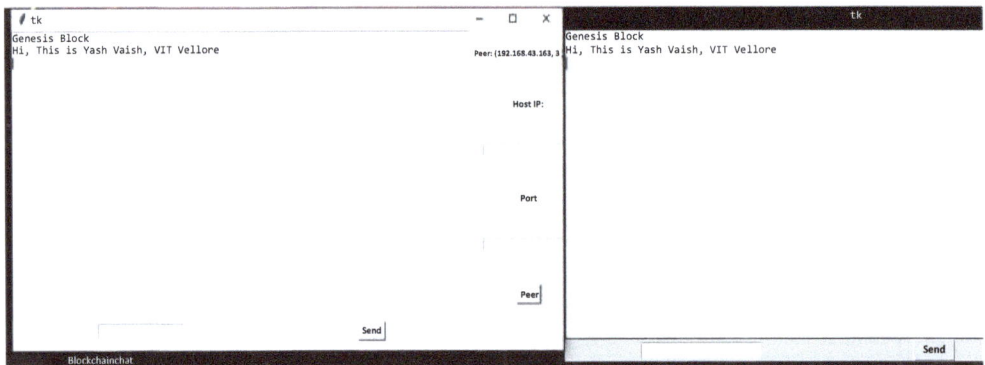

Fig. (15). Block Message received by the user.

The front end of the application displays the user's public identity, the port they are connected to, and their current status. The user can also specify the user they want to connect to by entering their public identity and the port they are connected to. The message is then hashed together with these values and sent across the network. The network searches for a node with the specified values in the header of the hash. None of the internal values, such as the message, are displayed to other peers in the network.

```
192.168.43.163 - - [10/May/2021 19:46:01] "GET /chain HTTP/1.1" 200 -

Genesis Block
Hi, This is Yash Vaish,VIT Vellore

Genesis Block
Hi, This is Yash Vaish,VIT Vellore

Genesis Block
Hi, This is Yash Vaish,VIT Vellore

Genesis Block
Hi, This is Yash Vaish,VIT Vellore

Genesis Block
Hi, This is Yash Vaish,VIT Vellore

Genesis Block
```

Fig. (16). Blockchain used in chat service.

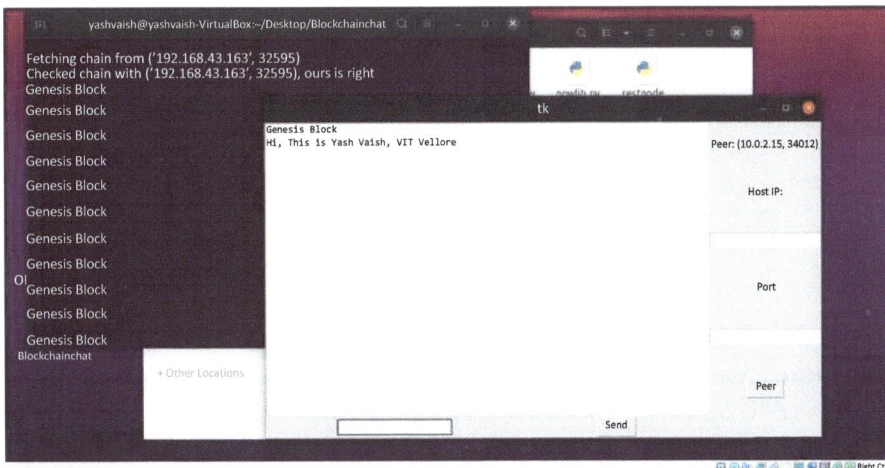

Fig. (17). A user terminal.

Fig. (18). Blockchain used in chat service.

The backend of the application runs the blockchain of the network, which is updated every few milliseconds. The application fetches header information from the blocks passing through it to check if the block is meant for the particular user. If the fetched block passes the match between the hash and the calculated value, the block is added to the blockchain of the user to be displayed as the message on the screen of the application.

When a peer request is made by any node, the request is flowed through each node and the same procedure of check and accept connection is done while connecting a node in the peer-to-peer network with other nodes.

Some of the security risks of blockchain:

Exchange hacks: Cryptocurrency exchanges are often targeted by hackers because they hold large amounts of cryptocurrency without adequate security measures. It is more secure to store funds through hardware wallets or paper wallets, which have fewer online touchpoints and can help to keep your money safe from hackers.

Social engineering attacks: These attacks can take many forms, but the goal is always to get your private keys, login information, or cryptocurrency. Phishing is one of the most common types of social engineering attacks. In a phishing attack, a malicious actor will impersonate someone you trust in an email, text message, or social media post in order to trick you into giving up your personal information.

Software flaws: Any software that uses blockchain technology should be thoroughly tested for security flaws. This includes code reviews, penetration testing, and smart contract audits. It is important to check if any blockchain-based software you use has been audited for defects or vulnerabilities by a third party. You should also take steps to secure your own devices and accounts.

Malware: Cryptojacking malware can cause performance problems, increase power consumption, and open the door to other malicious code. It is important to be careful about what software you install on your devices and to run regular security scans.

By being aware of these risks and taking steps to mitigate them, you can help protect your cryptocurrency and your data.

Exchange Spoof Attack

The author discusses a simple DNS spoofing attack that can be used to target patients who are making medical transactions online. In this attack, the attacker first spoofs the IP address of the DNS server that the patient is using. This means that the attacker is able to see all of the traffic that the patient is sending to and from the DNS server. The attacker can then modify this traffic, such as by redirecting the patient to a fake website. The attack is carried out in two phases: ARP spoofing and DNS spoofing. In the ARP spoofing phase, the attacker sends fake ARP messages to the patient's computer. These messages tell the patient's computer that the attacker's computer is actually the DNS server. This means that the patient's computer will send all of its DNS traffic to the attacker's computer. In the DNS spoofing phase, the attacker can then modify the DNS traffic that it is receiving from the patient's computer. For example, the attacker could redirect the patient to a fake website that looks like a real website.

In addition to DNS spoofing, the author also discusses social engineering attacks and software flaws. Social engineering attacks are attacks that exploit human psychology to trick the victim into giving up their personal information or clicking on a malicious link. Software flaws are errors in software that can be exploited by attackers to gain access to a system.

The author concludes by discussing malware, which is software that is designed to harm a computer system. Malware can be spread through email attachments, malicious links, or infected websites.

Some of the key points from the text:

DNS spoofing is an attack that can be used to redirect a victim's traffic to a fake website.

Social engineering attacks exploit human psychology to trick the victim into giving up their personal information or clicking on a malicious link.

Software flaws are errors in software that can be exploited by attackers to gain access to a system.

Malware is software that is designed to harm a computer system.

It is important to be aware of these attacks so that you can take steps to protect yourself. Some of the things you can do to protect yourself include:

Using a strong password and changing it regularly.

Not clicking on links in emails or on websites that you are not familiar with.

Keeping your software up to date.

Using a firewall and antivirus software.

CONCLUSION AND FUTURE WORK

Blockchain technology is still in its early stages of development, and there is a lot of excitement about its potential applications in a variety of industries. However, there are also some challenges that need to be addressed before blockchain can be widely adopted. One challenge is that blockchain applications are often vulnerable to attack. For example, the chat service described in the text could be attacked by a DNS spoofing attack, which would redirect users to a fake website. Malware attacks and software flaws could also be used to compromise the security of the chat service. Another challenge is that blockchain applications can be difficult to use. For example, the chat service described in the text requires users to have a strong understanding of blockchain technology in order to use it. This could make it difficult for businesses and individuals to adopt blockchain applications. Despite these challenges, there is still a lot of potential for blockchain technology. As the technology matures and the challenges are addressed, blockchain could have a major impact on a variety of industries.

REFERENCES

[1]   C. Aslanoglou, M. Konstantopoulos, N. Chondros, and M. Roussopoulos, "Take Back your Friends with DCS: A Decentralized Connectivity Service for private social communication apps", *2020 IEEE International Conference on Decentralized Applications and Infrastructures (DAPPS) Oxford, United Kingdom,* pp. 133-138, 2020.
[http://dx.doi.org/10.1109/DAPPS49028.2020.00017]

[2]   A. Shahnaz, U. Qamar, and A. Khalid, "Using Blockchain for Electronic Health Records", *IEEE Access,* vol. 7, pp. 147782-147795, 2019.
[http://dx.doi.org/10.1109/ACCESS.2019.2946373]

[3]   S. Wang, L. Ouyang, Y. Yuan, X. Ni, X. Han, and F.Y. Wang, "Blockchain-Enabled Smart Contracts: Architecture, Applications, and Future Trends", *IEEE Trans. Syst. Man Cybern. Syst.,* vol. 49, no. 11, pp. 2266-2277, 2019.
[http://dx.doi.org/10.1109/TSMC.2019.2895123]

[4]   S. Alexaki, G. Alexandris, V. Katos, and N.E. Petroulakis, "Blockchain-based Electronic Patient Records for Regulated Circular Healthcare Jurisdictions", *2018 IEEE 23rd International Workshop on Computer Aided Modeling and Design of Communication Links and Networks (CAMAD), Barcelona,* 2018.
[http://dx.doi.org/10.1109/CAMAD.2018.8514954]

[5]   S. Rajput, A. Singh, S. Khurana, T. Bansal, and S. Shreshtha, "Blockchain Technology and Cryptocurrencies", *2019 Amity International Conference on Artificial Intelligence (AICAI) Dubai, United Arab Emirates,* pp. 909-912, 2019.
[http://dx.doi.org/10.1109/AICAI.2019.8701371]

[6]   L. Böck, N. Alexopoulos, E. Saracoglu, M. Mühlhäuser, and E. Vasilomanolakis, "Assessing the Threat of Blockchain-based Botnets", *2019 APWG Symposium on Electronic Crime Research (eCrime), Pittsburgh, PA, USA,* pp. 1-11, 2019.
[http://dx.doi.org/10.1109/eCrime47957.2019.9037600]

[7]   S. Rouhani, and R. Deters, "Performance analysis of Ethereum transactions in a private blockchain", *2017 8th IEEE International Conference on Software Engineering and Service Science (ICSESS), Beijing,* pp. 70-74, 2017.
[http://dx.doi.org/10.1109/ICSESS.2017.8342866]

[8]   Azada Muhammad Ajmal, Arshadb Junaid, Mahmoud Shazia, and Salahc Khaled, "A Privacy-preserving Framework for Smart Context-aware Healthcare Applications",

[9]   S Chenthara, K Ahmed, H Wang, and F Whittaker, "Security and Privacy-Preserving Challenges of e-Health Solutions in Cloud Computing", In: *IEEE,* 2019.

[10]   MJ Swede, V Scovetta , and M Eugene-Colin, "Protecting Patient Data Is the New Scope of Practice: A Recommended Cybersecurity Curricula for Healthcare Students to Prepare for this Challenge", *J Allied Health.,* vol. 48, no. 2, pp. 148-155, 2019.

[11]   S.I. Attacks, S.J.S. Blockchain, S. Ruj, and D.B.E. Sipra, "A comprehensive survey on attacks, security issues and blockchain solutions for IoT and IIoT", *J. Netw. Comput. Appl.,* p. 18, 2020.

[12]   Bajrić S., "Data Security and Privacy Issues in Healthcare Samed BAJRIĆ", *Appl. Med. Inform.,* 2020.

[13]   Sudeep Tanwar, Parekha Karan, and Evans Richard, "Blockchain-based electronic Healthcare record system for Healthcare Elsevier Journal of Information Security and Applications",

[14]   Offner, K.L., Sitnikova, E., Joiner, K. and MacIntyre, C.R., "Towards understanding cybersecurity capability in Australian healthcare organisations: a systematic review of recent trends, threats and mitigation", *Health Security Intelligence,,* pp. 92-121, 2020.

[15]   M. Hölbl, M. Kompara, A. Kamišalić, and L. Nemec Zlatolas, "A systematic review of the use of blockchain in healthcare", *Symmetry (Basel),* vol. 10, no. 10, p. 470, 2018.
[http://dx.doi.org/10.3390/sym10100470]

[16] Y. Tribis, A. El Bouchti, and H. Bouayad, "Supply chain management based on blockchain: A systematic mapping study", *International Workshop on Transportation and Supply Chain Engineering,* vol. 200, MATEC Web of Conferences, 2018.
[http://dx.doi.org/10.1051/matecconf/201820000020]

[17] P. Helo, and A.H.M. Shamsuzzoha, "Real-time supply chain—a blockchain architecture for project deliveries", *Robot. Comput.-Integr. Manuf.,* vol. 63, p. 101909, 2020.
[http://dx.doi.org/10.1016/j.rcim.2019.101909]

[18] J. Andrew, D.P. Isravel, K.M. Sagayam, B. Bhushan, Y. Sei, and J. Eunice, "Blockchain for healthcare systems: Architecture, security challenges, trends and future directions", *J. Netw. Comput. Appl.,* p. 103633, 2023.

CHAPTER 8

IOT-Based Smart Healthcare System with Hybrid Key Generation and DNA Cryptography

Vidhya E.[1,*]

[1] *Padmavani Arts and Science College for Women, Salem, Tamil Nadu 636011, India*

Abstract: Many applications, such as smart health care, smart cities, smart homes, self-driving cars, IoT retail shops, tele-health, traffic management, and so on, will use IoT devices to generate information. In these tenders, smart health care is single of the most imperative because it generates sensitive information like disease managing, drug managing, secluded patient checking, defensive care, and so on. This large amount of information is acquired and recorded from a variety of sources (mobile phones, software, sensors, e-mail, applications and so on). These sources contain a basic encryption process, so hackers can easily hack the information and misuse it. These issues are taken by researchers, and they find solutions, but they do not fulfill the needs of encryption. Key generation is critical for encryption and decryption because a strong key increases the encryption and decryption level. In this chapter, the proposed system is designed and implemented with a strong key generation (KG) to encrypt (encr) and decrypt (decp) the information that is compatible with the limited processing capabilities of IoT devices. In this system, the mathematical key generation algorithm is created with the hybrid of prime numbers and pseudo random numbers using the Exclusive OR function. Besides, the DNA Cryptography algorithm is used to encrypt and decrypt the information. The above system makes it hard for hackers to break into. When paralleled with illustrious cryptographic schemes, the tentative outcomes of the proposed system show the best effects for every IoT scheme in terms of encryption time and key entropy. When equal to other surviving encryption schemes, the proposed system has a restored avalanche effect and key entropy value for achieving the security goals. The above security goals illustrate that such a scheme is able to protect IoT documents from present attacks.

Keywords: DNA Cryptography, IoT Devices, Pseudo Random Number, Prime Number.

INTRODUCTION

The Internet of Things is referred to as IoT, which was founded by Kevin Ashton in 1999. In the last 10 years, IoT has made any object internally connected and

* **Corresponding author Vidhya E.:** Padmavani Arts and Science College for Women, Salem, Tamil Nadu 636011, India; E-mail: vidhya11tamilarasi@gmail.com

L. Ashok Kumar, D. Karthika Renuka, Sonali Agarwal & Sheng-Lung Peng (Eds.)

has been considered the next technological revolution. The IoT is used by many applications such as smart health care, smart cities, smart homes, self-driving cars, IoT retail shops, tele-health, traffic management [1 - 8], and so on. In these applications, smart health care is unique and of the greatest significance because it generates sensitive information like disease management, remote patient monitoring, preventive care, drug management and so on. This large amount of information is acquired and recorded from a variety of sources (mobile phones, software, sensors, e-mail, applications and soon). IoT is really nothing more than associating processors to the internet *via* networks and sensors [9, 10]. These linked modules can be used in strength monitoring devices. The information is then conveyed to secluded locations *via* sensors such as M2M, which are machines for processors, technologies for people, handheld devices, or smartphones [11]. It is a humble, direct, much smarter, accessible, energy-efficient and interoperable method of following and enhancing care for any wellbeing issue. Currently, recent schemes provide a flexible border [12], assistant devices [13], and mental strength management [14] to help humans live a smarter lifetime. The IoT architecture is shown in the Fig. (**1**).

IoT devices generate structured and unstructured information based on their applications. This information needs a high level of security, but the IoT contains default encryption at a basic level, so it is not sufficient for this information [15]. Hackers can easily hack the information and misuse it, so the information is in a problem stage. This problem is studied by many researchers, and they find solutions, but they do not fulfill the needs of encryption because the level of encryption and decryption is based on the strength of the key generation. In this chapter, the proposed system is designed and implemented with a strong key generation to encrypt and decrypt the information that is compatible with the limited processing capabilities of IoT devices [16]. In this system, the mathematical key generation algorithm is created with the hybrid of prime numbers and pseudo random numbers using the Exclusive OR function. Besides, the DNA Cryptography algorithm is used to encrypt and decrypt the information [17]. The above system makes it hard for hackers to break into. When equaled to familiar cryptographic schemes, the tentative results of the proposed system show the best results for any IoT device in terms of encryption time, and key entropy [18]. When compared to other existing encryption systems, the proposed system has an improved avalanche effect and key entropy value for achieving the security goals. The above security goals illustrate that such a scheme is able to protect IoT documents from present attacks. The example for the Smart health care system is shown in the Fig. (**2**).

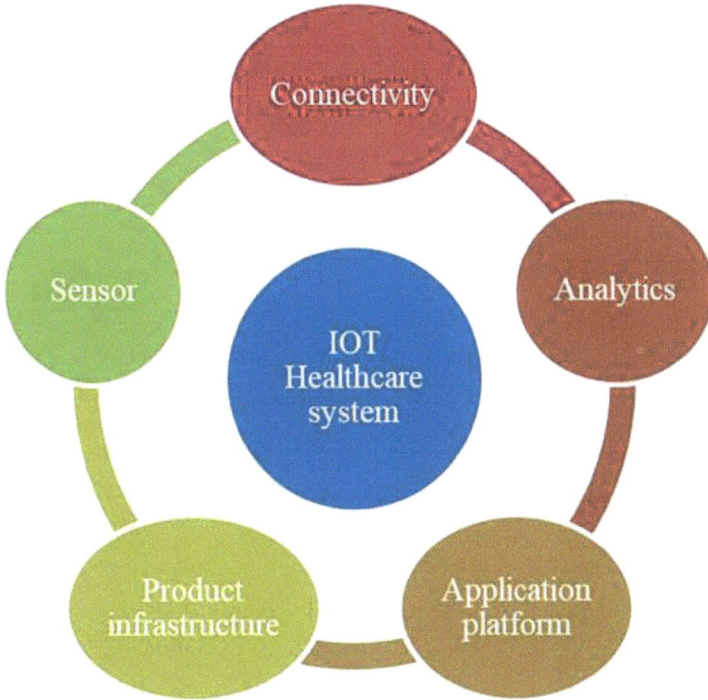

Fig. (1). IoT Health care system Architecture.

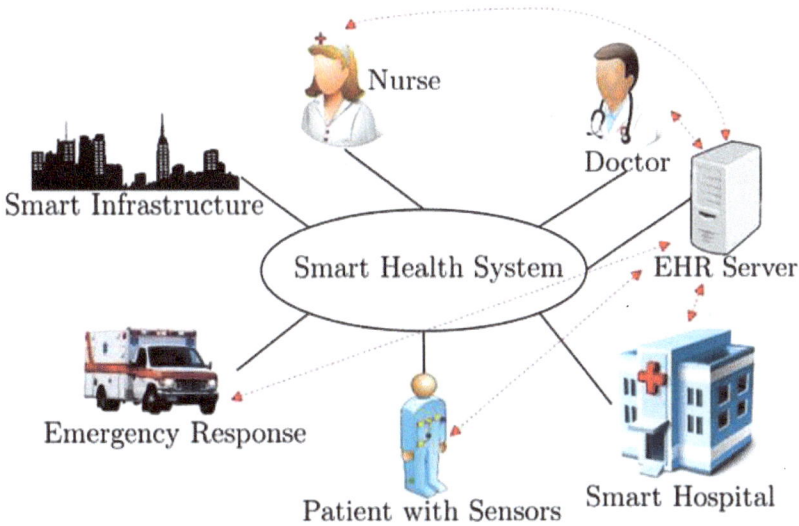

Fig. (2). Example Smart health care system.

PROPOSED WORK

The proposed work is described how to encrypt and decrypt the smart health care data by using DNA cryptography, which is generated by IoT devices and represented in Fig. (**3**).

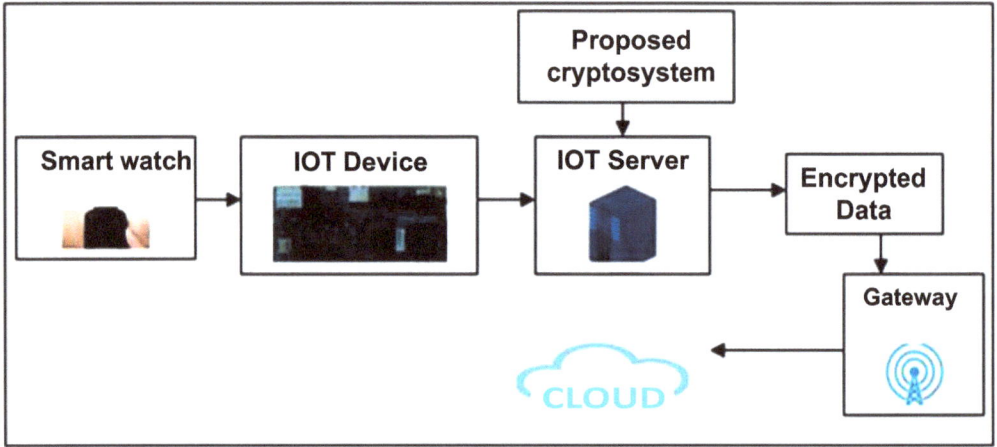

Fig. (3). Proposed Work Flow.

The data were collected from an IoT health care system and encrypted by using a new binary key, which is generated by XOR of prime numbers and pseudo-random numbers. The sender sends the encrypted data to the receiver. The receiver decrypts it by using the decrypt key and gets the plaintext.

The proposed work contains three processes. They are:

1. Key generation process [KGP]

2. Encryption process [EP]

3. Decryption process [DP]

Key Generation Process

In this process, the first step is to generate the prime number p using any one of the prime number generator algorithms like (Sieve of Eratosthenes, Sieve of Sundaram, Sieve of Atkin and so on). The second step is to generate a Pseudo random number q using a random function. The two numbers p and q are added using an Exclusive OR function and generate a new number. This number is converted to a binary number and saved by way of a binary key [bk] which is represented in Fig. (**4**).

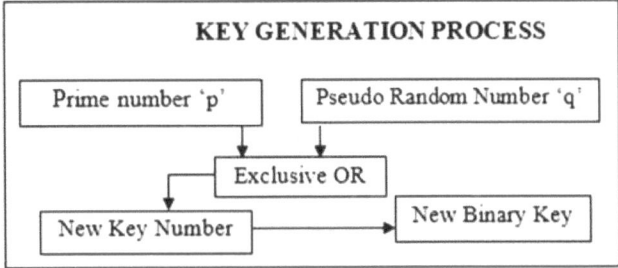

Fig. (4). Key Generation process.

Algorithm 1: Key Generation

HRKey_gen(SSB):
Begin:
1. q←random(n) // random number n-natural numbers
2. p ←prime(n)// prime number
3. BN← xor (q,p) // Exclusive OR
4. SBN← (BN)2 // BN to binary number
5. SSB ←(SBN % m) //m=1, Partition SBN into Single bit.
6. return (SSB)
End:

Encryption Process

In this process, the Smart Health care system generates data using smart IoT devices like smart watch contains pulse rate sensor, blood pressure sensor, temperature sensor and so on. These data are stored in an IoT server and encrypted using DNA cryptography. The encrypted data are sent to cloud using a Gateway. Fig. (**5**) represents an encryption process.

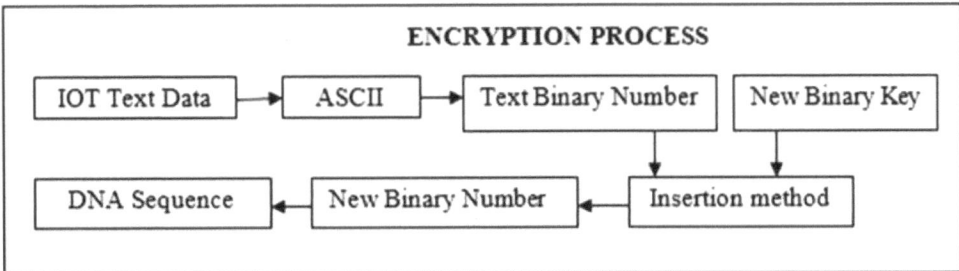

Fig. (5). Encryption process.

Decryption Process

The decryption process is the reversed process of encryption. In this, the receiver receives the DNA sequence and converts it to binary numbers. In those binary numbers, the key binary number is extracted from new binary numbers and the text binary number is returned. The binary number is converted to an ASCII value and to the original IoT text data. Fig. (**6**) represents a decryption process.

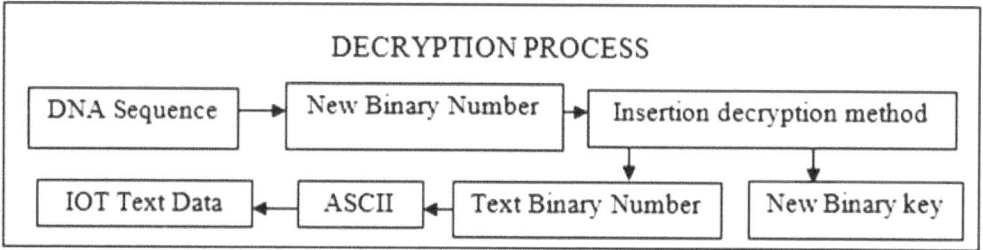

Fig. (6). Decryption process.

```
Algorithm 2: Encryption
Enc_alg(NDS):
Begin:
  1. DNA_enc(BN):
Begin:
        1. R ← read(PT || Image) // Read Plaintext.
        2. ST ← split(R)    //Split the plaintext string
        3. AS ← ASCII(ST)    // convert plaintext to ASCII values
        4. BN ← (AS)₂       // ASCII to Binary numbers
        5. return (BN)
End
  2. Insert_enc(BN):
     Begin:
        1. IN ← read(BN, SSB)  // Read BN and SSB
        2. BD ← (BN% k)  // BN in to segments with "k" number bits
        3. NBN ← insert(PB, DB)  // Insert BD into PB
        4. return (NBN)
  End:
  3. NDS ← DNA Code(NBN)
  4. return NDS
End:
```

Algorithm 3: Decryption
Dec_alg(PT):
Begin:
1. Rd ← read(NDS)
2. NBN ← (RD, DNAcode)
Insert_dec():
Begin:
1. $SE ← NBN\% k$ //k>=1<=n
2. SE1 ← extract(NBN, SBN)   //[remove SBN in NBN]
3. return (SE1)
End:
5. $AS ← (BN)_2$
6. $NPT ← chr(AS)$
7. $DNA\_Dec(PT):$
Begin:
1. $PT ← Chr(AS)$
2. $EI ← decode(AS)$
3. return (PT ‖ Image)
End:
End:

RESULTS AND DISCUSSION

The experimental results of the proposed system are presented in this section. The encryption and decryption outputs produced using the two levels of encryption are shown in the results. The proposed method is used to encrypt the text. The encryption simulation results are extremely noisy, indicating that no information about the corresponding original text can be retrieved from them. The proposed method provides good encryption results and is effective for encrypting text, according to the results of the proposed system.

As the key space of hybrid key generation is larger than 2218, it can easily prevent brute-force attacks. This large key space also supports resisting brute force attacks for a long period. Table **1** and Fig. (**7**) represent comparisons of the key space among the proposed hybrid method and other existing methods.

The Table **2** represents the Key entropy.

Table 1. Related works.

References	Cryptography Method	Techniques	Key Generation methods
A. Atito, A. Khalifa, & S. Z. Rida. (2012)	Asymmetric cryptography	Playfair, Insertion technique	Random
MandritaMondal (2017)	Asymmetric cryptography	DNA cryptography	Random
Animesh Hazra, Soumya Ghosh, & Sampad Jash. (2018)	Asymmetric cryptography	DNA cryptography	Random
M. Borda, O. Tornea (2010)	Symmetric cryptography	DNA cryptography, PCR	Random
L. XueJia, L. Mingxin (2010)	Asymmetric cryptography	DNA cryptography, PCR	Random
Deepak Kumar, Shailenda (2011)	Asymmetric cryptography	DNA cryptography, Biochip	Random
Z.yunpeng, Z. Yu (2011)	Symmetric cryptography	DNA Steganography	Random
M. Sabry, M. Hashem (2010)	Symmetric cryptography	AES, DNA cryptography	Random
B. Shimanovsky, J. Feng (2012)	Symmetric cryptography	Modify play-fair cipher, DNA cryptography	Random
H. I. Shiu, J. F. Fang (2010)	Asymmetric and Symmetric	Substitution, DNA cryptography	Random
S. Marwa, A. Shawi, K. Nagaty (2016)	Asymmetric and Symmetric cryptography	Modify Playfair cipher DNA Steganography	Random
Fasila, D. Antony (2014)	Symmetric cryptography	Matrix manipulation, DNA Steganography	Random
K. S. Sajisha, (2017)	Symmetric cryptography	AES, DNA Steganography,	Random
Alberto (2009)	Symmetric cryptography	DNA Cryptography, Fuzzy logic	Random
Ranbir (2010)	Asymmetric cryptography	DNA Cryptography, ECC	Random
Tatiana Hodoroge (2011)	Asymmetric cryptography	DNA Cryptography	Random
Zhang Yunpeng (2011)	Symmetric cryptography	DNA Cryptography	Random

(Table 1) cont.....

References	Cryptography Method	Techniques	Key Generation methods
Olga Tornea, Monica (2013)	Symmetric cryptography	DNA Cryptography	Random
Anchal Jain (2013)	Asymmetric cryptography	DNA Steganography	Random
Shipra Jain (2014)	Symmetric cryptography	DNA Cryptography.	Random
Sreeja C. S (2014)	Symmetric cryptography	Pseudo DNA cryptography	Random
Mona Sabry (2015)	Asymmetric cryptography	DNA cryptography	Random
AlaaKadhim (2016)	Asymmetric cryptography	DNA Cryptography	Random
Bismi Beegom (2017)	Asymmetric cryptography	RSA	Random
Md. Rafiu Biswas (2017)	Asymmetric cryptography	DNA Cryptography	Random
Ahgue (2018)	Symmetric cryptography	DNA Cryptography	Random
Zhang, Zhou, Niu (2018)	Symmetric cryptography	DNA Cryptography	Random
A. Khalifa, A. Atito (2012)	Asymmetric and Symmetric cryptography	Playfair-cipher DNA Steganography	Random

Table 2. Key entropy.

Existing Key						Hybrid Key					
Shift Key			Secret Key			Shift Key			Secret Key		
KS	LK	E	KS	LK	E	KS	LK	E	KS	LK	E
3.3	1.6	2.3	26.5	17.8	25.7	6.6	2.8	4.1	9.9	6.4	9.2
6.6	2.4	3.5	26.5	17.8	25.7	6.6	2.4	3.5	9.9	6.1	8.8
3.3	1.6	2.3	26.5	17.8	25.7	6.6	6.6	3.9	9.9	6.9	9.9
6.6	4.2	6.6	26.5	36.5	24.4	35.3	2.7	3.9	9.9	6.3	9.2
6.6	3.1	4.5	26.5	26.5	17.8	25.7	2.6	3.8	9.9	6.6	9.5
6.6	2.8	4.8	3.3	2.7	3.0	6.6	3.7	5.4	4.5	6.6	6.5
3.3	1.9	2.8	3.3	2.7	3.3	6.6	3.7	5.3	4.4	6.6	6.4
6.6	2.8	4.1	3.3	2.7	3.1	6.6	3.7	5.4	3.3	6.6	4.5
3.3	2.1	3.1	3.3	2.1	3.0	6.6	4.2	6.1	4.9	6.6	5.9

(Table 2) cont.....

Existing Key						Hybrid Key					
3.3	2.1	3.1	3.3	2.7	3.1	6.6	3.7	5.4	4.4	6.6	6.4
6.6	2.6	3.8	3.3	2.1	1.5	6.6	3.6	5.2	3.9	6.6	5.7
3.3	2.7	3.0	3.3	1.9	1.5	6.6	4.1	5.9	3.9	6.6	5.7
6.6	2.9	4.3	3.3	1.9	2.8	6.6	3.9	5.6	3.4	6.6	5.6

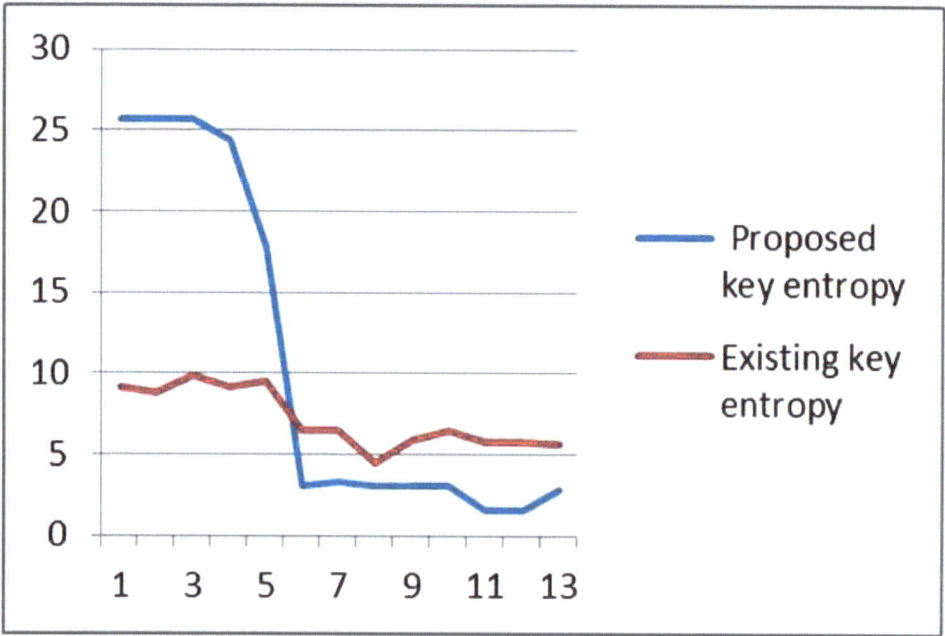

Fig. (7). Key entropy.

Table **3** shows that the encrypted data are completely different by lightly changing the encryption keys. However, in the existing schemes, the encrypted data are not completely different, when there are small changes in the secret key. This means that the secret keys are extremely sensitive in the proposed scheme.

Table 3. Avalanche effect.

Avalanche Effect											
Key Size		K1	K2	K3	K4	K5	K6	K7	K8	K9	K10
KB	PT										
	20	55	56	57	56	57	56	57	54	57	56
	51	56	58	58	57	59	59	59	57	59	60
	423	59	60	59	58	59	60	57	58	60	61
	664	60	61	60	57	58	59	60	59	57	60
	724	59	58	58	59	60	60	57	56	58	58
	752	60	58	58	58	56	59	58	58	60	56
MB	1.19	58	59	57	58	57	59	59	58	59	60
	5.43	58	59	58	58	59	58	58	59	57	58
	5.70	57	57	53	54	58	57	57	54	58	57
	8.59	56	54	57	58	53	57	56	53	55	58
GB	26.7	59	58	58	59	60	60	57	56	58	58
	46.5	60	58	58	58	56	59	58	58	60	56
	87.6	59	53	55	57	52	60	64	56	54	53

Table 4 shows the execution time for key generation, encryption and decryption. However, in the existing schemes, the encrypted data are not completely different when there are small changes in the secret key. This means that the secret keys are extremely sensitive in the proposed scheme.

Table 4. Execution time.

File in GB	DNA Sequence	Key Generation		Encryption time		Decryption Time	
	Existing	Existing	proposed	Existing	proposed	Existing	Proposed
20	41.16	2.59	15.1	82.	28.	93.	95.
51	165.8	2.78	35.7	85.	150	10	396
724	538.3	3.17	66.0	12	240	10	520
5.43	291.5	3.57	142.	17	441	13	161
26.7	1241.	5.12	201.	24	543	28	164

CONCLUSION AND FUTURE WORK

The leading neutral of this chapter was to develop the safety level of the material by using DNA cryptography. The future work is to encode the documents with a

DNA sequence and with an Insertion method procedure, the prime number and pseudorandom number for the key generation algorithm. The unauthorized individual cannot reach the unique information. This future work is to secure the text documents with a high level of surety by the quantity of key entropy values, avalanche effect and execution time.

REFERENCES

[1]   A. Rahaman, M. Islam, M. Islam, M. Sadi, and S. Nooruddin, "Developing IoT based smart health monitoring systems: A review", *Revue d'Intelligence Artificielle,* vol. 33, no. 6, pp. 435-440, 2019. [http://dx.doi.org/10.18280/ria.330605]

[2]   S.M. Riazul Islam, Daehan Kwak, M. Humaun Kabir, M. Hossain, and Kyung-Sup Kwak, "The internet of things for health care: A comprehensive survey", *IEEE Access,* vol. 3, pp. 678-708, 2015. [http://dx.doi.org/10.1109/ACCESS.2015.2437951]

[3]   T. Lin, H. Rivano, and F. Le Mouel, "A survey of smart parking solutions", *IEEE Trans. Intell. Transp. Syst.,* vol. 18, no. 12, pp. 3229-3253, 2017. [http://dx.doi.org/10.1109/TITS.2017.2685143]

[4]   A.R. Al-Ali, I.A. Zualkernan, M. Rashid, R. Gupta, and M. Alikarar, "A smart home energy management system using IoT and big data analytics approach", *IEEE Trans. Consum. Electron.,* vol. 63, no. 4, pp. 426-434, 2017. [http://dx.doi.org/10.1109/TCE.2017.015014]

[5]   A. Zanella, N. Bui, A. Castellani, L. Vangelista, and M. Zorzi, "Internet of Things for smart cities", *IEEE Internet Things J.,* vol. 1, no. 1, pp. 22-32, 2014. [http://dx.doi.org/10.1109/JIOT.2014.2306328]

[6]   G. Mois, S. Folea, and T. Sanislav, "Analysis of three IoT-based wireless sensors for environmental monitoring", *IEEE Trans. Instrum. Meas.,* vol. 66, no. 8, pp. 2056-2064, 2017. [http://dx.doi.org/10.1109/TIM.2017.2677619]

[7]   B. Chen, J. Wan, L. Shu, P. Li, M. Mukherjee, and B. Yin, "Smart factory of Industry 4.0: key technologies, application case, and challenges", *IEEE Access,* vol. 6, pp. 6505-6519, 2018. [http://dx.doi.org/10.1109/ACCESS.2017.2783682]

[8]   M. Ayaz, M. Ammad-Uddin, Z. Sharif, A. Mansour, and E.H.M. Aggoune, "Internet-of-Things (IoT)-based smart agriculture: toward making the felds talk", *IEEE Access,* vol. 7, pp. 129551-129583, 2019. [http://dx.doi.org/10.1109/ACCESS.2019.2932609]

[9]   M. Hasan, M.M. Islam, M.I.I. Zarif, and M.M.A. Hashem, "Attack and anomaly detection in IoT sensors in IoT sites using machine learning approaches", *Internet of Things,* vol. 7, p. 100059, 2019. [http://dx.doi.org/10.1016/j.iot.2019.100059]

[10]   S. Nooruddin, M. Milon Islam, and F.A. Sharna, "An IoT based device-type invariant fall detection system", *Internet of Things,* vol. 9, p. 100130, 2020. [http://dx.doi.org/10.1016/j.iot.2019.100130]

[11]   M Islam, N Neom, M Imtiaz, S Nooruddin, M Islam, and M. Islam, "A review on fall detection systems using data from smartphone sensors", *Ingénierie des systèmes d Inf.,* vol. 24, pp. 569-576, 2019. [http://dx.doi.org/10.18280/isi.240602]

[12]   S. Mahmud, X. Lin, J-H. Kim, H. Iqbal, M. Rahat-Uz-Zaman, S. Reza, and M.A. Rahman, "A multi-modal human machine interface for controlling a smart wheelchair", *2019 IEEE 7th conference on systems, process and control (ICSPC),* pp. 10-13, 2019. [http://dx.doi.org/10.1109/ICSPC47137.2019.9068027]

[13]   S. Mahmud, X. Lin, and J-H. Kim, "Interface for Human Machine Interaction for assistant devices: a

review", *2020 10th Annual computing and communication workshop and conference (CCWC),* pp. 768-773, 2020.
[http://dx.doi.org/10.1109/CCWC47524.2020.9031244]

[14]   X. Lin, S. Mahmud, E. Jones, A. Shaker, A. Miskinis, S. Kanan, and J-H. Kim, "Virtual reality-based musical therapy for mental health management", *2020 10th Annual Computing and Communication Workshop and Conference (CCWC)* Las Vegas, NV, USA, 2020, pp. 0948-0952.
[http://dx.doi.org/10.1109/CCWC47524.2020.9031157]

[15]   R. Rathipriya, and R. Vidhya, "Hybrid Key Generation for RSA and ECC", International Conference on Communication and Electronics Systems

[16]   E. Vidhya, and R. Rathipriya, "Key generation for dna cryptography using genetic operators and diffie-hellman key exchange algorithm", *Int. J. Math. Comput. Sci.,* vol. 15, no. 4, pp. 1109-1115, 2020.

[17]   E. Vidhya, and R. Rathipriya, "A study on unstructured data security issues", In: *IJIACS*, 2015, p. 61.

[18]   E. Vidhya, and R. Rathipriya, "Comparative Study of Hybrid RSA-ECC and Hybrid DNA-Insertion for Large Dataset", *Int. J. Grid Distrib. Comput.,* vol. 13, no. 1, pp. 2286-2303, 2020.

CHAPTER 9

Security Enhancement in Cloud and Edge Computing Through Blockchain Technology

Santanu Koley[1,*] and **Pinaki Pratim Acharjya**[1]

[1] *Department of CSE, Haldia Institute of Technology, Haldia -721607, India*

Abstract: The cloud computing (CC) network is designed to tackle the security and privacy challenges of centralized cloud services by distributing computing and storage resources among networked nodes. Cloud computing, on the other hand, is restricted by the performance of linked devices, posing problems in state authorization, stats encryption, consumer privacy and more. Blockchain technology (BT) is the most popular circulated network technology right now. It is utilized in numerous fields like bitcoin, IoT, *etc.*, to tackle the consistent issue of distributed data. The difficulties that CC networks present for security and privacy are covered in this chapter. Analysis and solutions brought to edge computing networks by BT in terms of data encryption, authentication and user privacy. In this chapter, the advantages of combining the cloud computing network with blockchain technology will be discussed. Finally, memory, workload, and latency problems for related future studies have been discussed.

Keywords: Blockchain, Cloud Computing, Security, Edge Computing.

INTRODUCTION

Service computing has seen an increasing number of applications in various areas recently. Topics include cloud computing, the digital economy, and the Internet of Things (IoT). The IoT is a good example. Through connected manufacturing of smart devices, healthcare, energy, and more, greater control can be achieved over the physical world, including industries. Despite its wide range of uses, there are some issues that need to be addressed to maximize its potential. Cloud computing is a service oriented architecture. In recent years, as the need for next-generation financial technology has increased, blockchain research is underway to enable the safe transaction.

Blockchain acts as a public ledger for transactions and protects against hackers when dealing with crypto currencies. It is a kind of distributed database, with an

---

[*] **Corresponding author Santanu Koley:** Department of CSE, Haldia Institute of Technology, Haldia -721607, India; Tel: 8944931442; E-mail: santanukoley@gmail.com

L. Ashok Kumar, D. Karthika Renuka, Sonali Agarwal & Sheng-Lung Peng (Eds.)

ever-expanding list of records, intended to prevent arbitrary manipulation by operators of distributed peers [1]. Blockchain software is installed on your computer to encrypt transaction records according to a set of rules. BT is used in electronic money, Bitcoin.

Comparing the use of blockchain with storing all data in a single database, the former can provide better security. Damage from database attacks can be avoided in terms of data storage and management. Furthermore, due to its openness attribute, blockchain [2] can provide data transparency when used in areas where data disclosure is required. These advantages allow it to be used in a variety of contexts, such as: Its potential applications could increase in the financial sector and IoT environment [3].

By consolidating transactions across the network into a single block, a digital currency lender completes a transaction record on the blockchain through a work-authentication process [4]. It is then verified and connected to the previous block to provide a hash value. This block will be updated periodically to reflect the electronic cash transaction information to convey the latest transaction details block. This procedure provides security for electronic currency exchanges while allowing the use of trustworthy mechanisms.

This chapter's sections are arranged as: Section 2 explains the fundamental ideas behind cloud computing. Section 3 explores privacy challenges in CC in more detail. The discussion on Blockchain and its benefits for security and privacy is in Section 4. Section 5 describes blockchain concepts. Section 6 elaborates on the concept of a secure solution for blockchain edge computing in cloud computing. In Section 7, it is discussed how blockchain adoption enhances edge computing security and privacy. Section 8 highlights the benefits of combining CC networks with BT. Finally, Section 9 concludes the study.

CLOUD COMPUTING

Transferring to the cloud, jogging through the clouds, these days, it seems like everything is taking place "on the cloud," whether it is being stored or accessed from there [5 - 10]. But what precisely is this hazy idea?

On the other end of the internet connection, there is a location where users may access apps and services and keep their data securely. The cloud is essential because of three things:

It does not require any effort to manage or maintain it. It should not worry about running out of space because its size is nearly infinite. Any device with an internet connection can be used to access cloud-based applications and services.

Fig. (**1**) depicts the cloud deployment model, which is a combination of private, public and hybrid cloud (combination of private and public). The server, storage and mobile devices attached as hardware components. Applications and databases are kept in separate software modules.

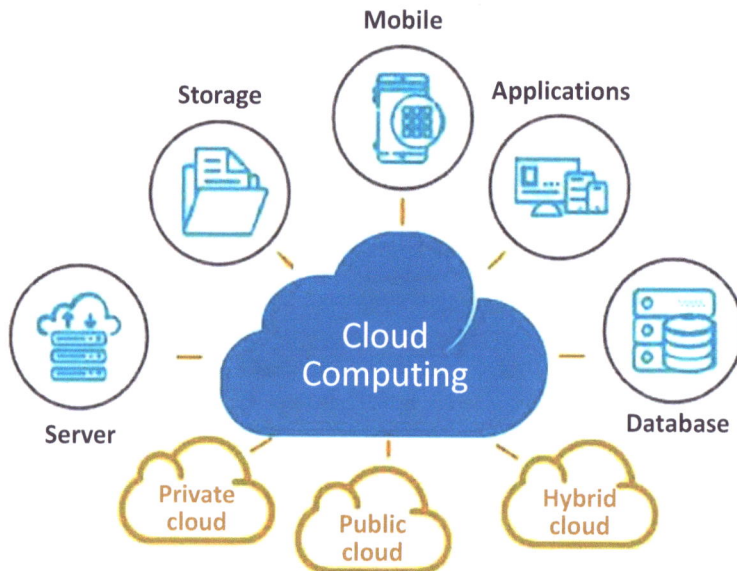

Fig. (1). Cloud Deployment Model.

Fig. (**2**) describes different parts of the cloud service model. This model is a mixture of diverse services of dissimilar software namely Software-as-a-Service (SaaS), the complete cloud platforms like H/W, S/W and infrastructure in lesser cost provided by Platform-as-a-Service (PaaS). Finally, Infrastructure-as-a-Service (IaaS) makes a variety of on-demand infrastructure services available to both enterprises and consumers *via* the cloud, including computing, storage, networking, and virtualization.

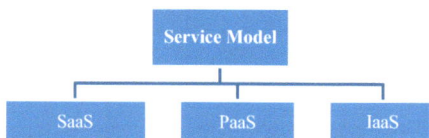

Fig. (2). Cloud Service Model.

PRIVACY CHALLENGES IN CLOUD COMPUTING

CC is an issue that is currently receiving attention from a variety of sectors, including academia, business, and research. It has become a hot topic at international conferences around the world. The vast amount of data processed and stored on computers is responsible for increasing employment opportunities. The convenience and simplicity of providing a large pool of shared computing resources is key to cloud concepts [10 - 16].

The rapid evolution of the cloud has increased product flexibility, cost efficiency and scalability, but it also poses significant privacy and security concerns. It's a relatively new concept and it's changing every day, so there are unknown vulnerabilities creeping in. These issues should be addressed as soon as they are identified. The top seven privacy concerns addressed by CC users are shown below.

Data Confidentiality Issues

Confidentiality of user data is an important consideration when outsourcing and offloading highly sensitive and sensitive data to cloud service providers. Persons without appropriate permissions should not be able to access personally identifiable information. Using strict access control policies and regulations is one way to ensure privacy. A major security risk that prevents many people from using cloud services is the lack of trust regarding data between users and cloud service providers or cloud database service providers.

Data Loss Issues

One of the biggest security issues facing cloud companies is data loss or data theft. Over 60% consumers refuse to use cloud services offered by providers if they have previously reported data loss or theft of critical or sensitive information. A loss of faith in these services at critical junctures was brought on by major failures in the cloud services of businesses like Dropbox, Microsoft, and Amazon. Furthermore, even if only one storage unit is hacked, it would be very easy for an attacker to access multiple storage units.

Geographical Data Storage Issues

Due to cloud infrastructure's global geographic distribution, users' data is frequently held in places that fall outside of their legal jurisdiction, which poses major accessibility issues as well as legal difficulties for users and local law enforcement. Data stored outside the region. The dynamic nature of the cloud makes it difficult for users to designate specific servers to use for cross-border data transfers, so users worry about violating local regulations.

Multi-Tenancy Security Issues

Multi-tenancy is the concept of distributing computing resources, data storage, applications, and services among numerous tenants. It is then hosted utilizing the same logical or physical platform at the cloud service provider's facilities. This strategy allows suppliers to maximize profits at the expense of their customers. Attackers can exploit the opportunity of having multiple apartments and launch a variety of attacks against other tenants, causing various privacy concerns.

Transparency Issues

The willingness of a cloud service provider to provide various details and characteristics on its level of security readiness is referred to as transparency in CC security. Some of these specifics violate security, privacy, and service level policies. When measuring transparency, it's crucial to include both willingness and disposition in addition to how easily accessible the data and information are regarding security readiness. No matter how readily available security information is, if it is not organized and presented in a way that cloud service customers and auditors can easily understand it, the organization's transparency can also be assessed as low.

Hypervisor Related Issues

The logical separation of computing resources from their physical constraints and limitations is known as virtualization. However, aspects such as user identification, billing and authorization face additional challenges. Hypervisors monitor large numbers of virtual machines, attracting the attention of adversaries. Virtual machines in the cloud typically reside on a single physical device controlled by the same hypervisor, as opposed to being independent of each other. Therefore, multiple virtual machines are at risk if the hypervisor is compromised. Additionally, hypervisor technology is new and provides features such as isolation, security hardening, and access control, increasing the opportunities for attackers to exploit systems.

Managerial Issues

Cloud privacy concerns come in technical and non-technical as well as administrative forms. Technical solutions to problems or products implemented without effective management will ultimately create vulnerabilities. Examples include lack of control, managing virtualization security and privacy, creating detailed service level agreements, and negotiating with cloud service providers and users.

BLOCKCHAIN

Blockchain is a hotly debated area of study. It records transactions [17 - 25] between users and resolves issues with the Byzantine Generals problem and inconsistent information consensus. The working procedure of a transaction through blockchain is shown in Fig. (**3**), where the entry of a new transaction is first requested, or the transaction itself. For each transaction, a different block is formed. Sending the block to each node, which guarantees the transaction's transmission to a global network of peer-to-peer computers, is the next task. The transaction's legitimacy is verified by this peer network of computers. The reward received by nodes must then be obtained in order to verify that genuine transactions are grouped into blocks. Eventually, the transaction is successfully completed after the blocks are chained together to provide a lengthy history of all transactions. Smart contracts, which are built on the blockchain platform, have made it possible to implement decentralization, automatic execution, and other features, enhancing the field of blockchain research and application. As an example, take the crypto-currency and BT, such as Bitcoin and Ethereum.

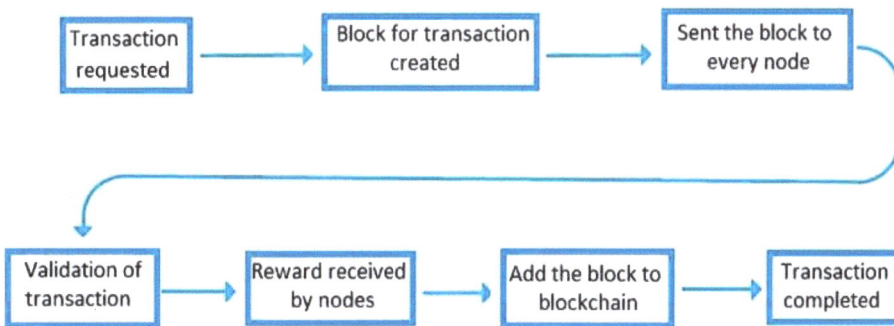

Fig. (3). The process by which a transaction enters the Blockchain.

Blockchain Introduces Benefits for Security and Privacy

With the distributed design of edge computing, BT enables a reliable method of communication between unreliable computer nodes. Three layers are usual for an edge network. Small sensors and gadgets make up the bottom tier, small servers with limited computing and storage power make up the middle tier (also known as cloudlets), and enormous data centres are constructed at the top. Because blockchain consensus methods have a significant processing cost and the underlying tiny devices perform poorly, blockchains are often hosted across numerous cloudlets in a central location [26 - 31].

Edge computing networks can be shielded from these dangers using BT. Similar to write permissions, read permissions can also be kept in blockchain blocks without the need for a central administrator to verify permissions, ensuring that users and local nodes are aware of how each server can access global data. Following is a description of an illustration of the community detection and blockchain-based data-sharing framework interaction process (Fig. **4**). Initialization, identity authorization, signature and verification, and data transfer are the four stages of the interaction process. Here, without the need to start a central node, programmatic operations distributed across nodes can be automatically implemented by decentralized smart contracts.

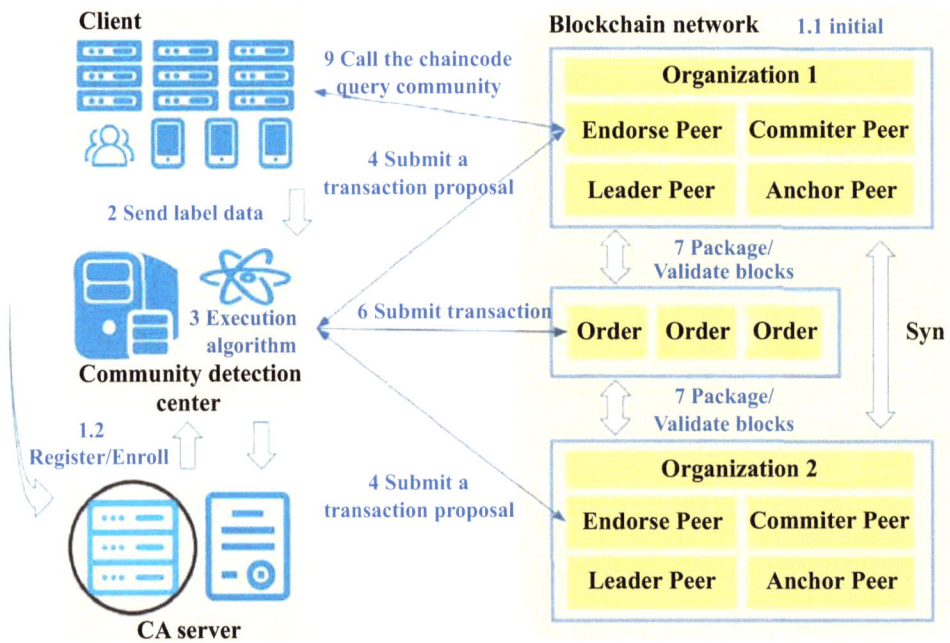

Fig. (4). Blockchain with detection and data layer [32].

BLOCKCHAIN RESEARCH AREAS FROM A SECURITY AND PRIVACY PERSPECTIVE

This section analyses the enhancements that BT makes to edge computing by summarizing some of the applications where it is used and by combining research cases.

Healthcare

Today, there is a demand for high-quality healthcare facilities that are supported by newer, more modern technologies. In this situation, Blockchain would be essential to revolutionising the healthcare industry. Additionally, the structure of the healthcare system is changing in favour of a patient-centered strategy that emphasises two key elements: readily available services and adequate healthcare resources at all times. Blockchain improves healthcare organisations' ability to deliver enough patient care and top-notch medical facilities. Another time-consuming, repetitive activity that raises expenses in the health industry is health information exchange, which may be resolved swiftly with the use of this technology. Participants in health research programmes can use Blockchain technology. Better research and data sharing on public wellness will also improve therapy for various populations. The management of the entire healthcare system and organisations is done through a single database. The three biggest issues in population health management up to this point have been data security, sharing, and interoperability. Blockchain technology makes this specific issue dependable. When used properly, this technology improves real-time updating, access, security, interoperability, data interchange, and integrity. Significant worries regarding data protection also exist, particularly in the areas of wearable technology and customised medicine. Blockchain technology is used to address these problems since patients and medical professionals need simple, secure ways to capture, send, and consult data *via* networks without security concerns.

Internet of Things

It is challenging to build trustworthy connections in this network because IoT devices and computing nodes do not trust one another. A distributed ledger on the blockchain is one practical choice [33]. Through an untrusted network, this keeps up a trustworthy communication relationship. However, IoT programme operations can be managed without the assistance of a central control node using decentralised and automatically deployed smart contracts [34]. The smart contract's output is then saved in the block. Program output and flow that are consistent prohibit questionable practices and ensure data security.

Vehicular Cloudlet

Automobiles distinguish themselves from other IoT devices by virtue of their mobility and spatiotemporal sensitivity. When moving vehicles are involved, it is extremely difficult to maintain data integrity and accuracy. Vehicles can instantly connect to the network, communicate in an encrypted fashion, and synchronize accurate vehicle data [35] to the blockchain consensus system by using the Roadside Unit.

Payment and Loan

The major application of BT is a digital currency with encryption. However, regular networks and servers are used to process the mining activity and transactions for digital currencies. The system's economy and mobility are improved through the inclusion of edge computing frameworks. The deployed smart contract can carry out automatic lending of money and transactions involving computing resources [36].

Privacy-Preserved Tracking

The system can gather more information and accurately forecast the general trend of users' movement by using the tracking function to characterize the user's movement trajectory. In order to lessen the sensitivity of the data while retaining accuracy, extra approaches are required because uploading raw user data into the system infringes privacy. User privacy must be protected by maintaining anonymity in the blockchain ecosystem, and the decentralized execution of smart contracts is essential to prevent malicious activity [37, 38].

BLOCKCHAIN IN HEALTHCARE

Beyond technological hurdles, building a strong hardware and network infrastructure is also necessary for the accomplishment of blockchain within the healthcare segment. Providentially, nowadays, with ICT structure, large companies offer specialised goods and services or specialised tools, greatly lowering the competent challenges. In order to safeguard patients' medical information from unauthorised access, blockchain networks are widely used in healthcare systems. Healthcare systems, however, face a number of security concerns, including inter-operability, accuracy, data distribution, and transmission of healthcare data, as a result of the absence of competent security measure design. Additionally, because there are so many hardware devices being developed, deployment and data management are the key blockchain in healthcare concerns.

Healthcare Implementation Using Blockchain

The term "health and medical data" refers to information gathered about patient care during the course of patient care and personal health prevention. Medical records and computing technology are integrated into the structure, which is a distributed structure. The three elements that make up the system are data service, data security, and data collecting. The data compilation section is utilised to gather medical data, the safety unit to create a defence system for the healthcare system, and the service unit to fulfil patient needs for healthcare related data.

The data service module, according to the aforementioned technical solution, consists of a data analysis module, a history case unit, a health supervision unit, and a patient evaluation unit. Comparing the medical and health information of patients with information from the blockchain research of medical associations that was carried out utilizing the data analysis module. The past healing of patients is kept in a historical case module. The patient assessment unit offers a stage for patients to assess medical associations, while the health supervision unit offers a stage for healthcare organisations to offer rehabilitative direction to patients.

The steps below make up one operational method for a blockchain-based system for sharing medical data:

Step 1: The mechanism for sharing medical data is employed to gather digital information while the patient is recovering.

Step 2: Safeguard and securely upload the EHR to the healthcare blockchain.

Step 3: Analyse the data saved on the blockchain and compare it to the newly created EHR. Then, upload the results.

Step 4: Creating the patient assessment stage.

Step 5: Adding the patient assessment stage to the healthcare blockchain.

EDGE COMPUTING

Edge computing is a distributed computing concept that moves computation and data storage closer to the data source. This reduces bandwidth usage and improves response time [39]. It's an architecture, not a specific technology [40]. This is a kind of distributed computing that depends on topology and location.

When content distribution networks were created in the late 1990s to transmit web and video material from edge servers near the consumer, the idea of edge computing was initially promoted. Early in the new millennium, networks were created that hosted applications, including store locators, shopping carts, real-time data aggregators, and search engines for inserting adverts [41]. An application edge server and its component applications are the end product. Fig. (**5**) depicts a use case for edge computing. In many instances, it would be incredibly beneficial to handle data on the device where it's generated. That's where edge computing comes in. Edge computing helps decentralize data processing and lower dependence on the cloud, as shown in Fig. (**5**).

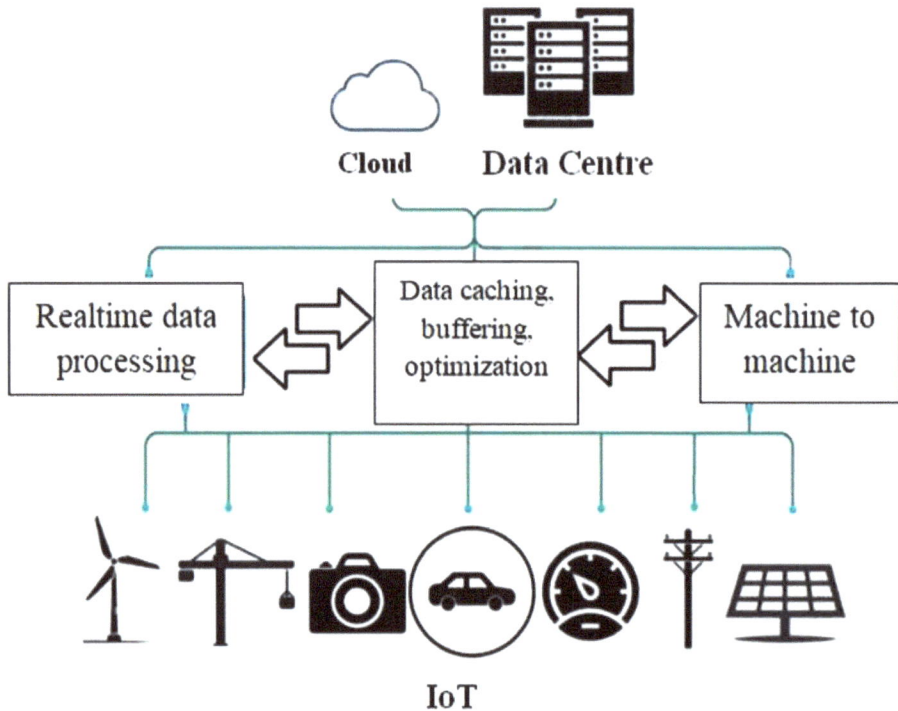

Fig. (5). Use cases for Edge Computing.

An instance of edge computing use cases is the IoT. The idea that edge and IoT are interchangeable is a popular one [42].

Any type of computer software that achieves minimal latency close to your requirements is considered to be an example of edge computing. Edge computing is everything that takes place at the network's edge, according to Karim Arabi, who first defined it in his IEEE DAC 2014 keynote speech [43] and later in his 2015 invited address at his MTL seminar at MIT [44]. It broadly referred to as non-cloud computing, more particularly in situations when real-time data processing is necessary. By definition, edge computing deals with "immediate data," or real-time data created by users and sensors, whereas CC deals with massive data. Fog computing and the phrase are frequently used interchangeably [45]. Edge computing concentrates on servers "near to the last mile network". This is according to the State of the Edge research. Anything that isn't a conventional data centre might be a "edge," according to Alex Reznik, Chair of the ETSI MEC ISG Standards Group [46]. A gamelet is an edge node used for game streaming that is typically 1-2 hops away from the client. In order to achieve real-time gaming reaction time requirements in cloud gaming situations, edge nodes are frequently one or two hops away from mobile clients, according to Anand and Edwin [47, 48]. Edge computing can benefit from virtualization technologies to make it easier to build and run a variety of applications on edge servers.

APPLYING BLOCKCHAIN IN EDGE COMPUTING TO IMPROVE SECURITY AND PRIVACY

An edge computing framework based on BT is generally shown in Fig. (6). It can consist of three layers. Edge devices that serve as data sources are found at the bottom user layer, whereas edge nodes with constrained processing and storage resources are found in the central edge layer. Most designs use huge data centres that act as a cloud layer on top of which they assume the role of blockchain miners, ensuring block synchronization and smart contract execution.

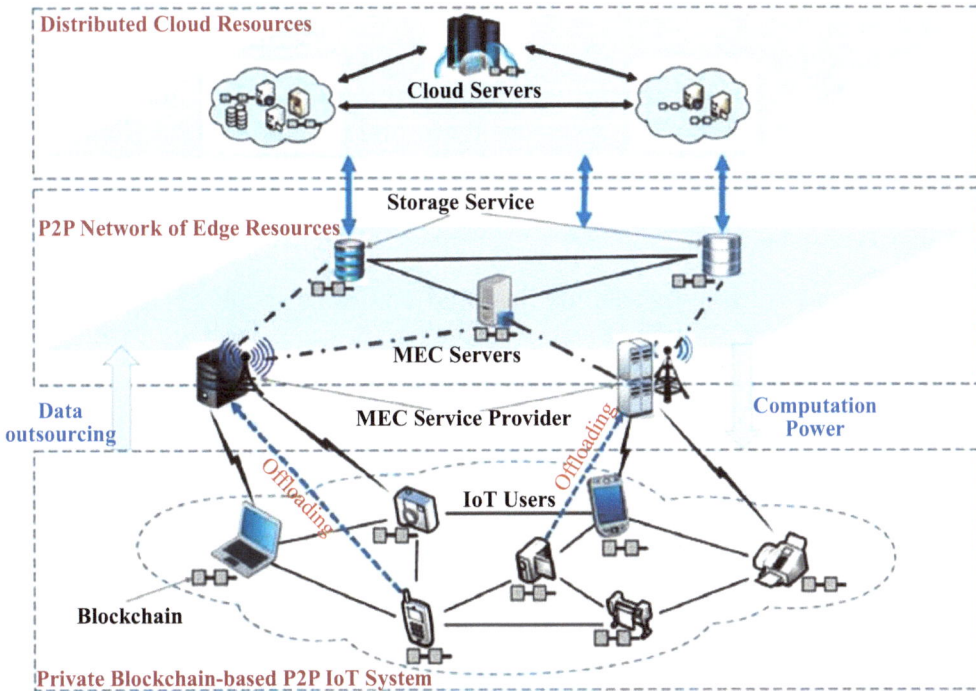

Fig. (6). Blockchain-based IoT framework with edge computing [69].

A blockchain-based edge computing system typically operates according to the following workflow. First off, the bottom edge devices offer activity information, including peer and edge node interactions. Middle edge nodes then validate this data and insert it into blocks using the blockchain's consensus algorithm. The necessary structural analysis and management is performed by the top-level main data center. The viability and benefits of edge computing systems built on blockchains from a security and privacy standpoint have been examined.

Anonymity

Anonymity is a crucial strategy for safeguarding users' and devices' identities in a distributed edge network environment. Devices can use smart contracts to verify their identities without revealing their identities to the server, and use the edge node server as an intermediary to send information. The secure and dependable connection between edge network devices and on-premises cloudlets depends on the entire design.

Top-level nodes in edge networks receive data from underlying devices. Information to identify underlying devices shouldn't be made available to other insecure networks. First-tier edge devices have a framework for centrally managing [49] and registering these underlying devices, and controlling communication and processing between these underlying devices. However, in such a plan, the layer 1 edge device acts as a local registry collector for the edge network. The anonymity of locally registered devices disappears as soon as collectors reveal these identifiers.

Blockchain gives the system anonymity and can make edge network devices' identities secret. Wang [50] suggested a blockchain-based strategy for verifying anonymous identities.

Authentication

In an edge network environment where device-generated data can travel across regions, it is necessary to manage device identities and data read and write permissions.

According to Wang's protocol [50], smart contract execution is a prerequisite for edge entity registration and data authorization [51]. Because only the registrar can link a device's genuine identity to its public key, authentication and communication between devices are safe [52]. Edge authentication of the system is supported by the dynamic domain name resolution approach proposed by Guo [53]. Blockchain is used to store domain name-related data for hedge terminals, and asymmetric cryptography technology based on elliptic curve cryptography is used to support communication between terminals. Similar to this, Jangirala's [54] light-weight blockchain-based identity verification protocol enables devices to authenticate one another and create a session key, effectively ensuring user identity privacy.

Protocol Security

More difficult and practical security challenges are present in the blockchain-based protocol design. All scenarios and requirements cannot be covered by a protocol design. For instance, it can be difficult to ensure identity in a lightweight protocol is untraceable. Therefore examine the protocol's security measures in light of particular scenarios. Jangirala [52] presented a lightweight RFID-based authentication protocol that supports blockchain that provides sufficient bandwidth for real-time data. The protocol is easy to use and balances communication and computational costs. A more universal, self-evolving, and spontaneous distributed network that is not limited to specific use cases. This network's Blockchain introduces Proof of Relay as an innovation in place of Proof of Work. This network can withstand different attacks like the Double Spend Attack and Denial-of-Service Attacks while consuming less energy and performing better, ensuring network security.

Security and Privacy in Architecture

There is also a need to demonstrate how blockchain contributes to edge fabric security and privacy from an architectural design perspective, in addition to the above protocol perspectives and specific application implementations. BT and mobile edge networks serve as the foundation of Rathore's decentralized network security architecture [55]. Blockchain can identify decentralized attacks, preventing the architecture from collapsing because of the failure of a single node.

Data Security

Using the term "data security" and examples from relevant case studies, the benefit factors of edge networks with blockchaining are—confidentiality, integrity, and availability—reflect the security of data. These three elements have more specific definitions in our scenario [56].

• **Confidentiality:** Data access is restricted to users who have the key that is encrypted and safeguarded at the edge node.

• **Integrity:** The consensus process of the edge node data in a distributed blockchain-based system must be resistant to attacks like Sybil and 51 percent attacks.

• **Availability:** Edge devices and top layer cloud services should always be able to access data thanks to edge nodes.

Confidentiality

For users to access data on edge nodes, an effective method of implying identity authentication is required. For the trading system, Ren [57] developed an identity authentication technique in which user identities are maintained in blocks to ensure data integrity and prevent tampering.

Integrity

The Proof of Work and Proof of Stake consensus methods used in the past require a lot of computer power. Inefficient hardware performance on edge devices or nodes makes it neither viable nor cost-effective to use them. Checking the device's repute is another technique to decide whether to write device data to blocks [58].

Availability

The availability of data has been significantly impacted by the heterogeneity of edge computing networks. Through software assistance and hardware virtualization techniques, it may harmonize communication between various edge network layers [59].

User Privacy

According to this work's definition of user privacy, data mining and cyber attacks do not reveal a user's identity or sensitive information [60]. Edge devices need to control who receives data, what data is sent to edge nodes, and how data is validated using encryption. How blockchain-based data encryption technology protects user privacy has been discussed. On both the Bitcoin and Ethereum systems, the Elliptic Curve Digital Signature Algorithm (ECDSA) [61] is a well-liked algorithm. Blockchain intrinsic cryptography provides users with digital signatures to verify and authenticate encrypted data without revealing the raw content. The needs of new situations, such as lowering computational costs for resource-constrained IoT devices, necessitate the use of lightweight bespoke protocols for applications like industrial IoT detection and outdoor drone data synchronization. The requirements of typical computer applications can be satisfied by these native cryptography techniques. Instead of using conventional encryption techniques, users can encrypt identities and sensitive data using the blockchain transaction system, attaining data security and offering privacy features.

In order to safeguard user privacy, eliminating identities and trajectory data is also an encryption technique. Identifiers and sensitive information that can be used to deduce the identities of users should be removed or replaced with noise before the source data is published. Social media platforms are highly popular today, and third companies track user activity on them and analyze data.

Despite the fact that each user's genuine identity is concealed, there is a distinct pattern to their activity that may be seen. This encryption strategy presents another potential problem. Strong anonymity reduces source data's usefulness and renders the information useless. Blockchain offers a compromise between usability and the encryption of critical data. The operating architecture of the smart grid was created by Keke [62, 63]. He employed pseudonyms to identify users in order to protect their real identities.

ADVANTAGES OF COMBINING THE CLOUD COMPUTING NETWORK WITH BLOCKCHAIN TECHNOLOGY

The utilization of BT in CC is one of the most innovative developments that is constantly being improved. Numerous industries exercise their storage on clouds. The BT is factored into the blend; the prospective consequences might completely upend certain industries. BT was utilised to generate Bitcoin, which receives the majority of media concentration. BT can be used in CC applications to manage and govern vast volumes of data in more accessible and secure ways. The various attributes of Blockchain, such as decentralization, transparency, and security, have made it a very significant and revolutionary technology for the current generation of numerous industrial applications.

One of those areas, the Cloud of Things, is made possible through a partnership between Iot and CC. Blockchain has shown to be an incredibly important solution that, through decentralization, may address the problems with the Cloud of Things, gives data privacy, and delivers network security. The scalability and adaptability of the Cloud of Things contribute to boosting the overall efficacy of blockchain operations. Therefore, combining blockchain and the Cloud of Things is quite advantageous. This technique, also known as BCoT, is currently thought to have several interesting industrial applications. This section describes and lists several important advantages of combining BT with CC.

Cloud Computing with Hyperledger Blockchains

Collaboration with "The Linux Foundation" resulted to the creation of the BT platform Hyperledger as open-source software. When there are distributed copies of a single BT record, it is farther complex to update data in an unauthorized way.

An accurate audit trail is produced by peer-to-peer networks used for decentralized record-keeping.

CC allows for the sharing of these records, and many parties can each keep a duplicate or a portion of it for audit verification. Contrary to cryptocurrencies, the hyper ledger's users have neither need nor desire for privacy. In practice, a small, acknowledged set of authorized users can be created using particular hyper ledger technologies.

Efficient Ownership Tracking

When BT and CC are joined, numerous occasions for further resourceful supervision of important stuff, such as stock ownership, real estate titles, and legal agreements of all types, are generated. For instance, the present, antiquated stock transfer clearing process through a Depository Trust Company (DTC), which takes three to six days to process, might be significantly sped up by using CC technologies to operate a hyper ledger system. These transfers might take place in just a few microseconds using hyper ledger blockchains or cloud storage. There are already active Hyperledger projects to enhance this procedure.

Decentralization

Many prospects for more effective management of valuable items, such as stock ownership, real estate titles, and legal agreements of all types, are created when BT and CC are combined. For instance, the present, antiquated stock transfer clearing process through a Depository Trust Company (DTC), which takes three to six days to process, might be significantly accelerated with the use of CC technologies administering a hyper ledger system. These transfers might take place in just a few microseconds using hyper ledger blockchains or cloud storage. There are already active Hyperledger projects to enhance this procedure.

Increased Data Security

IoT data storage in the cloud presents a significant challenge because it frequently contains the personal information of the homeowner, such as video footage, voice recordings, household goods, property, and personal habits. Personal security may be compromised if these details are made public, which could lead to theft, violence, and the unauthorized sale of personal data. These elements endanger the cloud infrastructure. The usage of blockchain in CC offers a solution to this issue and has the ability to increase the security of the entire architecture.

Fault Tolerance

In a network of computing devices that are firmly connected to one another by collaborative clouds, blockchain data can be duplicated over the cloud. This will enable for the preservation of services by lowering the chances of a single failure brought on by the disruption of any cloud node.

Scalability

Large-scale blockchain applications can result in very high transaction volumes in blockchain networks. Scalable blockchain services require reliable data processing services with high transaction execution rates. Due to its ability to grow, the cloud can offer blockchain activities the on-demand computational power they need. Therefore, a highly scalable integrated system can be produced by combining CC and blockchain.

Faster Disaster Recovery

BT makes it possible to widely share a transaction history. The fact that a blockchain is shared or made accessible to several authorized users is what makes it so beneficial. Failure of any network node has no effect on the subsequent blockchain iterations. Even when a node is offline, the remaining nodes carry on updating the blockchain. Any network node that encounters a failure can quickly catch up to the current blockchain database status when the node comes online thanks to the transactional record of the blockchain entries, especially if they include a secure timestamp.

Micro Transactions

The capacity and utility of CC systems to complete fewer transactions increases as their cost decreases. If the transaction's reward is more than its execution costs, blockchain nodes can only benefit very little. For instance, the cost of processing has made Bitcoin mining difficult. It is not economically feasible to mine Bitcoins if the cost of the required resources (utilities, processing power, *etc.*) exceeds the value of the currency. The need to manage programmes across an entire virtual server has been eliminated by the development of CC. Advanced CC just requires virtual servers that replicate the essential components of the operating system to process applications. Processing costs for CC are declining as a result of this trend. Micro transactions are now more practical as a result.

Distributed Supercomputing

Using millions of independent computer nodes, BT for CC enables the building of enormous computing platforms that mimic supercomputers. For projects requiring a significant amount of computer processing, the calculations can be divided, controlled, and distributed to the nodes in a cooperative effort, with each node getting paid according to its contribution to the proof of work. As BT develops in its connection with CC, powerful new applications for collaborative processing, edge-computational requirements for the IoT, and decentralized data storage are all actively growing.

Smartening Healthcare Sector

In the healthcare [64] industry, BCoT offers a lot of potential applications for upgrading and streamlining existing practices. Medical institutions and organizations are included in the healthcare [65] sector. The industry mostly deals with healthcare-related services, and medical devices, including ventilators, insurance, and other connected items. BCoT can address critical market issues in terms of security and service efficacy. It is possible to provide new intelligent services, such as CoT enabled Health data sharing, with the aid of BCoT integration in the healthcare industry. These services can create effective environments for exchanging healthcare data and reduce the amount of time needed for communication between connected devices and between patient devices and physicians. The use of Machine learning [66, 67] in the case of the Internet of Medical Things [68] is another upcoming chapter in smart healthcare systems.

Smart Manufacturing

A developing area where BCoT can contribute is smart manufacturing. The use of automated machines that can carry out particular jobs far more intelligently than current equipment is related to smart manufacturing. IoT, cloud manufacturing, and service-oriented manufacturing are the cornerstones of this sector. Centralized industrial networks and third-party-based authority are problems that smart manufacturing must address, nonetheless, given the existing environment. Lower flexibility, efficiency, and security are caused by centralized production designs. A potential response to these issues consists of the implementation of BCoT, which can improve security and establish a decentralized architecture.

CONCLUSION AND FUTURE WORK

Through the users who collectively store the transaction records and, ultimately, approve the transactions using P2P network technology, a Blockchain has eliminated the server to remove the function of the central authority. The distributed nature of the Blockchain makes use of the peer network and computational capacity of peers. Technical techniques like proof of work and proof of stack have been implemented to strengthen the security of Blockchain.

Blockchain security is continually being improved, however problems have remained and security research is always ongoing. An attacker tries multiple times to obtain a user's personal key, which is kept on the user's computer or Smartphone, in order to hack Bitcoin. The usage of a secure token or the safe storage of the personal key has both been studied.

A safe Blockchain usage and removal protocol was offered in this study to demonstrate how security is provided. It would seem that efficiency research is also necessary in addition to security research, given the environment in which a significant amount of information is exchanged.

ACKNOWLEDGEMENTS

The authors acknowledge the constant inspiration and encouragement from Professor (Dr.) Subhankar Joardar, Professor and HoD, Department of Computer Science and Engineering, Haldia Institute of Technology, West Bengal, India.

AUTHOR CONTRIBUTIONS

Pinaki Pratim Acharjya participated in the research, analysis, and writing of the article. Taking full responsibility of the documentation, review, comments, appraisal, *etc.* was Santanu Koley.

REFERENCES

[1]   M.S. Ali, M. Vecchio, M. Pincheira, K. Dolui, F. Antonelli, and M.H. Rehmani, "Applications of blockchains in the internet of things: A comprehensive survey", *IEEE Commun. Surv. Tutor.*, vol. 21, no. 2, pp. 1676-1717, 2019.
[http://dx.doi.org/10.1109/COMST.2018.2886932]

[2]   I-C. Lin, and T-C. Liao, "A survey of blockchain security issues and challenges", *Int. J. Netw. Secur.*, vol. 19, no. 5, pp. 653-659, 2017.

[3]   Z. Zheng, S. Xie, H.N. Dai, X. Chen, and H. Wang, "Blockchain challenges and opportunities: a survey", *Int. J. Web Grid Serv.*, vol. 14, no. 4, pp. 352-375, 2018.
[http://dx.doi.org/10.1504/IJWGS.2018.095647]

[4]   Z. Zheng, S. Xie, and H. Dai, "An overview of blockchain technology: architecture, consensus, and future trends", *IEEE 6th International Congress on Big Data,* IEEEIEEE: Honolulu, HI, USAPiscataway, NJ, USA, pp. 557-564, 2017.
[http://dx.doi.org/10.1109/BigDataCongress.2017.85]

[5]   S.B. Bele, "A Comprehensive Study on Cloud Computing", *International Journal of Information Research and Review.*, vol. 05, no. 03, pp. 5310-5313, 2018.

[6]   L. Conway, "The 10 most important cryptocurrencies other than bitcoin", Available from : https://www.investopedia.com/tech/most-important-cryptocurrencies-other-than-bitcoin/

[7]   A. Almutairi, M. Sarfraz, S. Basalamah, W. Aref, and A. Ghafoor, "A distributed access control architecture for cloud computing", *IEEE Softw.*, vol. 29, no. 2, pp. 36-44, 2012.
[http://dx.doi.org/10.1109/MS.2011.153]

[8]   K. Deepika, N.N. Prasad, S. Balamurugan, and S. Charanyaa, "Evolution of cloud computing: A state-

of-the-art survey", *Int. J. Innov. Res. Comput. Commun. Eng.,* vol. 3, no. 1, pp. 174-179, 2015.

[9]   T. Devi, and R. Ganesan, "Platform-as-a-service (paas): Model and security issues", *IJAAS,* vol. 15, no. 1, 2015.

[10]   J. Feng, and Y. Chen, "A fair non-repudiation framework for data integrity in cloud storage services", *Int. J. Cloud Comput.,* vol. 2, no. 1, pp. 20-47, 2013.
[http://dx.doi.org/10.1504/IJCC.2013.050954]

[11]   R. Giunta, F. Messina, G. Pappalardo, and E. Tramontana, "Enhancing applications with cloud services by means of aspects", *Int. J. Comput. Appl. Technol.,* vol. 51, no. 4, pp. 273-282, 2015.
[http://dx.doi.org/10.1504/IJCAT.2015.070490]

[12]   V.O. Gupta, and Y. Rai, "A survey paper: Threats and vulnerability in cloud computing", *National Conference Convergence,* vol. 2015, p. 28, 2015.

[13]   A. Srinivasan, M.A. Quadir, and V. Vijayakumar, "Era of cloud computing: a new insight to hybrid cloud", *Procedia Comput. Sci.,* vol. 50, pp. 42-51, 2015.
[http://dx.doi.org/10.1016/j.procs.2015.04.059]

[14]   W. Sun, W. Lou, Y.T. Hou, and H. Li, Privacy-preserving keyword search over encrypted data in cloud computing.*Secure Cloud Computing.,* S. Jajodia, Ed., Springer, 2015, pp. 189-212.

[15]   J. Kumar, S. Chaisiri, and R. Ko, *Data Security in Cloud Computing* The Institution of Engineering and Technology: London, United Kingdom, 2017.

[16]   J. Viega, "Cloud computing and the common man", *Computer,* vol. 42, no. 7, p. 3, 2009.
[http://dx.doi.org/10.1109/MC.2009.206]

[17]   A. Prashanth Joshi, M. Han, and Y. Wang, "A survey on security and privacy issues of blockchain technology", *Mathematical Foundations of Computing,* vol. 1, no. 2, pp. 121-147, 2018.
[http://dx.doi.org/10.3934/mfc.2018007]

[18]   X. Li, P. Jiang, T. Chen, X. Luo, and Q. Wen, "A survey on the security of blockchain systems", *Future Gener. Comput. Syst.,* vol. 107, pp. 841-853, 2020.
[http://dx.doi.org/10.1016/j.future.2017.08.020]

[19]   E.J. De Aguiar, B.S. Faiçal, B. Krishnamachari, and J. Ueyama, "A survey of blockchain- based strategies for healthcare", *ACM Comput. Surv.,* vol. 53, no. 2, pp. 1-27, 2021.
[http://dx.doi.org/10.1145/3376915]

[20]   H.T.M. Gamage, H.D. Weerasinghe, and N.G.J. Dias, "A survey on blockchain technology concepts, applications, and issues", *SN Computer Science,* vol. 1, no. 114, 2020.

[21]   D. Berdik, S. Otoum, N. Schmidt, D. Porter, and Y. Jararweh, "A survey on blockchain for information systems management and security", *Inf. Process. Manage.,* vol. 58, no. 1, p. 102397, 2021.
[http://dx.doi.org/10.1016/j.ipm.2020.102397]

[22]   S. Zhang, and J.H. Lee, "Analysis of the main consensus protocols of blockchain", *ICT Express,* vol. 6, no. 2, pp. 93-97, 2020.
[http://dx.doi.org/10.1016/j.icte.2019.08.001]

[23]   A.M. Antonopoulos, *Mastering Bitcoin* O'Reilly Media: Sebastopol, CA, USA, 2017.

[24]   W. Chen, Z. Xu, S. Shi, Y. Zhao, and J. Zhao, "A survey of blockchain applications in different domains", *International Conference on Blockchain Technology and Applications (ICBTA) New York, NY, USA,* ACM: Xi'an, China, pp. 17-21, 2018.
[http://dx.doi.org/10.1145/3301403.3301407]

[25]   D. Dave, S. Parikh, R. Patel, and N. Doshi, "A survey on blockchain technology and its proposed solutions", *Procedia Comput. Sci.,* vol. 160, pp. 740-745, 2019.
[http://dx.doi.org/10.1016/j.procs.2019.11.017]

[26]   A.A. Monrat, O. Schelen, and K. Andersson, "A survey of blockchain from the perspectives of applications, challenges, and opportunities", *IEEE Access,* vol. 7, pp. 117134-117151, 2019. [http://dx.doi.org/10.1109/ACCESS.2019.2936094]

[27]   W. Meng, E.W. Tischhauser, Q. Wang, Y. Wang, and J. Han, "When intrusion detection meets blockchain technology: a review", *IEEE Access,* vol. 6, pp. 10179-10188, 2018. [http://dx.doi.org/10.1109/ACCESS.2018.2799854]

[28]   V. Jesus, "Cloud computing enabling the future internet", *1st International Conference on Cloud Computing Munich, Germany,* pp. 19-21, 2009.

[29]   S. Walther Dane, "Akamai and Cloud Computing", *1st International Conference on Cloud Computing Munich, Germany,* pp. 19-21, 2009.

[30]   J. Chi, Y. Li, J. Huang, J. Liu, Y. Jin, C. Chen, and T. Qiu, "A secure and efficient data sharing scheme based on blockchain in industrial Internet of Things", *J. Netw. Comput. Appl,* vol. 167, p. 102710, 2020. [http://dx.doi.org/10.1016/j.jnca.2020.102710]

[31]   J. Leng, P. Jiang, K. Xu, Q. Liu, J.L. Zhao, Y. Bian, and R. Shi, "Makerchain: A blockchain with chemical signature for self-organizing process in social manufacturing", *J. Clean. Prod.,* vol. 234, pp. 767-778, 2019. [http://dx.doi.org/10.1016/j.jclepro.2019.06.265]

[32]   V. Urovi, V. Jaiman, A. Angerer, and M. Dumontier, "A secure and efficient data sharing scheme based on blockchain in industrial Internet of Things", *J. Netw. Comput. Appl.,* vol. 167, p. 102710, 2020. [http://dx.doi.org/10.1016/j.jnca.2020.102710]

[33]   Eric Hamilton, "LUCE: A blockchain-based data sharing platform for monitoring data License accoUntability and CompliancE", *Blockchain: Research and Applications,* vol. 3, 2022no. 4, p. 100102. ISSN 2096-7209 [http://dx.doi.org/10.1016/j.bcra.2022.100102]

[34]   "Gartner trend insights report 2018" (PDF). Gartner. Archived (PDF) from the original on 2020-12-18", Available From :https://www.gartner.com/imagesrv/pdf/special-report-calendar-2018.pdf (Accessed on 2019-05-14).

[35]   J. Dilley, B. Maggs, J. Parikh, H. Prokop, R. Sitaraman, and B. Weihl, "Globally distributed content delivery", *IEEE Internet Computing,* vol. 6, no. 5, 2002. [http://dx.doi.org/10.1109/MIC.2002.1036038]

[36]   E. Nygren, R. K. Sitaraman, and J. Sun, "The akamai network: A platform for high-performance internet applications", *ACM SIGOPS Operating Systems Review,* vol. 44, no. 3, pp. 2-19, 2010. [http://dx.doi.org/10.1145/1842733.1842736]

[37]   A. Davis, J. Parikh, and W. Weihl, "EdgeComputing: Extending Enterprise Applications to the Edge of the Internet", *13th International World Wide Web Conference,* 2004. [http://dx.doi.org/10.1145/1013367.1013397]

[38]   Gartner, "2021 Strategic roadmap for edge computing", Available From: www.gartner.com

[39]   IEEE DAC, "Keynote: Mobile computing opportunities, challenges and technology drivers", *Archived from the original,* 2021.

[40]   K. Arabi, Qualcomm, "Trends, opportunities and challenges driving architecture and design of next generation mobile computing and iot devices", *MTL Seminar Series,* 2021.

[41]   "What is fog and edge computing? Capgemini Worldwide", https ://www .capgemini.com/ insights/expert-perspectives/

[42]   Redhat, "What is IoT Edge computing?", https://www.redhat.com/en/topics/edge-computing/iot-ed-e-computing-need-to-work-together

[43]   B. Anand, and A.J. Edwin, "CloudHide: Towards latency hiding techniques for thin-client cloud gaming", *Thematic Workshops '17: Proceedings of the on Thematic Workshops of ACM Multimedia.,* pp. 144-152, 2022.

[44]   B. Anand, and A.J. Edwin, "Gamelets — Multiplayer mobile games with distributed micro-clouds", *2014 Seventh International Conference on Mobile Computing and Ubiquitous Networking (ICMU),* pp. 14-20, 2014.
[http://dx.doi.org/10.1109/ICMU.2014.6799051]

[45]   J. Leng, G. Ruan, P. Jiang, K. Xu, Q. Liu, X. Zhou, and C. Liu, "Blockchain-empowered sustainable manufacturing and product lifecycle management in industry 4.0: A survey", *Renew. Sustain. Energy Rev.,* vol. 132, p. 110112, 2020.
[http://dx.doi.org/10.1016/j.rser.2020.110112]

[46]   J. Leng, D. Yan, Q. Liu, K. Xu, J.L. Zhao, R. Shi, L. Wei, D. Zhang, and X. Chen, "ManuChain: combining permissioned blockchain with a holistic optimization model as Bi-level intelligence for smart manufacturing", *IEEE Trans. Syst. Man Cybern. Syst.,* vol. 50, no. 1, pp. 182-192, 2020.
[http://dx.doi.org/10.1109/TSMC.2019.2930418]

[47]   H. Poston, "Mapping the OWASP top ten to blockchain", *Procedia Comput. Sci.,* vol. 177, pp. 613-617, 2020.
[http://dx.doi.org/10.1016/j.procs.2020.10.087]

[48]   J. Park, and J. Park, "Ji.H. Park, Jo.H. Park, Blockchain security in cloud computing: use cases, challenges, and solutions", *Symmetry (Basel),* vol. 9, no. 8, p. 164, 2017.
[http://dx.doi.org/10.3390/sym9080164]

[49]   M. Usman, M.A. Jan, A. Jolfaei, M. Xu, X. He, and J. Chen, "AlirezaJolfaei, Min Xu, Xiangjian He, and Jinjun Chen. 2019. A distributed and anonymous data collection framework based on multilevel edge computing architecture", *IEEE Trans. Industr. Inform.,* vol. 16, no. 9, pp. 6114-6123, 2020.
[http://dx.doi.org/10.1109/TII.2019.2952645]

[50]   J. Wang, L. Wu, K.K.R. Choo, and D. He, "Blockchain-based anonymous authentication with key management for smart grid edge computing infrastructure", *IEEE Trans. Industr. Inform.,* vol. 16, no. 3, pp. 1984-1992, 2020.
[http://dx.doi.org/10.1109/TII.2019.2936278]

[51]   "ShaoyongGuo, Xing Hu, Song Guo, XuesongQiu, and Feng Qi. 2019. Blockchain meets edge computing: A distributed and trusted authentication system", *IEEE Trans. Industr. Inform.,* vol. 16, no. 3, pp. 1972-1983, 2019.

[52]   "SrinivasJangirala, Ashok Kumar Das, and Athanasios V Vasilakos. 2019. Designing secure lightweight blockchain-enabled RFID-based authentication protocol for supply chains in 5G mobile edge computing environment", *IEEE Trans. Industr. Inform.,* vol. 16, no. 11, pp. 7081-7093, 2019.

[53]   "Xuyun Zhang, HonghaoGao, Yuan Xue, Lianyong Qi, and Wanchun Dou. 2019. BeCome: Blockchain-enabled computation offloading for IoT in mobile edge computing", *IEEE Trans. Industr. Inform.,* vol. 16, no. 6, pp. 4187-4195, 2019.

[54]   J. Song, "Blockchain meets COVID-19: A framework for contact information sharing and risk notification system", *2021 IEEE 17th International Conference on Mobile Ad Hoc and Sensor Systems (MASS)* Denver, CO, USA, 2021, pp. 269-277.

[55]   "ByungWook Kwon, and Jong Hyuk Park. 2019. BlockSecIoTNet: Blockchain-based decentralized security architecture for IoT network", *J. Netw. Comput. Appl.,* vol. 143, pp. 167-177, 2019.

[56]   "Ricardo S Alonso, Juan M Corchado, Sara RodríguezGonzález, and Roberto Casado-Vara. 2019. A review of edge computing reference architectures and a new global edge proposal", *Future Gener. Comput. Syst.,* vol. 99, pp. 278-294, 2019.

[57]   Y. Ren, Q. Zhao, H. Guan, and Z. Lin, "A novel authentication scheme based on edge computing for blockchain-based distributed energy trading system", *EURASIP J. Wirel. Commun. Netw.,* vol. 2020,

no. 1, p. 152, 2020.
[http://dx.doi.org/10.1186/s13638-020-01762-w]

[58]   J. Kang, R. Yu, X. Huang, M. Wu, S. Maharjan, S. Xie, and Y. Zhang, "SabitaMaharjan, ShengliXie, and Yan Zhang. 2018. Blockchain for secure and efficient data sharing in vehicular edge computing and networks", *IEEE Internet Things J.,* vol. 6, no. 3, pp. 4660-4670, 2019.
[http://dx.doi.org/10.1109/JIOT.2018.2875542]

[59]   H. Zhou, and Z. Shi, "XueOuyang, and Zhiming Zhao. 2021. Building a blockchain-based decentralized ecosystem for cloud and edge computing: an ALLSTAR approach and empirical study", *Peer-to-Peer Netw. Appl.,* pp. 1-17, 2021.

[60]   Lei Xu, Chunxiao Jiang, Jian Wang, Jian Yuan, and Yong Ren, "Information security in big data: privacy and data mining", *IEEE Access,* vol. 2, pp. 1149-1176, 2014.
[http://dx.doi.org/10.1109/ACCESS.2014.2362522]

[61]   D. Johnson, A. Menezes, and S. Vanstone, "The elliptic curve digital signature algorithm (ECDSA)", *Int. J. Inf. Secur.,* vol. 1, no. 1, pp. 36-63, 2001.
[http://dx.doi.org/10.1007/s102070100002]

[62]   K. Gai, Y. Wu, L. Zhu, L. Xu, and Y. Zhang, "Permissioned blockchain and edge computing empowered privacy-preserving smart grid networks", *IEEE Internet Things J.,* vol. 6, no. 5, pp. 7992-8004, 2019.
[http://dx.doi.org/10.1109/JIOT.2019.2904303]

[63]   S. Sayeed, and H. Marco-Gisbert, "Assessing Blockchain Consensus and Security Mechanisms against the 51% Attack", *Appl. Sci. (Basel),* vol. 9, no. 9, p. 1788, 2019.
[http://dx.doi.org/10.3390/app9091788]

[64]   T. Kumari, R. Kumar, and R.K. Dwivedi, "Designing Blockchain Based Consensus Mechanism for Smart Healthcare IoT", *2023 International Conference on Intelligent and Innovative Technologies in Computing, Electrical and Electronics (IITCEE) Bengaluru, India,* pp. 878-884, 2023.
[http://dx.doi.org/10.1109/IITCEE57236.2023.10090882]

[65]   Takua Mokhamed, Manar Abu Talib, Mohammad Adel Moufti, Sohail Abbas, and Faheem Khan, "The potential of blockchain technology in dental healthcare: A literature review", *Sensors,* vol. 23, no. 6, p. 3277, 2023.
[http://dx.doi.org/10.3390/s23063277]

[66]   A.N. Abougreen, and C. Chakraborty, Applications of Machine Learning and Internet of Things in Agriculture.*Green Technological Innovation for Sustainable Smart Societies.,* C. Chakraborty, Ed., Springer: Cham, 2021.
[http://dx.doi.org/10.1007/978-3-030-73295-0_12]

[67]   C. Chakraborty, and A.N. Abougreen, "Intelligent internet of things and advanced machine learning techniques for Covid-19", *EAI Endorsed Trans. Pervasive Health Technol.,* vol. 7, p. 26, 2021.

[68]   W. Rafique, M. Khan, S. Khan, and J.S. Ally, "SecureMed: A Blockchain-Based Privacy-Preserving Framework for Internet of Medical Things", *Wirel. Commun. Mob. Comput.,* vol. 2023, pp. 1-14, 2023.
[http://dx.doi.org/10.1155/2023/2558469]

[69]   "Blockchain-Based Secure Storage Management with Edge Computing for IoT - Scientific Figure on ResearchGate", https ://www .researchgate .net/figure/Blockchain -based-IoT-framework-with-edge-computing_fig3_334711657

CHAPTER 10

Effective Automated Medical Image Segmentation Using Hybrid Computational Intelligence Technique

Manoranjan Dash[1,*], **Raghu Indrakanti**[2] and **M. Narayana**[2]

[1] *Department of Artificial Intelligence, Anurag University, Hyderabad, India*

[2] *Electronics and Communication Engineering Department, Anurag University, Hyderabad, India*

Abstract: In biomedical domain, magnetic resonance imaging (MRI) segmentation is highly essential for the treatment or prevention of disease. The demand for fast processing and high accurate results is necessary for medical diagnosis. This can be solved by using computational intelligence (CoIn) for data processing. The CoIn can be achieved by using well-known techniques such as fuzzy logic, genetic algorithm, evolutionary algorithms and neural networks. The computational complexity of a medical image segmentation depends on the characteristics of data as well as suitable algorithms. The selection of CoIn methods is very important for better segmentation of a medical image because each algorithm outperforms a different medical image data set. The hybrid CoIn (H-CoIn) is one of the solutions to overcome the problem of individual algorithms in medical image segmentation. The H-CoIn is a combination of two or more intelligence algorithms (like fuzzy logic, evolutionary algorithms and neural networks). The drawbacks of individual intelligence algorithms can be overcome by using H-CoIn. In a medical image segmentation process, two or more variables or objectives need to be optimized for H-CoIn. This problem can be solved by using multi-objective optimization techniques, where simultaneously minimization or maximization can be performed. In this chapter, the various CoIn algorithms' performance has been discussed in detail for medical image segmentation and compared with state-of-the-art techniques. The H-Coin algorithm has been implemented in a large medical dataset and attained an accuracy of 98.89%. Further, the H-Coin algorithm is reliable and suitable to overcome the inter-observer and intra-observer variability.

Keywords: Evolutionary Algorithms, Hybrid Computational Intelligence, MRI, Segmentation.

*Corresponding author Manoranjan Dash: Department of Artificial Intelligence, Anurag University, Hyderabad, India; E-mail: manoranjanai@anurag.edu.in

L. Ashok Kumar, D. Karthika Renuka, Sonali Agarwal & Sheng-Lung Peng (Eds.)

INTRODUCTION

The eighth critical organ of the human body is the sophisticated brain, which regulates the neurological system. Uncontrolled and erratic cell proliferation within the bladder might lead to a tumor. Primary and secondary tumors are the two main categories of breast tumors. Breast cancer has the greatest fatality rate of any disease in the world and does not correspond with population growth. Auxiliary brain tumors, which develop in one more part of the body and travel to the cerebrum through the circulatory system, grow in the brain tissues. In addition, if neglected, these could lead to a critical condition [1].

Early detection and classification are the most important steps in the diagnosis and treatment of brain cancers with good prognostic accuracy with which the patient's life can be saved. However, radiologists and medical professionals find it challenging to identify and localize malignancies and normal tissues from medical imaging due to the manual examination of brain MR images [2]. Systems for computer-aided diagnosis (CADx) are essential for resolving this problem.

It must be put into practice to lighten the strain and make it easier for doctors or radiologists to analyze medical images. A number of precise and dependable ways to automate the work of identifying and classifying breast cancers have previously been put forth by numerous researchers. Customary Artificial Intelligence based strategies are applied to the analysis of brain tumors. However, ML-based systems need human feature extraction and categorization and only employ tiny amounts of data. Deep learning (DL) consolidates feature extraction and grouping in a self-learning way on a lot of named information, essentially upgrading execution.

A version of DL called convolutional neural network (CNN) was also developed exclusively for two-dimensional (2D) problems. It mechanically extracts various features from MR images and only accepts datasets that have undergone a minimal amount of preparation [3]. Profound CNN models are most often utilized for the detection of brain tumors. Nonetheless, mind growth examination is very difficult and requires a strong DL-based cerebrum cancer investigation framework to help the radiologist's judgment because of the variable morphological construction, cancer appearance in a picture, and enlightenment impacts.

This chapter presents the related works reported in the literature, the methodology employed, results followed by conclusion and future work in the subsequent sections.

RELATED WORKS

Medical image analysis research spans a wide range of topics. These encompass a variety of imaging-related medical specialties, including segmentation, classification, and detection [4 - 8]. There is a requirement for novel ways of highlighting extraction, utilizing little and class-uneven MR imaging datasets of cerebrum malignant growths and cancers from different regions of the human body as companions for mind growth order are constructed [9, 10]. In the literature, binary classifications are crudely investigated to distinguish between benign and malignant tumor occurrences. Support vector machine (SVM) and genetic algorithm (GA) features were investigated by Kharrat *et al*. [11] for the categorization of brain tumors into normal, benign, and malignant groups. The suggested method allows for two-class categorization. It has limitations because new training is needed each time the image database is altered. Abdolmaleki *et al*. [12] constructed a shallow neural network to discriminate between benign and malignant tumors using thirteen distinctive features. These qualities were picked in light of the visual impression of radiologists. Their proposed method had classification accuracy for the harmful and elucidating cancers of 91% and 94%, individually. Papageorgiou *et al*. [13] used fuzzy cognitive mapping to differentiate between low-grade and high-grade gliomas.

Their study exhibited a 90.26% accuracy rate for low-grade brain tumors and a 93.22% accuracy rate for high-grade brain tumors. The feature selection approach was suggested by Zacharaki *et al*. [14] and then used with traditional machine learning. For this, they extracted characteristics such as the tumor's form, level of intensity, and invariant texture. SVM is used for feature selection and tumor classification. Their research had the highest classification accuracy for low- and high-grade gliomas, at 88%. The difficult benchmark dataset [15] of MRI scans of brain cancers, including meningioma, gliomas, and pituitary tumors, was used by several investigations. The picture enlargement utilized as the region of interest (ROI) and the expansion of the growth district in the ring structure are both parts of the multi-phase brain tumor categorization, reported by Cheng *et al*. [16]. Its proposed model was analyzed utilizing three distinct elements, and their precision rate was 82.31%. They performed better overall because of the use of a bag of the word (characteristics, even though the intricacy of the model expanded accordingly). Sultan *et al*. [17] proposed a profound CNN-based cerebrum cancer characterization model and utilized information expansion. They scored 96.13% accuracy in multi-class classification. Ahmet and Muhammad [18] were able to analyze brain tumors with 97.2% accuracy by utilizing a range of different CNN models while employing modified ResNet50 architecture. Khwaldeh *et al*. [19]

classified brain MRI images using several CNNs, and the accuracy was satisfactory. They get higher exactness of 97.2% by utilizing transformed pre-prepared Alexnet CNN.

DATABASE DETAILS

Normal and tumor photos for a brain tumor data set and dataset1 have been collected from the free and open-source Kaggle website (DS-1) [https://www.kaggle.com/datasets/navoneel/brain-mri-images-for-brain-tumor-detection]. Additionally, tumor images are acquired from a publically accessible dataset2 on the CE-MRI Figshare (DS-2) [15].

Our 6233 image collection, known as dataset 3 (DS-3), is so unbalanced and consists of 3233 images of malignancies and 3000 images of healthy individuals. The first phase of identification uses the DS-3 dataset, which consists of 6233 MR images, 3233 of tumor class, and 3000 of normal class. The taxonomy step separates the 3233 brain tumor MR images into the three families of glioma, meningioma, and pituitary tumors by means of the DS-2 algorithm. Examples of samples of the normal and tumors brain are shown in Fig. (1).

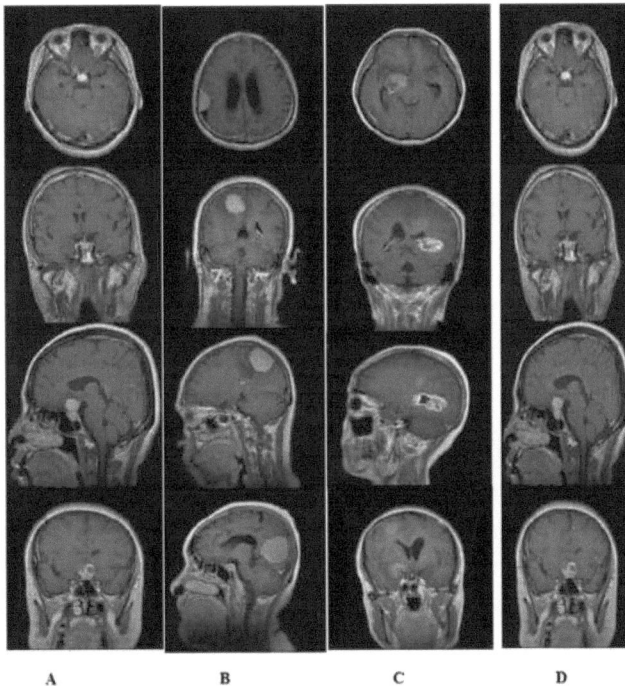

Fig. (1). Picture informational collection incorporates photos of cancers and ordinary tissue (A) Normal, (B) Glioma, (C) Meningioma, and (D) Pituitary.

METHODOLOGY

This section explains the planned U-NET framework's intricate architecture. Two phases make up the suggested framework. In the first phase, a U-NET [20] approach for brain tumor identification is suggested. The classification U-net alludes to the engineering shape, which appears to be like the letter set 'U'. The U-net design comprises contracting and separating ways associated with a U-shape. Using a cross-breed highlights combination-based mind cancer characterization model, the second stage entails classifying the tumor brain MR images discovered in the initial stage into three groups: meningioma, glioma, and pituitary. By using the unique KNN and SVM-based technique that has been proposed, distinct types of MR images are classified. It is possible to produce feature space variation by fusing static and dynamic structures. The proposed multi-stage cerebrum growth discovery and order system is displayed in Fig. (**2**).

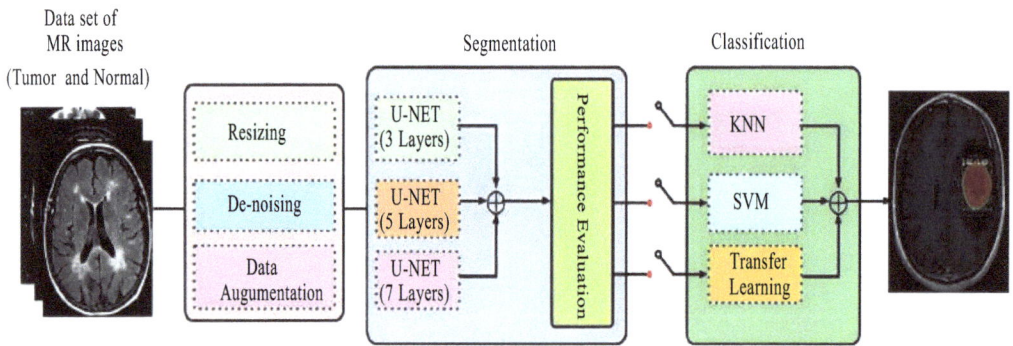

Fig. (2). Proposed Hybrid Computational Intelligence framework.

U-Net-based completely convolutional brain network is carried out for the programmed psoriasis skin sore division. The proposed network contains a profound completely convolutional network which performs 19 convolution tasks in simultaneousness with group standardization and a ReLU enactment capability. Further, max-pooling activity is performed to extricate the elements having spatial data. At last, to stay away from the overfitting issue inside the organization, dropout layers are utilized.

There are testing layers in both sections (contracting and expanding paths). The optimal extraction of   local   and   global   features   are   accomplished   in   contracting and expanding path respectively. There are back-to-back convolution layers which are used to learn and assemble more exact results in view of the examining highlights.

In this chapter, the comparative engineering of U-Net has additionally used bunch standardization at each step of convolution in both reaching and extending ways. The U-Net design has absolute 22 convolutional layers. Sigmoid enactment capability is utilized at the yield layer in a growing way.

RESULTS

The proposed U-Net-based calculation for the division was executed with Python 3.5 utilizing a tensor-stream backend. Picture handling has been finished utilizing the open-CV library. Every one of the investigations led on framework having Intel center i7, 2.20 GHz computer chip, GeForce GTX 1060 with 6GB illustrations memory. We have done minimal preprocessing. We basically resize the first picture to 128 ×128 and perform the training for 20 epochs.

The first stage involves distinguishing between those who have brain tumors and healthy people. The categorization of tumor data to other set classifications is completed in the second step. The successful cure procedure does not entirely depend on just tumor discovery; therefore, it is crucial to further categorize tumors into pertinent groups in order to provide effective and efficient therapy. Two experiments are conducted in order to assess the empirical efficiency of the suggested framework. By evaluating the effectiveness of DL and U-NET-based models, the first experiment is the task of detecting brain tumors. To assess the benefits of element space combination, melded dynamic and static component spaces are computed to isolate examples of assorted cerebrum growths in the subsequent stage.

The proposed approach has an accuracy of 98.89%. Table **1** depicts the different quantitative metrics, including accuracy (ACC). The other metric values like dice-coefficient (DSC), Jaccard Index (JI), Sensitivity (SE) and specificity (SP) also signify the efficacy of the proposed technique. The viability of the proposed U-Net based psoriasis sore division strategy has been assessed in this segment. To analyze the exhibition of the proposed strategy, we have measured the outcome utilizing four distinct records (Dice coefficient, awareness, particularity, and exactness) by contrasting the ground truth. Exactness characterizes the capability of isolating the injury and skin appropriately. Responsiveness and explicitness recreate the effectiveness of division autonomously.

Table 1. Performance evaluation metrics (in percentages).

ACC	DSC	JI	SE	SP
98.89	92.03	91.43	92.60	96.70

The graph between the number of iterations and DSC is provided in Fig. (**3**), which signifies the optimum attainment of DSC.

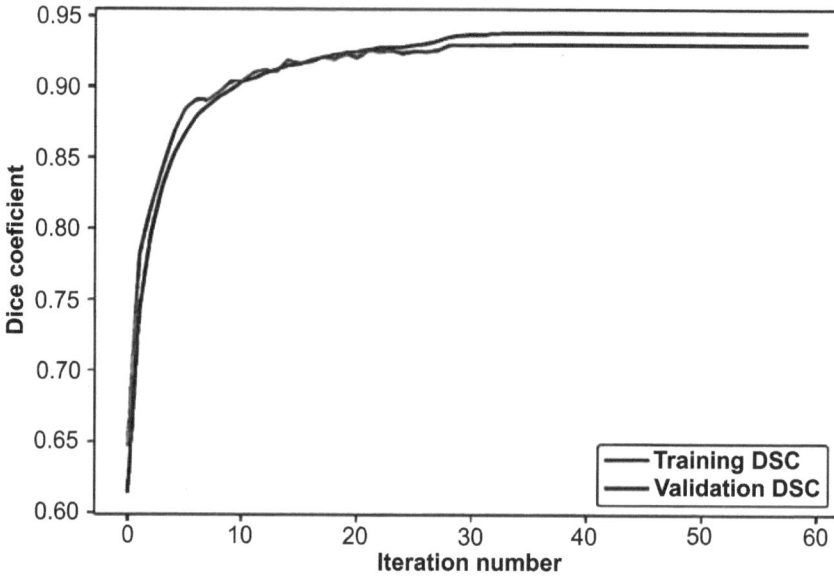

Fig. (3). DSC plot for training and validation.

Table **2** depicts the performance comparison of the proposed method with existing techniques. It can be observed that the proposed method outperforms the existing techniques in all five metrics.

Table 2. Comparison of performance of the proposed method with existing methods (in percentage).

Method	Metrics				
	ACC	DSC	JI	SE	SP
SVM [11]	81.27	84.11	77.29	84.58	82.77
CNN [17]	90.25	89.68	83.24	87.44	91.02
Proposed	98.89	92.03	91.43	92.60	96.70

CONCLUSION AND FUTURE WORK

For the patient to receive prompt treatment, a trustworthy brain tumor analysis framework is important. Another two-stage system for mind growth recognition and arrangement is made to further develop cerebrum cancer conclusion and decrease figuring intricacy. In the discovery stage, an original U-NET methodology has been proposed for separating brain cancer occasions from sound people with less misleading negatives, and execution is considered in contrast to the DL techniques currently being used. Experimental findings show that the suggested method performed better than expected by obtaining an accuracy of 98.89%. Further, the proposed algorithm can be more generalized by applying it to a larger real-time dataset.

REFERENCES

[1]   W. Rafique, M. Khan, S. Khan, and J.S. Ally, "SecureMed: A Blockchain-Based Privacy-Preserving Framework for Internet of Medical Things",
[http://dx.doi.org/10.1155/2023/2558469]

[2]   D.N. Louis, "World Health Organization, "classification of tumors of the central nervous system: A summary"", In: *Acta neuropathological,* vol. 131. , 2016, no. 6, pp. 803-820.

[3]   T. Kumari, R. Kumar, and R.K. Dwivedi, "Designing Blockchain Based Consensus Mechanism for Smart Healthcare IoT", Bengaluru, India. International Conference on Intelligent and Innovative Technologies in Computing, Electrical and Electronics (IITCEE), 2023.
[http://dx.doi.org/10.1109/IITCEE57236.2023.10090882]

[4]   S.H. Wang, K. Muhammad, P. Phillips, Z. Dong, and Y-D. Zhang, "Ductal carcinoma in situ detection in breast thermography by extreme learning machine and combination of statistical measure and fractal dimension", *J. Ambient Intell. Humaniz. Comput.,* pp. 1-11, 2017.
[http://dx.doi.org/10.1007/s12652-017-0639-5]

[5]   N.C.F. Codella, *"Skin lesion analysis toward melanoma detection": A challenge at the 2017 international symposium on biomedical imaging (isbi), hosted by the international skin imaging collaboration (isic).* IEEE, 2018.

[6]   S.H. Khan, "Segmentation of Shoulder Muscle MRI Using a New Region and Edge based Deep Auto-Encoder",

[7]   S.H. Khan, "Classification and region analysis of COVID-19 infection using lung CT images and deep convolutional neural networks", *arXiv: 2009.08864,* 2020.

[8]   M.M. Zafar, Z. Rauf, A. Sohail, A.R. Khan, M. Obaidullah, S.H. Khan, Y.S. Lee, and A. Khan, "Detection of tumour infiltrating lymphocytes in CD3 and CD8 stained histopathological images using a two-phase deep CNN", *Photodiagn. Photodyn. Ther.,* vol. 37, p. 102676, 2022.
[http://dx.doi.org/10.1016/j.pdpdt.2021.102676] [PMID: 34890783]

[9]   G. Litjens, T. Kooi, B.E. Bejnordi, A.A.A. Setio, F. Ciompi, M. Ghafoorian, J.A.W.M. van der Laak, B. van Ginneken, and C.I. Sánchez, "A survey on deep learning in medical image analysis", *Med. Image Anal.,* vol. 42, pp. 60-88, 2017.
[http://dx.doi.org/10.1016/j.media.2017.07.005] [PMID: 28778026]

[10] Z. Akkus, A. Galimzianova, A. Hoogi, D.L. Rubin, and B.J. Erickson, "Deep learning for brain MRI segmentation: state of the art and future directions", *J. Digit. Imaging,* vol. 30, no. 4, pp. 449-459, 2017.
[http://dx.doi.org/10.1007/s10278-017-9983-4] [PMID: 28577131]

[11]   C. Chakraborty, and A.N. Abougreen, "Intelligent internet of things and advanced machine learning techniques for Covid-19", *EAI Endorsed Trans. Pervasive Health Technol.,* vol. 7, no. 26, p. e1, 2021.

[12]   P. Abdolmaleki, F. Mihara, K. Masuda, and L.D. Buadu, "Neural networks analysis of astrocytic gliomas from MRI appearances", *Cancer Lett.,* vol. 118, no. 1, pp. 69-78, 1997.
[http://dx.doi.org/10.1016/S0304-3835(97)00233-4] [PMID: 9310262]

[13]   E.I. Papageorgiou, P.P. Spyridonos, D.T. Glotsos, C.D. Stylios, P. Ravazoula, G.N. Nikiforidis, and P.P. Groumpos, "Brain tumor characterization using the soft computing technique of fuzzy cognitive maps", *Appl. Soft Comput.,* vol. 8, no. 1, pp. 820-828, 2008.
[http://dx.doi.org/10.1016/j.asoc.2007.06.006]

[14]   E.I. Zacharaki, "Classification of brain tumor type and grade using mri texture and shape in a machine learning scheme. magnetic resonance in medicine", *An Official J. Inter. Soc. Mag. Res. Med.,* vol. 62, no. 6, pp. 1609-1618, 2009.

[15]   C. Jun, "brain tumor", Available from : https://figshare.com/articles/brain_tumor_dataset/1512427

[16]   J. Cheng, W. Huang, S. Cao, R. Yang, W. Yang, Z. Yun, Z. Wang, and Q. Feng, "Correction: Enhanced performance of brain tumor classification via tumor region augmentation and partition", *PLoS One,* vol. 10, no. 12, p. e0144479, 2015.
[http://dx.doi.org/10.1371/journal.pone.0144479] [PMID: 26629992]

[17]   H.H. Sultan, N.M. Salem, and W. Al-Atabany, "Multi-Classification of Brain Tumor Images Using Deep Neural Network", *IEEE Access,* vol. 7, pp. 69215-69225, 2019.
[http://dx.doi.org/10.1109/ACCESS.2019.2919122]

[18]   A. Çinar, and M. Yildirim, "Detection of tumors on brain MRI images using the hybrid convolutional neural network architecture", *Med. Hypotheses,* vol. 139, p. 109684, 2020.
[http://dx.doi.org/10.1016/j.mehy.2020.109684] [PMID: 32240877]

[19]   S. Khawaldeh, U. Pervaiz, A. Rafiq, and R. Alkhawaldeh, "Noninvasive grading of glioma tumor using magnetic resonance imaging with convolutional neural networks", *Appl. Sci. (Basel),* vol. 8, no. 1, p. 27, 2017.
[http://dx.doi.org/10.3390/app8010027]

[20]   N.D. Manoranjan Dash, S. Londhe, and S. Londhe, *"PsLSNet: Automated psoriasis skin lesion segmentation using modified U-Net-based fully convolutional network".* vol. Vol. 52. Biomed. Signal Process. Control, 2020, pp. 226-237.

CHAPTER 11

IoT-Botnet Detection and Mitigation for Smart Healthcare Systems using Advanced Machine Learning Techniques

S. Jayanthi[1,*] and **A. Valarmathi**[2]

[1] *Department of Computer Science and Engineering, Bit Campus, Anna University, Thiruchirappalli-24, India*

[2] *Department of Computer Applications Bit Campus, Anna University, Thiruchirappalli-24, India*

Abstract: The Internet of Things (IoT) age is quickly evolving, with millions of devices and many more intelligent systems, like healthcare. Attackers mostly aim for these IoT devices. These devices are infected with malware, which turns them into bots that are used by attackers to disrupt networks as well as steal important data. To address this issue, efficient machine learning combined with appropriate feature engineering is proposed to detect and protect the network against vulnerabilities. The proposed model will detect Distributed Denial of Service (DDOS)-based botnet attacks in the smart healthcare system. Hacktivists frequently use DDoS assaults to overwhelm networks and make them unusable. For healthcare providers who depend on network connections to enable efficient patient data access, this can be a serious problem. DDoS attacks are motivated by a social, political, ideological, or economic motive tied to a scenario that enrages cyber threat actors. Two modern Machine Learning (ML) methods, including (i) Support Vector Machine (SVM) and (ii) Light Gradient Boosting Machine (Light GBM), are used to validate the data set. From the extensive experimental analysis, feature-based algorithms are superior to other competing models in that they (i) have the highest detection rate with high accuracy, and (ii) have less computational complexity with minimal training and test time.

Keywords: Botnet, DDOS Attack, IoT, IoT Security, Light GBM, ML Algorithms, Smart Healthcare System, SVM.

INTRODUCTION

The Internet of Things (IoT) is promoting innovation and greater number of smart healthcare gadgets are getting associated with the internet. This permits more gadgets to possibly become botnet gadgets. This chapter aims to utilize the ML method to identify botnet assaults. A botnet comprises a few internet-associated

* **Corresponding author S. Jayanthi:** Department of Computer Science and Engineering, Bit Campus, Anna University, Thiruchirappalli-24, India; E-mail: dharsh02@yahoo.com

L. Ashok Kumar, D. Karthika Renuka, Sonali Agarwal & Sheng-Lung Peng (Eds.)

gadgets that might have been deliberately contaminated with malware from digital programmers. A botnet assault is a kind of malevolent assault that uses a progression of associated PCs to assault or bring down an organization, network gadget or site. It is executed with the sole purpose to upset typical working tasks or corrupt the general assistance of the objective framework [1]. Thus, the effective discovery and anticipation of botnets would have significant importance in PC security. As additional gadgets will possibly be botnet gadgets, the most common way of identifying and detecting these botnet gadgets should be possible utilizing different AI strategies. This section aims to detect botnets or pernicious traffic action on a shrewd medical care framework utilizing the arising ML strategies and give an improvement in accuracy over other related works [2].

Background Methodologies

I. Botnet

Botnet is an organization of various bots intended to bring about noxious exercises to the objective organization which are acquiring order and control conventions by the single unit called bot-herder. Bots are tainted PCs controlled from a distance by the bot-herder with no indication of being hacked and are employed to perform malignant exercises [3]. Hackers spread botnet malware and work secretly with practically no observable sign of their presence and can stay strong and work for quite a long time. The principal component in the botnet is the correspondence of the bot-herder with its related bots. Correspondence with the bots is fundamental to convey orders to the bots to carry out mean acts. Bot-herders generally remain stowed away involving low data transmission and offer secret types of assistance in the botnet network. Bot-herders generally impart orders and control servers to bots. The principal objective of bots is to stay concealed until they are expected to do the allocated undertakings. The existent pattern of a botnet comprises a few phases which includes spreading disease, secondary injection, association, order and control, update and maintenance [4].

II. DDoS attack

The most frequent cyber attack is a DDoS assault, in which many malicious packets are simultaneously sent from attacker's computer to the target server to overload the target network. DDoS attacks aim to seriously disrupt the target server's regular operations by saturating it with large amounts of traffic, such as false requests, to overwhelm its capacity and cause a disturbance or denial of service to the legitimate traffic [5]. DDoS attacks affect the server's CPU and memory, as well as their ability to overload the network's bandwidth with traffic. As a result, genuine PCs will experience service interruptions while the server is coping with the DDoS attack. Hackers perform DDoS attacks using a botnet. IoT devices that have been compromised by the malicious software that the attacker distributes online become targets of DDoS attacks. IoT devices that have been infected behave as bots and the attacker uses them to perform DDoS attacks [6].

III. Security vulnerabilities in IoT

Smart gadgets are used in many public and private sectors and are quickly becoming indispensable items for everyday life. So this results in high danger to data privacy. A computerized security system based on machine learning algorithms will be doomed in such a situation. Automated security systems that incorporate machine learning are necessary to stop threats like DDoS attacks, Man-in-the-Middle attacks, botnet attacks, eavesdropping and so forth [7]. Additionally, the majority of low-end IoT devices have inadequate security systems, making them targets for different security attacks or potentially serving as a botnet.

THEME OF WORK

All IoT devices are connected to the server continuously monitoring all devices. If the server has this facility installed, so, if they find any abnormalities in any connection, it immediately removes that device from the connected device. So, the malware should not spread across multiple devices.

LITERATURE REVIEW

IoT-related disciplines have produced a number of works. Researchers are still engaged in this area. IoT security research should be prioritized, according to Mahmud Hossain *et al* ., 2015, there are some unresolved issues in IoT and the IoT devices are insecure because of their limitations in mobility, usability and battery life.

Pahl *et al.*, 2018, proposed an IoT service firewall and anomaly detection mechanism. Different microservices have been integrated using clustering techniques BIRCH and K-Means. The distance among various clusters was the same as the standard deviation. The clustering concept is used to update online learning techniques. The author mimics this model and achieves an overall accuracy of 96.3% [7].

By making IoT devices as intelligent as bots, Zhang *et al.*, 2015, proposed an IoT defense algorithm that prevents DDoS assault while maintaining a portable and affordable solution. A node examines the consistency of the packet content to distinguish between a legitimate engine and a malicious request. Results indicated that this strategy aids in assault prevention, although it depends on each bot's finite resources. When monitoring a node, storage is needed to handle the increased demand [8].

Ukil *et al.*, 2016, examined the Internet of Things platform's ability to detect anomalies in the healthcare industry. He also pioneered the use of IoT sensors, predictive analysis, biomedical sensor analysis, big data mining, medical image analysis and a model for smartphone-based cardiac abnormality detection [9].

According to SikhaBagui and Kunqi Li *et al.*, 2021, six different datasets were subjected to five different types of resampling. The other three datasets can be viewed as less uneven than the first dataset, which is very unbalanced. The three datasets with the highest imbalance were KDD99, UNSW-NB15, and UNSW-NB18 (BoT-IoT). Additionally, it may be said that the three UNSW-NB17 datasets are less unbalanced. So, Machine Learning models trained on cybersecurity data are unbalanced and cannot distinguish minority data or assaults effectively [10].

Garg *et al.*, 2013, contrasted three machine learning methods to see if they can distinguish between botnets and regular traffic. This was accomplished by picking crucial components of network traffic, combining them in various ways, and then creating a number of test cases. Three algorithms were tested: J48, Naive Bayes, and K-Nearest Neighbor (IBk). Following independent testing of each algorithm for each instance, it was shown that the IBk and J48 algorithms had a detection accuracy that was superior to Naive Bayes. The drawbacks are that IBk and J48 required lengthy testing and training periods, respectively. The P2P botnets should be grateful for the high detection rates of more than 99% despite these shortcomings [11].

Anthi *et al.*, 2018, argued that the intrusion detection system should have rights in the Internet of Things. With the use of straightforward DoS attacks and scanner probes, he has effectively found several machine learning classifiers. Machine learning classifiers utilized Weka software [12].

"The cybersecurity in the development of IoT embedded technologies" by B. Usmonov *et al.*, 2017, highlighted the current issue of acquiring security when creating embedded technology for the IoT. The suggested methods include analyzing the data sent over the Internet of Things intellectually and using digital watermarks to transmit data between IoT devices [13].

"The Potential of Blockchain Technology in Dental Healthcare" (Mokhamed, Takua, Manar Abu Talib, Mohammad Adel Moufti, Sohail Abbas, and Faheem

Khan *et al.*, 2023) accomplished the Secure Electronic Health Records (EHR): Blockchain can provide a secure and immutable platform for storing and managing electronic health records. Patient data, including dental history, treatments, and radiographs can be stored on the blockchain, ensuring data integrity, privacy and controlled access. Blockchain-based EHRs can reduce the risk of data breaches and unauthorized modifications, allowing patients to have greater control over their health information [14].

"Toward Software-Defined Networking-Based IoT Frameworks: A Systematic Literature Review, Taxonomy, Open Challenges and Prospects" (Shahbaz Siddiqui *et al.*, 2022) discusses various dimensions and factors that influence the design of blockchain-based architectures for IoT, including consensus mechanisms, data management, security, privacy, scalability, and interoperability. The taxonomy provides a structured framework for understanding and comparing different blockchain-based architectures and their suitability for IoT applications [15].

There are various cutting-edge datasets available that are utilised for IDS and IPS training and testing on both traditional networks and IoT networks. The network traffic datasets that have been proposed over the last few years are still widely utilised today. A few of them are simulated datasets, which are created using simulation tools, while others are actual datasets, which are created using real-time systems. DARPA, KDD-99, NSL-KDD, DEFCON, LBNL, CAIDA, UNIBS, ISCX, and UNSW-NB15 are a few examples of cutting-edge datasets.

It is expensive and challenging to train and test IDS and IPS using network traffic datasets produced by real-time systems. However, by creating the dataset using a traffic generator tool, this conundrum can be resolved. Even though IDS technology is now very much advanced, it is insufficient for IoT systems. This is mostly due to the IoT nodes' poor processing and storage capabilities, which have been previously described as the key difficulty for host IDS [16, 17]. The communication protocols that IoT devices use (such as CoAP, MQTT, *etc.*) are rarely used in regular networks since each has unique security flaws and IDS requirements. The main goal of this effort is to produce a sizable and trustworthy dataset of IoT network traffic in order to construct IDS specifically for the IoT-based ICU setting. Any security lapse in such a situation could have a negative impact on the patient or, in certain cases, even result in death [18].

The original dataset was put forth in 1998 at MIT Lincoln Laboratory and is called DARPA . This dataset, which includes seven weeks' worth of recorded data, was created for the evaluation of IDS. It contains information about events linked to emails, FTP, Telnet, IRC, and SNMP. Using Windows and UNIX platforms, various attack types, including Denial of Service (DoS) assaults, Remote to Local (R2L) attacks, and User to Remote (U2R) attacks, are simulated. The absence of false positives is one of the dataset's oddities, along with the absence of real-time traffic [19].

Two versions of the DEFCON dataset—DEFCON-8 and DEFCON-10—were recorded during competitions for capturing the flags (hacking and anti-hacking) in 2000 and 2002, respectively. While DEFCON-8 covers buffer overflow and port scanning attacks, DEFCON-10 covers FTP, malicious packet, and port scanning threats. Two edge routers' inbound, outbound, and routing traffic were collected in 2004 to create the LBNL dataset. It only contained entire header files and was collected at a medium-sized site. It experiences severe anonymization [20].

The CAIDA dataset, which was gathered from a huge enterprise's Internet backbone, solely includes traffic headers without the payload. It includes particular assaults like DDoS assaults [21]. There was no additional processing done to the recorded information to produce new attributes that would have helped distinguish between legitimate and fraudulent traffic. Additionally, it is labelled, making it useless for IDS's immediate performance evaluation because labelling requires preprocessing [22-24].

Twenty workstations' worth of traffic from the router's tcpdump were used to record the UNIBS dataset. There was only the DoS attack in focus. In 2012, ISCX was created utilizing actual network configurations. Real network traffic was being simulated by a group of people. It is a dataset with labels that include various assault scenarios [25]. It has two profiles: the Beta-profile for ordinary traffic and the Alpha-profile for multi-stage assault scenarios. It contains the entire packet payloads of many protocols, including HTTP, FTP, SMTP, and others. It does not, however, include HTTPS, which accounts for 70% of traffic in the modern day [26]. By using the IXIA storm to create both malicious and benign traffic in a commercial penetration testing environment, the UNSWNB-15 dataset was gathered. The dataset Bot-IoT includes simulated IoT network traffic as well as attacks of various kinds [27, 28].

These studies demonstrate the usefulness and effectiveness of machine learning in detecting botnets. The objective of this work is to develop a botnet detection model utilizing machine learning's classification method.

PROPOSED DETECTION METHOD

In this approach, the proposed model suggests employing machine learning to identify IoT botnet assaults. Obtaining malicious datasets for a botnet is challenging in the real world. The proposed work attempts to produce network traffic traces that include both malicious and legitimate activities in order to evaluate our system. These traffic traces are gathered from well-known network apps. Due to the fact that both malefic and non-malefic traffic happened at the same time, they are jumbled together. Following that, the datasets for malefic and non-malefic traffic traces were divided. In this, the dataset that was taken directly from the traffic data is trained and tested. This allows us to identify server irregularities.

A. ARCHITECTURE DIAGRAM

Fig. (**1**) represents the Architecture diagram for the proposed model.

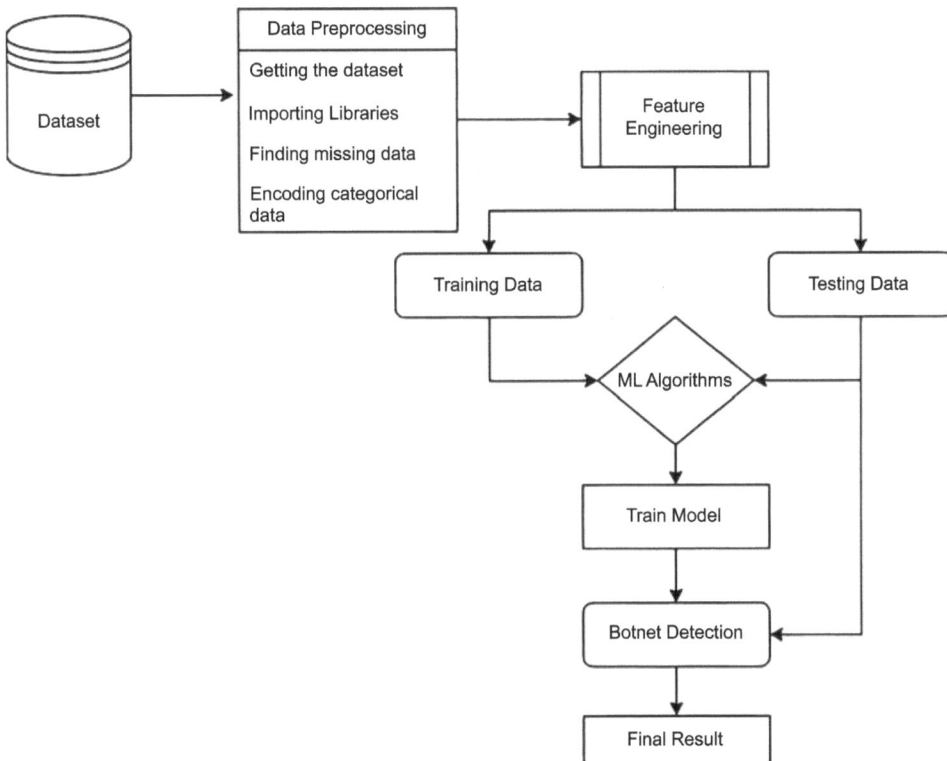

Fig. (1). Architecture Diagram.

This method consists of the following main stages:

1. Collection of Dataset
2. Data Pre-Processing
3. Feature Engineering

4. Training and Testing data

Fig. (**2**) represents the stages involved in the developed system.

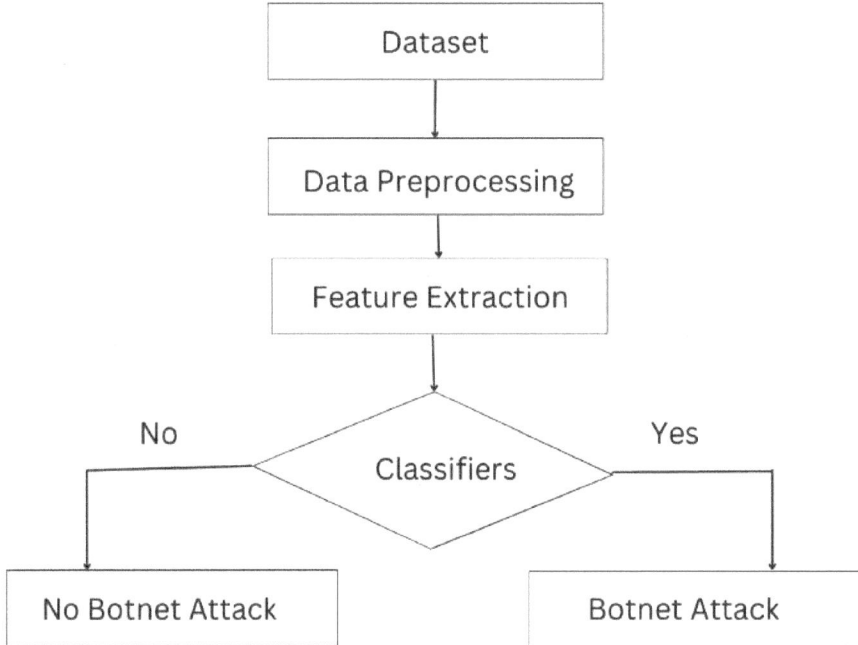

Fig. (2). Stages of the developed system.

1. Collection of Dataset

A data set is a grouping of associated sets of information that is made up of several components yet may be handled as a whole. The information or data needed for data science or machine learning is referred to as a dataset.

Typically, historical observations are used to get the data.

In a scheme, there are often two or three datasets: a training dataset, a development dataset, and either a validation or test dataset. Models are built using training datasets. The remaining datasets are used to fine-tune the proposed models, choose the one that performs the best, and assess how well the selected model generalises to new situations.

The proposed work uses the "Internet of Things (IoT) Botnet attacked (DDOS)" dataset in the dynamic environment of the Kaggle. KAGGLE dataset is an open source dataset platform helpful for data science projects stored as CSV files. To improve the performance, the proposed model utilizes an advanced machine learning algorithm.

Data Source: https://www.kaggle.com/datasets/siddharthm1698/ddos-botnet-attack-on-iot-devices

SVM and Light GBM are used to validate the dataset, and finally, we have the validation data having less computational complexity with minimal training and testing time.

2. Data Pre-processing

This model utilizes port mirroring on the switch and organizational traffic flows to acquire data from network traffic data. Data cleaning is used to identify the proper data by locating the missing values when records are partial, noisy or inconsistent. Inaccurate data might produce subpar results.

The dataset is extremely noisy, and hence proper care is taken to replace the missing values with the global most common attribute value from each column to fill the NAN (Not a Number) values as a data pre-processing task to make it ready for applications. After pre-processing of data, the model extract the attributes in the dataset from noises, null values and missing attributes.

3. Feature Engineering

Feature engineering techniques are performed on the attributes to reduce the amount of redundant data. In this work, it has undergone a 'for loop' condition to reduce the columns in the dataset. If the condition is satisfied, the datatype of data is '0', then prints the attributes. Tests of correlation among the features were performed. Logistic regression technique was used for the feature significance detection test.

4. Training and Testing Data

In this model, the data is initially separated into training and testing sets. Training dataset is used to train the model using Machine Learning algorithms. Testing dataset is used to measure performance and accuracy.

The relation between its input compression ensures that the network learns meaningful concepts when applying unseen traffic models to minimize the false positive rate and maximize the true positive rate.

5. Splitting of Data

This model transforms the data and fits the data in the model for training. 'train_test-split' is the syntax word used for splitting the rows (x) and column (y) as training and testing data.

B. SUPPORT VECTOR MACHINE

Support Vector Machine (SVM) is a technique in supervised machine learning that is used for both classification and regression. Categorization is the most appropriate term, the proposed work often refers to regression concerns. It is effective in high-dimensional contexts, that is when there are more dimensions than samples. It is memory-efficient since it only employs a fraction of the training data (also referred to as support vectors) in the decision function.

C. MULTI-LAYER PERCEPTRON (MLP) CLASSIFIERS

A fully connected class of feedforward artificial neural network models that produce a set of outputs from a set of inputs is the multilayer perceptron (MLP). Numerous research works have presented early stopping criteria that make use of a unique validation set and regularisation techniques in order to improve the performance of the MLP neural network model's generalisation capability by limiting overtraining. The MLP classifier's early stopping criteria provide a rough estimate of how many iterations can be run before the model starts to overfit.

D. LIGHT GRADIENT BOOSTER MACHINE

A cutting-edge open-source machine learning technique called Light Gradient Boosting Algorithm (Light GBM) is used to create an immediate anti-malware strategy at both the host and network tiers. This can be done without any human involvement. The findings have pointed to a viable method for identifying and categorising malware with a high degree of accuracy (90%) for both the network and host. Large-scale data may be handled by Light GBM, and its operation uses less memory. The popularity of Light GBM is also attributed to its emphasis on precise results. LGBM is frequently used by data scientists to construct data science applications since it also enables GPU learning.

E. PSEUDOCODE

1. Import libraries (NumPy, Pandas)
2. Import data/dataset

3. Verify the dim (Rows/Col)
4. Designate 0 as a DDOS attack and/1 as a non-DDOS attack for the quality
5. Combine two datasets using the label
6. Final output is " label"
7. Import sklearn model for svc, light GBM, MLP classifiers
8. Train and test data using test-train split
9. Train_x -> x-axis training | Train_y -> y-axis training test_x -> x-axistesting | y_test-> y-axis testing
10. A suitable model
11. Discover accuracy (using testing model) -> (test_x, test_y)

PROPOSED APPROACH

All experiments are performed using Python on an HP laptop with 8GB RAM and 2.67GHz CPU in a Windows 10 environment. The KAGGLE dataset, which has 1, 75, 413 training samples and 27 characteristics, is initially gathered from the Google Online Platform Machine Repository. The dataset is rather noisy, thus, enough care is taken to replace the NaN (Not a Number) values by replacing the missing values with the attribute values that are most commonly found globally across all columns as part of the data pre-processing technique to make the dataset suitable for applications. Furthermore, the best features are also discovered using the feature engineering technique. It goes without saying that the admin will be able to make effective selections if the best features are paired with the appropriate machine learning. Multi-Layer Perceptron (MLP) Classifiers Support Vector Machine (SVM) and Light Gradient Booster Machine (Light GBM) Classifiers are employed in this instance to understand the effectiveness of the suggested technique.

Table **1** represents the best features selected for the detection of BOTNET Attack.

Table 1. Best Feature Selected for Detection of BOTNET Attack.

Name	Type	Feature Description
Dt	Integer	Data table
Switch	Integer	Switch
PKT count	Float	Packet Count
Byte Count	Float	No. of Bytes in Frame
Duration	Integer	Time taken from source to Destination
Dur NSEC	Integer	Duration in Nano seconds
Tot_Duration	Integer	Total Duration per second

(Table 1) cont.....

Name	Type	Feature Description
Flows	Integer	No. of flows in Frame
packet ins	Integer	Packet transmitted in Inception point
packet per Flow	Integer	No. of packets per flow
Byte per Flow	Integer	No. of bytes per flow
Pocket Rate	Integer	Total packet per second in transaction
port No	Integer	Port Number
Tx_Bytes	Integer	Transmitted data in Bytes
Rx_Bytes	Integer	Received data in Bytes
Tx_kbps	Integer	Transmit data rate in kbps
Rx_kbps	Integer	Receive data rate in kbps
tot_kbps	Integer	Total data rate in kbps

RESULTS & ANALYSIS

The best features found in each classifier are used in this work.

The result summary is presented in Table **2.**

Table 2. Comparison of Training and Testing Accuracy of the Existing System.

CLASSIFIERS	NUMBER OF ATTRIBUTES	TRAINING ACCURACY	TESTING ACCURACY
Decision Tree	43	99.28%	98.87%
KNN	42	90.5%	82.14%

It is apparent that the Support Vector Machine (SVM) classifier's performance values were often the lowest when compared to those of other models. This model stated that testing and training accuracies were 87.78% and 88.01%, respectively.

For the Multi-Layer Perceptron (MLP) classifier, the proposed model compares fairly well with other models like SVM, where the testing and training accuracy were 99.60% and 99.85%, respectively.

However, the Light Gradient Booster (Light GBM) classifier finds that the proposed model is effective for categorizing botnet assaults. This model outperforms other classifiers due to the use of the entire data set and the best performance values. By using advanced Machine Learning techniques, the outcomes are best with 100% accuracy. Statistically speaking, the Light GBM classifier model could distinguish between malicious traffic and legitimate traffic more specifically. This work can be used to enhance the performance of other machine learning models that have been suggested in the literature.

Table **2** represents the comparison of training and testing accuracy of the existing model.

Table **3** represents the comparison of training and testing accuracy of the developed model.

Table 3. Comparison of Training and Testing Accuracy for the Proposed System.

CLASSIFIERS	NUMBER OF ATTRIBUTES	TRAINING ACCURACY	TESTING ACCURACY
SVM	19	88.01%	87.78%
MLP	19	99.85%	99.60%
LIGHT GBM	19	100%	100%

These findings make it clear that the Light GBM model, which has a total of 27 attributes linked to it, offered the greatest training and testing accuracy of 100%.

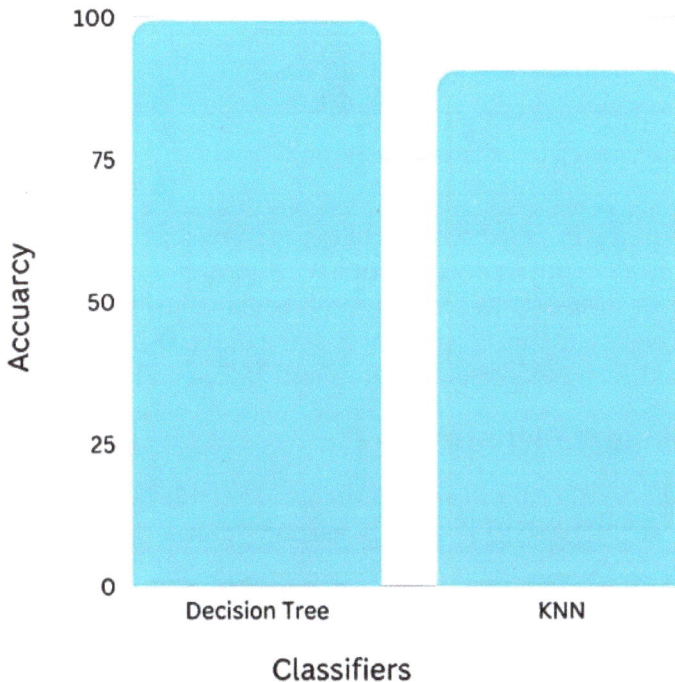

Fig. (3). Accuracy *vs* Classifiers for the Existing System.

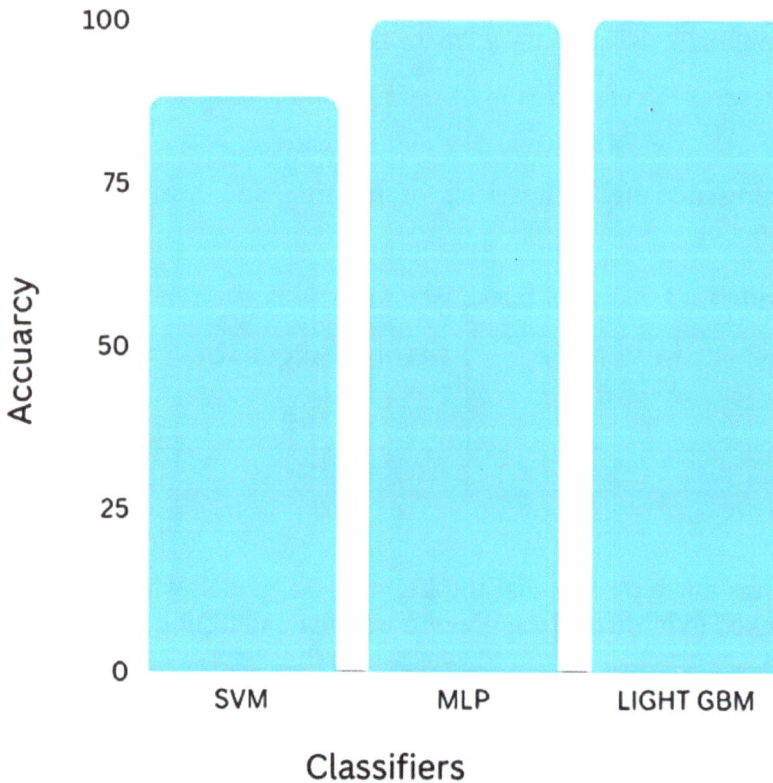

Fig. (4). Accuracy *vs* Classifiers for the Proposed System.

Our model can perform against novel data mentioned in the above graph Fig. **(4)** since we proposed a generalized model with proper evaluation and validation, testing on datasets. Models trained on the Kaggle dataset are typically optimized for the property and patterns of the training data. Kaggle datasets are often carefully curated and preprocessed to ensure high-quality data for analysis.

Research Challenges Addressed

1. Concluding and gathering the ones that are available is difficult. However, this article uses the KAGGLE dataset, a more current source of data, for its experimental work.
2. Effective feature engineering models are needed in order to solve the resource consumption of complex models, which is effectively handled in this research.
3. To prevent issues brought on by unbalanced data, a different classifier model is used to handle lower detection accuracy.
4. The detection of IoT-Botnet attacks using a lightweight model in the healthcare system was effectively addressed using the recommended technique, which

required little processing power, little training time, little testing time, and a high detection rate.

5. Despite the fact that this field is the subject of research, the performance in actual use is poor. To investigate further options, more studies must be conducted.

Table **4** represents the comparison of the average accuracy score for training and testing scores of the developed model with the existing model.

Table 4. Comparison of average accuracy score for training and testing scores.

CLASSIFIERS	SVM	MLP	LIGHT GBM
ACCURACY	87.5%	99.2%	100%

The graph representation of the accuracy score is shown in Fig. (**3**).

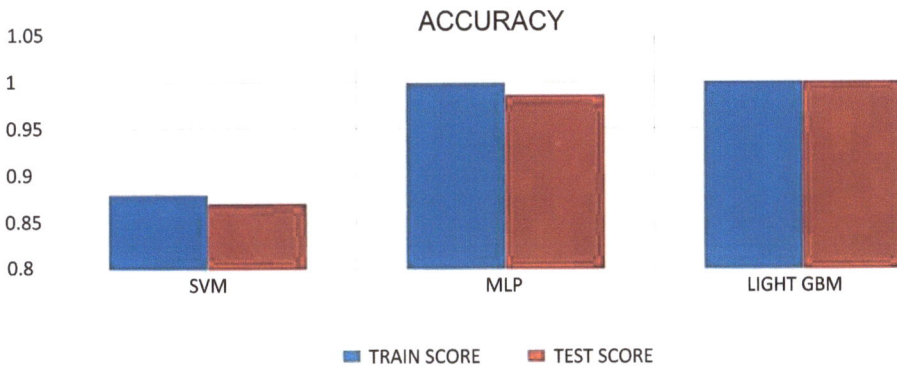

Fig. (5). Graph representation for accuracy score.

The above graph represents the accuracy score of the proposed model, which has the high accuracy than the existing model.

CONCLUSION & FUTURE WORK

Recently, a vast array of IoT devices and apps have been developed, with many of them being used in the healthcare industry. Attackers may target these devices because they handle sensitive and private information, such as information on a person's wellness. It is crucial to recognize the ideas of security needs and characteristics of IoT for healthcare. As a result, the machine learning and approach pre-processing strategies described in this study have a significant accuracy in the Healthcare IoT botnet. From the extensive experimental analysis, feature-based algorithms are superior to other competing models in that they (i) have the highest detection rate with high accuracy, and (ii) have less computational complexity with minimal training and test time. To improve the algorithm's performance against various botnet assaults on the healthcare system, this experiment might be expanded in future work to incorporate additional fresh datasets. Additionally, the supervised learning techniques utilised in this study may be contrasted with unsupervised learning techniques like clustering. To further hone these outcomes, alternative feature selection techniques might be investigated. Finally, the machine learning model may be evaluated in a real-time driven smart healthcare environment to see how well it performs and responds to various risks, including zero-day threats.

REFERENCES

[1]   S. Dange, and M. Chatterjee, *IoT botnet: The largest threat to the IoT network,"* in *DataCommunication and Networks.,* L.C. Jain, Ed., vol. Vol. 1049. Springer: Singapore, 2020, pp. 137-157.

[2]   S. Bagui, and K. Li, "Resampling imbalanced data for network intrusion detection datasets", *J. Big Data,* vol. 8, no. 1, p. 6, 2021.
[http://dx.doi.org/10.1186/s40537-020-00390-x] [PMID: 33425651]

[3]   B. Usmonov, O. Evsutin, A. Iskhakov, A. Shelupanov, A. Iskhakova, and R. Meshcheryakov, "The cybersecurity in development of IoT embedded technologies", *Proc. Int. Conf. Inf. Sci. Commun. Technol. (ICISCT),* pp. 1-4, 2017.
[http://dx.doi.org/10.1109/ICISCT.2017.8188589]

[4]   W.S. Hamza, H.M. Ibrahim, M.A. Shyaa, and J. Stephan, "IoT botnet detection: Challenges andissues", *Test Eng. Manage.,* vol. 83, pp. 15092-15097, 2020.

[5]   M. Hasan, M. M. Islam, M. I. I. Zarif, and M. M. A. Hashem, "Attack and anomaly detection in IoT sensors in IoT sites using machine learning approaches", *Internet Things,* vol. 7, 2019.
[http://dx.doi.org/10.1016/j.iot.2019.100059]

[6]   P. Gope, and T. Hwang, "BSN-care: A secure IoT-based modern healthcare system using body sensor network", *IEEE Sens. J.,* vol. 16, no. 5, pp. 1368-1376, 2016.
[http://dx.doi.org/10.1109/JSEN.2015.2502401]

[7]   S.L. Keoh, S.S. Kumar, and H. Tschofenig, "Securing the Internet of Things: A Standardization Perspective", *IEEE Internet Things J.,* vol. 1, no. 3, pp. 265-275, 2014.
[http://dx.doi.org/10.1109/JIOT.2014.2323395]

[8]   D. Metcalf, S.T.J. Milliard, M. Gomez, and M. Schwartz, "Wearables and the Internet of Things for Health: Wearable, Interconnected Devices Promise More Efficient and Comprehensive Health Care", *IEEE Pulse,* vol. 7, no. 5, pp. 35-39, 2016.
[http://dx.doi.org/10.1109/MPUL.2016.2592260] [PMID: 28113167]

[9]   T. Mohamed, T. Otsuka, and T. Ito, *Towards machine learning based IoT intrusion detection service,"* in *Recent Trends and Future Technology in Applied Intelligence.,* M. Mouhoub, S. Sadaoui, O.A. Mohamed, M. Ali, Eds., vol. 10868. Springer: Cham, Switzerland, 2018, pp. 580-585.
[http://dx.doi.org/10.1007/978-3-319-92058-0_56]

[10]   J.P. Chapman, E. Gerhards-Padilla, and F. Govaers, "Network traffic characteristics for detecting future Botnets", *Proceedings of the Communications and Information Systems Conference (MCC) IEEE,* pp. 1-10, 2012.

[11]   X. Dong, J. Hu, and Y. Cui, "Overview of Botnet Detection Based on Machine Learning", *International Conference on Mechanical, Control and Computer Engineering, Huhhot,* pp. 476-479,

2018.
[http://dx.doi.org/10.1109/ICMCCE.2018.00106]

[12]   S. Haq, and Y. Singh, "Botnet Detection using Machine Learning", *International Conference on Parallel, Distributed and Grid Computing (PDGC) India,* pp. 240-245, 2018.

[13]   R. Khan, R. Kumar, M. Alazab, and X. Zhang, "A Hybrid Technique To Detect Botnets, Based on P2P Traffic Similarity", *Cybersecurity and Cyberforensics Conference (CCC) Melbourne, Australia,* pp. 136-142, 2019.
[http://dx.doi.org/10.1109/CCC.2019.00008]

[14]   M. Stevanovic, and J. Pedersen, "An efficient flow-based botnet detection using supervised machine learning", *International Conference on Computing, Networking and Communications HI,* pp. 797-801, 2014.
[http://dx.doi.org/10.1109/ICCNC.2014.6785439]

[15]   N. Koroniotis, N. Moustafa, E. Sitnikova, and B. Turnbull, "Towards the development of realistic botnet dataset in the Internet of Things for network forensic analytics: Bot-IoT dataset", *Future Gener. Comput. Syst.,* vol. 100, pp. 779-796, 2019.
[http://dx.doi.org/10.1016/j.future.2019.05.041]

[16]   M. Bailey, E. Cooke, F. Jahanian, Y. Xu, and M. Karir, "A survey of Botnet technology and defenses", IEEE. In Proceedings of the Cybersecurity Applications & Technology Conference for Homeland Security (CATCH), 2009.

[17]   V.L. Thing, M. Sloman, and N. Dulay, *A survey of bots used for distributed denial of service attacks," New Approaches for Security, Privacy and Trust in Complex Environments.* Springer US, 2007, pp. 229-240.

[18]   L. Jing, X. Yang, G. Kaveh, D. Hongmei, and Z. Jingyuan, "Botnet: Classification, attacks, detection, tracing, and preventive measures", *Proceedings of the 4th International Conference on Innovative Computing, Information and Control IEEE Computer Society,* pp. 1184-1187, 2009.

[19]   F. Hussain, S.G. Abbas, G.A. Shah, I.M. Pires, U.U. Fayyaz, F. Shahzad, N.M. Garcia, and E. Zdravevski, "A Framework for Malicious Traffic Detection in IoT Healthcare Environment", *Sensors (Basel),* vol. 21, no. 9, p. 3025, 2021.
[http://dx.doi.org/10.3390/s21093025] [PMID: 33925813]

[20]   D.I. Dogaru, and I. Dumitrache, "Cyber security in healthcare networks", *Proceeding of The 6th IEEE International Conference on E-Health and Bioengineering Conference (EHB) Sinaia.* IEEE: Romania, 2017, pp. 414-417.

[21]   S.M.R. Islam, D. Kwak, M.H. Kabir, M. Hossain, and K-S. Kwak, "The Internet of Things for HealthCare: A Comprehensive Survey," in ", In: *IEEE* vol. 3. , 2015, pp. 678-708.
[http://dx.doi.org/10.1109/ACCESS.2015.2437951]

[22]   C. Zhang, and R. Green, "Communication security in internet of thing: preventive measure and avoid DDoS attack over IoT network", *In Proceedings of the 18th symposium on communications & networking,* 2015pp. 8-15 .

[23]   E. Anthi, L. Williams, and P. Burnap, "Pulse: An adaptive intrusion detection for the internet of things Pahl M.O. and Aubet F.X. 2018, November. All eyes on you: Distributed Multi-Dimensional IoT microservice anomaly detection", *In 2018 14th International Conference on Network and Service Management (CNSM,* pp. 72-80, 2018.
[http://dx.doi.org/10.1049/cp.2018.0035]

[24]   A. Ukil, S. Bandyoapdhyay, C. Puri, and A. Pal, "IoT healthcare analytics: The importance of anomaly detection", *In 2016 IEEE 30th international conference on advanced information networking and applications (AINA) ,* pp. 994-997, 2016.

[25]   S. Garg, A.K. Singh, A.K. Sarje, and S.K. Peddoju, "Behaviour analysis of machine learning algorithms for detecting P2P botnets", *In 2013 15th international conference on advanced computing*

technologies (icact) , pp. 1-4, 2013.

[26]   T. Mokhamed, M.A. Talib, M.A. Moufti, S. Abbas, and F. Khan, "The Potential of Blockchain Technology in Dental Healthcare: A Literature Review", *Sensors (Basel),* vol. 23, no. 6, p. 3277, 2023. [http://dx.doi.org/10.3390/s23063277] [PMID: 36991986]

[27]   W. Rafique, M. Khan, S. Khan, and J.S. Ally, "SecureMed: A Blockchain-Based Privacy-Preserving Framework for Internet of Medical Things", *Wireless Communications and Mobile Computing,,* p. 14, 2023.

[28]   Siddiqui S., Hameed S., Shah S. A., Ahmad I., Aneiba A., Draheim D., & Dustdar S. "Towards Software-Defined Networking-based IoT Frameworks: A Systematic Literature Review, Taxonomy, Open Challenges and Prospects". *IEEE Access*, 2022 [http://dx.doi.org/10.1109/ACCESS.2022.3188311]

CHAPTER 12

Smart Healthcare Classifier - Skin Lesion Detection using a Revolutionary Light Weight Deep Learning Framework

Sanjay Vasudevan[1,*], **Suresh Kumar Nagarajan**[2] and **Sarvana Kumar Selvaraj**[3]

[1] *School of Computer Science and Engineering, Vellore Institute of Technology, Vellore, India*

[2] *Department of Computer Applications, Kalasalingam Academy of Research and Education, Krishnankoil, Tamilnadu, India*

[3] *Department of Computer Science and Engineering, Jain University, Bangalore, India*

Abstract: Skin lesion diagnosis has recently gotten a lot of attention. Physicians spend a lot of time analyzing these skin lesions because of their striking similarities. Clinicians can use a deep learning-based automated classification system to identify the type of skin lesion and enhance the quality of medical services. As deep learning architecture progresses, skin lesion categorization has become a popular study topic. In this work, a modern skin lesion detection system is provided using a new segmentation approach known as wide-ShuffleNet. The entropy-based weighting technique is first computed, and a first-order cumulative moment algorithm is implemented for the skin picture. These illustrations are used to differentiate the lesion from the surrounding area. The type of melanoma is then established by sending the segmentation result into the wide-ShuffleNet, a new deep-learning structure. The proposed technique was evaluated using multiple huge datasets, including ISIC2019 and HAM10000. According to the statistics, EWA and CAFO wide-ShuffleNet are more accurate than the state-of-the-art approaches. The suggested technology is incredibly light, making it ideal for flexible healthcare management.

Keywords: Big Data, Computer Vision, Portable Health Service, Second Machine Intelligence.

INTRODUCTION

Skin cancer, which develops from lesions (abnormal changes in the interstation of the skin), is one of the deadliest forms of cancer. There are two main categories of skin cancer: melanomas and non-melanomas. Death and morbidity rates from melanoma lesions, the worst form of the disease, have skyrocketed in recent years

---

* **Corresponding author Sanjay Vasudevan:** School of Computer Science and Engineering, Vellore Institute of Technology, Vellore, India; E-mail: sanjay.researcher@gmail.com

L. Ashok Kumar, D. Karthika Renuka, Sonali Agarwal & Sheng-Lung Peng (Eds.)

[1]. Recovery times can be halved if cancers are detected early [2]. The similarity between various skin lesion types also makes it hard to conduct a thorough screening for melanoma, which can lead to incorrect diagnoses. The problem of inaccurate lesion picture recognition in healthcare [3] and image analysis [4] can be solved by applying machine learning.

With about a million cases of cell carcinoma lesions per year, about 3 million cases of skin lesions that are not melanomas are recorded each year. Approximately 2.5 million people died in 2012 from sun exposure, according to the world health organization. Infections of the skin account for more than 80 percent of all cases of fatal skin cancer [5]. The concept of prostate cancer, and in particular melanoma, was already linked to a history of scorching before this study was conducted. Patients with gliomas have a better prognosis if their tumors are diagnosed at an early stage [6]. In order to account for inter-observer variations, technicians are encouraged to manually diagnose melanoma. Consequently, the accuracy and timeliness of cancer diagnoses are improved by an automated analysis procedure.

Melanoma, especially in its early stages, can have a similar appearance to benign moles (even for qualified dermatologists [7]). Artificial intelligence (AI) and human-made systems have both been offered as possible solutions to these issues.

Border, color, and visual texture were used as early low-level clues to differentiate melanoma from other tumors [8]. However, the results of Celebi *et al.* [9], who also relied on form, color, and texture cues, were subpar because of the significant infraclass similarity between the training and test sets. Segmentation, as explained [10], is another way to get rid of extraneous details and background. The images were first binary-mask partitioned, and then labelled using a support vector machine. The results of using Gabor filter masks to generate thresholding values, like in [11]'s segmentation approach, are usually unsatisfactory.

The second method is the use of artificial intelligence, which has many uses in fields including mining, ecology, and city planning. There are two main categories of artificial intelligence (AI): machine learning and deep learning [12]. [13 - 15] Algorithms capable of data recognition and prediction are the product of machine learning. The various architectures that DL can utilise to probe linked image components and extract features are constantly expanding. Large datasets are no problem for DL, which may be utilised to examine them [16 - 22]. Particularly useful in video and image processing since the advent of multiprocessor unit computers is the deep neural network DL model. A recent study [23 - 25] found that CGI is a useful technique for evaluating bioimages.

Since skin cancer is so common, early diagnosis is essential. Machine analytic approaches are still not commonly applied in therapeutic settings, despite much studies to the contrary. Machine learning and deep learning models confront various challenges, including a shortage of data for correct lesion classifications and the necessity for qualified people to operate the equipment [26]. Therefore, it is crucial to have models that are both reliable and efficient and can run on distributed nodes. Parameter-heavy, desktop-centric deep learning algorithms aren't well suited to mobile devices [27]. Consequently, setting up the infrastructure for a portable device is a challenging task. We detail a novel method for classifying skin lesions that, in contrast to previous approaches, makes use of a few variables without sacrificing accuracy [28]. An example of a system where this method would be useful is a mobile healthcare system. We used a novel wide-ShuffleNet in conjunction with an original segmentation method to detect skin lesions. The proposed method of segmentation outperforms traditional approaches and aids the infrastructure in recognizing the local feature item during classification [29].

Insights gained from this research include the following:

• Combining the entropy-based weighting technique with the first-order cumulative moment algorithm, we present a novel method for segmenting skin images.

• Before moving on to a two-dimensional wide-ShuffleNet network, the point cloud is initially identified using an entropy-based weighting technique and the first-order cumulative moment algorithm. We found that the proposed method outperformed the entropy-based weighting method, the first cumulative instant algorithm, and the full Shuffle Net when it came to accumulating Datasets.

Here is how the rest of the chapter is structured. It discusses previous work, the methodology provided, numerical results, and future directions for study.

RELATED WORKS

KNN is a guided machine learning algorithm for prediction [30]. Accuracy is high using the nearest neighbor method [31]. Another automated skin cancer diagnostic method based on K-nearest neighbors was proposed by Sajid *et al.* [32]. Their method involves applying a median filter to an image and then using other statistical and textural data to reduce noise. Statistical information was gleaned from lesion images, while sensory data was extracted using a discrete wavelet region. This proposed method could also identify potentially cancerous images.

The KNN model's computation-intensive predictions make it inappropriate for use with huge data sets. Further, the KNN method is inadequate for skin lesion classification because of its poor performance on high-dimensional input data with erroneous feature information [33].

In order to identify eczema, Alam *et al.* [34] used support vector machines. In a study [35], you can change many different aspects of the image. In order to diagnose eczema, images must undergo segmentation, texture-based feature determination, and support vector machine analysis. The local feature parameters of the direction histogram, slope, and position were recovered by Upadhyay *et al.* [36]. All of these characteristics were combined using the SVM algorithm, and then classified as malignant or noncancerous. When dealing with skewed input images, SVM methodology breaks out [37]. When there are fewer data points available for analysis than there are unique features in the field being studied, SVM excels.

Bayesian methods [38] are also used in skin lesion classification with several skin ImageNet datasets used for training. Bringing the Naive Bayes method into a multi-objective setting is challenging. Among the many applications of the clustering algorithm model, the classification of skin lesions, cervical cancer detection and the prediction of lower-extremity lesions are two examples. For the detection of malignant melanoma, Arasi *et al.* utilized intelligence approaches, judgement tree branches, and Nave Bayesian. A kernel principal component analysis and a composite wavelet transform were used to extract the characteristics of interest. Selective networks and Nave Bayesian are only two of the classification methods that employ these features to determine whether or not a tumour is malignant. The decision tree approach requires a lot of training data to be effective methods that don't rely on segmentation.

Conventional DL classifier approaches for skin recognition include non-segmentation algorithms and abstraction layers.

Menegola *et al.* analysed six public datasets to classify lesion images. In this study, we used state-of-the-art methods based on robust predictive topologies to identify hydroxyl groups in bulbs, basal cell carcinomas, and nevi. It was also established that better classification accuracy is achieved when more training data is made available through the combination of datasets. Resnet-152 was proposed for pathological image classification by Han *et al.*. Basal cell carcinoma, colorectal cancer, keratosis caused by exposure to metal halides, fibrotic sarcomas, and myeloid tumours are all examples of these lesions. Lesion detectability is affected by two factors: visual contrast and genetics.

Esteva *et al.* used the Inception v3 classification framework to divide the lesion into three kinds. The method begins by classifying keratinocyte carcinomas and seborrheic keratoses into benign and malignant subtypes. This information can aid in the diagnosis of moles, both benign and malignant.

DL Segmentation Techniques

Gonzalez-Diaz outlined three techniques: segmentation, structural segmentation, and skin lesion detection. First, the skin scan is partitioned, and the resulting data is used as input for morphological segmentation. In the end, the evaluation processes use information gathered throughout the procedure to classify the skin condition. Creating a tagged training database is the primary obstacle in building a structure segmentation network that uses ground truth for each image. As dermatologists must draw the boundaries between the segments by hand, this annotation is typically challenging.

In the study, deep learning was used to construct a segmentation model to create a representation of the image sequence, collect areas of aberrant skin, and then feed that information into a classification algorithm. Also, Son and coworkers built the cluster boundaries using the U-Net output mask and then cropped them using the convex hull method. Each cluster was then fed into an Efficient Net in an effort to make a prediction about the lesion kind.

Al-Masni *et al.* suggested a system for efficiently isolating and labelling boundaries in picture data. We started by utilizing a deep learning comprehensive convolutional network to segment the edges of the local features (FrCN). A CNN processor was used to categorize the segmentation expansions. Because it records the most prominent characteristics of various skin lesions, segmentation is a crucial step in local feature diagnosis.

METHODOLOGY

Here, we introduce the EWM-CMFO segmentation technique and a unique wide-ShuffleNet for skin lesion categorization. In order to help the network recognise the skin lesion object, the segmentation step separates the lesion from the background. Using Wide-ShuffleNet, we segmented the data, extracted features, and categorised them Fig. (**1**) depicts the overall structure of the suggested technique. We demonstrate the synergistic benefits of combining the EWA with the cumulative moment first, to create the novel EWA-CMFO feature extraction technique (Section 3.1). In Section 3.2, the wide-ShuffleNet is presented The suggested Architecture are shown in the below Fig. (**2**).

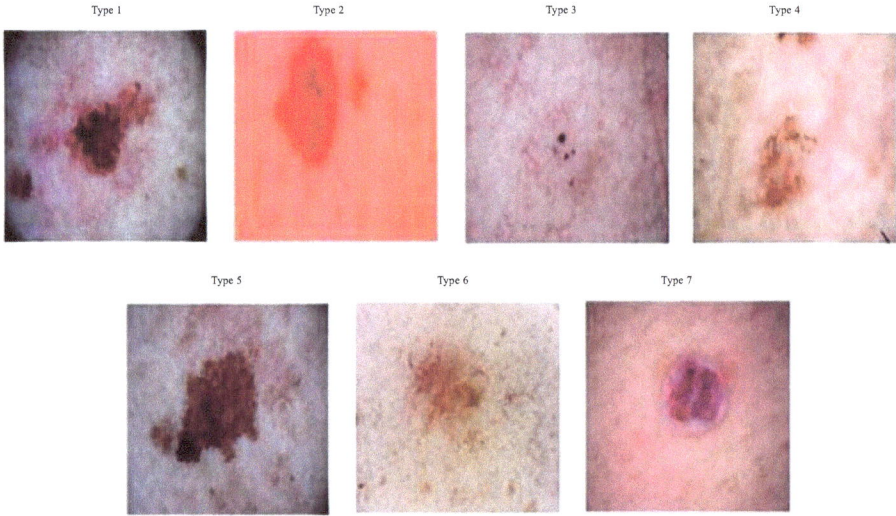

Fig. (1). Sample Dataset Skin Lesions.

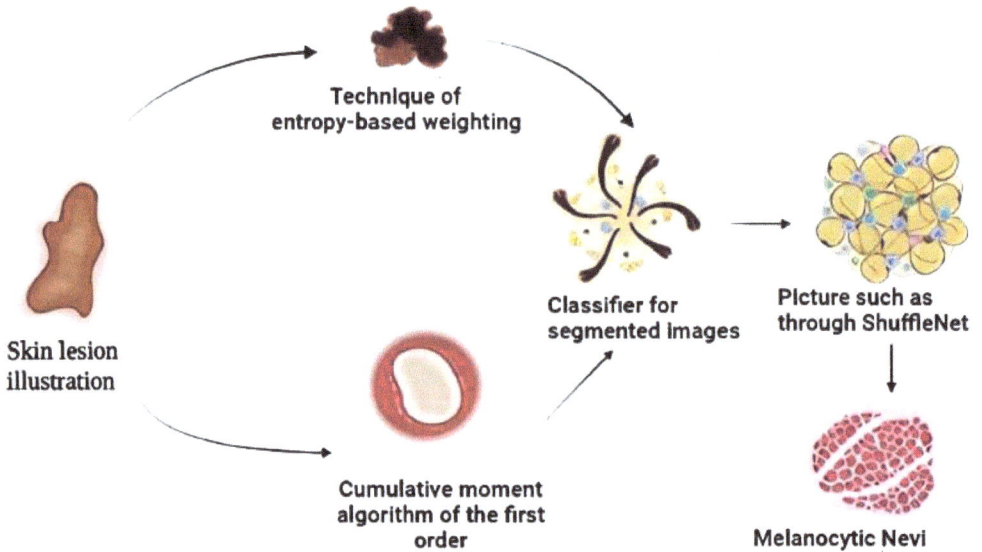

Fig. (2). Schematic of the Suggested Architecture.

A stochastic optimization model, the entropy-based weighting technique, mimics the social behaviour of a flock by analysing the statistical characteristics of the population. Like EA, it takes into account a population and assigns a fitness function to each member of that group. The arithmetic crossover operator of the

EWMs resembles the adjustment formula of the EWMs, adding further complexity. EMW is influenced by more than simply natural selection when it comes to social behaviour simulation. The fact that no one in EAs learns anything from the past is another key distinction. The ease with which EWM may be implemented has made it a popular tool for solving both discrete and continuous optimization problems [21].

As part of EWM, a group of people (called particles) congregate in and around the search zone. A different optimal solution to the problem is represented by each individual particle. Particles take cues for their locations not only from their own best position, but also from the best position of other particles in the vicinity. Generally speaking, the swarm's best particle is the one that happens to be in the nicest potential neighbourhood. G on best EWM is the name given to the final algorithm. It's been called the "best EWM for tiny neighbourhoods." Particle separation affects the fitness function, which in turn affects the optimization strategy and the final, optimal solution.

Current position of the particle: a_i

The current velocity of the particle: b_i

In the best possible configuration, a particle would be: c_i

The best place for the particle to be in the immediate area: $\hat{b}_i$

A particle's optimum position is the one that maximises its own fitness, or the position that the particle finds itself in most often. Consider the objective function to be f [22]. Then, the new best for a particle is calculated as (1) at time step t:

$$db_i(s+2) = \begin{cases} db_i(s) & if\ wg\big(a_i(s+2)\big) > dg\big(b_i(s)\big) \\ da_i(s+2) & if\ wg(a_i(s+2)) < dg(b_i(s)) \end{cases} \tag{1}$$

Every member of the swarm voted on which particle would make the best model. by picking one's optimal best position. In the event that the location of the best particle in the world is signified by the vector $\hat{b}$, then (2):

$$\check{b}\{b_0, b_1 \dots b_k\} = \min\{g\big(b_1(s)\big), \dots, (b_k(s))\} \tag{2}$$

Where the swarm size is shown as k.

The velocity update step is defined for all dimensionalities (j = 1,...,Nd). So, the jth component of the velocity vector for the ith particle is denoted by bi, j. To calculate the particle's speed I, we utilise the following equation (3):

$$b_{i,j}(s+1) = qb_{i,j}(s) + c_1m_{1,j}(s)b_{i,j}(s)) - b_{i,j}(s)) + c_2m_{2,j}(s)(\overline{b(s)} - b_{i,j}(s)) \qquad (3)$$

Inertia weight $=w$, acceleration constants are c1 and c2 and $c_1m_{1,j}(s)$, $m_{2,j}{\sim}U$ (0, 1).

Number-theoretic First-order Cumulative Moment Algorithm

Every training round involves a weak learner and uses the first-order Cumulative moment algorithm. After training, the algorithm boosts sample weights, which is expected to be a misclassification, and a drop in sample weight, which is correctly identified. Through this mechanism, the likelihood of using correctly categorised samples decreases from one iteration to the next, while the likelihood of using poorly classified samples increases [23].

The first-order cumulative moment algorithm employs the formula S=a (1,)b 1. Training samples of size N are represented as (a n,b n), where a i is an attribute variable for a subset of space P, and b i is the label for that sample in the label space Q [27].

The weights are first initialised uniformly across the training set before the algorithm begins iteration; in each iteration, the weights of all examples that were incorrectly classified are increased. This is how a poor learner would focus on the most extreme examples in the data set.

First-order cumulative moment algorithms on training data use a weight vector to update the weights of each training sample with each iteration (4).

S=a (1,)b 1. (a n,b n) is the basis of the first-order cumulative moment algorithm, where an I is an attribute variable for the subset space P and b I is the label for each sample an I in the label space Q.

The weights are first initialised uniformly across the training set before the algorithm begins iteration; in each iteration, the weights of all examples that were incorrectly classified are increased. This is how a poor learner would focus on the most extreme examples in the data set.

The first-order cumulative moment algorithm on the training samples uses a weight vector to update the weights of each sample with each iteration of the algorithm (4).

$$R_{s+1,i} = R_{s,i} A_s^{1-bi} \tag{4}$$

An error rate j of this classifier is calculated for each sample weighted by its likelihood in (5) [27] and then used to fine-tune the probability distribution of training samples.

$$\in = \sum_{i-1} W_{s,i}^{bi} \tag{5}$$

When building a powerful final classifier, it's helpful to give each classifier some weight based on how well it performs during training (x). Therefore, the algorithm is tuned to analyse samples of challenging patterns. Issues of simple yes/no classification are the topic of this research. Q = {-2 + 2}.

The algorithm's pseudo code is as follows [27]:

Specify M cases $(a_1 b_1), \ldots (a_i b_i) \ldots \ldots, (a_m b_m)$

Suppose $b_i \in \{-2,2\}$

Initialize $R_{1,t} = {}^1\!/_{2d}, {}^1\!/_{2z} \, for \, b_i = 2$

Where d and z are the number of unfavorable and favourable atoms, respectively.

For qs=1........Tv do

   (1) Create a classifier for each feature j using trainaclassifierk j

   (2) Examine the blunder minimal amount of flaw $\epsilon_t = \sum_{i=0} K, R_{s,i} b^i$

   (3) For best results, choose the classifier V s with the smallest error. ϵ_t

Correction of mass $R_{s+1,i} = R_{s,i} A_s^{1-bi}$

   Where $b_i = 0$ if $V_s(a_i) = z_i b_i = 1$

   WhereA_s $= \epsilon_s/(1 - \epsilon_s)$

End for

Classifier with high output

$$V(x) = \begin{cases} 1 \; if sign \left(\sum_{i=0} \alpha, \beta_s^{1-b} {}_s v_s \right) \\ -1 \qquad\qquad\qquad otherwise \end{cases}$$

With $\alpha_s = log(1/\beta_s)$

RESULTS AND DISCUSSION

Here we employ a variety of shuffle networks, including the ANN-ShuffleNet, KNN-ShuffleNet, CNN-ShuffleNet, EW-ShuffleNet, FCM-ShuffleNet, and EMA-CAFO-ShuffleNet. Both the total number of classification trees (which can be anywhere from 25 to 300) and their depth can be optimised (from 1 to 6). Data are summarised in Table **1**.

Table 1. Result Analysis.

Classification	F-Measure	Sensitivity	Specificity	Accuracy
ANN-ShuffleNet	65.05	68.3	70.04	73.02
KNN-ShuffleNet	62.3	55.4	65.05	70.03
CNN-ShuffleNet	73.03	68.05	92.28	93.03
EW-ShuffleNet	72.03	75.05	84.27	90.07
FCM-ShuffleNet	78.06	75.05	86.5	92.2
EW-FCM-ShuffleNet	85.05	87.56	89.05	94.05

The accuracy of the classification (represented by F-Measure values) is shown in Fig. (**3**) through 5.

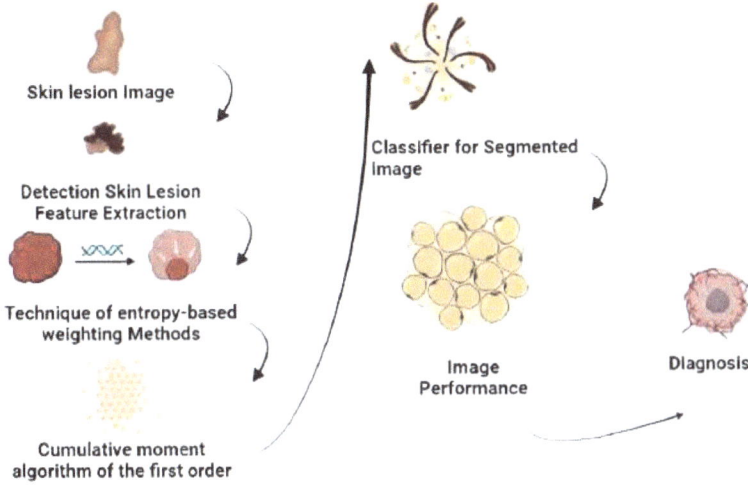

Fig. (3). The Proposed EWM-CAFO Rerouting Network.

Fig. (**4**) shows that compared to the KNN-ShuffleNet, the ANN-ShuffleNet improves F-Measure categorization by 20.46%, the CNN-ShuffleNet by 11.64%, the EW-ShuffleNet by 3.31%, and the EMA-CAFO-ShuffleNet by 5.63%.

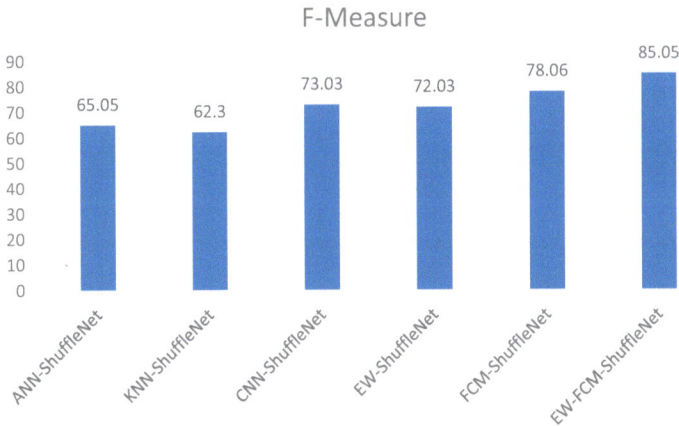

Fig. (4). F-Score for the EWA-CAFO ShuffleNet.

Fig. (**5**) shows that compared to the KNN-ShuffleNet, CNN-ShuffleNet, EW-ShuffleNet, and EMA-CAFO-ShuffleNet, the ANN-Shuffle Net achieves a 17.47% higher classification accuracy.

Classification Accuracy

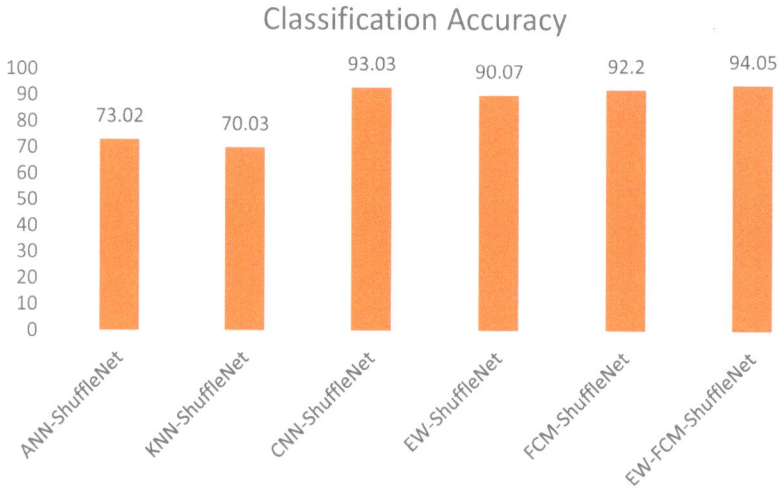

Fig. (5). Effectiveness of the ShuffleNet in the EWA-CAFO.

Fig. **(6)** demonstrates that the EMA-CAFO-ShuffleNet outperformed the CNN-ShuffleNet, KNN-ShuffleNet, EW-ShuffleNet, and EMA-CAFO-ShuffleNet when it came to detecting skin lesions.

Classification

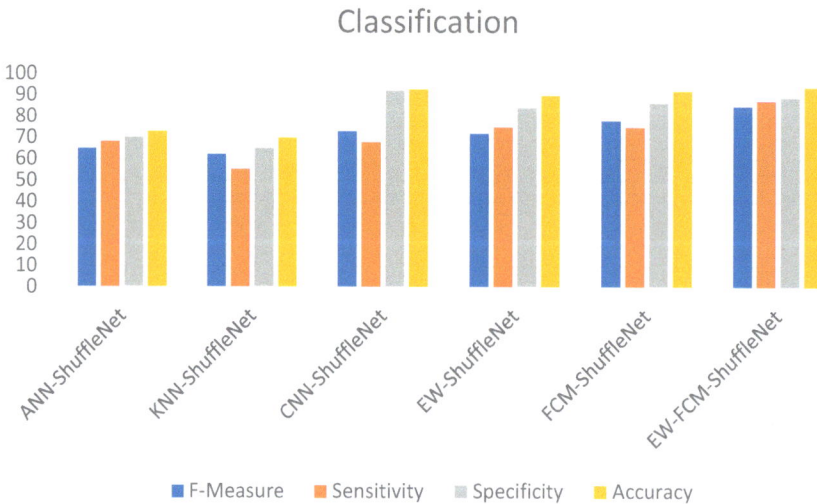

Fig. (6). Realized Motion Detection of Skin Disease.

CONCLUSION

Skin cancer is one of the most lethal forms of cancer in humans. Using DL to automate the classification of skin lesions will save doctors' time and increase their rate of success. Normal DL frameworks have too many parameters to be practical on a mobile device. Therefore, it is essential to propose a skin lesion classification using a minimal DL framework. In this research, we introduce a novel method for categorising entities. Because of this limitation, we provide a straightforward method for analysing a larger number of regional feature samples. In terms of efficiency and accuracy, the suggested framework is shown to be superior by the numerical results to the other 20 methods considered. The proposed solution maintains superior accuracy while reducing the number of alternatives by roughly 79 times compared to another approach (VGG19). The suggested method improves accuracy while also simplifying Differential-logic segmentation differential-Logic edge detection Non-deterministic logic feature extraction. It also offers DL clustering algorithm-scale estimation solutions. Additional nodes will be added in the future to conform to the conceptual approach. Future research and development could also focus on finding ways to implement the proposed method in real-world settings like mobility health care.

REFERENCES

[1]   T. Kumari, R. Kumar, and R.K. Dwivedi, "Designing Blockchain Based Consensus Mechanism for Smart Healthcare IoT", *2023 International Conference on Intelligent and Innovative Technologies in Computing, Electrical and Electronics (IITCEE) Bengaluru, India,* pp. 878-884, 2023.
[http://dx.doi.org/10.1109/IITCEE57236.2023.10090882]

[2]   S. Saravanan, "Skin lesion detection with a healthcare information classifier using a unique lightweight deep learning framework", *NeuroQuantology,* vol. 20, no. 5, pp. 4349-4358, 2022.

[3]   T. Mokhamed, M.A. Talib, M.A. Moufti, S. Abbas, and F. Khan, "The Potential of Blockchain Technology in Dental Healthcare: A Literature Review", *Sensors (Basel),* vol. 23, no. 6, p. 3277, 2023.
[http://dx.doi.org/10.3390/s23063277] [PMID: 36991986]

[4]   A.N. Abougreen, and C. Chakraborty, Applications of Machine Learning and Internet of Things in Agriculture.*Green Technological Innovation for Sustainable Smart Societies.,* C. Chakraborty, Ed., Springer: Cham, 2021.
[http://dx.doi.org/10.1007/978-3-030-73295-0_12]

[5]   C. Chakraborty, and A.N. Abougreen, "Intelligent internet of things and advanced machine learning techniques for Covid-19", *EAI Endorsed Trans. Pervasive Health Technol.,* vol. 7, no. 26, p. e1, 2021.

[6]   W. Rafique, M. Khan, S. Khan, and J.S. Ally, "SecureMed: A blockchain-based privacy-preserving framework for internet of medical things", *Wireless Communications and Mobile Computing,* vol. 2023, 2023.
[http://dx.doi.org/10.1155/2023/2558469]

[7]   L. Rey-Barroso, S. Peña-Gutiérrez, C. Yáñez, F.J. Burgos-Fernández, M. Vilaseca, and S. Royo, "Optical technologies for the improvement of skin cancer diagnosis: A review", *Sensors (Basel),* vol. 21, no. 1, p. 252, 2021.
[http://dx.doi.org/10.3390/s21010252] [PMID: 33401739]

[8]   K.M. Hosny, M.A. Kassem, and M.M. Foaud, "Classification of skin lesions using transfer learning and augmentation with Alex-net", *PLoS One,* vol. 14, no. 5, p. e0217293, 2019.
[http://dx.doi.org/10.1371/journal.pone.0217293] [PMID: 31112591]

[9]   R.V. Zicari, S. Ahmed, J. Amann, S.A. Braun, J. Brodersen, F. Bruneault, J. Brusseau, E. Campano, M. Coffee, A. Dengel, B. Düdder, A. Gallucci, T.K. Gilbert, P. Gottfrois, E. Goffi, C.B. Haase, T. Hagendorff, E. Hickman, E. Hildt, S. Holm, P. Kringen, U. Kühne, A. Lucieri, V.I. Madai, P.A. Moreno-Sánchez, O. Medlicott, M. Ozols, E. Schnebel, A. Spezzatti, J.J. Tithi, S. Umbrello, D. Vetter, H. Volland, M. Westerlund, and R. Wurth, "Co-Design of a trustworthy AI System in healthcare: Deep learning based skin lesion classifier", *Frontiers in Human Dynamics,* vol. 3, p. 688152, 2021.
[http://dx.doi.org/10.3389/fhumd.2021.688152]

[10]   N. Mishra, and M. Celebi, "An overview of melanoma detection in dermoscopy images using image processing and machine learning", *arXiv:1601.07843,* 2016.

[11]   World Health Organization, "Radiation: Ultraviolet (UV) Radiation and skin cancer", Available From: https ://www.who.int / news-room/questions-and-answers/item/radiation-ultraviolet -(uv)-radiati-n-and -skin- cancer

[12]   A.F. Jerant, J.T. Johnson, C.D. Sheridan, and T.J. Caffrey, "Early detection and treatment of skin cancer", *Am. Fam. Physician,* vol. 62, no. 2, pp. 357-368, 375-376, 381-382, 2000.
[PMID: 10929700]

[13]   J. Trufant, and E. Jones, Skin cancer for primary care.*Common Dermatologic Conditions in Primary Care.,* J.R. John, F.R. Edward Jr, Eds., Springer: Cham, Switzerland, 2019, pp. 171-208.
[http://dx.doi.org/10.1007/978-3-030-18065-2_17]

[14]   C. Barata, M.E. Celebi, and J.S. Marques, "A survey of feature extraction in dermoscopy image analysis of skin cancer", *IEEE J. Biomed. Health Inform.,* vol. 23, no. 3, pp. 1096-1109, 2019.
[http://dx.doi.org/10.1109/JBHI.2018.2845939] [PMID: 29994234]

[15]   M.E. Celebi, H.A. Kingravi, B. Uddin, H. Iyatomi, Y.A. Aslandogan, W.V. Stoecker, and R.H. Moss, "A methodological approach to the classification of dermoscopy images", *Comput. Med. Imaging Graph.,* vol. 31, no. 6, pp. 362-373, 2007.
[http://dx.doi.org/10.1016/j.compmedimag.2007.01.003] [PMID: 17387001]

[16]   T. Tommasi, E. La Torre, and B. Caputo, "Melanoma recognition using representative and discriminative kernel classifiers", *Proceedings of the International Workshop on Computer Vision Approaches to Medical Image Analysis (CVAMIA) Graz, Austria,* pp. 1-12, 2006.
[http://dx.doi.org/10.1007/11889762_1]

[17]   S. Pathan, K.G. Prabhu, and P.C. Siddalingaswamy, "A methodological approach to classify typical and atypical pigment network patterns for melanoma diagnosis", *Biomed. Signal Process. Control,* vol. 44, pp. 25-37, 2018.
[http://dx.doi.org/10.1016/j.bspc.2018.03.017]

[18]   A. Taner, Y.B. Öztekin, and H. Duran, "Performance analysis of deep learning CNN models for variety classification in hazelnut", *Sustainability (Basel),* vol. 13, no. 12, p. 6527, 2021.
[http://dx.doi.org/10.3390/su13126527]

[19]   W. Wang, and K. Siau, "Artificial intelligence, machine learning, automation, robotics, future of work and future of humanity: A review and research agenda", *J. Database Manage.,* vol. 30, no. 1, pp. 61-79, 2019.
[http://dx.doi.org/10.4018/JDM.2019010104]

[20]   A.L. Samuel, Some studies in machine learning using the game of checkers. II—Recent progress.*Computer Games I.* Springer: Berlin/Heidelberg, Germany, 1988, pp. 366-400.
[http://dx.doi.org/10.1007/978-1-4613-8716-9_15]

[21]   W. Liu, Z. Wang, X. Liu, N. Zeng, Y. Liu, and F.E. Alsaadi, "A survey of deep neural network architectures and their applications", *Neurocomputing,* vol. 234, pp. 11-26, 2017.

[http://dx.doi.org/10.1016/j.neucom.2016.12.038]

[22]   Z. Qiu, J. Chen, Y. Zhao, S. Zhu, Y. He, and C. Zhang, "Variety identification of single rice seed using hyperspectral imaging combined with convolutional neural network", *Appl. Sci. (Basel),* vol. 8, no. 2, p. 212, 2018.
[http://dx.doi.org/10.3390/app8020212]

[23]   J. Acquarelli, T. van Laarhoven, J. Gerretzen, T.N. Tran, L.M.C. Buydens, and E. Marchiori, "Convolutional neural networks for vibrational spectroscopic data analysis", *Anal. Chim. Acta,* vol. 954, pp. 22-31, 2017.
[http://dx.doi.org/10.1016/j.aca.2016.12.010] [PMID: 28081811]

[24]   X. Zhang, T. Lin, J. Xu, X. Luo, and Y. Ying, "DeepSpectra: An end-to-end deep learning approach for quantitative spectral analysis", *Anal. Chim. Acta,* vol. 1058, pp. 48-57, 2019.
[http://dx.doi.org/10.1016/j.aca.2019.01.002] [PMID: 30851853]

[25]   X. Yang, Y. Ye, X. Li, R.Y.K. Lau, X. Zhang, and X. Huang, "Hyperspectral image classification with deep learning models", *IEEE Trans. Geosci. Remote Sens.,* vol. 56, no. 9, pp. 5408-5423, 2018.
[http://dx.doi.org/10.1109/TGRS.2018.2815613]

[26]   X. Yu, L. Tang, X. Wu, and H. Lu, "Nondestructive freshness discriminating of shrimp using visible/near-infrared hyperspectral imaging technique and deep learning algorithm", *Food Anal. Methods,* vol. 11, no. 3, pp. 768-780, 2018.
[http://dx.doi.org/10.1007/s12161-017-1050-8]

[27]   J. Yue, S. Mao, and M. Li, "A deep learning framework for hyperspectral image classification using spatial pyramid pooling", *Remote Sens. Lett.,* vol. 7, no. 9, pp. 875-884, 2016.
[http://dx.doi.org/10.1080/2150704X.2016.1193793]

[28]   A. Signoroni, M. Savardi, A. Baronio, and S. Benini, "Deep learning meets hyperspectral image analysis: A multidisciplinary review", *J. Imaging,* vol. 5, no. 5, p. 52, 2019.
[http://dx.doi.org/10.3390/jimaging5050052] [PMID: 34460490]

[29]   K. Thurnhofer-Hemsi, E. López-Rubio, E. Domínguez, and D.A. Elizondo, "Skin lesion classification by ensembles of deep convolutional networks and regularly spaced shifting", *IEEE Access,* vol. 9, pp. 112193-112205, 2021.
[http://dx.doi.org/10.1109/ACCESS.2021.3103410]

[30]   G. Litjens, T. Kooi, B.E. Bejnordi, A.A.A. Setio, F. Ciompi, M. Ghafoorian, J.A.W.M. van der Laak, B. van Ginneken, and C.I. Sánchez, "A survey on deep learning in medical image analysis", *Med. Image Anal.,* vol. 42, pp. 60-88, 2017.
[http://dx.doi.org/10.1016/j.media.2017.07.005] [PMID: 28778026]

[31]   C. Cui, K. Thurnhofer-Hemsi, R. Soroushmehr, A. Mishra, J. Gryak, E. Dominguez, K. Najarian, and E. Lopez-Rubio, "Diabetic wound segmentation using convolutional neural networks", *Proceedings of the 41th Annual International Conference of the IEEE Engineering in Medicine and Biology Society (EMBC) Berlin, Germany,* pp. 1002-1005, 2019.
[http://dx.doi.org/10.1109/EMBC.2019.8856665]

[32]   K. Thurnhofer-Hemsi, and E. Domínguez, Analyzing digital image by deep learning for melanoma diagnosis.*Advances in Computational Intelligence.,* I. Rojas, G. Joya, A. Catala, Eds., Springer: Cham, Switzerland, 2019, pp. 270-279.
[http://dx.doi.org/10.1007/978-3-030-20518-8_23]

[33]   K. Thurnhofer-Hemsi, and E. Domínguez, "A convolutional neural network framework for accurate skin cancer detection", *Neural Process. Lett.,* vol. 53, no. 5, pp. 3073-3093, 2021.
[http://dx.doi.org/10.1007/s11063-020-10364-y]

[34]   N.C. Codella, D. Gutman, M.E. Celebi, B. Helba, M.A. Marchetti, S.W. Dusza, and A. Halpern, "Skin lesion analysis toward melanoma detection: A challenge at the 2017 international symposium on biomedical imaging (ISBI), hosted by the international skin imaging collaboration (ISIC)", *Proceedings of the 2018 IEEE 15th International Symposium on Biomedical Imaging (ISBI 2018)*

Washington, DC, USA, pp. 168-172, 2018.

[35] P.N. Srinivasu, J.G. SivaSai, M.F. Ijaz, A.K. Bhoi, W. Kim, and J.J. Kang, "SivaSai, J.G.; Ijaz, M.F.; Bhoi, A.K.; Kim, W.; Kang, J.J. Classification of skin disease using deep learning neural networks with MobileNet V2 and LSTM", *Sensors (Basel),* vol. 21, no. 8, p. 2852, 2021.
[http://dx.doi.org/10.3390/s21082852] [PMID: 33919583]

[36] Y. Dang, N. Jiang, H. Hu, Z. Ji, and W. Zhang, "Image classification based on quantum K-Neares--Neighbor algorithm", *Quantum Inform. Process.,* vol. 17, no. 9, p. 239, 2018.
[http://dx.doi.org/10.1007/s11128-018-2004-9]

[37] R. Sumithra, M. Suhil, and D.S. Guru, "Segmentation and classification of skin lesions for disease diagnosis", *Procedia Comput. Sci.,* vol. 45, pp. 76-85, 2015.
[http://dx.doi.org/10.1016/j.procs.2015.03.090]

[38] P.M. Sajid, and D.A. Rajesh, "Performance evaluation of classifiers for automatic early detection of skin cancer", *J. Adv. Res. Dyn. Control. Syst.,* vol. 10, pp. 454-461, 2018.

CHAPTER 13

Recent Trends in Telemedicine, Challenges and Opportunities

S. Kannadhasan[1,*], R. Nagarajan[2] and M. Shanmuganantham[3]

[1] *Study World College of Engineering Coimbatore, Tamilnadu, India*

[2] *Gnanamani College of Technology, Tamilnadu, India*

[3] *Tamilnadu Government Polytechnic College, Tamilnadu, India*

Abstract: Recent networking advancements in a variety of areas have encouraged the introduction of applications for the Internet of Things (IoT) and Artificial Intelligence (AI). This article analyses the implications of technologies like IoT and AI in Healthcare *via* a careful analysis of 85 peer-reviewed scientific journal publications. The study shows a previously unheard-of rise in the number of publications written in the last ten years, a wide range of publishing sources, a wide range of authors, and several technical papers in philosophy and architecture, all of which point to an evolving field with plenty of room for publication in the years to come. Medical research is currently combining the administration and analysis of telemedicine data as well as the development and use of artificial intelligence in numerous fields and enterprises (AI). Due to the difficulty of implementing telemedicine, it has been required to develop cutting-edge methods and expand its capabilities.

Keywords: Healthcare , Industry Sector, Machine Learning and Applications, Telemedicine.

INTRODUCTION

With the extension of the sharing of patient information to remote patient visits, medical evaluations and procedures, and doctor-patient relationships, the study's objective is to encourage the participation of new researchers in this field by recognizing the fundamental techniques and applications that will enable more telemedicine in their research. In an attempt to reverse the troubling tendency of categorizing raw physiological data, modern machine learning algorithms are being enhanced. In addition to responding to and adapting to the changing social needs and conditions for health, it incorporates new scientific breakthroughs. The main goals of telemedicine were to lessen the communication and coordination

---

[*] **Corresponding author S. Kannadhasan:** Study World College of Engineering Coimbatore, Tamilnadu, India; E-mail: kannadhasan.ece@gmail.com

L. Ashok Kumar, D. Karthika Renuka, Sonali Agarwal & Sheng-Lung Peng (Eds.)

gaps in the medical industry, as well as the escalating shortages and complicated pricing. Wireless technology has been developed for sensors and applications for case studies, including electronic health records and home monitoring, during the last 10 years. The medical community has conducted a study on the cost and use of this technology, which is included in this. One of the four fields where networks using information and communication technology (ICT) have been developed most extensively is teleradiology, which sends digital radiological images (such as X-ray images) from one site to another [1 - 6].

Clinical evaluations and/or consultations over the phone and/or through video chat are included in telepsychiatry in order to assess and interpret telepresence and video. Digital pathological observations are sent through telepath logy. Telepath logy transmits diagnostic data pertaining to skin issues. Since it has been around for such a long time, artificial intelligence technology is widely employed in a variety of fields. The software can be used in a variety of health care settings, such as creating a system for evaluating patient knowledge to pinpoint error causes and develop remedies for current clinical outcomes as well as streamlining procedures by utilizing computerized knowledge to enhance medical supplies and services [7 - 12].

TELEMEDICINE

Patient monitoring is one of telemedicine's oldest and most popular uses. It provides a simpler, more cost-effective way to carry out typical doctor-to-patient visits to ascertain the patient's current state and clinical results from a distance. This has been designed to resemble face-to-face interaction by using video conferencing and the attachment of interactive medical equipment to gather and monitor the patient's clinical information. Flexibility, convenience, quality, and cost savings over traditional physical patient monitoring is shown in Fig. (**1**). The most current telepresence robot designs are intended to be remotely controlled by a device interface that links the user to the robot through a Wi-Fi connection, enabling the robot to independently roam around hallways and rooms. This newly created method makes use of both AI and visual technologies to enable the traversing of barriers and their identification. The use of telemedicine as a flexible tool may include adding additional patients or choosing the ideal location for a treatment that will have an impact on many people's lives. Artificial intelligence has allowed telemedicine to keep up with developments, but certain problems still need to be resolved. The biggest benefit from these studies would come from their application, thus it is critical to start searching for ways to lower the cost of this technology so that it may be utilized in underdeveloped medical facilities and rural areas.

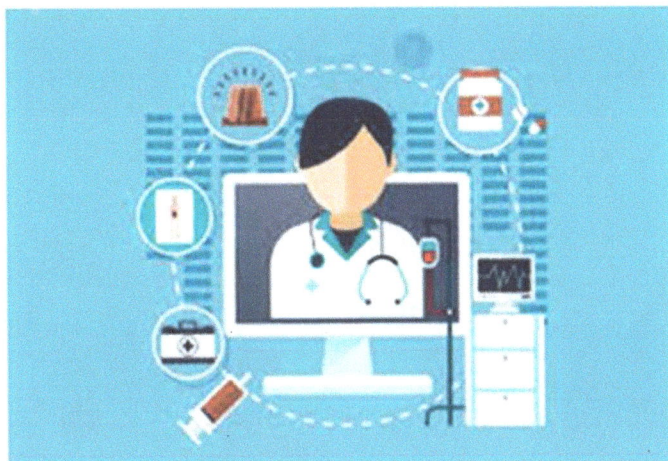

Fig. (1). Telemedicine in Biomedical Sector.

HEALTHCARE

EHRs were created by Cure because, according to an American College of Physicians survey, doctors spend 80% of their time working at their workstations and utilizing them. By substituting a chat interface for the time-consuming procedure of testing important patients, documenting the findings, and reporting them to the doctor, this device efficiently maintains medical information. It is thus easier to provide prescriptions and other paperwork to the customer, who may also submit directly for assessment images or videos.

It would be challenging to obtain and manage medical data given the large volume of health information acquired not just through manual registration in hospitals but also *via* the growing usage of self-diagnosis technologies. Given that telemedicine attempts to link patients and medical specialists from across the world, it is imperative that all involved organizations create a standardized record-keeping system using state-of-the-art techniques for accurately gathering electronic Healthcare data, such as "big data mining" and "neural networks." AI is increasingly being used to systematize data recovery and assessment, which often tackles problems with health care systems.

Two significant new advances in robotic technology are the utilization of mechanical support components and the intelligent diagnostic use of patient knowledge and data. Both traits work to support the new Healthcare system by assisting patients-either psychologically or by evaluating the initial medical diagnostic. These methods might be used to deep learning and programmable neural networks. Continuous implementation advances using the data and results connected to the plan. Intelligent diagnostics was used for tele-health self-diagnosis technologies in different app and mobile application formats. Modern advancements are being used is shown in Fig. (**2**).

Fig. (2).   Healthcare in Various Sectors.

There have been several potential Digital Technology Directives in the field of health knowledge due to the challenges involved with protecting its secrecy and security during telemedicine consultation and operations. As previously noted in the context of Healthcare information management, there is also a protection and confidentiality risk when linkages like satellites and the Internet are used. The full potential of these studies has not yet been realized, and it will take some time for them to adapt to actual telemedicine systems [13 - 17].

INDUSTRY SECTOR

In spite of the industry's constant need to cut costs owing to an increasingly obese population, IoT and AI have a substantial impact on the Healthcare sector, whether used alone or in combination. These advancements will let Healthcare professionals take full use of the opportunities that a society that is growing more open and networked presents. When the market is able to promote improved connectivity in a shared environment, consumers, physicians, payers, and drug manufacturers stand to gain greatly. Thanks to IoT devices like smart pills, wearable watches, and sensors, Healthcare providers can collect data continuously. AI applications may help interpret this data to spot changes in a patient's condition, suggest therapeutic alternatives, and spot patterns, which will help patients stick to their treatment plans, improve their outcomes, and speed up research into and access to novel therapies. Wearable sensors and computer synchronization are the main concepts behind technology improvements in healthcare. The essential skills needed to develop mobile healthcare solutions. Among these tools are remote telemedicine and remote diagnostic systems, which are essential for identifying emergencies, managing medication-related information, providing counseling and medical direction, and cross-organizational assistance. They also consist of patient surveillance and monitoring with wearable technology.

Physicians can now diagnose and treat a wider range of issues than in the past. Even with years of experience, they could struggle to accurately create the right diagnosis. IoT and AI technologies will be essential in offering effective tools for selecting the most appropriate treatment and a diagnosis in this situation. Artificial intelligence (AI) systems like neural networks will be able to swiftly analyze the vast amount of knowledge that is now accessible to physicians, speed up the diagnosis process, and help eliminate mistakes by fusing past information with essential patient data. This is crucial given that several sources will soon be supplying enormous volumes of health data, such as IOT medical devices that might provide data in real time makes it harder to understand and recognize human behavior is shown in Fig. (**3**).

Fig. (3). Healthcare in Industry Sectors.

MACHINE LEARNING

Using data, probability, and other sorts of uncertainty, machine learning, a subfield of AI, may tackle issues that conventional computer scientists think challenging. The body of research has shown that AI has great promise for a wide range of applications to solve complicated problems, especially in industries with vast volumes of data but little theory. Various roles for AI have been performed in scientific study. The application of AI approaches in biomedical engineering and informatics has lately attracted more attention. Applications range from understanding and investigating novel biological information for sickness treatment to using evidence-based reasoning to categories disorders.

A certain consequence is anticipated based on an input in categorization. The outcome is predicted by the algorithm using a training collection, which consists of a set of traits and the relevant result (also known as the goal or prediction attribute). The algorithm searches for connections between the traits that might be used to predict the outcome. Then, a data set that has never been seen before is given to an algorithm known as the prediction set. This algorithm's prediction set has the same features as the previous set, with the exception of the prediction attribute, which is still unknown. The programmed analyses the data and generates a prediction.

How consistently the prediction is produced determines how "good" the algorithm is. Although the many classifiers in use today provide various classification results for the same issue set, they all fail to account for the various outcomes for other problem sets.

In an effort to solve the shortcomings of traditional computer-aided diagnosis, researchers have created programmers that closely mimic expert human thinking is shown in Fig. (4). Expectations that such an approach would result in therapeutically useful programmers were not reached, even though many of the issues blocking the production of effective artificial intelligence programmes were overcome.

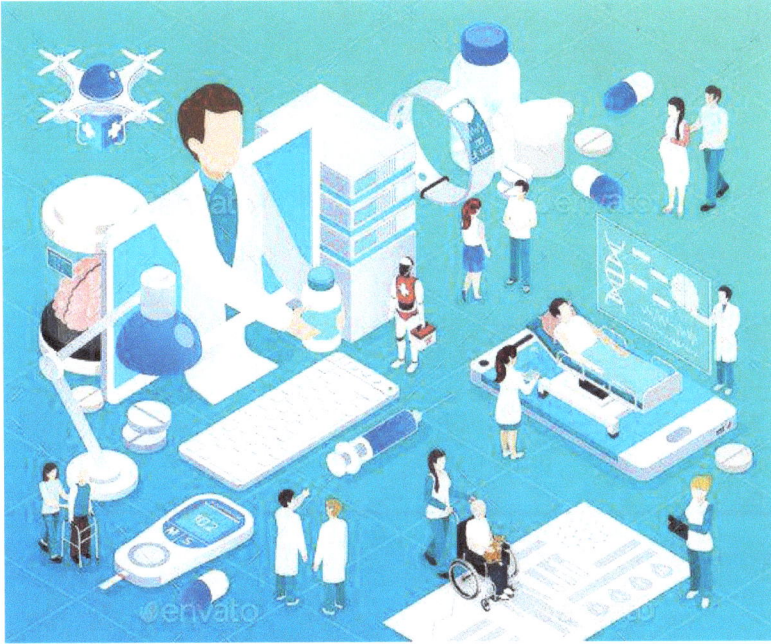

Fig. (4). Machine Learning in Industry Sectors.

APPLICATIONS OF BIOMEDICAL SECTOR

The analysis of diverse medical pictures really makes extensive use of software techniques for image identification and visualization. The primary use of syntactic pattern recognition methods for the investigation and early identification of certain organ issues is the study of specific forms of medical imaging. The following procedures are carried out upon initially seeing the analyzed images:

1. Separating pictures.

2. A complete skeletonization that looks into and verifies any apparent implications of the skeleton. The aberrant items that appear on the exterior boundaries of the organs under examination may be caused by pancreatic duct or skeletonization ramifications.

3. The exterior boundaries of the organs being studied are converted from two-dimensional regions into two-dimensional diagrams of width, revealing the outlines of the straightened organs. This serves as the starting point for their subsequent examination and diagnosis using pattern recognition syntactic techniques.

Artificial intelligence, EEG, ECG, and EMG may be used to analyze biological signs, such as for creating control signals, assisting with illness, and so forth. By contrasting the received waveform with the waveform that has previously been recorded, the waveform may be comprehended. The biological signal must be cleaned out of some of the branded components since AI requires particular data to train its network. But this network is now undergoing a test using brand-new data.

Because outcome prediction is a key focus of healthcare reform, networks have been used often. An artificial neural network (ANN) model, rather than logistic regression (LR) or the combination of age, prostate-specific antigen (PSA), body mass index (BMI), digital rectal examination (DRE), trans-rectal ultrasound (TRUS), Gleason sum biopsy, and Gleason sum primary biopsy, can more precisely predict the pathological staging of prostate cancer in patients before they undergo radical prostatectomy.

Artificial intelligence is a modern branch of science and technology (AI). At all socioeconomic levels, including those of people, social classes, businesses, and countries, it already has an impact on a broad variety of human behaviors. Since the beginning of the twenty-first century, artificial intelligence (AI) has significantly impacted almost every sector of business, economics, and society, include computer technology, engineering, space exploration, remote sensing, security and safety, transportation, and automobiles.

The speedy and successful advancement of AI is supported by a number of reasons. They involve the availability of efficient and reasonably priced computational (processing) tools, hardware (like graphics processing units), apps, and applications on consumer-grade personal computers and mobile devices, as well as huge (big) data sets with a variety of knowledge styles and formats, both online and cloud networks, produced in real time by wearable users and intermediaries. Block chain and AI integration would greatly advance market development, research, and transformation in the healthcare industry. Auto routing and traffic management benefit from decentralized AI. It guarantees the elimination of the current congestion and also works to avoid it. It is used in biomedical science and healthcare to speed up biomedical research, allow patients to manage their own data, and give elderly people with robotics-assisted care.

AI has uses in regulated fields including data security, research, and medicine. However, these well-established organizations are under risk because to the quick and inventive pace at which AI is evolving. A key question is whether AI should be governed as a separate industry or whether other regulatory areas should be examined in light of AI's possible repercussions. A lot of people have spoken about how important it is to provide scientists, doctors, and politicians the tools they need.

Users may be able to evaluate their own illnesses and, if required, take care of themselves thanks to applications for AI wellness. Artificial intelligence (AI) programmes created to help people with impairments or long-term health difficulties may improve people's sense of independence, dignity, and quality of life while enabling those who may otherwise have been admitted to care facilities to stay at home. AI systems, for instance, may have a detrimental influence on human autonomy by restricting options based on risk assessments or what is best for the consumer. The ability of the patient to make free, informed clinical choices may be compromised if AI programmes are utilized to make a prediction or build a treatment plan but the Healthcare provider doesn't explain how it was done.

Artificial intelligence aims to build computer programmes capable of abstract reasoning and global generalization. Machine learning, the discipline of developing performance-improving algorithms, seems to be developing gradually, despite the fact that general artificial intelligence is still a long way off. Deep learning, a kind of machine learning that employs multi-layer networks, has gained popularity in recent years due to its capacity to tackle difficult problems utilizing vast quantities of data. Since it was first presented in the 1980s, the idea of employing artificial intelligence to perform jobs in scientific research and clinical care has drawn academics' attention as an example of the growing potential of such technological breakthroughs. Medicine is now ready for the application of such technologies, which have evolved beyond the knowledge of humans, thanks to the emergence of massive volumes of multidimensional data. Research on the use of artificial intelligence in medicine has covered a broad variety of topics, including algorithms to forecast radiological imaging results, dermatological diagnoses, and patient outcomes based on data from electronic medical records.

Since imaging is a vital analytical tool in medicine, improving data analysis will save time and money. In a dual-energy computed tomography (CT) image obtained only from the low-energy channel, the neural network design is modified to account for a difference between the two directions. This enables the estimate of a high-energy signal using just single-energy CT systems as opposed to dual-energy CT systems, which are more common in clinical imaging. As shown in Fig. (**5**), the recommended technique will make it easier to get CT imaging data while increasing scanning doses and lowering noise. In Table **1**, articles published in 2015 through 2020 are listed. The articles released between 2015 and 2020 are shown in Fig. (**6**).

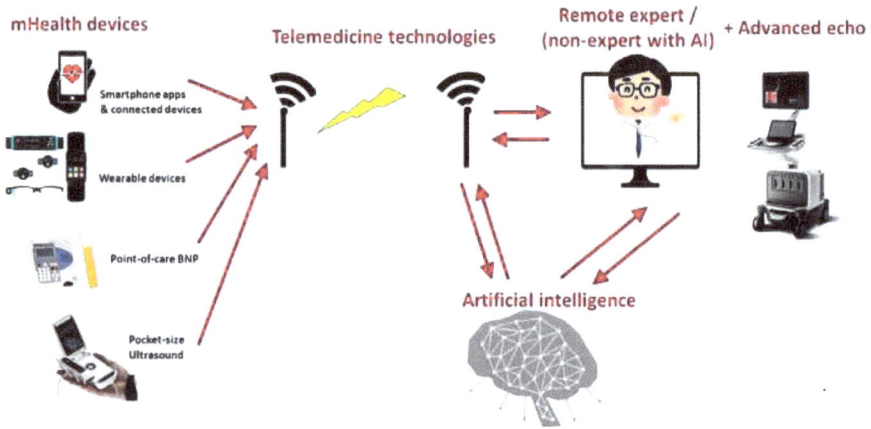

Fig. (5). Applications in Telemedicine.

Table 1. Number of Papers Published in 2015-2020.

Year	Number of Papers Published					
	IEEE	IET	ELSERVIER	SPRINGER	WILEY	ACM
2015	10	18	28	29	10	14
2016	15	12	29	30	20	16
2017	20	18	30	35	20	18
2018	22	20	22	34	10	12
2019	24	18	28	38	10	15
2020	26	22	22	40	20	16

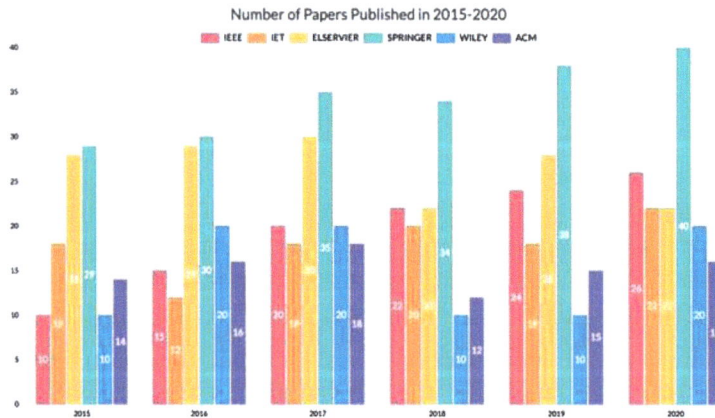

Fig. (6). Published Paper in the Year of 2015-2020.

CONCLUSION AND FUTURE WORK

This research highlights the AI model's amazing versatility and its potential to function across a range of areas with great diagnostic accuracy. The scientific community has made tremendous progress in recent decades to making AI-based systems a realistic reality for people, even if more research still needs to be done. Artificial intelligence (AI) systems are utilised or investigated in the domains of health and science for a number of reasons, including the development of medications, the treatment of chronic illnesses, the prevention of illness, and the provision of clinical services. AI advancements may help us combat them more successfully. However, the extent of serious health disorders could be limited by the validity of easily accessible health information and AI's lack of empathy. The use of AI raises a number of legal and societal issues, many of which overlap with more general issues caused by technological advancements in healthcare applications. Any future regulation of AI technology must make sure that AI is developed and utilised transparently, in accordance with the public interest, and in a way that supports and promotes the field's development.

REFERENCES

[1]   K. Kristian, "Machine Learning and Artificial Intelligence", *Two Fellow Travelers on the Quest for Intelligent Behavior in Machines Frontiers in Big Data,* p. 1, 2018.

[2]   V.L. Patel, E.H. Shortliffe, M. Stefanelli, P. Szolovits, M.R. Berthold, R. Bellazzi, and A. Abu-Hanna, "The coming of age of artificial intelligence in medicine", *Artif. Intell. Med.,* vol. 46, no. 1, pp. 5-17, 2009.
[http://dx.doi.org/10.1016/j.artmed.2008.07.017] [PMID: 18790621]

[3]   E.J. Topol, "High-performance medicine: the convergence of human and artificial intelligence", *Nat. Med.,* vol. 25, no. 1, pp. 44-56, 2019.
[http://dx.doi.org/10.1038/s41591-018-0300-7] [PMID: 30617339]

[4]   I.Y. Chen, M. Agrawal, S. Horng, and D. Sontag, "Robustly Extracting Medical Knowledge from EHRs: A Case Study of Learning a Health Knowledge Graph", *Pac. Symp. Biocomput.,* vol. 25, pp. 19-30, 2020.
[PMID: 31797583]

[5]   L. Brand, K. Nichols, H. Wang, H. Huang, and L. Shen, "Predicting Longitudinal Outcomes of Alzheimer's Disease via a Tensor-Based Joint Classification and Regression Model", *Pac. Symp. Biocomput.,* vol. 25, pp. 7-18, 2020.
[PMID: 31797582]

[6]   K. Yu, M. Zhang, T. Cui, and M. Hauskrecht, "Monitoring ICU Mortality Risk with A Long Short-Term Memory Recurrent Neural Network", *Pac. Symp. Biocomput.,* vol. 25, pp. 103-114, 2020.
[PMID: 31797590]

[7]   X. Zeng, Y. Feng, S. Moosavinasab, D. Lin, S. Lin, and C. Liu, "Multilevel Self-Attention Model and its Use on Medical Risk Prediction", *Pac. Symp. Biocomput.,* vol. 25, pp. 115-126, 2020.
[PMID: 31797591]

[8]   K. Salah, *Block chain for AI: Review and Open Research Challenges.* vol. Vol. 7. IEEE, 2019, pp. 10127-10149.

[9]   A. Maxmen, *AI Researchers Embrace Bitcoin Technology to Share Medical Data,*

2018.www.nature.com/articles/d41586
[http://dx.doi.org/10.1038/d41586-018-02641-7]

[10]   A. Dubovitskaya, Z. Xu, S. Ryu, M. Schumacher, and F. Wang, "Secure and Trustable Electronic Medical Records Sharing using Block chain", arXiv preprint arXiv:1709.06528, (2017).

[11]   K. Peterson, R. Deeduvanu, and P. Kanjamala, *Health Care (Don Mills),* vol. 20, no. 1, pp. 1-10, 2016.

[12]   Professor Hamid Jahankhani, "The age of AI,block chain and internet of everything",12th international conference on global security,safety and sustainability", *IEEE,,* 2019.

[13]   T. Kumari, R. Kumar, and R.K. Dwivedi, "Designing Blockchain Based Consensus Mechanism for Smart Healthcare IoT", *2023 International Conference on Intelligent and Innovative Technologies in Computing, Electrical and Electronics (IITCEE) Bengaluru, India,* pp. 878-884, 2023.
[http://dx.doi.org/10.1109/IITCEE57236.2023.10090882]

[14]   T. Mokhamed, M.A. Talib, M.A. Moufti, S. Abbas, and F. Khan, "The Potential of Blockchain Technology in Dental Healthcare: A Literature Review", *Sensors (Basel),* vol. 23, no. 6, p. 3277, 2023.
[http://dx.doi.org/10.3390/s23063277] [PMID: 36991986]

[15]   A.N. Abougreen, and C. Chakraborty, Applications of Machine Learning and Internet of Things in Agriculture.*Green Technological Innovation for Sustainable Smart Societies.,* C. Chakraborty, Ed., Springer: Cham, 2021.
[http://dx.doi.org/10.1007/978-3-030-73295-0_12]

[16]   C. Chakraborty, and A.N. Abougreen, "Intelligent internet of things and advanced machine learning techniques for Covid-19", *EAI Endorsed Trans. Pervasive Health Technol.,* vol. 7, no. 26, p. e1, 2021.

[17]   W. Rafique, M. Khan, S. Khan, and J.S. Ally, *SecureMed: A Blockchain-Based Privacy-Preserving Framework for Internet of Medical Things*, 2023.
[http://dx.doi.org/10.1155/2023/2558469]

CHAPTER 14

Sustainable Development for Smart Healthcare using Privacy-preserving Blockchain-based FL Framework

D. Karthika Renuka[1,*]**, R. Anusuya**[2] **and L. Ashok Kumar**[2]

[1] *Department of IT, PSG College of Technology, Coimbatore, Tamilnadu, India*

[2] *Department of EEE, PSG College of Technology Coimbatore, Tamilnadu, India*

Abstract: Artificial Intelligence (AI) methods need to learn from an adequately large dataset to achieve clinical-grade accuracy and validation, which is vital in the healthcare field. However, sensitive medical data is usually fragmented, and not shared due to security and patient privacy policies. In this context, our work aims at classifying abdominal and chest radiographs by applying Federated Learning (FL) without exchanging patient data. FL framework has been implemented on distributed data across multiple clients. In the framework, a multilayer perceptron is used as a deep learning model for the classification task. FL is a novel approach in which machine learning models are built with the collaboration of multiple clients controlled by a central server or service provider. FL model ensures data privacy and security by retaining the training data decentralized. FL model provides security and privacy for patients by training individual models in distributed clients and sharing merely the model weights.

Keywords: Classification, Deep Learning, Federated Learning, Machine Learning, Privacy-Preserving.

INTRODUCTION

Federated learning is a method for allowing distant clients to build a shared machine-learning technique cooperatively without having to share their training data. Its primary benefit is that it enables the construction of statistical models over long distances while keeping data localized. Although this minimizes data privacy threats, privacy concerns remain because trained model weights or parameters can leak training dataset information [1 - 10]. As a result, developing federated learning algorithms that build high-accuracy models while maintaining

* **Corresponding author D. Karthika Renuka:** Department of IT, PSG College of Technology, Coimbatore, Tamilnadu, India; Tel: 9976128726; E-mail: dkr.it@psgtech.ac.in

privacy is critical. Establishing a federated learning environment, particularly one with confidentiality assurances, is a time-consuming procedure with a variety of variables and parameters. To demonstrate that collaboration is possible and for improving model accuracy, clients must use a simulation framework that preserves privacy and is secure. Giving privacy to sensitive images using deep learning [11] and federated learning algorithms is achieved in this work. To address privacy issues during data sharing, an excellent backup framework will be used to maintain data sharing. Federated learning privacy algorithms with convolutional neural networks (CNN) are used to protect privacy.

In Machine Learning, data is gathered from a variety of edge devices, such as mobile phones, laptops, and other computers and then centralized. Machine Learning systems then use this data and train themselves, eventually predicting outcomes for new data. Google, Amazon, and Microsoft, among others, dominate the AI market with cloud-based AI solutions and APIs. Sensitive user data is transferred to servers where models are trained *via* typical AI approaches. With the increased awareness of user privacy across different devices and platforms, AI developers should not ignore the fact that their model is accessing and using data that is user sensitive.

Federated Learning is the result of the convergence of on-device AI, blockchain [13], and edge computing/IoT [14] technologies. FL can be utilized in the healthcare [15] industry for collaborative analysis. Decentralized training can be done here without any privacy concerns. To tighten privacy, some privacy preservation algorithms can be federated learning. Federated learning can be implemented using several frameworks. To select the best framework for FL implementation, 2 frameworks such as Flower and Pysyft are considered and the best one is chosen. Though federated learning provides some privacy, there may be some issues when updating gradients. So, privacy generally refers to unintentional disclosure of personal information. Privacy is divided into 2 categories. Privacy on the server side and privacy on the client side. Privacy at server side is necessary because when the server broadcasts the aggregated parameters to clients for model synchronizing, this information may leak as there may exist eavesdroppers. The parameters sent from the client to the server should be secured by encrypting it so that an attacker will find it difficult to get information about the user. For privacy protection on the Client-Side, perturbation is done, which adds noise to the shared parameters of the server so that attackers cannot restore the data or at least not be able to get the identity of the user.

CNN and modified auto encoder [16] require much time to analyze information, hyperparameter tuning, and validation of the model well before developing a genuine model in an effort to keep secrecy when analyzing massive data.

Asymmetric cryptosystems make use of the need for more memory. In terms of speed, safety, and energy usage, it is not a good option. The asymmetric approach is extremely complicated and, depending on the energy consumed, more cost.

RELATED WORKS

The growing popularity of in-depth cloud-based learning raises the issue of accurate predictions and data privacy. Previous research has used it to predict privacy in simple neural networks. Since sophisticated neural networks require more than a computer, the existing privacy assumptions schemes do not work well.

A) The article titled "**Blockchain-based federated learning methodologies in smart environments**" [18] suggested the CrowdSFL crowdsourcing technology. The work integrates blockchain with FL and claims to enhance validity, security, and computational time. It does not use a reliable dataset.

B) The article titled "**Secure and Provenance Enhanced Internet of Health Things Framework: A Blockchain Managed Federated Learning Approach**" [19] suggested a cooperative training data sharing system based on games and made the updated model accessible on the blockchain. It provides model training, full dataset encryption, and inference operations. The blockchain aggregates the updated model parameters while each federated edge node executes additive encryption, however, accuracy and loss metrics are poor.

C) The article titled "**End-to-end privacy-preserving deep learning on multi-institutional medical imaging**" [20] created a PRIMIA framework incorporating differentially private federated model training with encrypted aggregation of model updates as well as encrypted remote inference. It evaluates the framework's performance and privacy guarantees and demonstrates that the protections provided prevent the reconstruction of usable data by a gradient-based model inversion attack, but the success of FL models is largely dependent on high data quality.

D) The article titled "**Blockchain-based Privacy-Preserved Federated Learning for Medical Images: A Case Study of COVID-19 CT Scans**" [21] proposed a framework that integrates privacy-preserving federated learning over the decentralized blockchain. It secures the local model through the homomorphic encryption scheme, which helps build an intelligent model without leaking the data provider's privacy and creating trust in the data training process, but it does not enhance the latency of the blockchain and minimize the cost-effective solution.

E) The article entitled "**Blockchain-Federated-Learning and Deep Learning Models for COVID-19 detection using CT Imaging**" [22] suggested a framework that gathers a modest quantity of data from diverse sources (hospitals) and uses blockchain-based federated learning to build a global deep learning model. It proposed a method for normalizing data, used segmentation and classification based on Capsule Networks, and trained a global model using blockchain technology and federated learning.

PROPOSED METHODOLOGY

i. Methodology Used

Initially, the suitable framework is identified for our work from a vast variety of frameworks for federated learning implementation. After choosing a suitable framework, federated learning is implemented using that framework with the help of virtual workers. To enhance privacy, privacy preservation algorithms for both client and server side have been included and compared their performance. These algorithms make communication frequently to the server [24]. To make communication efficient between client and server, it is possible to decrease the updating of gradients for every round for every client. To implement it, communication efficient algorithms like fedavg and fedprox have been used. The detailed architecture is given in Fig. (**1**).

ii. Modules Identified

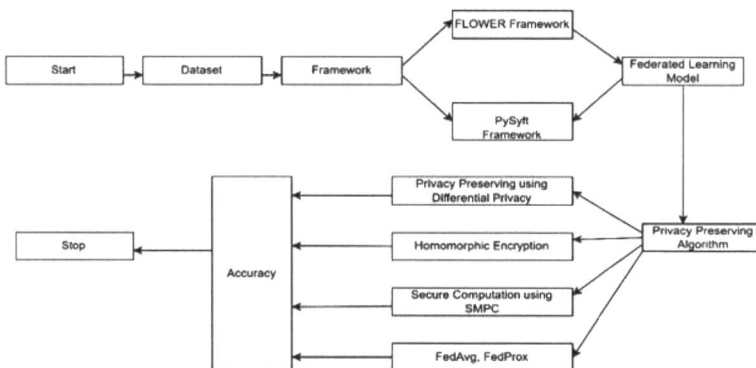

Fig. (1). Architecture of the proposed work.

iii. Modules For Framework Selection

Module 1: FL with Flower framework.

Module 2: FL with Pysyft framework.

iv. Modules For Privacy Preservation

Module 1: FL with Secure Multiparty Computation.

Module 2: FL with Secure aggregation.

Module 3: FL with Differential Privacy.

v. Module For Communication Efficient

Implemented Fedavg and Fedprox for communication efficient FL

A). DATASET DESCRIPTION

The MNIST dataset is an acronym that stands for the Modified National Institute of Standards and Technology dataset. This dataset contains 70,000 small square 28×28-pixel grayscale images of handwritten single digits between 0 and 9. The dataset is split into 60,000 for training and 10,000 for testing images. It is a widely used and deeply understood dataset. The dataset can be downloaded from https://www.kaggle.com/datasets/scolianni/mnistasjpg

B). IMPLEMENTATION: MODULE 1-FL WITH FLOWER FRAME-WORK

Flower is a user-friendly framework designed for implementing the Federated Learning approach. Flower is a recent framework for Federated Learning, created in 2020. Contrary to TensorFlow Federated and PySyft, which are linked to a single framework, Flower can be used with all of them by design. It focuses on giving tools for applying Federated Learning efficiently and allows you to focus on the training itself. Implementing a basic Federated setting with Flower is simple (20 lines of code is enough) and the rewriting needed to adapt a centralised code to a federated one is minimal. The design of Flower is based on a few guiding principles such as Customizable, Extendable, Framework-agnostic, and Understandable.

I). ALGORITHM

Server

1. Import libraries.

2. Create the strategy Function .

3. Using the FedAvg algorithm, the flower framework averages all the models together.

4. The aggregated weights are stored in a numpy library.

5. Run the server and get the port number as a command line argument.

Client

1. Import libraries.

2. Start Flower client and get the port number as a command line argument.

3. Using the fit method, get parameters and config, after that, train and fit the model.

4. Return current model weights.

5. Using evaluate method, print performance of the current model.

II). IMPLEMENTATION

In the flower framework, the client is an object that extends on Numpy Client class. The Client has three methods such as get parameters, fit, and evaluate. The get parameter method is used for downloading the current state of the model from the server. Fit is a method used to take downloaded weights and train the model on top of it, so it uses the private data and trains the model that is in the device currently and sends it back to the server once training is completed. The Evaluate method is called by the server to test the current model for analysing its performance. The server contains the averaging algorithm, which determines how to average out the various models that the server has got from different devices and client and server connecting using gRPC connection and the gRPC connection is completely secure. Once the minimum number of clients is connected to the server using a gRPC connection then the server starts the training process.

C). MODULE 2-FL WITH PYSYFT FRAMEWORK

PySyft is a free and open-source library for Federated Learning and Privacy Protection. It allows users to do Deep Learning in a private and safe manner. It's based on certain deep learning packages, including PyTorch, Keras, and Tensorflow. An abstraction called the SyftTensor is at the heart of PySyft. Syft Tensors are meant to represent a state or transformation of the data and can be chained together. The chain structure always has at its head the PyTorch tensor, and the transformations or states embodied by the Syft Tensors are accessed downward using the child attribute and upward using the parent attribute.

I). ALGORITHM

1. Import libraries.

2. Define virtual workers.

3. Define model specifications.

4. Load data and send to workers.

5. CNN Specification.

6. Define train and test functions.

7. Launch the training.

8. Accuracy calculation.

II). IMPLEMENTATION

Many privacy algorithms can be easily implemented using pysyft framework. Whereas algorithms such as Differential Privacy cannot be implemented using Flower Framework. Hence other modules have been implemented with pysyft framework.

D). MODULE 3-FL WITH SECURE MULTIPARTY COMPUTATION

Secure multi-party computation is a subfield of cryptography with the goal of creating methods for parties to jointly compute a function over their inputs while keeping those inputs private. Secret sharing in SMPC can protect both model's parameters and training/inference data. Machine learning as a Service is one of the most significant use-cases of SMPC as it would allow companies to offer their models to perform inference on private data sent by their clients, while ensuring the utmost privacy.

I). ALGORITHM

Define a crypto provider as a virtual worker.

Encrypting the data and sharing the private data among the virtual workers.

Encrypting the entire model.

Define train and test functions.

Launch the training and testing function.

Calculate accuracy.

II). IMPLEMENTATION

The working of SMPC is depicted in Fig. (**2**). Consider that the server and user would like to train the model on some data held by n workers. The server secret shares the model and sends each share to a worker. The workers also share their private data and exchange it between them. In the configuration, there are 2 workers: Alice and Bob. After exchanging shares, each of them now has their own shares, one share of the other worker, and one share of the model. Computation can now start to privately train the model using the appropriate crypto protocols. Once the model is trained, all the shares can be sent back to the server to decrypt it.

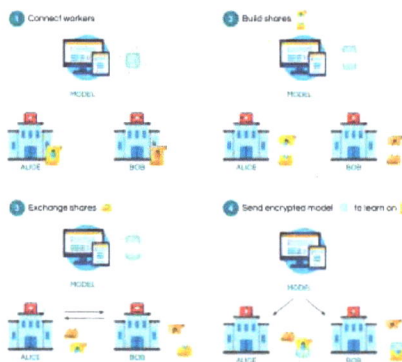

Fig. (2). Working of Secure Multiparty Computation.

E). MODULE 5: FL WITH DIFFERENTIAL PRIVACY

Federated learning allows models to be trained without openly sharing patient data, alleviating some of the confidentiality and privacy concerns that come with clinical data. Differential privacy adds quantitative constraints on the amount of privacy granted.

I). ALGORITHM

1. Import libraries.

2. Define virtual workers.

3. Define model specifications.

4. Load data and send to workers.

5. CNN specification.

6. Define train and test functions.

7. Add noise to the gradients.

8. Launch training.

9. Calculate accuracy.

II). IMPLEMENTATION

Differential privacy [13, 14] is a method that allows researchers and database analysts to acquire meaningful information from databases containing people's personal information while maintaining their anonymity. This can be accomplished by introducing minimal distractions to the database's information. The introduced distraction is immense enough that it can protect privacy and, at the same time, is limited enough so that providing information to analysts is still useful. As a simple definition, differential privacy forms data anonymously *via* injecting noise into the dataset studiously. It allows data experts to execute all possible (useful) statistical analyses without identifying any personal information. The working of DP is illustrated in Fig. (**3**).

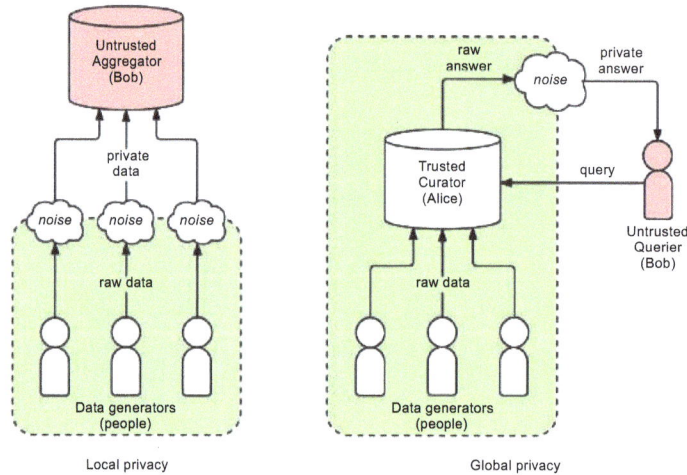

Fig. (3). Working of Differential Privacy.

Differential Privacy to protect individuals' privacy is to add noise to the data. It aims to reduce the impact of any one individual's data on the overall result. This means that one would make the same inference about an individual's data, whether it was present in the input of the analysis. Differential privacy mathematically guarantees that anyone seeing the result of a differentially private analysis will essentially make the same inference about any individual's private information, whether that individual's private information is included in the input to the analysis. DP provides a mathematically provable guarantee of privacy protection against a wide range of privacy attacks (including differencing attacks, linkage attacks, and reconstruction attacks).

In the specific case of training machine learning models on different data sets, DP mostly consists of two injections: Adding noise to the model parameters and clipping the maximum model parameters updates.

DP is a smart way of adding noise to sensitive data. It includes many factors, like a model that contains architecture, loss value, weights, *etc*. The goal is that the network does not memorise the data. In DP, noise can be added to input data, weights of the model and the loss function.

F). MATHEMATICAL EXPLANATION

The fundamental tenet of DP is that privacy should be seen as a resource, one that is depleted as data is extracted from a dataset. Private data analysis is to obtain as much helpful information as possible while compromising privacy as little as is practical. Consider a database D, which is merely a collection of data points, and a probabilistic function M working on databases, known as a mechanism, to formalise this idea. If the mechanism is (ε, δ) -differentially private for all subsets of outputs S⊆Range(M) and for all pairings of databases D and D′ that differ by one element, then.

Eq. (1) predicts that if one data point in the database is altered, the results of M will have a distribution that is almost identical when both have very small positive values. In other words, it's highly unlikely that adding one patient's data to a disproportionately private study will have any impact on the findings.

$$\Pr[M(D) \in S] \le \exp(\varepsilon)\Pr[M(D') \in S] + \delta.$$

(1)

Equation 1: Equation of Differential Privacy.

G). MODULE 6: COMMUNICATION EFFICIENT ALGORITHM

Federated Averaging (FedAvg) is a communication efficient algorithm for distributed training with many clients. In FedAvg, clients keep their data locally for privacy protection; a central parameter server is used to communicate between clients. This central server distributes parameters to each client and collects updated parameters from the client. FedAvg is studied mostly in a centralised fashion, requiring massive amounts of communication between the server and the client in each communication.

FedProx: FedProx can be viewed as a generalisation and re-parameterization of FedAvg, the current state-of-the-art method for federated learning. Although it makes only minor modifications to the re-parameterization method, these modifications have important implications both in theory and in practice.

I). ALGORITHM

Import the libraries.

Data loading and visualisation.

CNN classification and model building.

Defining an Aggregation strategy.

Using two strategies like FedAvg and FedProx.

FedAvg is the simplest and standard aggregation strategy where learning is performed in rounds.

Another aggregation strategy is FedProx which is a generalisation of FedAvg with some modifications to address the heterogeneity of data and .systems Federated training with FedAvg and FedProx.

Launching the train and test function and calculating and comparing the Accuracies.

II). IMPLEMENTATION

In federated averaging (FedAvg), learning is performed in rounds. In each round, the server samples a set of m clients (out of a total of K clients) that will be considered for the current iteration and sends them the current global model. These clients update the parameters of their local copy of the model by optimising the loss of Fk on their local training data using SGD for E epochs. At the end of the round, local parameters are sent to the server, which aggregates them by performing a weighted average. The aggregated parameters define the global model for the next round.

In FedProx, which is an improvised aggregation of Fedavg, the learning is done again in rounds. In each round, the server samples a set of m clients and sends them the current global model. Unlike FedAvg, here, clients optimise a regular loss with a proximal period. In particular, the new function $Fk(\omega)+\mu2\|\omega-\omega t\|2$, where Fk is the loss, is the local parameter to optimise, and t is the global parameter at time t. In addition, local optimizations is executed for a variable number of epochs according to system resources (so that even the slowest clients can contribute to training with a small number of epochs). For FedAvg, local parameters are sent to the server and aggregated.

EVALUATION AND ANALYSIS

A). Performance Evaluation

Evaluation is of key importance to our project because it allows us to compare different algorithms and come up with the best modules that give the most accurate results. Metrics were used in testing modules that tested an effective model for image safety and disease prognosis.

Accuracy- *Accuracy is an accurate performance measure and is simply a prediction of accurately predicted predictions for all observations.*

Fig. (**4**) represents the accuracy graph of training the model on the 3 clients, using the FedProx aggregation strategy.

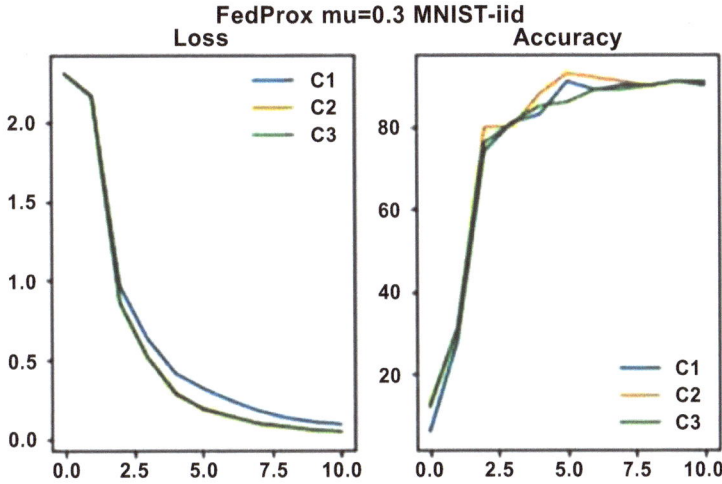

Fig. (4). Accuracy and loss of FedProx.

Our work has distributed a federated learning process as privacy preserving FL and communication efficient FL. The privacy algorithms come under privacy preserving FL, whereas the communication efficient FL consists of algorithms such as Fedavg and the modified version of Fed Avg called as FedProx. In FedAvg, clients keep their data locally for privacy protection; a central parameter server is used to communicate between clients. FedProx is a generalisation of FedAvg with some modifications to address the heterogeneity of data and systems. The learning is again performed in rounds. At each round, the server samples a set of m clients and sends them the current global model. Both algorithms gave an accuracy of 90.6% each. Federated learning and SMPC were performed with medical dataset, Chest X-Ray dataset, which gave an accuracy of 98%.

B). ATTACKS

Securing data aggregation is to protect data aggregation, one of the basic primitives of sensor networks for communication efficiency, against security attacks such as eavesdropping and forging aggregated results. Differentially private training algorithms provide protection against one of the most popular attacks in machine learning: the membership inference attack. However, these privacy algorithms incur a loss of the model's classification accuracy, therefore creating a privacy-utility trade-off. Secure Multi Party computation is a part of secure computation technology that enables computation while keeping data encrypted. Data is kept secret here even while it is in computation. It prevents data leakage.

CONCLUSION AND FUTURE WORK

Conventional Machine Learning models require the training data to be accumulated at a particular data centre or on a specific machine, which leads to data leakage. The proposed work has developed a federated deep learning algorithm for the privacy of data. Here, only updated models are sent to the cloud, all training data remains on local devices. However, sharing other information, such as model updates, as part of the training process, can also potentially reveal sensitive information. To overcome security vulnerabilities, our work has implemented various algorithms like secure aggregation and differential privacy. Using a communication efficient algorithm, the frequent communication between server and client has been reduced. In future, our work will propose to develop a hybrid model combining all the privacy-preserving algorithms to enhance the privacy and security of the data.

REFERENCES

[1]   Nguyen Truong, "Privacy preservation in federated learning: An insightful survey from the GDPR perspective", *Compu. & Security.*, vol. 110, p. 102402, 2021.

[2]   W. Cheng, W. Ou, X. Yin, W. Yan, D. Liu, and C. Liu, "A privacy-protection model for patients", *Secur. Commun. Netw.*, vol. 2020, no. Dec, pp. 1-12, 2020.
[http://dx.doi.org/10.1155/2020/6647562]

[3]   J. Liu, "Projected federated averaging with heterogeneous differential privacy", *Proc. VLDB Endow.*, vol. vol. 15, no. 4, pp. 828-840, 2021.
[http://dx.doi.org/10.14778/3503585.3503592]

[4]   V. Subramaniam, "Federated learning an introduction. Medium", Available at: https ://medium.com /secure-and   -private-ai-   writing-challenge/federated-learning-an-introduction-93bc0167f916 (Retrieved on: May 9, 2022).

[5]   J. Marks, "Differential privacy applied to smart meters: A mapping study", *Proceedings of the 36th Annual ACM Symposium on Applied Computing, ACM.*, pp. 761-70, 2021.
[http://dx.doi.org/10.1145/3412841.3442360]

[6]   M. Moreau, "Differentially private federated learning with flower and opacus", *Medium, Towards Data Science.*, 2021. Available at: https://towardsdatascience.com/differentially-private-federat-d-learning-with-flower-and-opacus-e14fb0d2d229

[7]   M. Rehman, *Federated Learning Systems.* Springer Nature, 2021.
[http://dx.doi.org/10.1007/978-3-030-70604-3]

[8]   V. Dwivedi, "Solve real-world problems using Deep Learning & Artificial Intelligence", Available at: https ://towardsdatascience .com/solve-real-world-problems-using-deep- learning-artificial-intelligence -f2f8e842c9f4 (Retrieved on: May 9, 2022).

[9]   H. Jakub Konečn , H. Brendan McMahan, Felix X. Yu, Peter. Richtarik, Ananda Theertha Suresh, and Dave Bacon, "Federated learning: Strategies for improving communication efficiency", *fed.commun.NIPS16,* 2016.

[10]   K. Wei, J-G. Li, M. Ding, C. Ma, H. Su, B. Zhang, and H.V. Poor, "Performance analysis and optimization in privacy-preserving federated learning", *arXiv,* 2020.https://arxiv.org/abs/2003.00229

[12]   R. Fantacci, and B. Picano, "Federated learning framework for mobile edge computing networks", *CAAI Trans. Intell. Technol.,* vol. 5, no. 1, pp. 15-21, 2020.
[http://dx.doi.org/10.1049/trit.2019.0049]

[13]   J. Qian, X. Fafoutis, and L. Kai Hansen, "Towards federated learning: Robustness analytics to data heterogeneity", *arXiv.,* 2020.http://arxiv.org/abs/2002.05038

[14]   D.C. Nguyen, "Federated learning for internet of things: A comprehensive survey", *IEEE Commun. Surveys & Tutor.,* vol. 23, no. 3, pp. 1622-1658, 2021.
[http://dx.doi.org/10.1109/COMST.2021.3075439]

[15]   Jie Xu, "Federated learning for healthcare informatics", *J. Healthc Inform. Res.,* vol. 5, no. 1, pp. 1-19, 2021.
[http://dx.doi.org/10.1007/s41666-020-00082-4]

[16]   G. Long, "Federated learning for privacy-preserving open innovation future on digital health", *Compu. Sci.,* 2021.http://arxiv.org/abs/2108.10761
[http://dx.doi.org/10.48550/arXiv.2108.10761]

[18]   Dong Li, "Blockchain-based federated learning methodologies in smart environments", *Cluster Comput.,* vol. 25, no. 4, pp. 2585-2599, 2021.
[http://dx.doi.org/10.1007/s10586-021-03424-y] [PMID: 34744493]

[19]   M.A. Rahman, "Secure and provenance enhanced internet of health things framework: A blockchain managed federated learning approach", *IEEE Access.,* vol. Vol. 8, pp. 205071-205087, 2020.
[http://dx.doi.org/10.1109/ACCESS.2020.3037474]

[20]   G. Kaissis, A. Ziller, J. Passerat-Palmbach, T. Ryffel, D. Usynin, A. Trask, I. Lima Jr, J. Mancuso, F. Jungmann, M-M. Steinborn, A. Saleh, M. Makowski, D. Rueckert, and R. Braren, "End-to-end privacy preserving deep learning on multi-institutional medical imaging", *Nat. Mach. Intell.,* vol. 3, no. 6, pp. 473-484, 2021.
[http://dx.doi.org/10.1038/s42256-021-00337-8]

[21]   R. Kumar, "Blockchain based privacy-preserved federated learning for medical images: A case study of COVID-19 CT scans", *Compu.Sci.,* vol. 1, no. 2, p. 15, 2021.http://arxiv.org/abs/2104.10903
[http://dx.doi.org/10.48550/arXiv.2104.10903]

CHAPTER 15

Smart Ambulance for Emergency Cases to be Reported to Hospitals at the Earliest using Deep Learning Algorithms and Blockchain-based Distributed Health Record Transactions for smart Cities

V. Kavitha[1,*] and **Partheeban Pon**[2]

[1] *Computer Science and Engineering, University College of Engineering, Kancheepuram, India*

[2] *Computer Science and Engineering, Stella Mary's College of Engineering, Aauthenganvilai, Kanyakumari, India*

Abstract: The everyday eating habits and lifestyle choices that people make have a significant impact on how long they live on the planet. Ancient people ate food that had an acceptable ratio of fat, vitamins, minerals, and carbohydrates, which helped them live a long life. Nowadays, individuals live shorter lives and experience many crises like heart attacks and mental despair that cause them to drive carelessly and cause accidents. This is due to our current diets of junk food and style of life. For the people and the individuals, this results in a tremendous loss. Here, saving people's lives depends largely on the passage of time. The extent of the injury or the patient's emergency situation, the amount of traffic that makes it difficult for the ambulance to reach its destination, and the hospital's capacity to accept patients and save lives are just a few of the many factors that affect the time limitations. In the current situation, hospitals are using the available services to meet time restrictions, which correctly route the ambulance. The main disadvantage of this system is that hospitals handle all the data, making it easy to tamper with medical records and risk losing the integrity of the data. The goal of intelligent ambulances is to forecast the shortest amount of time needed to admit the patient to the local hospitals that have the resources to care for them, preventing the need to transfer patients to other hospitals, as well as to determine the most efficient route to the destination. The patient's life can be saved as a result. The aforementioned can be accomplished by using a deep learning algorithm to predict the injury and the time limit to admit the patient to the hospital, matching the injury with the treatment options available in the hospital and mapping the appropriate hospital, as well as by finding the quickest route with the least amount of traffic to get to the destination within the allotted time limit, giving first aid in the ambulance, and handling the data transfer of health records in a secure manner. Therefore, in a smart city, the smart ambulance can quickly save lives.

---

[*] **Corresponding author V. Kavitha:** Computer Science and Engineering, University College of Engineering, Kancheepuram, India; Tel: 9487116703; E-mail: kavinayav@gmail.com

L. Ashok Kumar, D. Karthika Renuka, Sonali Agarwal & Sheng-Lung Peng (Eds.)

Keywords: Blockchain, Emergency Systems, e-Health, m-Health, Smart Ambulance.

INTRODUCTION

Emergency calls and responses have recently highlighted characteristics of great stress in India. Millions of calls indicate an issue with emergency call protocols. This has led to a decrease in the percentage of disaster response transportations at the point of impact and lengthier response times when combined with a growing community and budget cuts at the national level. Thus, we highpoint the key problems with providing assistance in emergency and provide a summary of the aforementioned solutions. In order to improve, we create a brand-new method called the Smart Ambulance System (SAS). The main goal of SAS is to help people recover by enhancing communication between victims and first responders. Increasing the capacity of emergency communication while minimising problems with emergency call systems and causing emergency help are the two objectives of employing the most recent technologies and SAS algorithms. Using SAS's complex technologies and algorithms, the emergency response system will be made more profitable while also improving the effectiveness of emergency communication. Through computerised contacts with emergency services and the management of force data stored on a personal smartphone as well as inside tracked data, SAS aims to improve the spoken data effectively and securely, eventually reducing communication backups. SAS places a lot of focus on live communication techniques to improve first conversations between patients and emergency personnel. A predecessor to this approach has developed. A first usability, dependability, and communication performance analysis of the system has been conducted.

One of the major goals of our contemporary civilization is to increase the effectiveness of biomedical and healthcare policy. As a result, it is crucial to offer patients high-quality medical care while also lowering the expense of healthcare assistance and resolving the scarcity of nursing faculty. In fact, in the Knowledge Era of the twenty-first century, we use computational capabilities of all kinds for a variety of daily goals (such as managing household appliances and tracking endurance use), which has led to the collection and transmission of enormous amounts of personal data on a continuous basis. Sadly, reaching someone in an emergency remains a significant challenge despite the sudden surge in technology. This unresolved problem necessitates more rigorous work because it limits the patient's location to a narrow, searchable significant caller who can provide that information to the emergency call operator. We have investigated this issue in depth, digging out layouts that are being tested or that are just starting to take shape and giving them a critical analysis of their approaches.

Sonali *et al.* proposed integrating Blockchain and machine learning algorithms into healthcare in 2019. Health records are extremely sensitive data, thus, Blockchain, which operates on distributed networks and each node has a copy of the distributed ledger, provides transaction security. The transaction's integrity and authenticity are achieved by the hash code. In order to provide secure transactions across all domains, blockchain technology has been applied in the following areas: agricultural domain, funding, money transfer, lending, borrowing, stock market, educational areas, supply chain management, *etc.*

In terms of online or digital transactions, the health care industry has undergone a significant transformation. To access records on a worldwide scale, the health care industry must make billion-dollar investments. Therefore, blockchain technology has a broad application in the health sector. Dr. B. Arunkumar and others used machine learning algorithms to extract pertinent facts for generating intelligent decisions from the raw data. Many Artificial Intelligent apps that are user-friendly and easily incorporated into each person's daily life have been produced as a result of the combination of Machine Learning and Deep Learning Algorithm. To ensure the security of all such applications that conduct business with numerous end users, where the number of healthcare data breaches is significant in 2018 (3 2019 July).

AI *VS* ML *VS* DL

Artificial intelligence is the capacity of a computer to perform functions carried out by humans by adding human intelligence through the process of machine learning. AI can significantly enhance people's lives by advancing technology. Hard challenges that occur around the world can be solved with the help of meaningful interpretation of the raw data. AI is nothing more than a machine-processed emulation of the human intellect, particularly as it relates to computer systems.

Artificial intelligence is a subset that creates machine learning and aids in decision-making. With the aid of deep learning algorithms and machine learning ideas, data science helps to comprehend and analyse raw data. For businesses to succeed, data scientists and analysts need to understand algorithms and be able to evaluate forecasts.

An illustration of the significance of machine learning is shown. Ram likes music with a fast tempo and strong intensity (soaring). Therefore, when a new song is released, we can determine whether Ram likes the music based on the intensity and tempo of the song. When a song with a low speed and light intensity is released, it is obvious that Ram won't like it. But it might be very challenging to determine whether Ram loves a song when it is released because of its medium intensity and medium tempo. This situation calls for the use of machine learning. Machine learning assists us in determining whether somebody likes or dislikes music by taking into account the neighbourhood songs that people like and dislike. There are three types of machine learning: supervised, unsupervised, and reinforcement learning.

These algorithms use input and output data to learn while being supervised. Throughout the learning process, a target/output (Label) is defined. Regression and classification are additional categories under which supervised algorithms fall. Unsupervised algorithms pick up information from unstructured, unclear data. The raw data is categorised or grouped. Classification and relationships are the two categories of unsupervised algorithms. Clustering and SVM.

Algorithms that use reinforcement learning learn from their surroundings. Every step taken in the direction of the goal is rewarded; otherwise, the error is evaluated based on feedback.

Machine learning belongs to the subset of deep learning. It depends on the study of computer based algorithms. These are dependent on the basic principles, whereas it makes use of artificial neural networks that are designed to replicate how these people think and learn. The form of complexity in these neural networks was limited by computer power. Thanks to advancements in big data analysis, which allow computers to watch, understand, and react to such complex natural events more quickly when compared to other people; larger and more complex neural networks are now feasible. Deep learning has been useful for speech recognition, language translation, and image categorization. It can tackle any pattern based recognition problem without any of these human interactions.

Artificial neural networks have several layers where Deep neural networks (DNNs) are an example of such networks. These layers of a DNN carry out complex linear operations like representation and abstraction, which makes use of voice, text, and image data. Deep learning is used by many companies for the creation of innovative business models. Deep learning is recognised as the machine learning sector. Layers of nodes like the human brain consist of neurons. Layer nodes that are close to one another are connected. The clarity depends on the number of layers. The human brain receives many signals from nearby neurons. In an artificial network, signals between nodes travel, which are dependent on complementary weight. This influence depends on the nodes which have a larger weight. The last layer effectively combines the weighted inputs producing an output. Deep learning provides powerful hardware processing a larger amount of data and a number of mathematical operations. These advanced equipment and deep learning training computations may take weeks.

BLOCKCHAIN

Each machine serves as a replica of the network in this distributed ledger that is shared over peer-to-peer networks. This eliminates the possibility of a single point of failure. Each piece of data is then mathematically encrypted and added as a new block to the chain of earlier records once all transactions are verified by consensus techniques. The success of blockchain technology is demonstrated by the fact that all of the aforementioned transactions can be added to a block without the need for a central authority. This, by default, thwarts harmful behaviour; the process of extremes began in antiquity. Silver and gold were the first metals used to coin money. The Tange Dinarsity in China adopted more paper money. Italian banking developed in the early Renaissance and during the Middle Ages. The gold standard was adopted in Britain. Later, credit cards were developed, and the US was the first nation to introduce internet banking. The concept of a blockchain has fundamentally altered how individuals and businesses conduct cryptocurrency-related transactions. The blockchain is essentially a distributed, replicated digital ledger of transactions that covers the whole network. Legitimate transaction batches are simply encoded into trees and saved in blocks after being hashed. A timestamp and a cryptographic hash of the previous block are included in each block. The genesis block, which is the first block, has other nodes as children.

In this work, we are running our blockchain with Ethereum on the Ropsten Testnet in exchange for a transaction fee. To add or retrieve hospital data from blockchain, we need two different types of functions. We will create a transaction key for each transaction using the necessary information from our blockchain. We use Deep Learning algorithms created specifically for this purpose to obtain scores based on patient criteria after obtaining data from the blockchain.

LITERATURE SURVEY

Based on characteristics like agility and simplicity of accessibility for various applications, cloud assisted systems play a dominant role in the provision of support in the present era. Due to recent improvements, the use of cloud services has increased, making it appropriate for real-time applications [1]. These are better suited for large companies when the number of organisations that exceeds the bound. Data handling is crucial because of the enormous amount of data that is generated daily from numerous sources, including mobile devices, archives, and other sources. A sudden data explosion could lead to system failure in the devices [2, 3]. Cloud computing is suitable for such problems as it provides better storage with minimal resource usage to the customers. Additionally, this makes it easier to reduce the system overhead brought on by the massive data explosion.

Additionally, the transactional data that lies on succeeding nodes needs to be handled with the utmost care. The usability of the services requires users of the cloud to have access to, transact with, and share data for the different purposes that cloud-based devices can serve [4]. when data is transferred to the cloud, the user loses direct access to the resources' operations. These types of exchanges are also carried out by users in a matter of seconds when they conduct transactions, which puts the network's massive amounts of data at risk. The transferred data include extremely valuable information that is necessary to provide the end user with high-quality services.

Traditional approaches produce falsely intolerable user responses in cloud-based environments. According to analysis, the current pattern in utility services indicates that users' sensitive data is being exploited [6-8]. This has a negative impact on the user's privacy and produces adversarial variations in the original data from the invaders. In order to provide the consumer with superior data transaction services, distributed, decentralised algorithms are used. Users lose trust in the system's operations when sensitive data they share with it is compromised [9-11]. As a result, disagreements and danger to the privacy of users' data are problems in the system. The currently used methods make use of a number of security elements such as key, agreement, password, and cryptography like data standard for encryption, blowfish, twofish, and so on. These techniques have a number of problems, including data loss, data tampering, and attacker-caused fault data incursion. Additionally, the cloud-based systems' significant problems include reduced resource utilisation and a lack of containment and administration costs. In some techniques, it is incorrect to employ knowledge or to oversee or govern all data services. Additionally, when data is transferred from local storage to the cloud, the system does not achieve sufficient compliance, and enterprises struggle to manage different clouds throughout the network [12-15].

Only the application of an effective, trustworthy, tamper-resistant system will be able to address the aforementioned problems. Blockchain has recently come to light as a security option for cloud-based systems. Blockchains are more suited to cloud-based systems because of their inherent tamper resistance and decentralised data sharing [16-18]. The cloud-based services also need the following additional fundamental qualities: confidentiality, trust, authentication, mobile security, access control, and other enforcements. Thus, these characteristics necessitate method that meets the requirements for improving cloud-based systems [19-21]. Due to the vulnerabilities created in traditional cryptography procedures, blockchain technology is now being used in the most recent cloud-based methods. Additionally, machine learning (ML) in cloud computing shows to be a successful algorithm that provides improved utility services for the system's end user. This technique can identify unauthorised communications and system intrusions. It can also be combined with the blockchain to give users of the cloud system improved data transactions and secure services.

The primary concerns surrounding the topic are outlined in this part, along with an overview of emergency systems, their purposes, and any connected challenges. Additionally, we look into emergency system-related work and solutions, as well as cutting-edge technologies in such areas.

CALL SYSTEMS DURING EMERGENCY

A need for trustworthy emergency numbers became clear as phone networks developed and became more difficult and problematic. Almost every region in the world has at least one emergency phone number as of right now. Our designed application will have safeguards in place that will lessen the likelihood of accidental dialling while still considering the value of being able to quickly call a number. We will be able to do this by accounting for elements like button positioning and human times for these responses.

Issues in Call Systems

Here, we make an effort to condense the various situations involving the emergency call channel and the network effect by adding complexity or producing inefficiency. Some common questions, *e.g.*, "What are you calling for?", "From where are you calling?" and "What urge do you have?", are the barriers with call systems, which start to appear. Emergency group responses will consequently depend heavily on the location and nature of the emergency because they are prerogatives in accordance with these values. For instance, a patient in a chronic crisis would be given priority for emergency care over a patient who was grieving. Therefore, in order to possibly protect beings, positive and accurate responses to the aforementioned questions are required.

Caller Location

Caller location is one of the most prominent details to have during an emergency since it tells the operator where to send help. The response time increases with the speed at which this information is retrieved. Callers may occasionally find it challenging to vocally describe their location. To locate a caller in this circumstance, operators will require additional tools. Since phone numbers are associated with specific addresses, it is easiest to trace landline calls; mobile calls, which make up 60% of all emergency calls, are more challenging. A mobile device's location can be ascertained in three different methods. These are:

Cell Tower - Mobile stations often use local towers to send and receive calls, therefore it is possible to locate them by focusing on the area that each tower's signal covers, which is typically close by. These results can be obtained by triangulating signals on phones from many cell towers.

Global Positioning System - Since cellphones come equipped with a GPS transmitter, it is possible to use this technology to determine communication with the emergency operator. The most exact position, with a maximum inaccuracy of a few metres, would be determined by the caller's latitude and longitude. The limited utility of GPS as a result of frequency blackouts is a problem.

Choosing the Right Number - Anywhere in the world, before making an emergency call, a caller must first be aware of the emergency service they need and the contact information for that service. From a global viewpoint, this can be challenging because different countries have different emergency phone numbers—for example, India uses 100, the U.S. uses 911, where some nations have individual lines for ambulances, police, and fire services. Numerous numbers are provided for less catastrophic circumstances as well. For instance, in India, the following numbers are accessible:

1. 100 - Police

2. 108 - Ambulance

3. 101 - Fire Brigade

Alternative non-emergency numbers that provide telephone guidance have been set up in order to decrease the overuse of 108 call systems. However, there is no proof that these numbers lessen the volume of 108 calls. Lack of knowledge of the various numbers could be a contributing factor, but it has been recommended that a better option for dispatching response vehicles in response to non-serious calls is to offer telephone help. The primary remedy to this issue seems to be better education about when to call. Users can use a set of questions to determine whether they should call and, if so, which number to dial. The goal of the proposed system development is to incorporate all of the different service numbers. In order to provide a place for genuine emergencies, this is intended to assist in filtering out or redirecting less serious crises.

FRAMEWORK FOR SMART AMBULANCE SYSTEM

The proposed Smart Ambulance System (SAS), as shown in Fig. (**1**), intends to boost emergency service efficiency by delivering a quicker response time by utilising the technology built within smartphones (for example, sensors and location services). The key objective of SAS is to transfer patients' information rather than the more customary practice of having callers verbally input their information on the phone. In the end, SAS will work to speed up during emergency calls made and received by minimising the multiple steps now engaged in the process. A quicker response time, increased calls for the operators, and improved efficiency based on caller information should be the results of streamlining these processes.

The strategy we take in creating the SAS is based on looking into the problems with the call system as well as elements that may be created to enhance the conventional manner of calling for emergencies. As a result, we examine the systems put in place for patient and operator contacts as well as the systems utilised by both parties to collect data to benefit both parties. These systems involve the caller's (the patient) usage of mobile applications and the operator's use of web platforms (*i.e.*, doctors and paramedics).

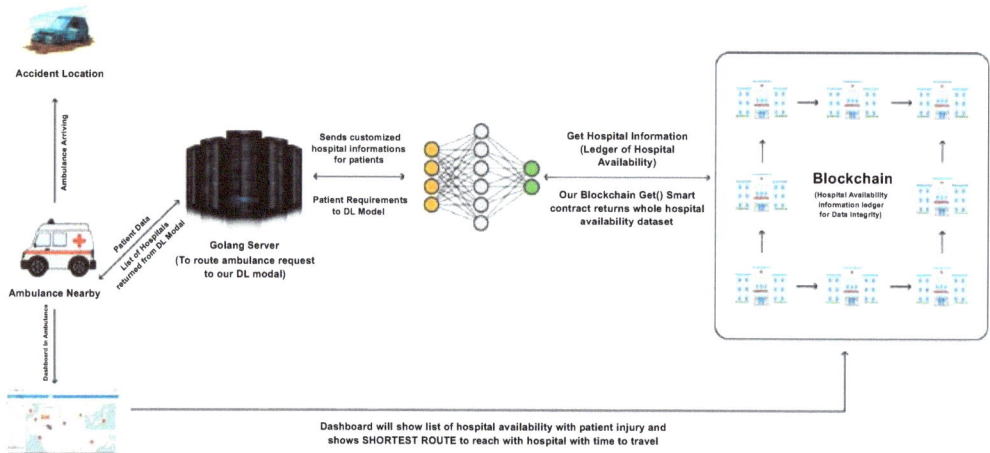

Fig. (1). Smart Ambulance Framework.

The primary processes that the system uses to gather and handle the necessary data from callers are depicted in the above diagram. We have identified three individuals who have a function in the system based on who would utilise it. Every one of these user groups has various requirements for the system. Additionally, they will make use of the system in other ways. The following are the roles of the user groups:

1. The caller is the individual who contacts the SAS for assistance.

2. The person that is contacted for assistance is the Operator.

3. The responder goes to the caller to assist them.

The caller system uses two methods to gather data. Patients' data are first collected by the system using a mobile application, and operator data are then collected by the system through an operator web platform. Data is collected for processing that are sent to the data center, and then made available to the operator wherever they are, whenever they need it. The general data flow can be thought of as a two-way flow between the platforms used by the operator and the patients, or more precisely, it should also include the data centre layer, or patients' data centre operator. The process of requesting an ambulance is depicted in the image.

The logic of starting SAS determines if the patient is a first-time user or not when the SAS programme is launched. When a user logs in for the first time, registration is required so that the system has a unique identity to use when requesting an emergency. Additionally, since users' locations on their mobile devices may be traced, this might assist avoid malicious requests. The algorithm will go into greater detail when the user has been identified to describe the standard practises for taking patients in an emergency and submitting the request. As a result, all of this data is sent (Wi-Fi, 3G, 4G, *etc.)* to a data centre, and made accessible to an approved healthcare provider. Finally, an online platform that displays patient requests is connected to the data centre. It is anticipated that the operator platform will display a variety of information and statistics, with a focus on user identification, GPS data, and other patient status-related information. Additionally, this information must be presented appropriately. For instance, the patient's GPS coordinates should be displayed on a mapview, and the symptom data should be displayed using the proper charts, such as a line chart for the heart rate.

IMPLEMENTATION METHODOLOGY

The algorithm for incident handling at the accident site is presented below and the implementation methodology is presented in Fig. (**2**).

ALGORITHM: Request from ambulance

BEGIN PROCEDURE

STEP 1: Get the current location *via* GPS.

STEP 2: Investigate the type of injury and necessary treatment required.

STEP 3: Send the location and injury data to the server.

STEP 4: Await data from the server

END PROCEDURE

REST API SERVER

Algorithm for handling requests from ambulances at the server. Machine learning algorithms based on KNN and Decision Tree algorithms are used in Recommendation systems nowadays.

ALGORITHM: Process request

BEGIN PROCEDURE

STEP 1: Get the location data and the injury type.

STEP 2: Get the list of hospitals which support the injury type from blockchain.

STEP 3: Bundle the necessary data into JSON format.

STEP 4: Send it to the Deep Learning Algorithm.

STEP 5: Get the results from the neural network.

STEP 6: Sort the Results based on

Shortest Path [[Departments in Hospital === Patient Injury]]

STEP 7: Send the Results back to the server.

END PROCEDURE

DATA EXTRACTION PHASE

Algorithm for getting and setting data from block chain

Algorithm: Reading block-chain data

BEGIN PROCEDURE

STEP 1: Get the query to process.

STEP 2: Check if the query parameters are valid.

STEP 3: If VALID then,

STEP 3.1: Filter data in chain based on query.

STEP 3.2: Read The Filtered Data Back to the buffer.

STEP 4: ELSE send an invalid query error.

STEP 5: Send the data in the buffer back to the server.

END PROCEDURE

Algorithm: Writing Data into block-chain

STEP 1: Get the data to be written.

STEP 2: Write the data

```python
def make_score(node, current):

    r_client.delete("loc")

    c_lat, c_lon = current
    n_lat, n_lon = node

    r_client.geoadd(
        "loc"
        , (c_lon, c_lat, "current"
        , n_lon, n_lat, "next")
    )

    ret = r_client.geodist("loc", "current", "next", "km")
    r_client.delete("loc")

    return ret

@app_server.route('/', methods=["POST"])
def processRequest():
    resp_data = request.get_json()

    data = resp_data.get('data')
    cur_loc = resp_data.get('cur_loc')
    inj_type = resp_data.get('inj_type')

    fields = ['name', 'addr', 'phone', 'lat', 'lon', 'dept']

    inj_avl = filter(lambda x: inj_type in x[-1], data)
    inj_avl = list(inj_avl)

    new_data = []
    for i in inj_avl:
        node_data = zip(fields, i)
        node_data = list(node_data)
        node_data = dict(node_data)
        node_loc = node_data['lat'], node_data['lon']
        new_data.append(node_data)
        new_data[-1]['score'] = make_score(node_loc, cur_loc)

    resp_data = sorted(new_data, key = lambda x: x['score'], reverse=True)

    return {'data': resp_data}
```

Fig. (2). Implementation Methodology.

RESPONSE AND DATA VISUALIZATION PHASE

Mapbox can be used to visualise map data with time predictions and navigation routing for hospitals that need to transport patients with Deep Learning Model. Fig. (**3**) presents data visualization.

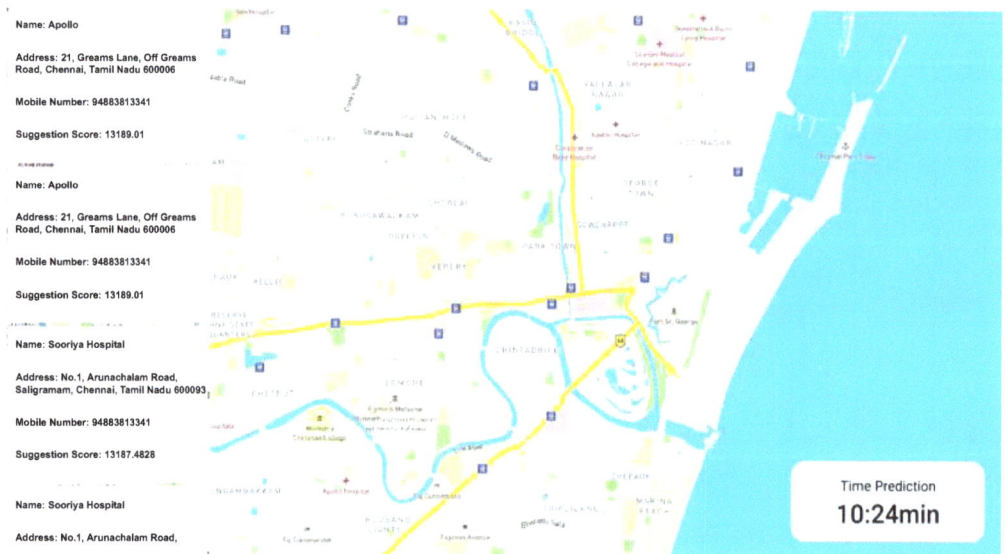

Fig. (3). Data Visualization.

CONCLUSION AND FUTURE WORK

The growing elderly population in India has significantly altered the present population structure. The emergency services response methods will undoubtedly experience more stress in the next years due to population growth and a rise in the number of elderly persons who live longer and are known to need more emergency resources. This is already clear from the vastly increasing number of unanswered calls, which cause numerous fatalities each year. Deaths continue to happen due to the longer ambulance response times, despite answered and responded calls. Therefore, this article suggests the Smart Ambulance System (SAS) as a new method for handling public requests for emergency response in place of the current emergency response protocols. Despite the fact that SAS prototype development and the features contained therein were successful, we have found features that might be added to the system in the future. Through iterative design, these features would make the system better. An indoor position tracker, for instance, could be crucial for locating the patient if voice connections between the patient and emergency services are disrupted. Multi-language support is another example of a feature that would increase the system's usability. As was previously said, it's critical that SAS be usable by as many potential users as possible, independent of their smartphone's operating system. It is extremely expected that the use of IoT devices in the healthcare industry will continue to rise as technology becomes more widely available and affordable, especially as we enter the Internet of Things (IoT) era. Overall, as more academics show interest in the healthcare crossover domains, it gives much potential for future expansion, openings, and additional research.

REFERENCES

[1]   C. Stergiou, K.E. Psannis, B.G. Kim, and B. Gupta, "Secure integration of IoT and cloud computing", *Future Gener. Comput. Syst.,* vol. 78, pp. 964-975, 2018.
[http://dx.doi.org/10.1016/j.future.2016.11.031]

[2]   B. Varghese, and R. Buyya, "Next generation cloud computing: New trends and research directions", *Future Gener. Comput. Syst.,* vol. 79, pp. 849-861, 2018.
[http://dx.doi.org/10.1016/j.future.2017.09.020]

[3]   P. Li, J. Li, Z. Huang, C.Z. Gao, W.B. Chen, and K. Chen, "Privacy-preserving outsourced classification in cloud computing", *Cluster Comput.,* vol. 21, no. 1, pp. 277-286, 2018.
[http://dx.doi.org/10.1007/s10586-017-0849-9]

[4]   N. Subramanian, and A. Jeyaraj, "Recent security challenges in cloud computing", *Comput. Electr. Eng.,* vol. 71, pp. 28-42, 2018.
[http://dx.doi.org/10.1016/j.compeleceng.2018.06.006]

[5]   M. Abdel-Basset, M. Mohamed, and V. Chang, "NMCDA: A framework for evaluating cloud computing services", *Future Gener. Comput. Syst.,* vol. 86, pp. 12-29, 2018.
[http://dx.doi.org/10.1016/j.future.2018.03.014]

[6]   J. Li, Y. Zhang, X. Chen, and Y. Xiang, "Secure attribute-based data sharing for resource-limited users in cloud computing", *Comput. Secur.,* vol. 72, pp. 1-12, 2018.
[http://dx.doi.org/10.1016/j.cose.2017.08.007]

[7]   S. Xie, Z. Zheng, W. Chen, J. Wu, H.N. Dai, and M. Imran, "Blockchain for cloud exchange: A survey", *Comput. Electr. Eng.,* vol. 81, p. 106526, 2020.
[http://dx.doi.org/10.1016/j.compeleceng.2019.106526]

[8]   X. Liang, J. Zhao, S. Shetty, and D. Li, "Towards data assurance and resilience in IoT using blockchain", *MILCOM 2017 - 2017 IEEE Military Communications Conference (MILCOM)* *Baltimore, MD, USA.,* 2017.
[http://dx.doi.org/10.1109/MILCOM.2017.8170858]

[9]   H. Liu, Y. Zhang, and T. Yang, "Blockchain-enabled security in electric vehicles cloud and edge computing", *IEEE Netw.,* vol. 32, no. 3, pp. 78-83, 2018.
[http://dx.doi.org/10.1109/MNET.2018.1700344]

[10]   W. Liang, Y. Fan, K.C. Li, D. Zhang, and J.L. Gaudiot, "Secure data storage and recovery in industrial blockchain network environments", *IEEE Trans. Industr. Inform.,* vol. 16, no. 10, pp. 6543-6552, 2020.
[http://dx.doi.org/10.1109/TII.2020.2966069]

[11]   J. Li, Z. Liu, L. Chen, P. Chen, and J. Wu, "Blockchain-based security architecture for distributed cloud storage", *2017 IEEE International Symposium on Parallel and Distributed Processing with Applications and 2017 IEEE International Conference on Ubiquitous Computing and Communications (ISPA/IUCC) Guangzhou, China.,* 2017.
[http://dx.doi.org/10.1109/ISPA/IUCC.2017.00065]

[12] Y. Zhang, X. Lin, and C. Xu, "Blockchain-based secure data provenance for cloud storage", In: *Proceedings of the International Conference on Information and Communications Security.,* D. Naccache, Ed., Springer: Cham, 2018, pp. 3-19.
[http://dx.doi.org/10.1007/978-3-030-01950-1_1]

[13] U.U. Uchibeke, K.A. Schneider, S.H. Kassani, and R. Deters, "Blockchain access control ecosystem for big data security", *2018 IEEE International Conference on Internet of Things (iThings) and IEEE Green Computing and Communications (GreenCom) and IEEE Cyber, Physical and Social Computing (CPSCom) and IEEE Smart Data (SmartData) Halifax, NS, Canada.,* 2018.
[http://dx.doi.org/10.1109/Cybermatics_2018.2018.00236]

[14] D. Guha Roy, P. Das, D. De, and R. Buyya, "QoS-aware secure transaction framework for internet of things using blockchain mechanism", *J. Netw. Comput. Appl.,* vol. 144, pp. 59-78, 2019.
[http://dx.doi.org/10.1016/j.jnca.2019.06.014]

[15] S. Desai, O. Deshmukh, R. Shelke, H. Choudhary, S.S. Sambhare, and A. Yadav, "Blockchain based secure data storage and access control system using cloud", *2019 5th International Conference On Computing, Communication, Control And Automation (ICCUBEA) Pune, India.,* 2019.
[http://dx.doi.org/10.1109/ICCUBEA47591.2019.9129015]

[16] P. Yousefi, H. Fekriazgomi, M.A. Demir, J.J. Prevost, and M. Jamshidi, "Data-driven fault detection of un-manned aerial vehicles using supervised learning over cloud networks", *Proceedings of the 2018 World Automation Congress (WAC) Stevenson, WA, USA.,* pp. 1-6, 2018.
[http://dx.doi.org/10.23919/WAC.2018.8430428]

[17] P. Li, T. Li, H. Ye, J. Li, X. Chen, and Y. Xiang, "Privacy-preserving machine learning with multiple data providers", *Future Gener. Comput. Syst.,* vol. 87, pp. 341-350, 2018.
[http://dx.doi.org/10.1016/j.future.2018.04.076]

[18] Z. He, T. Zhang, and R.B. Lee, "Machine learning based DDoS attack detection from source side in cloud", *Proceedings of the 2017 IEEE 4th International Conference on Cyber Security and Cloud Computing (CSCloud) New York, NY, USA.,* pp. 114-120, 2017.
[http://dx.doi.org/10.1109/CSCloud.2017.58]

[19] C. Lin, D. He, X. Huang, X. Xie, and K.K.R. Choo, "Blockchain-based system for secure outsourcing of bilinear pairings", *Inf. Sci.,* vol. 527, pp. 590-601, 2020.
[http://dx.doi.org/10.1016/j.ins.2018.12.043]

[20] L. Zhu, Y. Wu, K. Gai, and K.K.R. Choo, "Controllable and trustworthy blockchain-based cloud data management", *Future Gener. Comput. Syst.,* vol. 91, pp. 527-535, 2019.
[http://dx.doi.org/10.1016/j.future.2018.09.019]

[21] A. Theodouli, S. Arakliotis, K. Moschou, K. Votis, and D. Tzovaras, "On the design of a blockchain-based system to facilitate healthcare data sharing", *2018 17th IEEE International Conference On Trust, Security And Privacy In Computing And Communications/ 12th IEEE International Conference On Big Data Science And Engineering (TrustCom/BigDataSE) New York, NY, USA.,* 2018.
[http://dx.doi.org/10.1109/TrustCom/BigDataSE.2018.00190]

[22] Y. Qian, Y. Jiang, and J. Chen, "Towards decentralized IoT security enhancement: A blockchain approach", *Comput. Electr. Eng.,* vol. 72, pp. 266-273, 2018.
[http://dx.doi.org/10.1016/j.compeleceng.2018.08.021]

[23] J. Weng, J. Weng, J. Zhang, M. Li, Y. Zhang, and W. Luo, "Deepchain: auditable and privacy-preserving deep learning with blockchain-based incentive", *IEEE Trans. Depend. Secure Comput.,* vol. 18, no. 5, pp. 2438-2455, 2019.
[http://dx.doi.org/10.1109/TDSC.2019.2952332]

[24] W. Xiong, and L. Xiong, "Smart contract based data trading mode using blockchain and machine learning", *IEEE Access.,* vol. 7, pp. 102331-102344, 2019.
[http://dx.doi.org/10.1109/ACCESS.2019.2928325]

[25]   M. Shen, J. Duan, L. Zhu, J. Zhang, X. Du, and M. Guizani, "Blockchain-based incentives for secure and collaborative data sharing in multiple clouds", *IEEE J. Sel. Areas Comm.,* vol. 38, no. 6, pp. 1229-1241, 2020.
[http://dx.doi.org/10.1109/JSAC.2020.2986619]

CHAPTER 16

Authentication Techniques for Human Monitoring in Closed Environment

V. Vishu[1,*] and **R. Manimegalai**[2]

[1] *Department of Computer Applications, Coimbatore Institute of Technology, Coimbatore, Tamil Nadu 641014, India*

[2] *Department of Computer Science and Engineering, PSG Institute of Technology and Applied Research, Neelambur, Tamil Nadu 641062, India*

Abstract: Human monitoring and trailing in a blocked or closed environment such as a jail or psychological shelter is an important research concern. Industry 4.0 has enabled the monitoring of physically or mentally challenged people in asylums and criminals who are sentenced to serve their terms in jails with various tools such as sensors, wireless systems and sophisticated cameras. The hidden nature of monitoring and reporting in closed environments without any new technologies such as IoT, RFID, *etc.*, may lead to ill-treatment of the inmates in the above-mentioned places. The traditional physical monitoring system can end up with wrong reports about the inmates and can hide the real scenarios. Personal opinions and characteristics of officials as well as the prisoners may vary based on their health and behavioral patterns. The automation of human monitoring involves monitoring of security, activity, fitness, and health factors of the inmates in the closed environment. The human-activity monitoring is carried out by acquiring and analyzing the body signals of the inmates. Passive tags are attached to the wristband of each person in the RFID human monitoring systems. Minimal human intervention and effort is one of the biggest advantages of the human monitoring system. Authentication, intelligent decision making and minimum use of resources are the main challenges in designing a human monitoring system. Intelligent decision making algorithms are applied to predict human behavioral patterns. This work gives a summary of different authentication protocols and methodologies used with the Internet of Things (IoT) and RFID devices in human monitoring systems. It presents the components and infrastructure of a typical human monitoring system and summarizes the sensors and IoT devices used for the same. A wide investigation is conducted on security and privacy issues while storing the private and confidential details of the inmates. A comprehensive survey on different authentication techniques and data security issues in closed human monitoring is presented in this work.

Keywords: Authentication, Closed Human Monitoring, IoT, RF-ID, Sensors.

---

[*] **Corresponding author V. Vishu:** Department of Computer Applications, Coimbatore Institute of Technology, Coimbatore, Tamil Nadu 641014, India; E-mail: vishu.cta.cit@gmail.com

INTRODUCTION

Human Monitoring system provides intelligent information and alerts to the users through the control devices such as Radio Frequency Identification (RFID), IoT and sensors. In traditional human monitoring systems, the limited access to the stored data in human monitoring systems at remote locations may lead to ill-treatment of the inmates [1]. The design of human monitoring system becomes more challenging for analyzing the data received from wearable sensors and devices. As the data handled by monitoring systems are sensitive and private, there is a need for more efficient authentication techniques. IoT and sensors play a major role in improving the security and prediction of human activities accurately. The values from sensors, RFID tags and IoT devices create the percept history and are combined to propose a key which is used in authentication and decision making, as shown in Fig. (**1**).

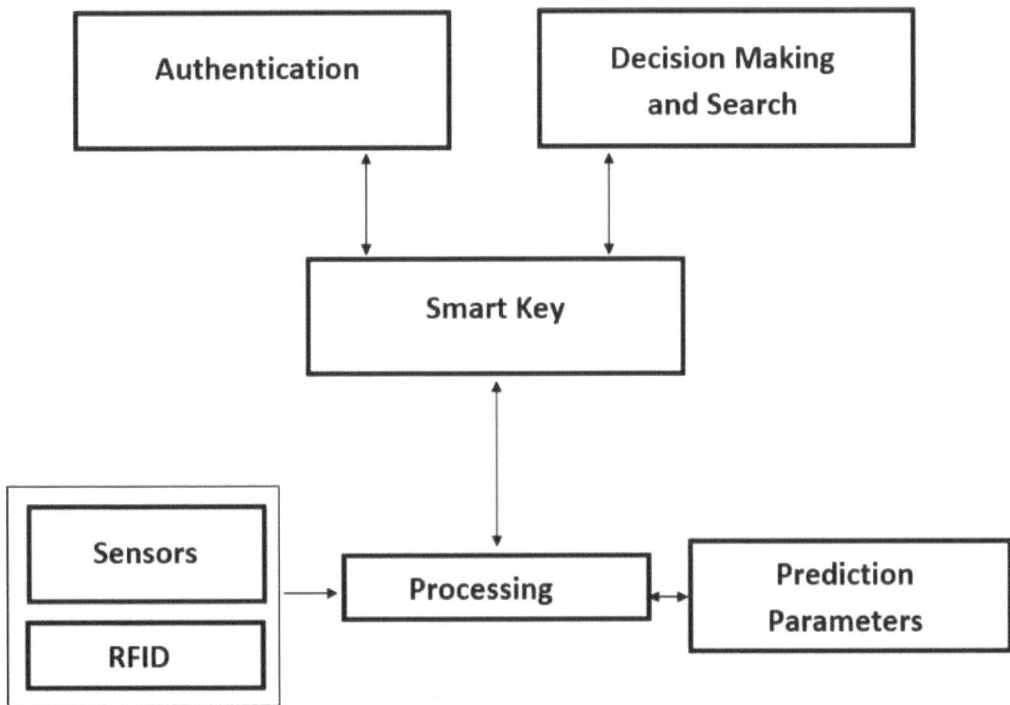

Fig. (1). Block Diagram of a Typical Human Monitoring System.

The human monitoring techniques have high computation and communication costs and are prone to a range of known attacks, which decrease their significance for applicability in real-world environments. There are various techniques for performing authentication, such as the use of text passwords or cipher texts. The combination of one or two authentication, called multi-factor authentication, is also one of the best solutions in the human monitoring environment [2]. Intelligent agents facilitate the prediction of physical and mental condition and behaviors of the inmates. Alarms are produced based on age, deceases, and unusual activities. RFID tag traces the inmate's physical and health conditions and recognizes the presence of any electronic device. When an inmate leaves a region, the nearby RFID reader beside the door scans the tags connected to the wristband and generates an alarm if the entry is limited to the particular inmate. Intelligent sensors and readers are placed in each entrance and common areas. Once the antenna identifies a passive tag, the RFID reader finds the position and reminds the officials with a message or voice through the interactive podium [3].

RADIO FREQUENCY IDENTIFICATION IN HUMAN MONITORING

Radio Frequency Identification (RFID) technology uses radio frequency signals to acquire data dynamically from tags within reading range. The data is then used for a variety of purposes, such as opening doors and gates, paying tolls, tracking equipment, materials and human beings. The RFID system consists of a reader and a transponder component called a tag, which is associated with the corresponding object. Tags are classified into passive tags and active tags [4]. The RFID systems are designed based on the transmission of radio signals. Identification of human beings is done on the basis of a unique identifier, which is stored on the tag. RFID tags are used in various environments, such as water, dust, oil *etc*. It is possible to read multiple RFID tags simultaneously through multiple objects. RFID tags are devices that contain identification and other information that is communicated to a reader from a distance [5].

An RFID tag is a microchip combined with an antenna and is packaged so that it can be attached to the human body. The reader is connected to the power source and a COM port and connected to server machines. RS 232 protocol is used to enable serial communication and Putty is used for the interface between transmitter and receiver [6]. The reader network commands such as DHCP, IP address, Net mask, Gateway, and DNS are used for interactive and autonomous mode communication. The interactive mode uses active tags, whereas the autonomous mode uses the continuous conversation style. Various triggers are incorporated in the alien RFID readers. Notifications are made whenever a new tag comes into visibility, addition and deletion of tags, and customizing the tag values. Notifications are generated from a reader in different formats, such as plain text messages, 16-bit values, XML, *etc*. Readers are classified as enterprise readers, handheld readers and commercial readers. ALR-F800, ALR-F800, ALR-9900+, and ALE 9650 are some of the available enterprise readers. A jail environment with a minimum number of 8 readers and a maximum number of 24 antennas is considered. A reader usually supports 4 antennas, and each antenna is placed in different gates and identifies the values from where it is recorded [7].

Each antenna has a different number and responsibilities assigned to it. Some antennas only record the entries, whereas other antennas have the responsibility of authentication alone. Programming of antennas through a reader interface is possible [8]. Squiggle tags are the best for applications that need accurate results. These types of tags allow the applications to read from documents and files where the accuracy of reading is a major issue. Places such as the library and offices encourage squiggle tag usage. The missed tag reading values are very less in squiggle tags. While glasses or liquids are considered in the field of RFID, high dielectric and automotive tags are popularly used. In metallic environments, the unwanted tag information is read due to reflections. In order to avoid such unwanted multiple readings of tags, high-performance tags are used in handheld readers. Health and medical field of study uses form-factor tags. Form factor tags are used where RFID has a minimal chance of implementation and success. A square form-factor tag is used for tracking larger goods or trucks with close proximity and accuracy. Form factor tags are designed to read all possible angles with random orientations. Different applications use square tags for implementation, such as gas cylinder tracking and guest tracking. The square tags are used for small read-range and environments that need more accuracy. Materials and assets that are in motion are tracked using square tags [9].

SENSORS USED IN HUMAN MONITORING

Sensors inside the jail environment play a major role as they collect, pass, and store details of the inmates to create the knowledge base. Two categories of sensors are physically attached sensors and environmental sensors. The sensors that are attached either to the human body or fabric are known as physical sensors and the sensors that are attached to the walls, outdoor objects, and fences are considered environmental sensors. Active and passive sensors are used based on the requirements. Active sensors do not require external power for the operations, whereas the passive sensors need exterior power. Inside the jail, various sensors such as surface sensors, ECG monitoring sensors, pulse monitoring sensors, respiration sensors, and activity sensors are used based on the requirements of different locations and inmates [10].

PREDICTION PARAMETERS IN HUMAN MONITORING

Human Monitoring Systems need to predict or help the inmates with some instructions or intimations. The monitoring system makes use of decision-making techniques with prediction parameters. Intelligent agent programs make use of these parameters in decision-making. A dynamic intelligent agent helps to make the right decision without human intervention. RFID and sensor values are passed on to agent programs to predict the right choice from the available options [11]. The automation of human monitoring system for a jail environment combines the inmates' thinking and activities to predict human behavior. Language is not considered a barrier as the intelligent agent program provides natural language processing and converts thinking and activities into percept history and knowledge. Comparisons are made based on daily activities, problem-solving methods and reasoning capabilities of the inmates to identify whether the proposed intelligent agent makes predictions accurately. The representation of this information after processing is called knowledge representation in jail intelligence [12-14].

The jail environment is divided into multiple locations and each location is set with many constraints. The intelligent agent programs accept the information from RFID tags as well as the sensors. The intelligent agent program receives a set of actions from readers and sensors. The correct representation of each state received from readers as well as sensors decides the number of states, the number of operators, and the types of decision factors. The cost of deciding the best solution in the smallest amount of time is the main advantage of combining RFID and intelligent sensors. In an alpha-beta pruning algorithm, the node that is closest to the solution is analyzed first to get an optimized solution [15, 16].

DECISION-MAKING AND SEARCH IN HUMAN MONITORING

The Human Monitoring environment receives many decision-making parameters that act as inputs to intelligent agents in searching for the best solution. Right decisions are to be made and given in the automated human monitoring system. Behavior patterns are made from the sensor information as the first step in decision-making [17 - 19]. State space search techniques are considered to analyze the same. The proposed smart key is a combination of values such as RFID tag values with personal information, sensor values, decision-making, and intelligence. Passive class 2 RFID tags are used so that individual information is predefined and attached to the wristband. The portability controller sets the permissions for movements and activities and stored tag values within the premises [20].

Inmates' movement to different locations is based on the rules provided to them as well as their hobbies and mood swings. The main factor considered in human decision making is reasoning ability. The agent considers past actions, rules, environments, and their past life situations for right decision making. High probability of solution and a less probability alternative solution is considered for accuracy. In this particular jail environment, the multi-decision values that give a high probability of success are considered $x=(x_1,x_2,x_3.....x_n)$ and are compared with the expected value set $z=(z_1,z_2,z_3.....z_n)$. These comparison results are given as a sparse matrix of 0's and 1's. The server records the location of inmates and behavioral patterns. The intelligent agent based method solves multiple tag identification within short range and collision due to metallic environments. The intelligent agent identifies signals from a variety of sensors, such as medical sensors, environmental sensors, and RFID readers and applies pattern recognition techniques to make out the behavioral and health parameters of the inmates. Location tracking, inmate's entry-exit, and standard activities are recorded by all the RFID readers.

INFRASTRUCTURE OF THE CLOSED HUMAN MONITORING ENVIRONMENT

Closed human environment automations consider the infrastructure to be compatible with the IoT or RFID device functionalities to avoid vulnerabilities [18]. The human monitoring environments considered in an RFID environment consist of different segments such as office, administrator, smoke rooms, inmate's cells, kitchen, and entertainment, work sections, dining and parking areas. Four Alien RFID readers are positioned in diverse locations of the jail. Every reader has four antennas and sixteen antennas are placed at each entry-exit point to different areas to record the movements. The jail has two different ways of fencing at the exterior. Three office rooms have the central power along with the administrator room. Different sensors are placed in the exterior, human body, and electronic devices, which continuously monitor and record the ideals. The recorded ideals are used to predict human behavior. The recorded data are used as proof by the officials. The distinctive jail infrastructure for the proposed human monitoring system is shown in Fig. (2). The jail surroundings are controlled by three office sections. The middle reader records at different entry-exit points. Administrators continuously check the central servers and monitoring systems. Different regions, such as kitchens, cells and reading rooms in which inmates are authorized for movement, are positioned with different sets of sensors.

The movements made by inmates are helpful in identifying the living style and preferences of those inmates. All the readers are connected to the server and in case of unauthorized entry-exits, alarms are generated and all officials are intimated. The outer layer of the cell is covered with a fence and the inner layer is connected with the planned RFID monitoring system. Each cell opens to a general corridor where entry and exit points are limited with automatic gates. The primary objective of this intelligent plan is to make the living of the inmates more well-organized and comfortable. The proposed monitoring system presents both location tracing and health alarms. The security issues of an IoT-based human monitoring system principally depend on the category of the application. Basic needs are confidentiality, reliability and authentication. Authentication and integrity are the key requirements in an IoT application [21, 22]. The cryptographic techniques designed for large memory devices do not support resource limited IoT devices. Providing better ambiance in the jail by reducing the occurrences of persistent and troublesome behaviors, aggression, pressure and anxiety is one of the primary objectives of a closed human monitoring system. The outer layer of the cell is covered with a fence and the inner layer is connected with the planned RFID monitoring system. Each cell opens to a general corridor where entry exit points are limited with automatic gates.

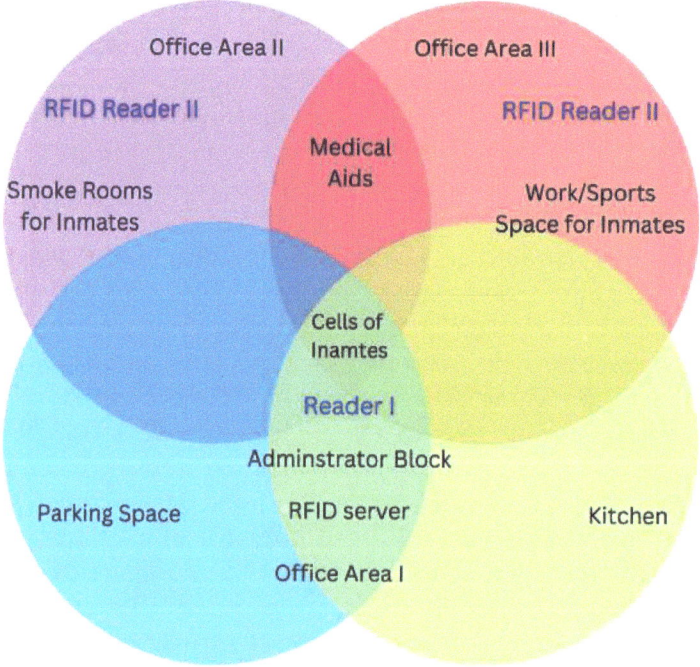

Fig. (2). Structure of Proposed Human Monitoring Systems.

EXISTING   TECHNOLOGIES   AND   TOOLS   FOR   HUMAN MONITORING

The review of general approaches in a closed human monitoring environment brought light on IoT and RFID technologies to offer an efficient supervising system. The day-to-day activities are guided through the IoT or RFID wearable devices in closed areas [23]. Visually challenged people stumble on carrying out their regular work inside different closed environments such as hospitals and jails. RFID is used in the incessant monitoring of animals within farms. The rising size of the animal units is the main issue considered. The execution of Ultra High Frequency (UHF) RFID helps the animal monitoring systems and alters information handling in competent mode. The UHF RFID authentication protocol improves competence in terms of animal health analysis, cost, and security [24]. An RFID authentication method is proposed for storing individual actions with RFID wireless networks. The continuous monitoring is made inside the closed environment using RFID readers and tags. The authentication competence is measured with different AES algorithm versions, and proposed a technique that increases the authentication efficiency in terms of time and number of transitions the proposed technique increases the authentication. The authentication process in IoT devices is shown in Fig. (**3**).

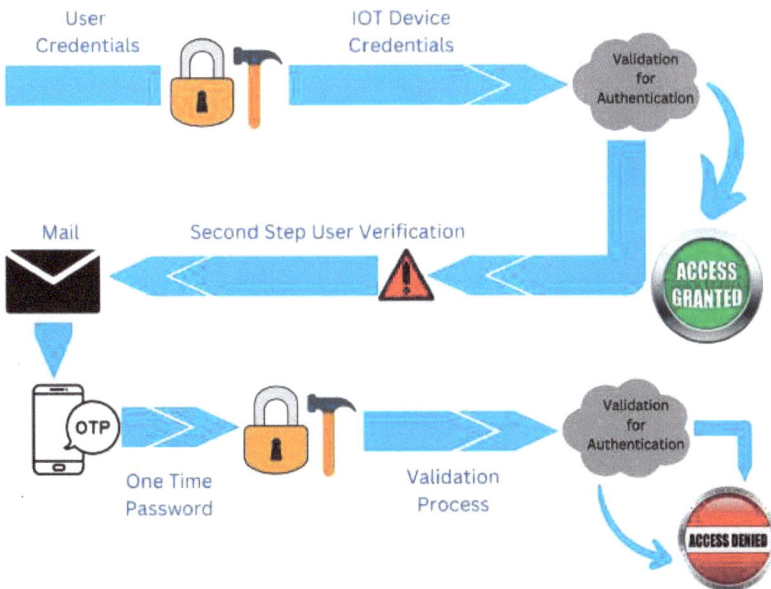

Fig. (3). Authentication Process Involved in Human Monitoring Systems at the IoT Device Level.

The smart parking systems are taken into contemplation to learn whether RFID is ideal for human interactive environments. M N Kamel *et al.* [12] have proposed various profitable and practical aspects to give more protected RFID parking surroundings. Ultra-high frequency is used in general areas as it is considered to give more consistent outcomes. The system gathers information regarding available parking spaces and timing and gives proper instructions to drivers. The billing system utilizes routine RFID technology. Java and Google Cloud messaging expertise are used in this application. These technologies apply a central server to accumulate and route the information and provide a variety of alerts [24].

The data examination in agriculture and health is done through wearable RFID wireless tags. The wearable RFID tags increase the effectiveness in terms of security, right communication among the users, and timely revision between different RFID control mechanisms. The relative study of RFID in the different application vicinity such as healthcare, retail management, supply chain management, billing systems, and agriculture is done. The classification issue and the combination of radio frequency identification techniques are examined in [10] with biometric devices. The estimation of RFID with conservative ID tools is done to boost authentication performance. Every utility translates into an accurate RFID method and constraints. Techniques comprise frequency compilation, tag power delivery, and tag writing capabilities. Information exchange issues of identifier process in retails are analyzed and structured for choosing an auto ID system in a supply chain [25].

The monitoring services are designed for the manufacturer of RFID. RFID developers need a functional tool to assist them in creating novel RFID product functions. The lessons showed the QT Kano mould approach, which put together three supervision tools, renowned function employment, the hypothesis of inspired problem-solving and a refined Kano's model to create original invention functions of RFID goods. To decrease the high stoppage velocity in fresh commodities development procedures, an advanced Kano's model is functional to suggest a better understanding from the customer's viewpoint and to assist service designers in focusing on the majority of attributes that need to be enhanced. The genuine case of RFID innovation function growth is established to show the effectiveness of the proposed model. B D Deebak *et al.* presented a literature review on different authentication techniques to compare according to different parameters and ways to distinguish the efficient ones for different circumstances. Single and multi-factor authentication techniques are compared to suggest the best for human monitoring system. User authentication is major in the IoT atmosphere as it permits the user to exchange information with the mechanism securely. Combination of authentication expertise with IoT guarantees the secure data retrieval and robust access control. This study assist to recognize the general challenging security concerns in the existing authentication protocols for human monitoring system [26].

The human monitoring studies based on sensors and IoT for relevant applications were re-evaluated and analyzed to observe these technologies and provide researchers with a clear vision of security and privacy in Chandrakar P *et al.*, 2018. The major research concerns in the authentication model are security and privacy. Features such as movement speed, body temperature and frequent choices of diversions are considered to make an intelligent prediction on the behavioral blueprints. Recording all particulars about the inmates, besides the visitor preferences, helps to witness inmates' behavioral patterns, health, and to fix the expected levels of freedom. The missed tag reading values are very less in squiggle tags and readers are very closely placed. While glasses or liquids are considered in the field of RFID, high dielectric and automotive tags are best. When metallic environments are considered unwanted, tags are read due to reflections. To avoid such multiple reading of tags, high-performance tags are used in handheld readers. The analysis of the safety measures on the Gen2 protocol and the implementations in the context is done based on time-based attackers. The firm interaction timings mentioned in the Gen2 protocol alleviate different kinds of attacks. The movable implementations with time limits on industrial invaders and limited time constraints enable tags to give the efficiency of the particular time control. RFID tools are found to be functional all through the industrialized methods to trail central stuff. An involuntary monitoring prototype is used to translate RFID facts into significant information.

Two major challenges are addressed, such as modeling complexity and observing efficiency. When the association between high-point untagged fundamentals and low-level tagged basics becomes complicated, it becomes hard to describe, uphold, and motivate by only using a conventional rule-based occurrence giving out approach. To resolve the difficulty, the model-based techniques are used to check important fundamentals by approximation of their most likely condition according to RFID particulars and the constraint-based replica. The inadequate quantity of jail security persons, it is a demanding mission for jail guards to observe the bulky amount of criminals in jail. It is complicated to expect the motion localizations of the inmates exactly. It is significant to assume information expertise to check the prisoners' performance. RFID feature with the potential of multi objective recognition, exact spot, and rapid appreciation, is an enviable device for the monitoring of jail inmates. An active RFID technology foundation hostage localization system is planned and used. In order to progress the localization correctness, the pathway failure exponent, which reproduces the ecological failure exponent, is brought in to lessen the inaccuracy caused by neighboring environment issues. The testing is performed to authenticate the algorithm and the administration validation system.

Prosanta Gope *et al* have discussed the benefits of combining WSN and RFID. An original scheme for gas compactness, observing and forecasting is based on a passive RFID sensor tag and a Convolutional neural networks (CNN) algorithm. The wireless sensor is the foundation of the electronic product code (EPC) generation2 (G2) protocol, and the antenna data are entrenched into the identification (ID) particulars of the RFID chip. The wireless sensor contains an interactive section, a radio-frequency (RF) physical section, and a dynamic section. The interaction is applied to carry out the broadcast and response of wireless technologies. The RF physical sector is approved to supply the firm electrical energy for other fractions. The dynamic section is working to obtain sensor data and rule the general procedure of the wireless sensor based on the EPC procedure. The diverse disturbances decrease the correctness throughout the procedure of wireless transmission, and the CNN algorithm is used to pull out the vigorous characteristic from raw statistical data. The dimension grades illustrate that the subjugated RFID sensor realizes a maximum reading distance of 10.3 m and can determine and foretell the gas thickness in an underground mine. The RFID sensor knowledge is a helpful up-to-date alternative monitoring system. With the growing population and crime count face, the number of jail inmates increased and led to the increased need for jail managing.

The wireless management system is led to enable the intelligent management of prison [9]. Research on the construction of prison wireless management systems based on active RFID wireless sensors is conducted and found beneficial. The analyzed RFID tools brought the benefits of active and passive sensors in jail wireless monitoring tools and brought the options of developing wireless monitoring methods as well as the right to use control management inside jails, regional observing procedures, and prison inmate's location tracing rules and methods and secondary systems. On this foundation, the analysis and implementations combined RFID and software systems to create the supervision system and get better the sub-module functions and consistency of the jail management methods. RFID implementations acquiescent to the EPC global Generation-2 (Gen2) passive UHF RFID protocol are being organized in a wide range of implementations, including the right of entry control, computerized tolling, individual detection, and supply chain administration. The implementations insist on the increasing needs of RFID tag performances, and safety on the tag has become a significant facilitating functionality in many implementations [13]. To deal with the marketplace need, EPCglobal is initiating a benchmark safety structure within which safety functionalities are included flawlessly into the Gen2 protocol.

The proposed Gen 2 safety structure and the cryptographic techniques to show how to use the structure and to offer a variety of safety measures The analysis of the safety measures on the Gen2 protocol and the implementations in the context is done based on time-based attackers is done in the firm interaction timings mentioned in the Gen2 protocol alleviate different kinds of attacks. The movable implementations with time limits on industrial invaders and limited time constraints enable tags to give the efficiency of the particular time control. RFID tools are found functional all through the industrialized methods to trail the central staff. An involuntary monitoring prototype is used to translate RFID facts into significant information. Two major challenges are addressed, such as modeling complexity and observing efficiency. When the association between high-point untagged fundamentals and low-level tagged basics becomes complicated, it becomes hard to describe, uphold, and motivate by only using a conventional rule-based occurrence giving out approach.

To resolve the difficulty, the model-based techniques are used to check important fundamentals by approximation of their most likely condition according to RFID particulars and the constraint-based replica is described. The structure encloses two stages as the model-based programming mode that honors RFID parameters and agreeably implants them into the structure that identifies the monitoring rules and regulations. The model-based monitoring stage depicts the structure and calculates the required stages effectively. The RFID built-up units are competent in reacting in a sensible manner to unforeseen turbulence. The security necessities of an IoT based human monitoring system principally depend on the category of applications it handles. Basic needs are confidentiality, reliability and authentication. Authentication is measured as a key requirement for IoT; integrity of the devices considered in an IoT network is very important for the accurate working of the network. The real nature of IoT devices makes the existing authentication methods unreliable. The cryptographic techniques designed for large memory devices do not support resource-limited IoT devices. The appearance of insubstantial authentication methods; some of them are specific to the context of IoT or to the RFID devices, which can be considered suitable for IoT. The major point of the planned monitoring solution is to get better the ambiance in the jail by reducing the occurrences of persistent and troublesome behaviors, aggression, pressure and anxiety.

The SACS algorithm is applied to explain genuine RFID network development issues in the search for solutions in a study by S Otoum *et al.*, 2019. The trial results show that the proposed algorithm acquires improved answers for the RFID network setting up problem than all former adaptive cuckoo search alternatives in terms of optimization and stoutness. The fine points of the progress of an Arimaa program prototype, a board game with extremely uncomplicated and instinctive regulations to humans, except which are very multifarious for computers. With the intention of the enhanced way of handling this difficulty, the game is examined, learning its representative narration, how it participates, and the difficulties accessible when indoctrinating it. The latest alternative of the cuckoo search algorithm, called the Self Adaptive Cuckoo Search algorithm, is vigorously accustomed according to the growth of optimization procedure and is considered for analysis.

This survey is done to recognize the general challenging security concerns in the existing authentication protocols for human monitoring systems. The human monitoring studies based on sensors and IoT for relevant applications were re-evaluated and analyzed to observe these technologies and provide researchers with a clear vision of security and privacy. The major research concerns in the authentication model are security and privacy. Features such as movement speed, body temperature and frequent choices of diversions are considered to make an intelligent prediction on the behavioral blueprints.

AUTHENTICATION TECHNIQUES IN HUMAN MONITORING SYSTEMS

Automation of human monitoring systems leads to security and privacy issues in data storage, processing and retrieval. The observed data need to be secure and communicated with proper authentication. In every monitoring scheme, authentication and security are provided with different encryption approaches. The encryption process is divided into two categories as symmetric and asymmetric encryption. Symmetric keys ensure secure data transfer between the sender and the receiver with the same key for encryption and decryption. Asymmetric keys use separate keys for encryption and decryption. The computational time for key generation includes encryption decryption time, key generation time and the key exchange time between sender and receiver. The time is measured when converting a plain text file into a cipher text file. Any key generation time depends on the size of the key length, which is different for symmetric and asymmetric cryptography.

Encrypted cipher text exchange time depends on the communication channel between the sender and the receiver. The DES algorithm is not quicker for software, but the efficiency of DES is good on hardware. F. Al-Turjman described the examination on the ground of encryption algorithms, directed on private key block ciphers, which are normally used for mass data, a link encryption practice.

Primarily surveyed some of the accepted and capable encryption algorithms currently used. The principal focus is on the different encryption techniques that are evolved, and a comparative study is done with the same. This study extends to the performance parameters used in encryption processes and analyzes their protection issues. Cryptography is the tradition and revision of thrashing in sequence. Earlier cryptography was almost identical to encryption and the translation of information from a legible state to an indecipherable state. With the purpose of avoiding discarded persons being able to study the information, senders hold the facility to decrypt the information. The revision of the accepted symmetric key encryption algorithms such as DES, AES and Blowfish is done. The symmetric key encryption provides additional safety measures. The routine assessment of particular symmetric algorithms is leading toward the RFID and intelligence combination. The existing recreation of the AES has better performance than other algorithms in terms of security, cost, and efficiency. AES has benefits over the DES in terms of performance and decryption period, except Blowfish. The 128-bit approach to the Data Encryption Standard cipher using the symmetric block cipher is described. Many methods are hacked in order to split the cipher and find the plaintext communication, explicitly through brute force attacks. To get better its security, and have made modifications to the benchmark bit size, wherein it is doubled from a size of 64-bits to 128-bits on the key arrangement and plaintext block. The size of a range of tables, functions, keys, and swaps during the process of the unique DES are also subject to this replication in size.

Chaudhry S A *et al.* defined the Data Encryption Standard two times as general as its predecessor. By increasing the large collection of the cipher, it is much longer for an invader to avoid safety during the exploit of brute force. DES has been the most widely used encryption algorithm paradigm in recent times. Encryption and decryption comprise cryptography standards and measures. The cryptography method used in the encryption standards covers the original content. DES is a cipher-based algorithm for every data block. Data encryption is being used to conceal the true sense of data, so that it is very hard to assault. The reproduction and mixture grades of implemented DES algorithm give a better result. Investigation of performance gives the best execution time of 12 seconds. The step-by-step examination gives better results.

The idea of cryptography extended with encryption and decryption is analyzed. DES has 16 rounds of the process. The plaintext is occupied to 16 rounds of operation, which produces a cipher key. With the same key and data, and performance, it produces the same output. Data Encryption Standard has improved the stage of safety because of the 16 rounds of function. It is complicated for the unconstitutional party to attack and break. Encryption is the progression to safe classified data to transmit over insecure channels. Data is not secure because of attackers and intruders. The DES is an apprehensive algorithm because of its 8 bits fixed keys. The proposed modification simplifies the DES algorithm to secure data. The random number based generation of keys makes the S-DES algorithm more secure. When corresponding with another individual, the risk regarding protection finds out a solution to make a more secure S-DES algorithm. Chaudhry S A *et al*. explained the integration of RFID tags in an ample diversity of areas increases the necessity for formulating certain safety and solitude of the unit with which these tags are associated. This is a very active region, as demonstrated by the huge number of connected available research literature.

Gutub A *et al*. have proposed a shared authentication protocol for RFID. This procedure has a basic defect that can be eagerly taken advantage of by an inventive opponent, which indicates the features of a new protocol for these attacks. Shaping the safety of AES is an innermost difficulty in cryptanalysis, but development in this region had been dawdling, and only a handful of cryptanalytic techniques led to important advancement. C Xu *et al*. presented an original nature of distinguisher for AES, such as structures, but so far, all the published attacks which were based on this distinguisher were less than before known threats in their convolution. The practice of N Ellouze *et al*. with some other techniques to get the finest recognized key revival attack on 5 round AES in the particular key representation dropping its general complication from about 232 to about 222.5. Extending the techniques to 7 round AES has provided the most excellent known results on AES-192, which utilize sensible amounts of facts and memory violation. The evidence for such threats, which are obtained in the past by the standard square attack, are identified. Table **1** summarizes various encryption techniques that are used for human monitoring systems.

Table 1. Comparison of Authentication Techniques in Human Monitoring Environments.

Num.	Layer	Proposed Solutions	Access Control	Issues Addressed	Context Credentials	Pros and Cons of The Existing Solution
1	Application Layer	Authorization Framework, Decisions Based on Base Data and Environment Factors [1]	Multi User	Node Capture, Fake Nodes, Mass Node Authentication	IoT, RFID, Sensors, Authentication	Significant Flexibility to the Access Control Models

(Table 1) cont.....

Num.	Layer	Proposed Solutions	Access Control	Issues Addressed	Context Credentials	Pros and Cons of The Existing Solution
2	Presentation Layer	An Architecture IoT-OAS Targeting Http/COAP Services Flexible, Highly Configurable, and Easy To Implement [2]	Single User	Threats Involving The Node Security	IoT Authentication	Flexible, Highly Configurable, Easy to Integrate With Existing Services, Lower Processing Load
3	Application Layer	Proposed A Mechanism For Privacy Protection That Is Preference-Based for the IoT [3]	Multi User	Confidentiality Service, Key Management	IoT, Sensors	Ensure Desirable Level of User Privacy
4	Application Layer	Suggested An Inter-Device Authentication and Session Key Distribution System [4]		Lightweight Authentication and Key Establishment In Wireless Sensor Networks	Sensors	Prevented Replay Attacks, Man-In The Middle Attacks, Estimated The Session Key in Prior
5	Network Layer	An Enforcement Security Policy Is Suggested For Addressing The Privacy and Security Challenges [5]	Multi User	Data Access and Authentication, DoS Attacks, Secured Communication Session	RFID, Authentication	Provided Optimal Communication Between the IoT Devices
6	Application Layer	A Mechanism That Supports end-t--end Secure Communication Between Internet and IP Sensor Networks [6]	Multi User	Access Control and Authorization Issues in Interconnected Devices	IoT	Secure and Efficient
7	Network Layer	Detection Algorithm In Which The Sensors Can Identify Their Status In The Distributed Environment As "Good" or "Faulty" [7]	Multi User	Users Privacy Protection	IoT	Maximum Accuracy

(Table 1) cont.....

Num.	Layer	Proposed Solutions	Access Control	Issues Addressed	Context Credentials	Pros and Cons of The Existing Solution
8	Presentation Layer	Proposed An Improved Protocol for Radio Frequency Identification Security [8]	Multi User	Security Policy to Address the Privacy Challenges	IoT	Computationally Efficient, Prevents Disclosure and Resynchronization Attacks.
9	Network Layer	Lightweight Encryption Scheme [9]	Multi User	Inter-Device Authentication Issues and Session-Key Distribution Issues	IoT	Efficiency and Reduced Communication Cost
10	Application Layer	Pervasive Authentication Protocol and A Key Establishment Scheme [10]	Multi User	Data Authentication Between The Cloud and The Smart Devices	IoT	End-Users Can Authenticate Themselves To The Sensor Nodes Directly And Acquire Sensed Data And Services. Uses Three Factor Authentication And Privacy Preserving Is Considered. Resistance To Replay, MITM, Active, Passive, Forgery, User Traceability

The experimentally recognized key revival attack on 5 round AES dropping its whole convolution varies from 232 to 222.5. The extended attack to 7 round AES obtained the most excellent key revival threats on the 192- and 256-bit versions of this crypto scheme, which have sensible information and memory complexities. The recent mobile devices show high ability and convenience, bringing bring in supplementary stress in terms of protection validation. By means of the extensively known deprived use of PINs, active authentication is planned to defeat the elementary concern of practical and protected authentication during the operation of biometric-based procedures to endlessly validate user individuality. The novel text-based multi-biometric use linguistic investigation, keystroke statistics, and behavioral patterns. Investigational results indicate that individuals can be distinguished by text-based way, with a standard Equal Error Rate of 3.3%. These conclusions ensure a structure that is competent to offer healthy, constant, and clear authentication. The structure is analyzed to scrutinize the usefulness of providing safety and user handiness. The effect illustrated that the structure is capable of providing a 91% decrease in the number of invasive authentication needs necessary for high security applications. N Ellouze *et al*. [10] have found turn-based scheme games that affect the investigation to enable artificial players with the regulations presented by developers with several test cases.

CONCLUSION

This chapter presents a survey on various RFID and IoT-based authentication techniques in closed human monitoring environments. The human monitoring techniques available in the literature have identified the following issues: threats involved in data handling, data reliability and inter-device authentication issues. To address these issues, various authorization frameworks, data recovery methods, and pervasive authentication protocols are suggested in the application layer, presentation layer and network layer of the authentication process. The proposed authentication techniques evaluate optimal authentication solutions to mitigate middle attacks in data processing and improve load efficiency.

REFERENCES

[1]   B.D. Deebak, Turjman Fadi Al, and Omar Alfandi MoayadAloqail, "'An Authentic- Based Privacy Preservation Protocol for Smart E-Healthcare Systems in IoT'", *IEEE Journal on Security and Privacy in Emerging Decentralized Communication Environments,* vol. 7, pp. 135632-135649, 2019.

[2]   M. Wazid, A.K. Das, N. Kumar, A.V. Vasilakos, and J.J.P.C. Rodrigues, "Design and Analysis of Secure Lightweight Remote User Authentication and Key Agreement Scheme in Internet of Drones Deployment", *IEEE Internet Things J.,* vol. 6, no. 2, pp. 3572-3584, 2019.
[http://dx.doi.org/10.1109/JIOT.2018.2888821]

[3]   S. Otoum, and B. Kantarci, "HMouftah, 'Empowering Reinforcement Learning on Big Sensed Data for Intrusion Detection", *IEEE International Conference on Communications,* pp. 1-7, 2019.

[4]   S. Vankamamidi, Sivaranjani Reddit. Naresh, and V E S Murthy. Nistala, *'Secure Lightweight IoT Integrated RFID Mobile Healthcare System',* Journal of Wireless Communications and Mobile Computing,, vol. 20, pp. 1-13, 2020.

[5]   F. Al-Turjman, "Intelligence and security in big 5G-oriented IoNT: An overview", *Future Gener. Comput. Syst.,* vol. 102, pp. 357-368, 2020.
[http://dx.doi.org/10.1016/j.future.2019.08.009]

[6]   Jemin Lee. ProsantaGope, and S Quek Tony Q, "'Lightweight and Practical Anonymous Authentication Protocol for RFID Systems using Physically unclonable Functions'", *IEEE Trans. Inf. Forensics Security,* vol. 13, no. 11, pp. 2831-2843, 2018.

[7]   P. Chandrakar, and H. Om, "An extended ECC-based anonymity-preserving 3-factor remote authentication scheme usable in TMIS", *Int. J. Commun. Syst.,* vol. 31, no. 8, p. e3540, 2018.
[http://dx.doi.org/10.1002/dac.3540]

[8]   S.A. Chaudhry, H. Naqvi, and M.K. Khan, "An enhanced lightweight anonymous biometric based authentication scheme for TMIS", *Multimedia Tools Appl.,* vol. 77, no. 5, pp. 5503-5524, 2018.
[http://dx.doi.org/10.1007/s11042-017-4464-9]

[9]   A. Gutub, "Al-Juaid 'Multi-bits Stego-system for hiding Text in Multimedia Images based on User Security Priority'", *Journal of Computer Hardware Engg.,* vol. 1, no. 2, pp. 1-9, 2018.

[10]   H. Luo, G. Wen, J. Su, and Z. Huang, "SLAP: Succinct and Lightweight Authentication Protocol for low-cost RFID system", *Wirel. Netw.,* vol. 24, no. 1, pp. 69-78, 2018.
[http://dx.doi.org/10.1007/s11276-016-1323-y]

[11]   T. Adame, A. Bel, A. Carreras, and J. Meli, "'A-Segu'ı, M. Oliver, and R. Pous, 'Cui-dats: An RFID–WSN Hybrid Monitoring system for Smart Health Care Environ-ments,'", *Future Gener. Comput. Syst.,* vol. 78, pp. 602-615, 2018.
[http://dx.doi.org/10.1016/j.future.2016.12.023]

[12]   H. Bangui, M. Ge, and B. Buhnova, "Exploring Big Data Clustering Algorithms for Internet of Things Applications,", *In Proceedings of the 3rd Interna-tional Conference on Internet of Things, Big Data and Security, IoTBDS,* 2018.
[http://dx.doi.org/10.5220/0006773402690276]

[13]   Portugal. Madeira, "2018, pp.269–276.T. Adame, A. Bel, A. Carreras, J. Meli'a-Segu'ı, M. Oliver, and R. Pous, 'An RFID–WSN Hybrid Monitoring System for Smart Health care Environments,'", *Future Gener. Comput. Syst.,* vol. 78, pp. 602-615, 2018.

[14]   H. Bangui, M. Ge, and B. Buhnova, "Exploring Big Data Clustering Algorithms for Internet of Things Applications,", *Proceedings of the 3rd International Conference on Internet of Things, Big Data and Security, IoTBDS 2018 Madeira, Portugal,* pp. 269-276, 2018.
[http://dx.doi.org/10.5220/0006773402690276]

[15]   N. Ellouze, S. Rekhis, N. Boudriga, and M. Allouche, "Powerless security for Cardiac Implantable Medical Devices: Use of Wireless Identification and Sensing Platform", *J. Netw. Comput. Appl.,* vol. 107, no. 1, pp. 1-21, 2018.
[http://dx.doi.org/10.1016/j.jnca.2018.01.009]

[16]   C. Xu, K. Wang, and M. Guo, "Intelligent resource management in block chain-based cloud data centers", *IEEE Cloud Computing,* vol. 4, no. 6, pp. 50-59, 2017.
[http://dx.doi.org/10.1109/MCC.2018.1081060]

[17]   B.M.N. Kamel, J.T. Wilson, and K.A. Clauson, "Geospatial BlockChain: Promises, Challenges, and Scenarios in Health and Healthcare", *Int. J. Health Geogr.,* vol. 17, no. 1, pp. 1-19, 2018.
[PMID: 29329535]

[18]   J.H. Tseng, Y.C. Liao, B. Chong, and S. Liao, "Governance on the Drug Supply Chain via Gcoin Blockchain", *Int. J. Environ. Res. Public Health,* vol. 15, no. 6, pp. 1055-1067, 2018.
[http://dx.doi.org/10.3390/ijerph15061055] [PMID: 29882861]

[19]   H. Kaur, M.A. Alam, R. Jameel, A.K. Mourya, and V. Chang, "A proposed solution and future direction for block chain-based heterogeneous medicare data in cloud environment", *J. Med. Syst.,* vol. 42, no. 8, pp. 156-167, 2018.
[http://dx.doi.org/10.1007/s10916-018-1007-5] [PMID: 29987560]

[20]   M. Weyrich, and C. Ebert, "Architectures for the Internet of Things'", In: *IEEE Transactions on software* vol. 33. , 2016, pp. 112-126.

[21]   G.P. Bhalla, R. Amin, S K. Hafizul Islam , and Bhalla. Neeraj Kumar, "'Lightweight and Privacy-Preserving RFID Authentication Scheme for Distributed IoT Infrastructure with Secure Localization Services for Smart City Environment'", *Future Gener Comput Syst.,* vol. 83, pp. 629-637, 2017.

[22]   M. El-hajj, M. Chamoun, M. Fadlallah, and A. Serhrouchni, "Taxonomy of authentication techniques in Internet of Things (IoT)'", *Proceedings of the IEEE 15th Student Conference on Research and Development,* pp. 67-71, 2017.

[23]   P. Gope, R. Amin, S.K. Hafizul Islam, N. Kumar, and V.K. Bhalla, "Lightweight and privacy-preserving RFID authentication scheme for distributed IoT infrastructure with secure localization services for smart city environment", *Future Gener. Comput. Syst.,* vol. 83, pp. 629-637, 2018.
[http://dx.doi.org/10.1016/j.future.2017.06.023]

[24]   S. Mejjaouli, and R.F. Babiceanu, "RF Integrated Monitoring and Control System for Production,

Supply Chain, and Logistics Operations", *International Conference on Flexible Automation and Intelligent Manufacturing,* pp. 378-381, 2014.

[25]   S. Zhou, W. Sheng, F. Deng, X. Wu, and Z. Fu, "A Novel Passive Wireless Sensing Method for Concrete Chloride Ion Concentration Monitoring", *Sensors (Basel),* vol. 17, no. 12, p. 2871, 2017.
[http://dx.doi.org/10.3390/s17122871] [PMID: 29232901]

[26]   P.K. Sadhu, V.P. Yanambaka, A. Abdelgawad, and K. Yelamarthi, "NAHAP: PUF-Based Three Factor Authentication System for Internet of Medical Things", *IEEE Consum. Electron. Mag.,* vol. 12, no. 3, pp. 107-115, 2023.
[http://dx.doi.org/10.1109/MCE.2022.3176420]

[27]   P.K. Sadhu, A. Baul, V.P. Yanambaka, and A. Abdelgawad, "MOuth: A Single Message Identification Method of Internet of Medical Things", *2022 IEEE Global Conference on Artificial Intelligence and Internet of Things (GCAIoT) Alamein New City, Egypt,* pp. 130-137, 2022.

[28]   P.K. Sadhu, A. Baul, V.P. Yanambaka, and A. Abdelgawad, "Machine learning and PUF based authentication framework for internet of medical things", *2022 International Conference on Microelectronics (ICM) Casablanca, Morocco,* pp. 160-163, 2022.
[http://dx.doi.org/10.1109/ICM56065.2022.10005380]

ABBREVIATION

AR	Augmented Reality
AI	Artificial Intelligence
ANN	Artificial Neural Network
ABE	Attribute-Based Encryption
API	Application Programming Interface
AHS	Artificial Healthcare System
AV	Autonomous Vehicle
BIoT	Blockchain of Things
BK	Binary Key
BT	Blockchain Technology
BMI	Body Mass Index
BFT	Byzantine Fault Tolerance
BCCOT	Blockchain Technology and Cloud of Things
BCIOT	Blockchain Technology and Internet of Things
BCTFOT	Blockchain Technology and Fog of Things
BASN	Body Area Sensor Networks
CNN	Convolutional Neural Networks
CT	Computed Tomography
COPD	Chronic Bronchitis and Emphysema
CC	Cloud Computing
CoIn	Computational Intelligence
CADx	Computer-aided Diagnosis
CAT	Computed Tomography
CPS	Cyber-Physical Systems
CORE	Common Open Research Emulator
DS	Digital Signature
DLT	Distributed Ledger Technology
DDoS	Distributed Denial-of-Service
DEX	Decentralized Exchange
DAG	Directed Acyclic Graph
DPoW	Delegated Proof of Work
DP	Decryption Process

DTC	Depository Trust Company
DL	Deep learning
DRE	Rigital Rectal Examination
DP	Differential Privacy
DNN	Deep Neural Networks
EHD	Electronic Health Records
EHRs	Electronic Health Data
EMR	Electronic Medical Record
EP	Encryption Process
EVM	Ethereum Virtual Machine
ECDSA	Elliptic Curve Digital Signature Algorithm
EPC	Electronic Product Code
FL	Federated Learning
FedAvg	Federated Averaging
GA	Genetic Algorithm
GDPR	General Data Protection Regulation
G2V	Grid to Vehicle
HIPAA	Health Insurance Portability and Accountability Act
H-CoIn	Hybrid CoIn
HLF	Hyperledger Fabric
IoT	Internet of Things
IoE	Internet of Everything
IoMT	Internet of Medical Things
ICT	Information and Communication Technology
IPFS	Interplanetary File System
KG	Key Generation
KGP	Key Generation Process
LAN	Local Area Network
LightGBM	Light Gradient Boosting Machine
LR	Logistic Regression
LEA	Lightweight Encryption Algorithm
LSTM	Long Short-Term Memory
MRI	Magnetic Resonance Imaging
ML	Machine Learning
MLP	Multi-Layer Perceptron

M2M	Machine-to-Machine
MAS	Multi
NC	Nanocrystalline
NOS	Network Operating System
NFV	Network Function Virtualization
OBU	On Board Unit
Pow	Proof of Work
PoS	Proof of Stake
PoA	Proof of Authority
P2P	Peer to Peer
PoET	Proof of Elapsed Time
PKI	Private/public Key Infrastructure
PSA	Prostate-Specific Antigen
PKC	Public Key Cryptograph
PoET	Proof of Elapsed Time
PCA	Patient Centric Agent
PoBT	Proof of Block Trade
QoS	Quality of Service
RFID	Radio-Frequency Identification
ROI	Return on Investment
RL	Read Latency
RPM	Remote Patient Monitoring
SQL	Structured Query Language
SVM	Support Vector Machine
SAS	Smart Ambulance System
SAT	Security Access Token
SGX	Intel Software Guard Extensions
SWF	Simple Workflow Services
SC	Smart Contract
SDN	Software Defined Network
TRT	Transaction and Read Throughput
TRL	Transaction and Read Latency
UHF	Ultra High Frequency
VANET	Vehicular Distributed Ad-hoc
VR	Virtual Reality
V2G	Vehicle to Grid
WSN	Wireless Sensor Network

SUBJECT INDEX

A

AI-powered digital therapy 3
Air conditioners 60
Algorithm(s) 174, 186, 201, 202, 203, 208, 209, 222, 234, 235, 236, 241, 253, 254, 270, 273
  cipher-based 273
  outperforms 174
Alzheimer's disease 16
Applications 65, 151
  cloud-based 151
  high-performance blockchain technology 65
Architecture, blockchain-based 187
Artificial intelligence 2, 3, 5, 27, 218
  and blockchain 27
  in healthcare 2
  techniques 3
  technology 218
  tool 5
Artificial neural network (ANN) 192, 224, 247
Asymmetric 144, 145, 231
  cryptosystems 231
  and symmetric cryptography 144, 145
Asymmetric cryptography 70, 144, 145, 162, 272
  technology 162
AtomNet's technology 4
Automated security systems 185
Automation 86, 264, 272
  -blockchain concepts 86
  of human monitoring systems 264, 272

B

Basal cell carcinoma 42, 204
Bitcoin 70, 164, 167
  and Ethereum systems 164
  blockchain 70
  mining 167
Block hashing techniques 72

Blockchain 19, 20, 31, 32, 39, 42, 48, 59, 61, 64, 65, 70, 71, 84, 88, 89, 90, 94, 96, 100, 103, 107, 108, 124, 134, 151, 164, 231, 246
  aggregates 231
  algorithms 64
  and IoT technology 103
  applications 31, 32, 94, 108, 134
  community 64
  consortium 19, 20, 64
  economy 124
  fusing 39
  integrating 84, 88, 89, 90, 246
  internet of things (BIoT) 39, 61
  IoT Applications 59
  processes data 64
  security analysis 70
  software 107, 151
  systems 42, 48, 70, 96, 100
  technology device 65
  transaction system 164
  transactions 71
Blockchain-based 42, 59, 65, 104, 159, 161, 162, 164
  access control system 65
  data encryption technology 164
  edge computing system 162
  IoT 59, 161
  systems 42, 104, 159
Blockchain consensus 155, 157
  methods 155
  system 157
Blockchain technology 48, 54, 60, 65, 72, 84, 91
  applications of 60, 65, 91
  deploying 72
  integrating 48, 54, 84
Body mass index (BMI) 224
Brain tumors 175, 176, 179
Breast tumors 175